Aust
The Da
Symposium

Edited by Stephen R. Graubard

Originally published as an issue of *Daedalus,*
the Journal of the
American Academy of Arts and Sciences

ANGUS
& ROBERTSON
PUBLISHERS

ANGUS & ROBERTSON PUBLISHERS

*Unit 4, Eden Park, 31 Waterloo Road,
North Ryde, NSW, Australia 2113, and
16 Golden Square, London W1R 4BN,
United Kingdom*

*First published in Australia
by Angus & Robertson Publishers in 1985*

*The essays in this book appeared in
the Winter 1985 issue of* Daedalus,
*the Journal of the American Academy
of Arts and Sciences.*

*Published by arrangement with the
American Academy of Arts and Sciences*

*National Library of Australia
Cataloguing-in-publication data.*

Australia, the Dædalus symposium.

ISBN 0 207 15197 0.

*1. Australia — Social life and customs —
Addresses, essays, lectures. 2. Australia —
Social conditions — Addresses, essays, lectures.
I. Graubard, Stephen R. (Stephen Richards).*

994.06'3

*Printed in Australia by
The Dominion Press–Hedges & Bell*

Contents

ADVISORY GROUP

Henry S. Albinski, Geoffrey Blainey, Manning Clark, John Clive, Hugh Collins, Jill Conway, Zelman Cowen, Michael Davie, Donald Horne, K.S. Inglis, Gordon Jackson, Nicholas Jose, Leonie Kramer, T.B. Millar, Hugh Stretton, Richard Walsh, Bruce Williams, Judith Wright

Preface

THIS IS THE FIRST TIME that *Daedalus* has published an issue devoted entirely to a single country. Earlier *Daedalus* issues on Europe, Africa, and the five Nordic countries served many purposes, not least to confirm that even in the modern world, where communications are instantaneous and national differences are supposedly subsumed in a universal twentieth-century "global village" culture, institutional and intellectual diversity are far from extinct. What makes the study of Australia so compelling is precisely the distinctiveness of its society: Australia is not a carbon copy of other modern democracies, even of those with whom it has close and continuing relations and is constantly compared.

Only in the most superficial sense, for example, does Australia resemble the United Kingdom. Its substantially different political traditions, derived initially from the need to conquer an inhospitable land, led settlers to express needs and develop values little resembling those characteristic of the dominant classes of Victorian Britain. The adoption of a federal system guaranteed that Australian politics and administration would assume forms unknown in imperial England. So, also, with its economy: the continued salience of Australia's mining and rural exports, the need to invent patterns of investment and tariff control suited to a "developing" society, the entire mix of secondary and tertiary industries spawned by this novel economy—so substantially different from that of the first industrial and maritime power of the world—made improvisation both necessary and possible. Even the most cursory study of Australia's social institutions suggests that this is neither England nor Scotland nor Wales. While Irish blood may course through the veins of many Australians—a glance at a telephone directory tells in an instant how important Irish immigration once was—the Irish, in establishing themselves in Australia, did not seek to create a new Ireland in the South Pacific.

Does Australia then resemble the United States? Not at all; not, at least, in the view of this American observer, who starts from the premise that the United States today, despite its ethnicity and regionalism, is a continental and imperial society in a way that Australia is not. American culture is accessible to vast multitudes, including innumerable strangers, in a way that Australian culture has not been and may never be. Though much is made of Australia's new immigration policies, which, when contrasted with those common before the Second World War, are indeed both liberal and enlightened, Australia is able to control its immigration in a way that the United States cannot, and not only because of the existence of the Rio Grande. The population pressures are of a totally different order; so, also, are the extent and range of the tolerated violations of immigration laws. Sydney, for all its raffishness, is not New York; Melbourne, for all its nineteenth-century architectural elegance, is not Boston. The grinding misery of the American poor is totally unknown in Australia; it would be an unacceptable national insult, a humiliation inconceivable to a people schooled in certain communal values.

Those who stress Australia's Commonwealth associations may choose to see Canada as the more recognizable of Australia's close cousins; they may even delude themselves into believing that the physical hardships imposed by drought and heat are not fundamentally different from those created by frost and cold—that a common frontier experience, years of unremitting and dangerous combat in two great twentieth-century wars, and the simultaneous acquisition of dominion status under the provisions of the Statute of Westminster create psychic bonds that are all but indissoluble. Such analysis ignores intangibles; there is no irony in the suggestion that a twentieth-century country blessed with magnificent beaches in close proximity to the great population centers of the country will enjoy a way of life and experience opportunities and temptations not immediately available to men and women who for the most part are compelled to live out of sight of the open sea in a much less salubrious climate, in close proximity to a bumptious and powerful neighbor.

Australia is not Canada in the South Pacific, nor ought it ever to be confused with contemporary New Zealand, a much smaller, more homogeneous society. The last comparison, indeed, would be as unpalatable and unwelcome to many Australians as it would to many New Zealanders. Australians ought not to be thought of as Americanized English (or Irish), who are now deliberately opening their country to men and women of other races and nationalities, including some of their Asian neighbors, but are otherwise simply kith and kin of those who live in Wellington, New Zealand.

Australia has always been remote; it remains so even today when jet airliners are believed to render distance largely irrelevant. The major cities of Australia are situated thousands of miles away from the principal cities of the country's non-Commonwealth neighbors, which include, in relatively close proximity, Indonesia and the Philippines, and more distantly, Thailand, Vietnam, Cambodia, and Laos. A glance at the map that appears in this *Daedalus* issue—a document that merits attention—suggests that Australia is a largely empty continent with vast interior spaces, mostly desert, and only a handful of large cities, located principally on the southeast coast, that serve to link the country with its distant foreign trading clients. Another type of map, showing other features, might have emphasized the country's rich and various mineral resources, its extensive grazing lands. Even today, Australia is largely a white people's world, predominantly urban, in a sea populated, for the most part, by men and women of other races living mostly in rural villages.

Australia acquires concreteness only to the extent that its distinctiveness is both acknowledged and accepted. This requires, as this issue of *Daedalus* is intended to suggest, an acceptance also of the proposition that geography and history matter, as much today as at any other time, and that they shape a society as few other forces do. To assert this is to contradict the conventional wisdom that sees contemporary societies as able to mobilize a great variety of resources to achieve their "modernity," imagining that the articulation of large social purposes is the first major step towards the creation of a new reality. The proposition that societies are more substantially constrained, that their choices are as much a function of conditions created by nature and geography as they are of technology, and that they will often show the influence of their history—"the dead hand of the past"—can be disconcerting. Still, the proposition deserves consideration. In a new society particularly—and Australia is such, yesterday's creation—it is well to remember that while technology may tame nature, reducing its power and making it less absolute, nature is not thereby rendered a spent force. Nor, for that matter, ought it to be imagined that history, particularly in a "new nation," is necessarily an ephemeral thing, flimsy and insubstantial. Traditions die hard in Australia; they do not simply collapse before the power of reason or the insight of a vigorous social-engineering capability.

The suggestion that neither technology nor reason operates quite so effectively as is sometimes claimed—not even in supposedly new societies receptive to innovation and unencumbered by the customs of centuries—is deliberately provocative. Indeed, it may be one of the more important lessons that a country like Australia is capable of giving. Boxing Day and the queen do not make Australia British; skyscrapers and supermarkets do not make it American; vast tracts of uninhabited land and the remnants of an indigenous population do not make it Canadian; propinquity and decades of relative isolation, the principal fruits of the "tyranny of distance," do not make it New Zealand. Australia is what it is today because of the choices it has made; these have reflected, to an extraordinary degree, the ways in which Australians have perceived the opportunities provided them by geography. This people, as much as any other, lives by myths, of no great interest to outsiders, but vitally important to those who would understand the country's perception of itself and others.

Australia was chosen as a country to explore in depth less because it is exotic than because it is different. Australia is different today; it was different in the nineteenth century. It was prosperous, very prosperous, when many nations now wealthy were not so at all. Australia retains some residual memory of its earlier great affluence—an affluence based on speculation, built on hazard and greed. While international statistical comparisons suggest that the very rich are now to be found elsewhere in the world, Australians are concerned, as is evident in these pages, with what some see as a growing cupidity and materialism at home. A more fundamental concern, certainly, is whether Australia will continue to do well in the fiercely competitive economic world of the future, whether so easygoing a society will be able to accommodate itself to the demands of a new kind of industrial order, and how all this may serve to transform the country, leading it in wholly new directions.

Australia retains a memory of having once been enormously inventive politically. It is no accident that the term "Australian ballot"—secret ballot—bears the name that it does. Yet, if Australia in the nineteenth century had a booming economy based on gold and wool, and if its political forms were indeed exemplary, democratic in the most literal sense of the term, it was also a society legally closed to all but white settlers, principally from the British Isles. Today, when the country is open to men and women of all races, there is growing concern whether Australia may not soon become a brown or a yellow society, and whether such changes would not cause it to lose certain qualities it esteems and seeks to preserve. Many exult in the new mix of peoples; few ask whether there is indeed much "mixing," whether Australia is not threatened with becoming increasingly a society of largely separated ethnic and racial enclaves. The issue is significant precisely because it raises other, more fundamental questions—whom Australia chooses to relate to in the world today, how it defines those relations, how it perceives its future in Asia and in the Pacific more generally.

Australia seeks desperately to be independent, not only of the United Kingdom but also of the United States. The question, however, is whether Australia is prepared to pay the price for such independence, is in a position today to calculate its probable costs. The ambivalences are very real. Australia aspires to be modern, but remains curiously uncertain about how to achieve that objective. How much education, for example, ought it to provide its children? What ought the purposes of that education be? The country has not earned a reputation for making "educational opportunity" widely available. Whether this is explained as a residual nineteenth-century Australian contempt for certain kinds of book learning and certain elite forms of intellectuality is a moot and delicate point. It needs to be squared, in any case, with the remarkable Australian accomplishments at the highest levels in many fields of science, applied technology, literature, and the arts, which seem to flourish quite independently of what some insist is the mediocrity of the more general culture. Yet, with all the Australian self-confidence, the pleasure taken in a booming film industry that has made so deep an impression in great parts of the world, not to speak of the renown that has come to the country from its great athletic and sports achievements, why is it necessary for Australia constantly to seek justification elsewhere? Why, for example, is recognition more forthcoming at home when it is confirmed first by a conspicuous success in London or New York? Australians are much preoccupied with what they call "cultural cringe"; they resent what they sense to be the survival in themselves of a colonial mentality, of colonial attitudes.

To dwell on these points is to reflect also on who feels "liberated" in Australian society today, how that "liberation" defines and expresses itself. It is to ask also about the constraints in Australian society, constraints that derive in part from the values of a people who are not given to speaking too abstractly, who are constantly charged with not encouraging the growth of the "high timber" in their midst that so impresses outsiders. How are all these seeming contradictions to be explained? While Australia's "civil religion" is not a principal theme in this volume—it is perhaps an American concept, at least in its modern form—such religion exists in Australia, and Gallipoli is only one of its many major twentieth-century totems. Patriotism is not unfashionable in Australia, not unknown. To understand the Australian preoccupation with success and heroism, failure and defeat, equality and independence, is to know why those who see the country's twentieth-century religion principally as a worship of the sun are using a simple journalistic formula in a semi-jocular fashion. The questions conveniently avoided by such levity are whether new "religions" do exist, what they are, whether they are significant, what they reveal about contemporary Australian society.

In its new moral preoccupations—in its concern with the protection of Aboriginal rights, for example—Australia is clearly going beyond the political agenda established earlier in the century when so much of the Anglo-American world first became seized of certain kinds of economic and social issues. How "human rights" will figure in Australia, whether they will enjoy a salience that they are unlikely to command in less vulnerable and less egalitarian societies, is to raise issues of great complexity and delicacy. For, if Australians are renowned for their "plain speaking," for a willingness to use robust and explicit language in public debate to deflate the pompous and the self-important, to insist on certain kinds of candor, it must also be said that the country, for all its geographic size, is small. Candor has its price. Australia is cozy; intellectual "families" exist; enmities are best avoided. The questions that Victorian men of letters habitually asked about Britain in the nineteenth century concerning the adequacy of its representative institutions, the quality of its intellectual life, and the justice and sufficiency of its social organization, need to be asked again in the world once colonized by Britain.

Whether Australians today possess the self-esteem and self-awareness to pose such questions and to relate them to larger issues dealing with the complex problems of national security in a world of atomic arms, is to ask whether they are still capable of drawing on their much-discussed powers of political ingenuity and inventiveness, and whether their isolation still provides certain intellectual advantages. The Australian experience raises profound questions about the reality and meaning of national independence in the world today, but also about the continuing hazards of provincialism—not to speak of the unacknowledged power and influence of a recent colonial subordination.

This *Daedalus* issue is not intended to be read as a complete and authoritative manual on contemporary Australia. Such a volume cannot be composed. The society is much too complex for such easy compression. Also, any pretended search for "objectivity" would have required a suppression of much of the opinion that gives this issue its distinctive flavor. A *Daedalus* issue specifically on the arts, that treated Australian film and music, that considered Australian painting and architecture, would have told yet another story and might have raised yet other questions. Still, limits had to be imposed. Our aim was never to produce an almanac, but only to create the basis for an informed discussion of a society that is too little known.

Thanks are due to many individuals and institutions who helped with this issue. It was Professor John Clive's enthusiasm on returning from a first visit to Australia that started the enterprise going. Professor Geoffrey Blainey, who was then spending a term at Harvard, helped immensely with the initial planning of the issue. A small committee that included Professors Clive and Blainey, together with Professor Kenneth Inglis, Sir Bruce Williams, Sir Zelman Cowen, Dr. Richard Walsh, and President Jill Conway met with me at the House of the Academy in Cambridge to plan the issue, to identify topics and authors. Commissioning letters were prepared, and in April 1984, authors and planners sat together for four days at the University of Melbourne to discuss each of the drafts individually. We are grateful for the facilities of Melbourne University; the arrangements could not have been more agreeable.

Finding funds for this project was not easy. We feel a deep gratitude to those both in Australia and in the United States who have assisted us. To list the names of those who have made contributions is not even to begin to tell the whole story of this, the most difficult fund-raising effort that *Daedalus* has ever embarked on. Whether the explanation of the difficulty is a diminished American foundation interest in certain kinds of international questions, or whether it reveals an Australian preference for certain kinds of charity over other forms of philanthropy, the experience is worth noting because it may just possibly signal a more general problem that waits to be confronted. There are many reasons why, today more than ever, countries like Australia—one in a handful of modern democracies—need to be understood and, in fact, deserve to be known better.

Our sincere thanks go to Amatil, Ltd.; the Australia and New Zealand Banking Group; the Commonwealth Fund in New York; the Department of Foreign Affairs, Commonwealth of Australia; Esso; the Exxon Corporation; the Andrew W. Mellon Foundation; Price Waterhouse, Inc.; the Reserve Bank of Australia; and Westpac Banking Corporation for their generous support of this issue. Qantas Airways is to be thanked for assisting us with air transport expenses. The Melbourne conference could not have taken place without such assistance. Our planners and authors made very great efforts to sustain and advance this enterprise; we are much indebted to all of them.

S.R.G.

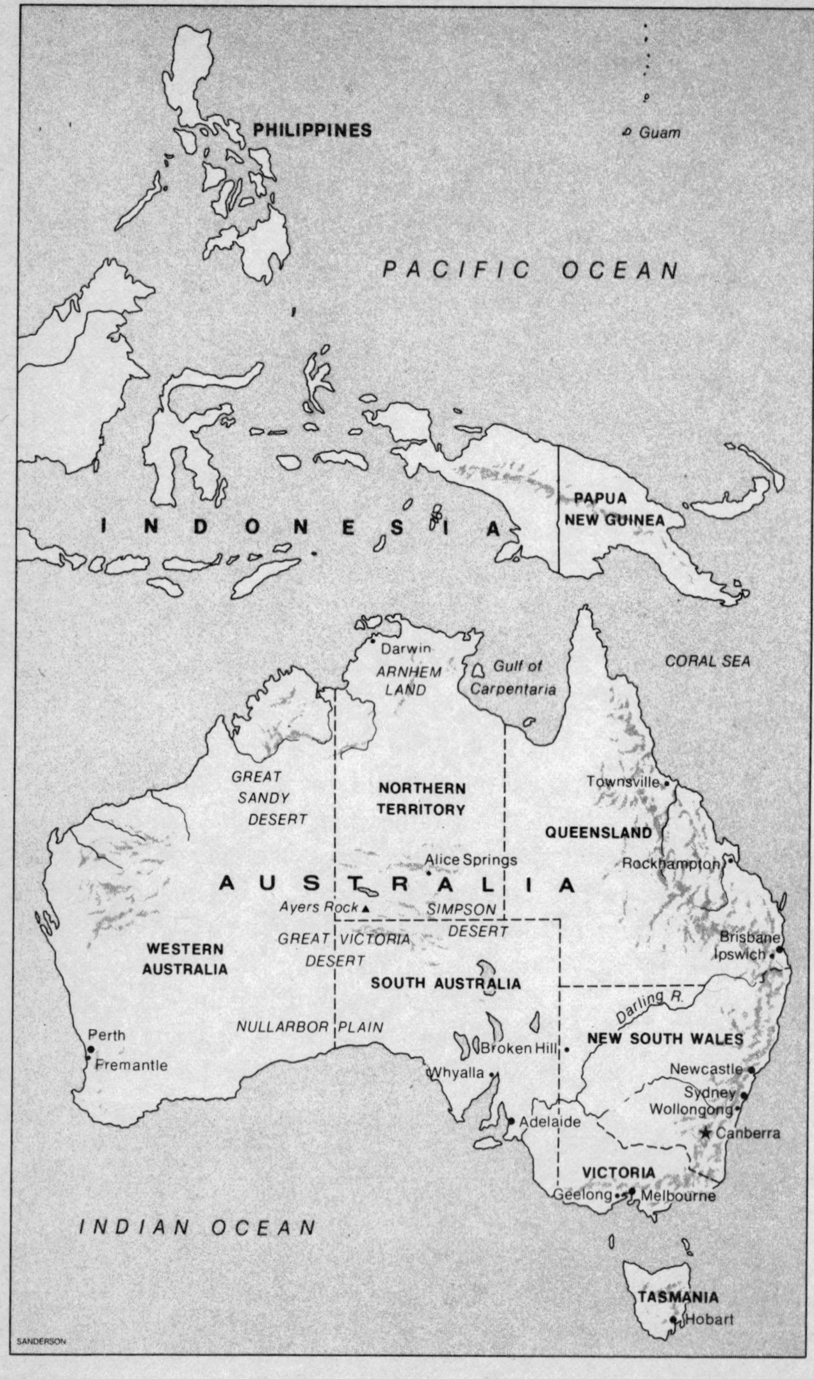

PHILIPPINES
Guam
PACIFIC OCEAN
INDONESIA
PAPUA NEW GUINEA
Darwin
ARNHEM LAND
Gulf of Carpentaria
CORAL SEA
GREAT SANDY DESERT
NORTHERN TERRITORY
Townsville
QUEENSLAND
Alice Springs
Rockhampton
AUSTRALIA
Ayers Rock
SIMPSON DESERT
GREAT VICTORIA DESERT
WESTERN AUSTRALIA
Brisbane
Ipswich
SOUTH AUSTRALIA
Darling R.
NULLARBOR PLAIN
Perth
Fremantle
Broken Hill
NEW SOUTH WALES
Whyalla
Newcastle
Sydney
Wollongong
Adelaide
Canberra
VICTORIA
Geelong
Melbourne
INDIAN OCEAN
TASMANIA
Hobart
SANDERSON

Geoffrey Blainey

Australia: A Bird's-Eye View

IN AN AGE WHEN EUROPE was reshaping the world, Australia was the last of the continents to be tugged into that world. This fact, perhaps more than any other, explains the recent history of Australia, its opportunities and dilemmas, its successes and failures. Long isolation has shaped much of the history of this smallest of continents, this largest of islands.

THE SETTING

Australia is larger than most world maps would suggest. The Mercator map, with its oblong rather than its global depiction of the world, enlarges the area near the poles and therefore relatively diminishes the area of lands such as Australia that do not extend into high latitudes. In area, the Commonwealth of Australia ranks sixth among the world's nations, exceeded only by the Soviet Union, Canada, China, the United States, and Brazil. Australia is also an empire—it held Papua New Guinea until 1975—and if its large claim in Antarctica is included, it is second in size only to the Soviet Union, having a total of 5.4 million square miles.[1] By the standards of Europe, the continent of Australia is vast. It is nearly twenty-five times the size of the British Isles and fourteen times the size of France. Sudan, Algeria, and the Congo, the biggest three countries in Africa, together do not equal Australia in area. The old forty-eight United States cover virtually the same area as Australia; it is only Alaska that makes the United States substantially larger. The typical Australian state—there are only six states and two territories—dwarfs the typical state of the United States. Thus, Western Australia is more than three times as large as Texas, and Queensland is more than four times as large as California. Even Tasmania, the smallest of the Australian states, is three times the combined areas of Massachusetts and Rhode Island. Part of the mystique of Australia, in the eyes of many young Americans, is this vastness, the sense of space; but the breathing space is of a higher quality than the soil.

There is in this land a dryness of which people in Europe and North America cannot easily conceive. Arizona and New Mexico are dry, but their area is small compared to the arid zone of Australia. Much of Mongolia is dry, but traveling across it by train can give an Australian the impression of relatively favorable pastoral country. In seven-tenths of Australia, the annual evaporation exceeds the rainfall. On a map of Australia, in the lower center, is a place called "Lake Eyre," a lake that theoretically drains one-sixth of all Australia but is normally waterless. For decades Australian geographers wondered whether Lake Eyre had ever held water.[2] In 1950, torrential rains in the interior actually filled the lake, and for a short time it was a wonderful sight with a myriad of birds on its banks. It has since been filled several times by great cloudbursts, and the surrounding country then resembles paradise for a month.

Death by thirst was a common experience in inland Australia in the nineteenth century. Explorers traveling in well-equipped parties entered dry country and found themselves desperate for water. Ernest Giles, exploring in central Australia in 1874, was saved by finding a tiny, newborn wallaby, the size of a mouse: "I pounced upon it and ate it, living, raw, dying—fur, skin, bones, skull, and all."[3] Three deserts occupy large parts of central Australia, and one of them, the Simpson Desert, was not even named until 1929, and not traversed until 1939. When we fly from Sydney to Europe and cross that desert with its parallel rows of sand dunes, like long rollers in a vast sea, we traverse in less than an hour a waterless terrain that the first explorer, C.T. Madigan, spent five weeks in crossing. The camel was introduced as a carrier in dry terrain, and in perhaps half of Australia it was the main form of transport in the period from the 1880s to the 1920s. Heavy loads were carried in flat-top wagons drawn by teams of eighteen or more camels and lighter loads were strapped to the pack camels that moved along in a slow, jolting procession. Most camel teams were run by men from the present Pakistan but they were generally known as Afghans. The railroad that, superseding the camel teams, ran from the southern coast to Alice Springs in central Australia, was for long known as "The Ghan."[4]

Statistics of annual rainfall in Australia are not always revealing. When exactly the rain falls, how torrentially it falls, and how long are the lapses between each fall of rain, are as significant as the total rains of the whole year. The annual rainfall in many parts of Australia—and it might fall in two of the 365 days—is pitiful. An intensely hot area around Lake Eyre receives four to six inches of rain in the average year. Troudaninna, over a span of nearly half a century, knew only one year in which the rain exceeded nine inches; between 1895 and 1903, its average rainfall was less than three inches a year. One memorable year, 1896, registered less than an inch, and it is possible that the inch fell in one day, rushing away before it could be conserved. Those years embraced the first devastating drought in the British history of this land: drought of an intensity for which people were unprepared. Even then, Australia held more sheep than any nation in the world's history, and in the space of one decade the number of sheep was exactly halved. The sheep population declined by fifty million, and cattle also perished by the million. It is a comment on how fragile is our understanding of this land, a land so new to us, that each major drought takes us by surprise. Recently, a long but not an unprecedented drought hit southeastern Australia, ending in 1983. It shocked people, even fifth-generation Australians. In a long drought, consisting not of one year but many years, the plowed wheatlands crumble into dust, and the wind whips the topsoil and carries it in dense red-brown clouds, even showering it on the snow of the New Zealand alps, more than a thousand miles away.

The coldest temperature ever recorded in Australia, minus eight degrees Fahrenheit, is experienced by the average resident of Chicago every year.[5] In the central deserts, the nights in winter are cold but are followed by days of warmth and brilliant light. Only Tasmania and a small area in the southeast of the continent receive snow; in a normal year, most Australians do not see even one light fall of snow. Australia lacks high mountains, and cars can be driven on most days of the year to the top of the continent's highest place, Mount Kosciusko, near Canberra. In economic terms, Australia pays a penalty for the lowness of its mountains. If the mountain ranges that form a spine along two thousand miles of the Pacific coast had been at least ten thousand feet high, the snowfields along most of that spine would, when melted in summer, provide a vital source of water. Australia is deficient in long rivers as well as high mountains. Maps show long rivers but most are dry for part of each year or dessicated into a chain of waterholes.

The longest river system in Australia is the Murray and its tributaries, the Darling and the Murrumbidgee. For most of its course, the Murray is narrow and slow-flowing: water takes two or three months to flow from Albury to the river mouth, a distance of eighteen hundred miles. The volume of river traffic has always been meager compared to the wide Mississippi's, partly because the Murray and Darling meander across dry plains, and partly because in drought years they become too shallow to allow the steamers to complete their voyage; steamers could be marooned for a year or more, waiting for the river to rise. By the 1880s, the heyday of the river traffic had passed, allowing more of the water to be diverted to irrigation. Two out of every three irrigated acres in Australia lie near the Murray and its tributaries, and since the 1960s much of the water in the Murray Basin has come from a giant hydroelectric and irrigation scheme that taps the short, swift Snowy River, and diverts to the inland plains water that previously flowed into the Pacific Ocean. During the periodic droughts, however, more sheep and cattle die from lack of grass and herbage than of water. Australia is the world's largest museum of soil deficiencies—soils deficient especially in phosphate but also in cobalt, zinc, copper, and other minerals—and that increases the rural sparseness.

The big city of every state is a seaport—we have no giant inland cities like Chicago or Pittsburgh. The biggest inland city in Australia is the federal capital of Canberra with a population approaching a quarter of a million; but it is less than a two hours' drive from the ocean and is, even more than Washington, D.C., a government-created city. The next largest inland cities—Toowoomba in southern Queensland and the old gold-rush city of Ballarat in Victoria—hold some seventy thousand people and are also less than a hundred miles from the Pacific Ocean. Alice Springs is the only large town near the center of Australia and its population barely exceeds twenty thousand. Draw a radius of five hundred miles around Alice Springs, and there exists in that large circle only two or three towns with more than five hundred people. Little of the income generated in Alice

Springs comes from the natural resources of the district, most of its food comes from the distant coast, and its assets are the tourists who come to see dry ranges and valleys of haunting beauty and that remarkable inselberg known as Ayers Rock, a massive outcrop of smooth rock.

In shape, Australia resembles a ragged square, but the real Australia where people live and work is a ribbon. Australia, economically, is more like Chile—a long coastal strip. The interior is largely deserted, and so too are most of the 12,200 miles of coast, but two strips of coast are settled more intensively. The most populous part of Australia is a curving strip, about two hundred miles at its widest and more than fourteen hundred miles long. It holds the country's biggest cities, Sydney and Melbourne, with a combined population of six million, out of Australia's fifteen million, people. This coastal strip holds most of the valuable farmlands, the best sheep pastures, most of the large tourist resorts, and almost eight out of every ten people. Occupying the southeast corner, it has sometimes been called the Boomerang Coast because of its shape. Another small strip occupies the southwest corner and includes Perth, the capital of Western Australia. Together these two strips of coast, occupying about one-tenth of Australian land, hold about nine-tenths of the people. Transpose these ribbons onto a map of the United States, and that would be the equivalent of nine-tenths of the American population living in a corridor of the east coast running from the Canadian border to Florida—not reaching as far west as Rochester, Pittsburgh, or Atlanta—with a small subsidiary strip stretching from Los Angeles to the Mexican border.

The dryness of the interior positively precluded that westward movement of peoples that marked the United States' history during much of the nineteenth century. The settling of the more favored parts of Australia called for short movements inland from the nearest port, not for a grand westwards sweep. A chain of little ports—many of them now deserted—were the spearheads for explorers, sheepmen, and miners to push inland. The barque, schooner, ketch, and small coastal steamship were vital agents of settlement in Australia, but through the influence of American western films, the covered wagon, the dray, and the pack horse have caught the imagination of Australians more than those coast-hugging vessels. Australia lacked long transcontinental routes. Virtually all traffic between the western and the eastern coasts of Australia—between the Pacific and the Indian oceans—went by sea until the time of the First World War when the railway linked Sydney, Melbourne, and Adelaide on the one side of the continent with Perth on the other side: even that railway ran close to the southern coast. As late as 1950, it was impractical to drive a truck or car from eastern to western Australia, but today a bitumen road runs around Australia, thus enabling an east-west crossing to be made at the northern and the southern end of the continent. There is no east-west route across the middle of Australia, not even a regular air route, but a road crosses the continent from south to north, linking Adelaide and Darwin. Isolation of the interior from the coast, like the isolation of the coast from the hub of the Western world, has shaped much of the human history of Australia.

THE TROPICS

Four-tenths of Australia lies within the tropics. Queensland and Western Australia have large tropical zones, and the Northern Territory is also mainly in the tropics. Australia's most northerly coast is as close to the equator as are Nicaragua, Curaçao, and Barbados.

In tropical Australia, a ribbon of fertile country on the Pacific coast, between the Great Dividing Range and the ocean, has long been closely settled; today, sugar is the main crop, but long before the sugar flourished, the shallow gold mines poured out their riches. Once travelers left that fertile tropical ribbon and went west, they entered a tropical region almost as large as India but with a sparse population and natural resources that are very scattered. The map of that tropical region shows many names, but most names signify not towns but huge pastoral stations with perhaps forty people on each station. As late as 1960, that tropical region west of the Great Dividing Range had only two towns with more than five thousand people: one was the port of Darwin and the other the mining town of Mount Isa, said at that time to be the only big underground field in the world's tropics to be worked entirely by European labor.

In 1890, the majority of people in tropical Australia had been Aboriginals, Chinese working on the gold fields, or Polynesians working in the sugarcane fields. After the Commonwealth of Australia was formed in 1901, most Melanesians were repatriated to their own islands, no more Chinese gold miners or Afghan camel drivers arrived, and the labor force of the far north became inadequate. The White Australia policy, in force from the 1880s to the 1940s, proclaimed that only those resources could be developed that paid the standard wages of the south and employed predominantly European labor. As there was a universal belief that Europeans could not do hard manual labor in the tropics, European labor was not forthcoming.

The controversial geographer Ellsworth Huntington, of Yale University, had long preached that climate was one of the profound influences on human history. In 1923, he came to Australia, intensely curious to see if "white people can live permanently within the tropics and can efficiently carry on all sorts of labor including physical and mental, and if women and children can stand the tropical climate without deterioration." Here, he believed, was one of the world's great human laboratories. At a time when much global history was still being written in terms of the Europeans capturing and occupying the whole world, the question of whether they could really occupy and live in the tropics—efficiently, independently, and if necessary without the help of colored laborers and servants—was vital. Tropical Australia was seen as the answer to this international question. Huntington especially looked forward to seeing the tropical port of Townsville. Lying nineteen degrees from the equator, almost the same distance as Bombay and Jamaica, Townsville was to climatologists and imperialists a special place, being "the largest purely white city within the tropics in any part of the world."[6] Its population? A mere twenty-one thousand.

The far north of Australia was especially retarded in that long era from about 1895 to 1955, when hard physical labor was needed to harvest the sugar cane, to work the underground gold and base-metal mines, to build the tropical railways, and to herd the cattle on the vast pastoral estates. Since the wages had to be high (except for Aboriginals, and they were willing to work only on the cattle stations), everything was dearer in the tropical north. The White Australia policy faded away in the late 1950s, and more immigrants came from Asia, but they had no particular wish to live in the tropics. A wonderful series of mineral discoveries in the 1950s and 1960s enabled a powerful mining industry to spread itself across the tropics, but with transport and wages so dear in those remote places, as much mechanization as possible was utilized in the mines and ports, and the minimum of labor employed. The tropics are now more productive, embracing on the northwest coast the most important iron-ore belt in the world, but they employ few people. Ellsworth Huntington's question has been answered. People of European descent certainly can work hard in the tropics but they prefer the cooler south, the big cities, and places where jobs are more diverse and abundant. There is no national policy to offer strong financial incentives to develop the tropics; the cost is too high. So long as Australia's relations with China are favorable, and so long as Japan is militarily weak, the old fears about the undefended northern coast rarely recur, although Indonesia is watched closely today by many Australians. At present, long stretches of Australia's isolated northern coast are not even patrolled each day by air or sea craft. Many parts of that coast are uninhabited, and along some five thousand miles of tropical coast the largest town holds fewer than a hundred thousand people.

CITIES ON THE RIM

Australians hug the rim of the continent: they stand like seagulls on the sea cliffs and beaches. In contrast, the far interior—known variously as the Outback, the inland, the Never-Never—is largely deserted. On the sea coast, the typical Australian lives within a mile of a doctor and several miles of a hospital. In the far outback, the typical inhabitants who live outside the towns are so far from a doctor that they use wireless to communicate with the doctor and in an emergency are visited by a flying doctor. This service began in 1928, when the first flying doctor escorted a miner injured in northwest Queensland to the nearest hospital by means of a little aircraft run by a company called Qantas. Qantas originally signified Queensland and Northern Territory Aerial Services, and it was a small outback airline long before it became Australia's international airline.

Australia has long been a nation of coastal cities. In 1900, a higher proportion of Australians than North Americans lived in cities. The typical Australian city straggles, like Los Angeles, with most city residents living within easy access to the countryside and beaches. The typical Australian has never seen the real Outback. He imagines it. That gives the Outback—the dry plains—a firm grip on the minds of people.

Our artists and intellectuals sometimes stress the difficulty of being a poet, short-story writer, or painter in a new land,[7] but in few countries of the modern world have creative artists so shaped the imagination and images of the people and shaped them so quickly. For the Australians of the coastal cities, the vision of who they are and what Australia is has been profoundly shaped by artists depicting in word and paint the life and the landscapes of that Outback where the horizon is never reached. It is fair to suggest that in the last century and a half, no English creative writer except Charles Dickens seized the imagination of the average Englishman in the same way as Adam Lindsay Gordon, Henry Lawson, and Banjo Paterson seized the imagination of the average Australian. Such landscape painters as Streeton, Tom Roberts, Nolan, Drysdale, and Fred Williams have a place in the public mind enjoyed by no living painter in England in the last hundred and fifty years. The artists in this new land have a special task: they must erect emotional signposts for people who still feel slightly lost, who lack a sense of belonging, in a land whose climate, vegetation, soil, and light are so different from those of Europe.

The Europeans were strangers in Australia in a way they were not in North America. If the eastern parts of North America, especially New England, had the vegetation and light and heat of Australia, the European immigrant would not have adapted so quickly. In climate and environment, New England was similar enough to England to make the first and crucial stage of adaptation relatively easy. In Australia, the same process of emotional assimilation was slow, even though most of it took place closer to the sea than to the dry interior. In contrast, the Aboriginals, especially those still living in their tribal lands, have a stronger sense than do the European Australians of belonging to the land.

THE THREE PHASES OF HISTORY

Australia carries the imprint of the three main phases of its human history. Divide the human history of Australia into a twelve-hour clock face, and the Aboriginals reigned during all but the last few minutes of that clock. The British, arriving at Sydney in 1788, came to dominate the second phase, and by the late 1840s the British peoples in Australia must have outnumbered the Aboriginals. The third phase, increasingly influential, began at the end of the Second World War when Australia moved rapidly away from its dependence on British migrants, capital, ideas, technology, and markets, and became a far more diverse society.

The first Aboriginals reached Australia at least fifty thousand years ago. The level of the world's oceans was lower then; Australia, New Guinea, and Tasmania formed one continent; and that continent was closer than the present Australia to the Indonesian archipelago and to Asia itself. Moving from island to island, the first Australians discovered this continent thousands of years before the human race set foot on North America. It is assumed, though at present it can in no way be certain, that the first immigrants to Australia were ancestors of the present Aboriginals. It is likely that many waves of immigrants reached the continent of Greater Australia while the seas were low and the gaps between the northwestern islands were short; and it is almost certain—judging from archaeological finds made in the 1960s and 1970s in the southeast of Australia—that several distinct racial groups reached Australia and, for thousands of years, lived in proximity.

About twenty thousand years ago, the climate of the world began to warm, the thick layers of ice in the far northern and southern hemispheres slowly melted, and the level of the sea rose, perhaps by 400 or 450 feet, nearly reaching its present level about six thousand years ago. During that dramatic rising of the seas, Australia was isolated from New Guinea when Torres Strait was formed. Tasmania—already inhabited—was similarly isolated from Australia. Thus, the old continent of Greater Australia was divided into three unequal parts and cut off, in varying degrees, from the outside world at the very time when the first domestication of plants and animals was transforming Asia and the Americas. Most parts of the world entered the neolithic revolution, during which people became more sedentary, their occupations became more specialized, and the first towns were formed; in Australia, however, life was unchanged. While the island of New Guinea was profoundly influenced by this revolution, and even practiced a form of agriculture in the highlands some eight thousand years ago, agriculture and herd-keeping did not reach Australia. Torres Strait, narrow and easily crossed by large canoes, remained—for reasons not easily understood—a barrier that was seemingly stronger than the Himalayas or the Sahara to the southward flow of the new way of life.[8]

In Australia, the Aboriginals remained nomads, moving camp frequently and systematically to take advantage of seasonal sources of food and shelter. They did not reap or sow, built no permanent houses, rarely hoarded food, and congregated only in small numbers and then only for short periods. They owned few possessions, because to travel lightly is the special logic of a nomadic society. Traveling lightly, they relied on a wonderful variety of skills in gathering plant foods and in hunting birds and animals, rather than on the equipment, the hardware, that is the essence of our society. No museum anywhere in the world has yet done justice to such a society as the Aboriginals had, for museums are still geared to the collecting and display of *objects*—they are jackdaws at heart—rather than to the recreation of skills. On the eve of the coming of the British, Aboriginal Australia was divided into several hundred republics, each with its own language or distinctive dialect, each with its patriotism and customs and traditions, and each making so little imprint on the territory it occupied that, to newcomers from Europe, the Aboriginals did not even seem to be occupying it. In fact, they occupied it, depended on it, exploited and harnessed it, loved it, and even worshiped it, but in a way we are only now beginning to appreciate. It is usually said that three hundred thousand Aboriginals lived in Australia and Tasmania in 1788, but some revisionists are now arguing that the figure may be closer to a million. It is a crucial argument and will not be easily resolved. My belief is that if the population was little more than three hundred thousand, then the standard of living in a normal year was high; higher than that of at least 70 percent of the population of Europe in 1788 when the industrial and agricultural revolutions had barely begun their work. If however, the new estimate of a million Aboriginals proves to be valid, we will probably have to discard the proposition that the Aboriginals lived in the midst of plenty. Our knowledge of Aboriginal history suffers from a paucity of evidence. Such a history is especially subject to drastic changes in interpretations when even a thimbleful of new evidence comes to light.

After the British arrived in 1788, and after they spread over the grasslands with their multiplying flocks of sheep, Aboriginal societies one after the other collapsed. The main killers were diseases to which they had no immunity. Smallpox, measles, influenza, venereal disease, and many other illnesses virtually wiped out entire tribes. The firearms of the new settlers were also effective. In many areas, Aboriginals resisted strongly, but their weapons were weak, and tribal rivalries usually prevented them from uniting to resist the invader. Alcohol increased their plight; as their old way of life collapsed, even the will to live seemed to fail. In the long term, the Aboriginals paid a high penalty simply because their way of life was nomadic. If, instead, they had passed through the neolithic revolution like people in nearly all parts of the world, and become diggers of gardens and keepers of herds, their mode of organization would have been tighter, their population would have been larger, and they would have offered powerful resistance to an invader. Moreover, their right to the land would have been recognized. As it was, they received virtually no right to the land because in the eyes of the newcomers they did not cultivate or fence it. The common name given to the Aboriginal lands by the incoming British was "waste lands." British lawyers thought that the political organization of the Aboriginal tribes was so frail—meaning that it was difficult to understand, being different from European nations—that even the negotiation of a treaty was extremely difficult. The British were puzzled by a society that had no recognized king, no princes, no single designated ruler, either within a tribe or in a cluster of tribes.

Dispossessed, landless, declining in numbers, the Aboriginals, it was said as late as 1914, were destined to vanish from the face of the earth. Charles Darwin cited the fate of the Aboriginals as an instance of what he imagined to be the iron law of nature: the fit races survived, the unfit vanished.

In the 1960s, the voice of the Aboriginals was increasingly heard. They had not died out, but the great majority of those who called themselves Aboriginals were partly of European or Asian ancestry. The rise of the Third World nations, some decline of a European-centered view of values and goals on the part of white Australian people, and increasing clamor for black rights in the United States were among the factors that aided the Aboriginals in their growing sense of their identity and in their call for land rights and adequate civil rights. Assimilation ceased to be an official government policy. Aboriginal spokesmen, often fluent and forceful, emerged, taking over from the white Australians who had earlier pleaded their cause. Neville Bonner, an Aboriginal, won a seat in the federal Senate in 1971. Respect for Aboriginals increased markedly, though the respect was highest in the cool south where Aboriginals were rarely seen or, if seen, were not easily identified, physically, as Aboriginals. Land rights were at last granted to Aboriginals, sometimes on terms that gave them a tighter control of their land than was permitted by law to landowners of European or Asian descent. By 1981, one-tenth of the land in Australia was owned by Aboriginals or reserved for their special use. In the Northern Territory, the Aboriginal stronghold, nearly one-quarter of the land was held by Aboriginals, and nearly all was freehold, and in South Australia and Western Australia the Aboriginals held nearly 10 percent. Most of these Aboriginal lands were very poor in soils and grasses, but in mineral potential they were possibly a little above the average of Australian land. As those calling themselves Aboriginals formed only 1.2 percent of the country's population, their share of the land was now relatively high. In the space of two decades, a revolution in attitudes to Aboriginals had occurred. The revolution was still only half a turn of the wheel. In education, housing, health, lifespan, and many other facets of social well-being they are relatively deprived. The deprivation, however, is no longer accepted as right or inevitable by most white people, although a minority of white people do wish for the old days of black subservience.

The second great wave of migration in Australia's history came from the British Isles, and this has left the largest imprint on the cities and the countryside, and on their institutions and culture. It is still the dominant influence on Australia, though the main influence no longer comes directly from Britain itself but from the layers of habits, attitudes, and rituals already embedded in Australian life. The British influence probably reached its peak in the 1920s and 1930s, and began to slump in the first months of the Pacific War of 1941–45. For a century and a half, the overwhelming proportion of immigrants came from the British Isles; the main religions and social customs came from the British Isles; and trade with Britain exceeded that of all other countries added together. Most of the outside investment came from Britain; the laws and books and most of the popular songs and sports came from Britain; and the latest international news—the telegraph had reached Australia in 1872—came from British sources along cables owned by British companies. Australia was defended mainly by the British Navy, though the last British garrison of soldiers in Australia was withdrawn as far back as 1870. Australia sent troops or ships to some of the overseas wars in which Britain was engaged—to the Maori wars in New Zealand in the 1860s, to the Sudan (after General Gordon was killed) in 1885, to the South African War in 1899–1902, to the Boxer Uprising in China in 1900, and to the two world wars. More Australian soldiers than United States soldiers were killed on the battlefields of Europe in the First World War, at which time the population of Australia was less than five million. The war in Vietnam was unusual in Australia's military history, being the first in which Australians fought but Britain did not. No instructions were given by the government in London ordering Australian troops to fight in those wars in foreign lands. The decision to fight was made by Australian government and volunteer troops, though on several occasions the decision to declare war was seen as automatic by the Australian government.

It is not easy to explain to Americans why a land so far from the British Isles should have retained such loyalties and such bonds. It is not even easy to explain the anomaly that lands that nominally belonged to England should, in practice, have been so independent. Perhaps the simplest answer is that the American War of Independence had a profound long-term effect on the way Britain viewed her colonies, especially colonies composed largely of British peoples, and that, in consequence, the Australian colonies were handled with caution, especially in trade and other volatile commercial issues. Concord, Bunker Hill, and Saratoga were battles in which the American colonists were not the only victors. The shot fired at Concord in 1775 was, as Emerson wrote, "heard round the world," and is still heard in Australia.

The queen of England is still the queen of Australia. At the grand ceremonial occasions in Australia, the English national anthem, "God Save the Queen," was still sung or played until 1984 when it was largely dethroned. The Australian flag depicts a southern cross but embraces in the top left corner the Union Jack, or English flag. In the constitution of the Commonwealth of Australia, the queen of Australia has the formal power to appoint the governor-general of Australia, and he in turn is the commander-in-chief of all the naval and military forces. And yet Australia, despite this constitution, is in practice a republic. The queen of Australia, no matter what her powers in theory, continues to hold office only because she exercises no power. Should she be seen to exercise power in Australia, she would probably cease to be the monarch of Australia. She is respected by a majority of—but not all—Australians partly because she respects the country's independence. Formal republicanism is growing in Australia, and in the next quarter-century Australia might well become a republic formally as well as in fact.

Australia, like the United States, has a federal system, and government in both the federal center and the states is elected by the people. The Chartist influences of the 1840s and 1850s were strong, and elections are held every three years for state and federal parliaments. There is no federal president. The most powerful citizen, called the prime minister, is the leader of the strongest party in the House of Representatives, our equivalent of Congress. He and his cabinet, in effect, appoint the governor-general who is the formal and ceremonial head of state. It sounds like a plot from a Gilbert and Sullivan opera. The plot is workable but not easily understood by a considerable number of Australian adults, let alone by visitors.

Behind the colonial-like facade of dependence is an independence that came more quickly to Australia than to the United States. In 1855, the main British colonies in Australia were granted self-government, with elected parliaments on the British system, and those colonies gained almost complete control of their economic policy—thus eliminating any chance of a Boston Tea Party. The colonies could even impose large duties on British imports; Victoria, which was then the most populous colony, became one of the most protectionist lands in the world at a time when Britain itself was an exponent and ideologue of free trade. In law, the British government had the reserve power of deferring or refusing to accept acts passed by the various Australian parliaments, but this right was rarely used. Foreign policy was the main field in which the British government was supreme, but even here various colonies pursued policies—for instance, the exclusion of Chinese immigrants by special taxes—that ran strongly against Britain's foreign policy. When in 1901 the new federation, the Commonwealth of Australia, came into being as a result of initiatives within Australia, the reserve powers were soon transferred from Britain to Australia. For a few years, foreign policy remained largely the monopoly of Britain, and such oversight was generally accepted as wise by Australian politicians and people. Since Britain paid most of the cost of defending its Australian and other colonies, it was entitled to decide what international risks it should run in pursuing its foreign policy.[9] In 1909, Australia and the other self-governing lands were permitted to run their own navies, and the Australian navy cooperated closely with Britain's. In London during the First World War, a war cabinet was created with the British prime minister in the chair, and Australia possessed a seat and a vote in that war cabinet. At the end of the war, Australia was represented at the Paris Peace Conference as a nation in her own right; and it was the Australian prime minister, William Morris Hughes, who, fearing future pressure from Japanese immigrants, strongly opposed President Woodrow Wilson's plea that a clause affirming racial equality be inserted in the covenant of the League of Nations. Hughes also insisted that Australia govern the German colony in New Guinea, captured by Australian forces in 1914.

Any doubts about the effective independence of Australia were removed when the British parliament in 1931 passed the Statute of Westminster, affirming that Australia and other self-governing British lands were autonomous. The new statute was seen as being of little practical consequence and even slightly subversive to the spirit of empire, and it was not adopted by the Australian parliament until 1942. By then, the great British warships had been sunk near Malaya, and the naval base and paper fortress at Singapore had fallen to the Japanese, and Britain was now clearly incapable of defending those parts of the world that she could once have defended simply by the threat of using her power. Australia was never so dependent, never so fragile, as in 1942—the year in which she nominally became independent.

Why then, in summary, did Australia not become a republic during her first century-and-a-half as a European settlement? Why did her history seem to deviate from that of the United States? Economic grievances, the most dangerous cause of division, could not become inflammable after the 1850s, because the Australian governments were even free to be anti-British in their economic policies. Political grievances were unlikely to reach burning temperature because Australia was independent in everything except foreign policy. As an important part of Britain's foreign policy was to defend Australia, that policy did not conflict with Australian wishes, nor did it hurt Australian purses. Australia possessed a long and vulnerable coastline, and that part of the coast which was least defensible faced China and Japan. Australians therefore needed a powerful western ally if they were to become independent of Britain. So long as Britain possessed the world's most powerful navy, it was the best ally Australia could desire. Even when, after the First World War, Britain's navy ceased to be so powerful, the only alternative ally for Australia was the United States, which was becoming increasingly isolationist.

The British alliance was emotional, convenient, and economical, but it had at least one weakness. The relationship was so pervasive, embracing everything from the latest news to the latest machine, that Australians saw the whole world too much through British eyes. They did not realize that as an industrial power Britain had been overtaken by both the United States and Germany before the First World War. They did not realize how overextended was Britain's empire in the 1920s and 1930s. Curiously, it was an Australian who, more than any articulate thinker of the late nineteenth century, foresaw that Europe's sway would probably end and that the subjected peoples of the tropics and the Orient would one day become powerful, and that therefore, by implication, a country as isolated as Australia might be marooned from effective help. This Australian thinker was Charles Henry Pearson, and his book of 1893 was called *National Life and Character*.[10] One American impressed by his message was Theodore Roosevelt, but few Englishmen were impressed by his "scare-mongering": he was half a century ahead of his time.[11] When the Japanese in 1941–42 captured most of southeast Asia with ease, and trapped a large Australian army defending the Malay peninsula, the incredulity and sense of shock in Australia was profound. Japan was believed to be, technologically, an infant.[12] "Made in Japan" had been seen as the symbol of the shoddy and second rate, the very antithesis of "Made in Birmingham."

To many Americans, the Australians' willingness to fight in foreign wars seems unusual. After all, Australia was so isolated, and most of the battlefields in which her soldiers fought—until the end of 1941—were far away. Most Australians killed in foreign wars lie in graves that are at least ten thousand miles away. Whereas the United States was very late in entering the First World War and late in entering the

Second World War, Australia entered as soon as those wars began. In explaining this contrast, one clue is apparent. The United States was a melting pot of peoples from every part of Europe, and therefore to take part in a European war could have divisive effects at home. But Australians were overwhelmingly British in their ancestry, and so to enter a major war on Britain's side was to exercise a unifying and cohesive rather than a divisive effect on the people at home. Similarly, Australia, being militarily weak compared to the United States, relied on its alliance with Britain, and to enter a war promptly on Britain's behalf is one way of reaffirming the value of the alliance. It is paying a debt before the interest even falls due. The same strong emphasis on the contractual side of an alliance can perhaps be seen in Australia's participation as an ally of the United States in the Korean and Vietnam wars. In addition, a strand of nationalism is visible in Australia's attitudes to overseas war, especially before 1945. War was an international theater, a tournament, in which a relatively unknown nation could prove itself, both to others and to itself. The United States felt less need to appear in such a theater because it had both won its independence through war and had maintained its unity through war, the terrible Civil War.

In the early 1940s, Australia slowly began to enter its post-British phase. From 1942 on, the United States replaced Britain as the main ally in defense. In the 1960s, Japan replaced Britain as the main outlet for Australian wool, foodstuffs, minerals, and other exports. The United States also replaced Britain as the main source of Australia's imported goods and became the main source of Australia's outside capital and new technology. In high culture, America challenged—though it did not surpass—the British influence: in popular culture, the American influence in the years since the movie boom of the 1920s and 1930s has been at least as powerful as the British.

Australia's web of outside links has been reshaped, and in no area is this more visible than in immigration. Between 1945 and 1970, more immigrants came to Australia than in all the previous history of the country, and only about half of them came from the British Isles, hitherto the predominant source of migrants. Whereas an Australian child of the 1930s could grow to the age of ten in many suburbs and rural districts and not once hear a sentence spoken in a foreign language, now Italian, Greek, German, Dutch, Polish, Yugoslav,

Turkish, Latvian, Chinese, Vietnamese and other languages are widely spoken and printed. This has been one of the most successful long-distance movements of people in recorded history. Some observers even argue that it has been too successful, and that the immigrants from non-British lands have assimilated too readily.

The postwar immigration has made Australia more like the United States in its ethnic composition, though most rural districts are still overwhelmingly Anglo-Celtic. It is widely believed that the new wave of migration has transformed the country. Certainly, it is less insular in attitude and more tolerant than it was in 1939. Certainly, the restaurants have altered, with Italian and Chinese cooking overtaking English cooking in popularity. It may well be that the typical migrants from continental Europe, especially those from Eastern Europe and the Baltic lands, were unusually suspicious of big government, thus helping to make Australia less collectivist in its politics and more enthusiastic about education. On the other hand, the non-British migration has probably helped to keep alive some facets of society that are traditionally seen as marking the old British Australia: a tightly knit family, a sympathy with religion, and a reluctance to criticize publicly the royal family.

SOME MYTHS, LEGENDS, AND FACTS

Australia has long been regarded by the United States as a land dominated by trade unions, a land that was "half-socialist" years before the Russian Revolution of 1917. There is some truth in these ideas. Australian unions are very powerful, and one stream of their influence is the Australian Labor Party, which in 1984 was the dominant party in the federal parliament and four of the six states: the present prime minister, Mr. Hawke, before entering parliament, was the head of the trade-union movement but that is an unusual succession of office. By the mid 1960s, about six out of every ten wage earners and salary earners in Australia were members of a trade union; membership in a trade union is especially common among government officers and high bureaucrats, among university professors, air pilots, and many of the professions. Strikes are frequent, but the overseas picture of Australia as a nation always about to strike is exaggerated. That picture was intensified in the United States in the 1920s when Harry Bridges, born in Melbourne in 1900, began to organize the longshoremen of San Francisco, introducing, in his own words, the "technique of Australian militant unionism." Australia is not the most strike-prone nation in the Western world: its record at industrial peace is certainly superior to Canada's.

The role of government in Australia has traditionally been high, but that was more true of the era 1895 to 1920, by world standards, than of the last twenty years. By 1920, a minimum wage and maximum weekly hours were ordained for workers in most industries, and if an employer could not pay that minimum wage he was forced to close his factory or shop. By 1920, the state governments paid pensions for the aged, built most of the hospitals, and provided free primary schooling (but not free secondary schooling nor free universities). Government intervened in industrial relations, setting up boards and arbitration courts to try to solve industrial disputes. The governments were busy in marketing primary products, partly because of the dislocation to shipping caused by the First World War. Several of the state governments ran—not always efficiently—business enterprises ranging from gold and coal mines, shipping services and tramways, to brickworks and butcher shops.

The state governments had, since the 1850s, built and operated nearly all the railways, financing them with long-term loans from private investors in Britain, and at one time turning them into the biggest business enterprises in Australia. The governments owned the telegraphs, telephones, many of the electric power plants, and supplied water. Neither right-wing nor left-wing governments had a strong objection to heavy government interference in industry and commerce, though each side interfered in a different way. Only in one area were governments less likely to interfere in Australia than in the United States: that was in the regulating of business trusts and cartels. Governments have also been active in building houses and acting as landlords, but this has often been accompanied by a policy of encouraging people to buy their own houses. In the five largest Australian cities, from 72 to 76 percent of the householders own—or are in the process of buying—the house in which they live.[13] This proportion—one index of a private enterprise system—is probably higher in Australia than in the United States.

It is not easy to find simple explanations for the fluctuating role of government in Australia. The role of government was high in the convict era: a convict society is inevitably controlled tightly. The government's active role possibly waned from the 1840s to the 1880s, but the depression of the 1890s—a series of bank crashes followed by long drought—affected the outlook of most Australians, forcing many to seek the aid of the state. That depression in Australia was more severe, more jolting, than any depression experienced in Europe or North America in the nineteenth century, and it led to increased calls for government regulation of economic and social activities.

Since 1945, the role of government in Australia has increased at a much slower pace than in most western European countries. Today the ratio of government expenditure to gross domestic product is lower in Australia than in England and West Germany and three-quarters of the member countries of the Organisation for Economic Cooperation and Development. The dominance of right-wing governments in the Commonwealth in four years out of five in the postwar era is part of the explanation, but that in itself is a product of other causes.

One difference between Australia and the United States is, in my view, crucial in explaining some of their diverging political attitudes. Australia was far from Europe; and the only hope of attracting immigrants, in competition with North America with its cheap land and cheap fares, was to subsidize the fares and even to select the migrants. The first migrants, British convicts, were very much selected; so were most of the free immigrants who came in the nineteenth century, the government paying their fare. Only in the gold rush of the 1850s—an event parallel in time and magnitude to the California gold rush—did the great majority of migrants pay their own way. Even in the 1950s and 1960s, the typical migrant to Australia—especially the British migrant—was subsidized almost to the full amount of the fare. In contrast, subsidized fares to the United States were unusual. The migrants there were self-selected and perhaps a little more enterprising, a little less likely to rely on government when they reached their new land. As most migrants to Australia were selected, it was understandable that British migrants would be preferred. Thus, from these linked facts—the distance of Australia from Europe, the dearness of the fare, and a voyage so long that a return to the homeland was unlikely—came many consequences: subsidized migrants who were more likely to lean on the government when they reached Australia; a predominance of British migrants; and a flow of immigrants that, in contrast to the United States, could be stemmed whenever unemployment became widespread in Australia[14]—the government simply subsidized fewer migrants in poor times. This saved government expenditure and at the same time appealed to wage-earners. Labor thus gained a much stronger bargaining position in Australia, because the gluts of labor were fewer and shorter than in countries with less-controlled immigration. This fact alone probably increased the bargaining position of workmen and so encouraged the formation of strong unions.

A SPORTING COUNTRY

A favorable bargaining position for labor and success in spectator sport are characteristics of Australia. Indeed, they are causally linked. The Australian sporting tradition arose at the same time as the strong trade unions. Of all the advantages that Australia in the period 1860 to 1890 offered to sport, the favorable outdoor climate and the provision of free government land for sporting fields—vital as they were—were not as important as the ample leisure of workingmen. Workingmen had long used their strong bargaining position to press for shorter hours. In 1856, many men in the building trades in Melbourne, the stonemasons leading the way, won the eight-hour day or forty-eight hour week, and henceforth the eight-hour day became the shining goal of trade unions and the occasion for strikes and petitions.[15] The governments were great employers of labor, especially in the building and operating of railways, and were pressed by populist politicians in the easy-money years to introduce a shorter working week. In the cities, the Saturday afternoon holiday was widespread by the 1880s, and huge crowds attended Saturday sporting events. The day of the great horse race, the Melbourne Cup, was the first Tuesday in November, and it too became a public holiday; in the 1880s, as many as a hundred thousand spectators watched that race. In Melbourne, the premier sporting city in Australia, cricket and Australian-rules football in the 1880s drew crowds such as were then unknown in England.

As Australia was so isolated, the best sportsmen did not have much chance to compete internationally, but their skills blossomed in an environment with such a fine climate, numerous sports grounds, ample leisure, and prosperity. Cricket and sculling were among the world's few international sports in the 1880s, and in these Australia could hold its own with England. When the modern Olympic Games began in 1896, only a few Australian athletes could afford to visit the games in the far-away northern hemisphere, but in swimming and athletics those few became prominent. Soon after the Davis Cup was instituted for international tennis in 1900, the combined team of Australia and New Zealand was the winner.

It is a commentary on our weak sense of history that when Australia won the America's Cup at Newport, Rhode Island, in 1983, the overwhelming belief, from the prime minister to sporting commentators, was that this was the greatest of all achievements in Australian sport, an occasion for national rejoicing and even for gloating. It is reasonable to suggest that many of the earlier achievements, made by an isolated nation of few people competing in sports far more widely contested than millionaire yachting, were victories of more merit against greater odds. At times, sport in Australia is a national obsession, and a focus for nationalism. That Australia in the late 1960s entered a more nationalist mood accounts perhaps for the jubilation over the America's Cup and the amnesia about the success of earlier Australian sportsmen.

The obsession with spectator sport and therefore with success in sport rather contradicts another oft-noticed Australian characteristic: a leveling tendency, a suspicion of the powerful, a mistrust of excellence, and an ambivalence towards training and education. These are old, not new, Australian characteristics. It is possible that these attitudes have been diluted by the postwar flow of migrants from continental Europe. Certainly, the old suspicion of education was weakened in the 1960s and 1970s by a dramatic increase in facilities for tertiary education, but the typical Australian still leaves school or college at a much younger age than the typical American. Australian life suffers at times from an inadequate respect for enterprise, originality, and talent. On the other hand, it also gains from the democratic and communal sense that "Jack is as good as his master"—if not better. Professor Russel Ward, at the end of one of the most influential of Australian books, *The Australian Legend*, argues that "it is possibly harder to imagine a Hitler, a Stalin or even a Perón flourishing here than in any other country on earth, including England itself."[16] If by chance a Perón should rise to power in

Australia, it is likely that he will have first made his mark as an athlete or an entertainer.

THE DECLINE OF ISOLATION

While isolation has powerfully influenced Australia's history, that influence is probably diminishing. So long as sea was the only method of travel, Australia remained isolated and few people of renown visited the country—unless they came before they were famous. Even prominent Australians rarely went overseas, and when Prime Minister J.H. Scullin decided to visit London in 1930, during the world depression, he was absent for fifteen weeks—a time of mounting political tension in Australia—and for most of those weeks he was at sea. It is significant that a reigning English monarch did not visit Australia until 1954 and an English prime minister until the following decade.

In the last quarter of a century, the world has shrunk. The jet and then the jumbo jet reduced the cost and time of travel, and the typical flight from London to Sydney now takes a little more than twenty-four hours. Satellites now send television pictures and telephone messages quickly across the world, and yet as recently as the year 1962 only sixteen international telephone calls were made to and from Australia in an average hour of the week.[17] Australians are now among the world's most energetic tourists; it may well be that one-third to one-half of the adult population born in Australia has now visited Europe or Asia. Australians, for instance, rank third among travelers to China, coming behind Japanese and American tourists.

This does not necessarily mean that Australians feel less isolated—isolation always was and always will be relative. Moreover, the distances have narrowed so quickly and so dramatically that perhaps we do not fully understand this fact. Isolationist strands of thought, particularly on the left side of politics, are more powerful now than at any period since perhaps the 1930s. Of course, isolationism comes in many forms and is sometimes masked or hidden and sometimes strident. In Australia, it is visible in influential attitudes to defense, to the mining of uranium, to foreign capital, to immigration, to the conservation of wilderness, and even education.

Australia's isolation has been reduced not only by the development of swift communication but also by changes in centers of power. The importance of the Pacific—the increasing power of Japan, China, Vietnam, and Indonesia and the increasing industrial strength of the West Coast of the United States—means that Australia is no longer so isolated from one of the hubs of commercial and military power. When the historian Russel Ward said how difficult it was to imagine a Hitler or Stalin flourishing in Australia, he was mirroring our traditional sense of security and the faith that our leaders would always arise from within the country rather than be imposed from outside. That faith, that sense of security, is at times too high in Australia. Isolation in one sense has tended to become as much a state of mind as a fact of geography.

How to cope with proximity to Asia has been Australia's main dilemma since the Second World War. The immigration policy reflects that dilemma. For some twenty years after that war, Australia brought in European immigrants on a large scale in the hope of more successfully defending the country with the aid of a larger population and a stronger industrial base. That motive faded away, to be replaced by a woolly policy supported more by parliaments than by public opinion. The new policy increasingly favored Asian immigrants in the hope that their presence would smooth political relations with Asia, attract Asian commerce, and provide—so some Australian employers hoped—a more highly motivated labor force than that composed of migrants from Britain and continental Europe. Asian migrants were few in number in the 1960s but by the mid-1970s they formed one quarter of all immigrants and have remained above that proportion. In the late 1970s, refugees from Indochina began to swell the Asian inflow.[18] It is almost certain that Australia, in proportion to the size of its population, has accepted more Indochinese refugees than has any country in the world. Unfortunately, they have arrived at a time when unemployment—peaking at about 10 percent—is more serious than it has been at any time in the last forty-five years. Moreover, the Asian refugees have congregated in those old manufacturing districts where jobs are scarcest.

In 1984, there was increasing hostility to this inflow. The government, instead of trying strenuously to persuade the public that the inflow might be in Australia's long-term interest, has appealed to the principle that its doors be open equally to all peoples. It has also applied its own strange definition of Asia, minimizing the extent of Asian immigration. At times it has suggested that the fast inflow is a temporary event and will slacken. It has been careful not to publicize statistics on net immigration, but the latest statistics on the long-term and permanent movement of population in and out of the country show that Asians constituted over 60 percent of the net immigration in 1983.

The immigration controversy highlights Australia's uncertainty about its relations with Asia and especially Southeast Asia. It mirrors the dilemma of whether Australia should continue to belong primarily to European civilization. It mirrors the vital question of whether it should remain a relatively cohesive society or whether it should—in line with government policies since the late 1970s—become a multicultural and multiracial society. It mirrors, too, the rising nationalism and a growing feeling for Australian traditions and history as well as an increasing sense that the world is one. With so many important principles and emotions at stake, such a controversy will not easily be solved.

ENDNOTES

[1]A. Grenfell Price, *Island Continent: Aspects of the Historical Geography of Australia and its Territories* (Sydney: Angus & Robertson, 1972), p. v.

[2]T.M. Perry, "Geography," in *Australia,* ed. C. Pearl (Berne: Kummerley & Frey, 1965), pp. 47–8.

[3]Geoffrey Blainey, *A Land Half Won* (Melbourne: Macmillan, 1980) p. 178.

[4]H.M. Barker, *Camels and the Outback* (Pitman: Melbourne, 1964), preface. One of the last camel drivers came to me in the early 1960s with a manuscript telling of his experiences, and I helped with his final version. His hope was that if a nuclear war was fought, and mankind were forced to begin afresh with a simple technology, a book on how to handle camels would be more useful than a book on motor mechanics.

[5]*Official Year Book of the Commonwealth of Australia* (Canberra: Commonwealth Bureau of Census and Statistics, 1964), p. 31.

[6]Ellsworth Huntington, *West of the Pacific* (New York: Charles Scribner's Sons, 1925), p. 334.

[7]Probably the only history of the arts in Australia is G. Serle, *From Deserts the Prophets Come: the Creative Spirit in Australia 1788–1972* (Melbourne: Heinemann, 1972).

[8]On the Aboriginals, see D.J. Mulvaney, *The Prehistory of Australia* (Melbourne: Penguin Books, 1975) and Kenelm Burridge, *Encountering Aborigines* (New

York: Pergamon, 1973) and Blainey, *Triumph of the Nomads: A History of Aboriginal Australia* (New York: Overlook Press, 1976).

[9]On the development of foreign policy, the best summary is P.G. Edwards, *Prime Ministers and Diplomats: The Making of Australian Foreign Policy 1901–1949* (Melbourne: Oxford University Press, 1983).

[10]C.H. Pearson, *National Life and Character: A Forecast* (London: Macmillan, 1893).

[11]John Tregenza, *Professor of Democracy: the Life of Charles Henry Pearson 1830–1894, Oxford Don and Australian Radical* (Melbourne: Melbourne University Press, 1968) pp. 231–2.

[12]Blainey, *The Causes of War*, rev. ed. (South Melbourne: Sun Books, 1977) p. 249.

[13]*Parochial Australia* (Melbourne: John Clemenger Pty Ltd., 1983) p. 38.

[14]Blainey, *The Tyranny of Distance: How Distances Shaped Australia's History* (London: Macmillan and History Book Club, 1968) chap. 7.

[15]K.S. Inglis, *The Australian Colonists: An Exploration of Social History 1788–1870* (Melbourne: Melbourne University Press, 1974) p. 117ff.

[16]Russel Ward, *The Australian Legend*, rev. ed. (Melbourne: Oxford University Press, 1978) p. 308.

[17]Blainey, *The Tyranny of Distance*, rev. ed. (Melbourne: Macmillan, 1982) p. 338ff.

[18]See Nancy Viviani, *The Long Journey: Vietnamese Migration and Settlement in Australia* (Melbourne: Melbourne University Press, 1984).

Judith Wright

Landscape and Dreaming

THE FIRST ARRIVAL OF THE BRITISH to set up a convict colony on the east coast of Australia—for reasons so occult that historians argue them today—was based on at least two misconceptions. One, set out by Cook in his journal, was that the Australian Aborigines had no "fix'd habitation," but "moved about from place to place like wild Beasts in search of food"—implying for the British government that they had no claim on the land or title to it through cultivation, management, or habitation. The second, provided by both Cook and Banks, was that Aborigines of the eastern coasts were few. As James Maria Matra put it,[1]

> Capt. Cook first coasted and surveyed the eastern side of that fine country . . . In this immense tract of more than 2,000 miles there was every variety of soil, and great parts of it were extremely fertile, peopled only by a few black inhabitants, who, in the rudest state of society, knew no other arts than such as were necessary to their mere animal existence, and which was almost entirely sustained by catching fish.

Cook had claimed only the eastern coast in the king's name. Reports of the west and northwest coasts, nearer by sea voyage to Britain and Asia, were not encouraging. Even the Dutch, whose ships had often been blown off course far enough to make contact, had made no attempt to occupy it, and Dampier in 1699 had coasted it without finding a harbor. His reports of it were bleak, finding nothing to commend; and his view of the inhabitants seemed to corroborate those of Cook and Banks. Accordingly, it was the east coast on which the British set up their new colony. It lay at the end of a journey that might take six months or more; but the eastern coast proved to be, and still is, the most favorable in soils, rainfall, and forests for European habitation.

The land the colonists occupied was a rocky and restricted coastal shelf, backed by a parapet of sandstone that resisted their attempts to cross it for decades to come. Nevertheless, even around Sydney Harbor, as early records and paintings attest, hills were green and open and trees spaced well apart. Elizabeth Macarthur wrote that the country looked like a nobleman's park;[2] that judgment was repeated later for country farther inland, beyond the resistant mountains of the Dividing Range. These open coastal forest lands were perfect hunting grounds for Aborigines and pastures for kangaroos and other marsupials; they were not good sheep country. The Macarthurs, and other early sheep breeders, found that the good grasses soon vanished under selective browsing, under the trampling of sharp hooves and the nibbling of myriads of teeth: the remaining grasses and shrubs were wiry and unpalatable and these increased and took over.[3]

With the disappearance of the Aborigines—victims of disease (especially smallpox) and undeclared war—and the spread of sheep and cattle more and more widely, not only soils and grasses deteriorated but unpalatable shrubs and eucalypts sprang up in new profusion. The fire that had once kept the pastures open for kangaroos was now prohibited for fear of burning the flocks and huts and houses. When fire occurred, from that time on, it was increasingly uncontrollable, increasingly hot and destructive, and resulted in an even thicker regeneration of fire-resistant vegetation, or in bared ground that eroded rapidly in rain or wind.

That, in brief, is the story of practically all the sheep-country occupied in the early times of historical Australia. Since for many decades sheep brought in most of the income of the colony of New South Wales, and of the separate colonies established later, it is impossible to understand the aspect of Australia today without taking into account the impact not only of sheep but of the less-damaging cattle, of timber-getters and gold-miners, and of the plagues of animals and plants that soon began to run wild and escape their introducers.

This is the first point to be remembered in looking at Australian landscape—that though the island continent holds some of the most recently European-occupied land in the world, especially in its northern and central arid and monsoonal lands, there is virtually no part of it that has not been influenced, often for the worse, by its European inhabitants.[4]

Yet human occupation stretches back for unknown millennia, certainly for more than forty thousand years, while European occupation dates back less than two centuries. Ignorance, and contempt, stand between us and the story of the millennia that preceded the European arrival; but now a little of the truth is emerging.

Fire was the most powerful and virtually the only tool used by Aborigines to change the face of the land. Hunting and gathering, fishing and moving from place to place as food supplies fluctuated, they left little other trace on it. Cook's and Banks's judgment of them, however, was certainly mistaken. Not only did they handle fire with judgment and intent, to keep pastures and watercourses clear of excess growth and accessible to marsupials, hunters, and gatherers, but in some places, where food supplies were reliable and climates harsh and cold, they built small villages[5]—thus belying Cook's view (based on very brief observation) that they had no fixed dwellings. (It is reported that along some of the northeastern rivers where fish supplies were plentiful, such villages were also found.) As to their relationship with the land, it is only gradually becoming understood—and neither our system of law nor our views of land-use and ownership can be made to tally with it.

For Aborigines, every part of the country they occupied, every mark and feature, was numinous with meaning. The spirit ancestors had made the country itself, in their travels, and fused each part of it into the "Dreamtime"—a continuum of past, present, and future—that was also the unchangeable Law by which the Aborigines lived. The spirits remained in the land, passing on their essence through the births and rebirths of Aborigines themselves, and still present in the telling of their stories.

> Dreamtime,
> The first ones lived, those of long ago . . .
> Where the sun climbs, over the hill and the river
> they came
> And they are with us in the land.[6]

The gulf between the Aboriginal way of seeing the landscape, and that of Europeans—most of whom came in earlier times as sentenced exiles, or in the days of wool-boom and gold-fever to plunder rather than to stay—is clearly almost unbridgeable. Yet it has been only in quite recent decades that any attempt to understand the Aboriginal viewpoint has been made. Few of us can say we have succeeded.

In fact, this very word "landscape" involves, from the beginning, an irreconcilable difference of viewpoint, and there seems no word in European languages to overcome the difficulty. It is a painter's term, implying an outside view, a separation, even a basis of criticism. We cannot set it against the reality of that earth-sky-water-tree-spirit-human complex existing in spacetime, which is the Aboriginal world. We have unraveled the original continuum into many different elements, and use the word not only in aesthetic contexts, but as a general vague term in geology, botany, and many other disciplines. To add the further elements of prehistory, history, and future that are bedded in the Dreamtime is to realize how far our world has been fragmented.

What we see in the landscape, then, is a partial, inadequate, and temporal vision, reflecting our own interests. Perhaps the problem can best be summed up in a single case: that of the great weather-sculptured heave of sandstone, ancient and red, that rises near the heart of Australia and that Aborigines have known and revered for millennia as Uluru. We have arrogantly renamed it Ayers Rock. The man whose name it bears was an immigrant Englishman, a nineteenth-century mining entrepreneur who rose to be premier in the government of South Australia at a time when what is now the Northern Territory was still part of that colony. The Aborigines who for untold time had held it sacred, still carried out on its slopes and in its caves secret ceremonies of totemic and ancestral spirits and decorated it with ceremonial paintings. The man it was renamed for, Sir Henry Ayers, if he ever visited it probably regarded it as an immense sandstone pebble of geological interest but of no use to the mining industry.

Ayers Rock, Uluru, has now been "returned" to the Aborigines under our land title, though, for them, it has never belonged to us. But since the growth of a tourist boom in Central Australia, it has become what is oddly known as a "tourist Mecca," though of course no sacred significance is attached to the term. The Hawke government's decision to grant Aborigines title to the rock has been greeted with rage by the tourist entrepreneurs and operators to whom it represents a source of income. For, the Aborigines who now officially own the rock can control access and direct tourists (with their litter and unmeaning graffiti) away from areas too sacred to be shown.

There are few places left in Australia where this ancient relationship to the land has not been fractured or destroyed. The last invasion of European industry and tourism has taken place in the once almost untouched northern and central areas, arid or monsoonal lands where even pastoral cattle enterprises have had to occupy enormous areas to make a profit. Elsewhere, the Ayers-Rock-Uluru metaphor of what has happened since the European arrival is far enough back in time to have been ignored and forgotten for most of the twentieth century, while the more fertile areas have been intensively occupied. Most of the new northern invasion is the result of a mining industry boom and therefore more or less ephemeral.

A glance at the population maps easily demonstrates where those more fertile areas lie. In the driest of continents, water is the chief limiting factor, soils are another. The "fertile arc" stretches from Cooktown in northern Queensland, in a widening sweep southwards and around the southern coast to Adelaide; there it is gapped by a great stretch of limestone, the Nullarbor Plain, with only a corner of southwest Western Australia carrying a high population beyond the Great Australian Bight. Population maps echo the distribution of water and more or less fertile soils, and of reliable rainfall. Inland of this arc, small clusters of population in isolated towns and townships depend on two industries, grazing and wheat farming, and the nomadic mining industry that is gradually mining itself out.

For that matter, both grazing and wheat farming are also in many places as precarious and exploitive. The arid and semi-arid lands cover, on a recent estimate, 5.3 million square kilometres, or 69 percent of Australia.[7] In a few decades of grazing, there has been extensive degradation of these lands, and large regions now are virtually abandoned to the feral animals that can survive there (cats, foxes, rabbits, camels, donkeys, and "brumby" horses maintain small populations, especially in good seasons) and to the arid-adapted animals that were there in the first place and have survived the impacts of change and of the introduced animals.

Recurrent drought and a high rate of evaporation away from the moister coasts will always limit occupation in the interior of the continent, but so does Australia's geological history. Up to the

Cretaceous period, the geological story of the lands that now form Australia was immensely complex and is only gradually being unraveled. The hypothetical Great Southern Continent known as Gondwanaland, which some geologists believe consisted of all the conjoined landmasses of the southern hemisphere and India,[8] has left little evidence of its existence. But the most stable and ancient of the land surfaces of Australia, the Pilbara and Yilgarn shields of gneiss and schist that now form a large part of Western Australia, date back to Archaean times and are thought to have formed part of that mysterious continent. As the landmasses drifted apart, rose and fell and vanished under the oceans, this nucleus of ancient rocks remained stable while sea invasions or mountain-building episodes changed the lands adjacent to it. It is among the oldest and longest-exposed land surfaces in the world, "having remained above sea-level almost continuously for 2500 million years or more."[9] Travelers from Perth in the west cross it, entering Yilgarnia at the Darling Range near the city, and do not leave it for almost five hundred miles. Its almost level distances are varied only by occasional low black hills of rock, and its dark low-growing trees are lit here and there by the apricot-colored trunks of taller salmon-gums.

The other lands that form Australia have had a history of repeated inundations of seas and lakes, but the most influential marks on the Australian interior date from the Jurassic and Cretaceous periods. From 130 to 120 million years ago, great channels opened from north to south, covering a huge area from the Gulf of Carpentaria south and west. These tremendous inundations for a time divided the continent into four or more islands, and "literally wiped Australia from the face of the earth."[10] It is these and other invasions of the sea and brackish waters that have bequeathed the huge areas of sedimentary rocks and sandy or clayey soils that cover so much of inland Australia and help to make it not only among the driest but among the most infertile of lands.

The dunes that run north-south in great parallel waves west of Cooper Creek and north of Lake Eyre—the Simpson Desert—are one of the legacies of the sea and of the wind. The fifty-mile stretch of Lake Eyre itself, and its neighboring smaller salt lakes, Callabonna, Gregory, Blanche, and Frome, and their surrounding salt pans are almost always dry. They glitter under mirage, their crusts of salt white in the dazzle of the inland heat; the mirages that haunt them can make them into hypnotic illusions of water, but around them the sands and dunes are almost bare of vegetation, except for the prickly spinifex *(Triodia)*, and no desert can look thirstier or more empty.

Between the Lake Eyre Basin, into which run the "vanishing rivers" of the Channel Country which feed the lake in the rare periods of great floods from the Queensland tablelands, and the deserts on the western side of the Lakes—the Great Victoria Desert, the Gibson Desert to its north, and the Great Sandy Desert bordered by Eighty-mile Beach in northwestern West Australia—lie the central ranges, Macdonnell and Musgrave. Each side of them, therefore, is arid country reminiscent of the great inundations of the past. But the arid lands can, nevertheless, in good years startle the eyes with flowering. Cassias, hopbush, emu-bush *(Eremophilas)*, many kinds of wattle, and many species of low-growing ephemeral ground-cover plants can spring into bloom in a few days after the rare rains, and seed and die as quickly. The Channel Country's flowerings are famous. This huge, mainly dry drainage basin, roughly following the direction of the old Cretaceous inundation, traces its way south towards Cooper Creek and the Warburton, which lead to Lake Eyre through some of the driest and flattest country in Australia, flanking the Simpson Desert.

Southwest of Lake Eyre Basin, the four-hundred-mile Nullarbor Plain borders the Southern Ocean. Here a Tertiary sea covered a subsidence of part of old Yilgarnia, and left great limestone deposits made by marine organisms—deposits that have gradually been eroded by underground water into a kind of sponge-work of caves, not all of which have even been discovered. The best-known of these is now Koonalda Cave, a great dome-shaped underground cavern in which Aboriginal occupation has been proved to have extended from twenty-four thousand years before present to fifteen thousand years ago. There, in what must have been total darkness except for fires and torches, flint was mined and curious marks and designs were traced or incised on the cave walls, probably twenty thousand or more years ago.[11] This Ice Age occupation depended on those underground waters, which also supported a small Aboriginal population when Europeans first arrived in the country.

But there is little water on the surface, all the way across the Nullarbor and as far east as Spencer Gulf in South Australia. Not until the strangely contorted rocky hills of the Flinders Range north of Adelaide break the levels, does the average rainfall (twenty inches annually) rise to a point beyond the definition of "arid." If Australia is the driest continent, South Australia is its driest state, depending as it does on the waters of the Murray River's lower reaches; for much of its supplies, Adelaide's lifeline is also a pipeline.

Low-growing mallee eucalypts—species which are many-stemmed and depend on a large tough underground rootstock to survive drought—clothe the brown soils and sandhills of the eastern part of the state and extend into western Victoria and New South Wales, lining the Murray and Darling. Such soils have proved capable of growing wheat in spite of their uncertain rainfall, and these semi-arid lands have been extensively cleared and plowed. In the droughts of the 1940s and 1960s, and especially in the four-year drought that ended in 1983, those loosened soils rose and blew eastward and southward, giving the coastal cities a taste of what it is like to live, as farmers and graziers of the southern inland must, with grit and sand in eyes and nostrils, food and clothing.

If the mallee country now grows wheat, it also supports many thousands of sheep. During the first few decades of the nineteenth-century wool boom, it was thought that sheep would never survive away from the moister climates of the eastern coast and highlands. Outbreaks of disease, and the eating out of near-coastal pastures, forced a move inland in good rainfall seasons, and it was found that sheep would in fact survive with far less water than the first sheepmen and shepherds had believed. The mallee and sandhill country, and the slopes and plains west of the Dividing Range, were accordingly invaded and sheep occupied almost the whole of the Murray-Darling catchment.

Since sheep have been the main influence in the degradation of the semi-arid lands of the south, the original plant associations were altered and the soils trampled and bared sometimes even before introduced rabbits multiplied and spread north from their introduction-point in western Victoria in the late 1860s. That brown sandy mallee soil, which covers much of the well-watered southern basin of the Murrumbidgee and Lachlan, and Wimmera and Murray, by 1879 was heavily infested. Rabbits were being reported as far west as Coorabie on the Nullarbor Plain, as far east as Hillston in southern New South Wales, and sporadically in many other places. By the end of 1887, writes Eric Rolls,[12] "the north-east of South Australia, in what should have been a good season, had been turned by rabbits into a terrifying desert," where "most trees and plants had been killed."

The story was repeated wherever seasons and food favored rabbits, and no state was spared—even Tasmania—though the hot north kept their numbers low or held them back altogether. Then, in 1950, the deadly virus myxomatosis was introduced, and "by the beginning of 1953, in little more than three years, most of Australia was virtually free of rabbits."[13] Though there are frightening signs that rabbits are developing strong resistance, numbers are still comparatively low.

But the plant cover of Australia had been changed and degraded to the point where, between rabbit invasions and overstocking by graziers, the arid and semi-arid lands of saltbush, bluebush, mulga, and mallee are probably nowhere in anything like their original condition. In many places, they are degraded to the point where regeneration may not be possible, or will be expensive beyond our means.[14] With the plants, of course, have gone the fauna they supported.

The idea of reserving land as national park or nature reserve came too late, and was too hotly resisted in areas that could be used for any other purpose, to save representative areas of the semi-arid inland pastures. The same can be said of the richer and moister lands of southeastern and central Queensland—the so-called "brigalow belts." Brigalow is a tall dark acacia that grows strongly and tenaciously on better soils where rainfall is fairly reliable. It became an enemy to pastoralists and governments early, since, like other acacias, it rapidly increased where grazing was heavy, and the soils it occupied were much coveted for agricultural production. With the great prickly-pear plague that took over huge tracts of Queensland, and favored similar soils, it virtually denied access to cattle and sheep; when the prickly-pear fell to an introduced enemy, the cactoblastis moth, the brigalow remained, and proved extraordinarily resistant to clearing. The advent of new heavy machinery after World War II changed the balance against it, and government subsidies lured farmers back to try again. Soon the brigalow and softwood communities of these favored soils began to vanish; and now the Queensland National Parks and Wildlife Service, surveying what remains, estimates that only half of one percent of the former brigalow-softwood communities remains, and very little can now be reserved.[15] These communities have joined the rainforests of the Eastern Highlands as endangered associations.

The Eastern Highlands and the coastal plain have supported European populations longer than anywhere else in Australia. The Dividing Range, which runs as a spine and watershed between the eastern-flowing coastal rivers and the western-flowing waters that feed into the Murray-Darling basin, was heavily forested on our arrival, from the rainforests of Cape York all the way south to Victoria and the Tasmanian mountains. Uncontrolled timber-cutting, ruthless exploitation of coveted species such as the red cedars—until now almost none are left—ringbarking and clearing for often short-lived farms, and a late and often nearly powerless control of the timber industry by state forestry authorities have deeply injured the original forests. But eucalypts are stubborn, and their regrowth, where they are permitted, often conceals the wounds. For that reason, the eucalypt forests are regarded by many people as the typical Australian landscape, and they are seen as much more widespread than in fact they are—for the high population of the eastern coasts and tablelands and the concentration of tourism in the "fertile arc" confuses popular perception. Wrote a forest scientist:

> Australians have tended to regard their country as heavily forested. But, compared with other countries, Australia is poorly endowed with forests, which cover only 4 percent of the area of the continent . . . The idea . . . probably arose from the fact that most of the forests are, or were, along the eastern coasts where settlement developed.[16]

In these well-watered and apparently fertile regions, the clearing of trees for farming was a herculean, often misguided, but highly approved attempt to follow early directives of government in Britain and Australia. A "yeoman class," it was thought, would occupy profitably the country's empty spaces, which greatly worried those who feared the designs of other countries on the colonies. Drought, flood, soil infertility, a succession of economic booms and busts, high-interest loans, and ignorance of soils and climates ended that dream, and often left farms abandoned and seriously deteriorated. Marginal farming seldom provides a livelihood anywhere in Australia; in the past it has resulted in what Webb calls "erosion gullies that are like savage claw-marks on our eastern mountains, and miserable slopes which grow only landslides and vegetable rubbish or support only timber-tombstones."[17]

Moreover, this "fertile arc" on which so much of Australia's population is concentrated has depended for its fertility on soils, especially alluvial soils, that are now in far heavier demand for urban expansion, tourist development, industry, and road and port development than their supply can support. Said the Report of the National Estate:

> Over the recent years, the land-use pattern in Australia has been radically altered. The rush to the cities has produced the vast urban conglomerations which now increasingly demand land for recreation, and in many cases, also for holiday living and "prestige" houses outside city limits. It is now possible to live seventy-five kilometres or more from one's work place. The pattern of settlement has tended to concentrate on well-watered river valleys and coastal areas . . . This has resulted in development pressures on near-urban land forcing many farmers out of prime agricultural lands . . . The forcing of farms into previously unused or lightly used lands has many costs and disbenefits . . . Some, at least, of the land is unsuitable for intensive agriculture because of soil infertility or fragility . . . Soil erosion, pasture and soil deterioration, higher flood levels, spread of introduced weeds, silting of streams, rivers, water storages and ports can all result.[18]

Certainly, the uncontrolled clearing of forests on the uplands and slopes has greatly contributed to the problem. Coastal (and inland) rivers are now heavily silted in many places; salination of soils often follows timber-clearing, and is especially a problem in the irrigated areas of the river-systems of the Murray-Murrumbidgee. The irony is that these problems are occurring in the only parts of the continent where climate, rainfall, and soils are favorable and reliable enough to support a heavy burden of population.

The rape of the forests set off little protest until the 1960s, though even a hundred years before it had attracted attention at least in the southern states. Then a Japanese woodchip industry moved into the forests of Tasmania, and later to the southern coastal mountains of New South Wales. We may not mind exterminating our own forests; but the scale and ruthlessness of the woodchip export projects set off a strong reaction. Western Australia's once-splendid forests of hardwood eucalypts, including the famous jarrah *(Eucalyptus marginata)*, whose tough, dark red wood was once the pride of Australia's timber export trade, were under threat, from both mining applications and another woodchipping project. Western Australia's forests grow in soils easily laterized when cleared, and it had been realized that extensive timber-clearing in the state had already begun to salinize most of the rivers running from cleared farmland. With very little fertile area except in the southwest, the woodchipping project and a large-scale operation for bauxite in the Darling Ranges have seriously increased the salt problem.

At present, only two rivers in southwestern Australia carry potable water. Forest regeneration is slow, and "dieback" fungal disease is practically epidemic in many forest areas. The most valuable of the timber species, the deep-rooting jarrah that once tapped the water table and helped maintain it in equilibrium, is particularly susceptible, and it has proved impossible so far to regenerate the mined lands with the eucalypt species that once grew there.

Increasing population and land-clearing for sheep and wheat-farming, with new methods of extending farming into formerly unrewarding soils and climates, have somewhat changed the face of Western Australia; but with two-thirds of the state classified either as arid or semi-arid, and with salt lakes scattered over the great inland plateau, the state likes to hope that its future lies with the mineral deposits of the Pre-Cambrian Shield rocks. Most of this mining so far has been for iron ore, in the richly colored hills and ravines of the Hamersley Ranges of the Pilbaraland. Little but spinifex ("porcupine grass") grows in the nearly waterless ranges, but their crimsons, browns, and mauves glow in banded layers through the heatwaves of the northwest.

In Tasmania, where the "southwest wilderness" has been the scene of a protracted and increasingly embittered battle between the forces of conservation, represented by the Tasmanian Wilderness Society with mainland backing, and the interests of industrialization represented by the Tasmanian Hydro-Electricity Commission and successive Tasmanian governments, forests were only part of the issue at stake, but the southwestern forests are nevertheless extraordinary. The southwest represents a remnant of old Gondwanaland, elsewhere in the Southern Ocean sunken underwater. Its southward-flowing wild rivers, running from the central mountains through gorges and valleys and between tall cliffs, are lined with dense, temperate rainforest in which the unique endemic Huon Pine once predominated. Many of these trees have been felled, where they were accessible to the "piners"—the Tasmanian equivalent of the Eastern Highlands cedar-getters. Some remain in a reserve on the Denison River, where Olegas Truchanas, most revered figure of the battle for the wilderness, succeeded against all odds in forcing the hand of the Hydro-Electricity Commission and having a thousand-acre Huon Pine Scenic Reserve declared on the river—a reserve now known by his name.

The Tasmanian Aborigines were long thought to have occupied the island only during the period of the last Ice Age, eight to ten thousand years ago, when Bass Strait islands were linked with the mainland by the locking of waters in the ice caps. The peril of the Gordon and Franklin Rivers posed by the dam proposals set off more exploration by archeologists; and in at least two caves remarkable assemblages of artifacts and hearths were found. Carbon-dating in Deena-Reena Cave, deep in the limestone cliffs of the Franklin River, proved occupation as far back as twenty thousand years—the earlier Ice Age, when Koonalda Cave in the Nullarbor was also occupied.

This southmost occupation not only by Australian Aborigines, but by any peoples during the ice of that period makes Deena-Reena and other caves on which little archeological work has yet been done of the greatest significance in the piecing together of human prehistory. "The courage and skill of these Tasmanian Aborigines, braving the ice, snow and freezing cold to hunt wallabies within sight of glaciers, is eloquent testimony to the indomitable spirit of early humans."[19]

This discovery proved of immense help to the Commonwealth government in its High Court case to obtain an injunction against the building of the dam, under the World Heritage legislation it had introduced. If the magnificent rivers and forests of southwest Tasmania are now nationally—and internationally—protected against the bulldozers' advance, so is the memory of their first inhabitants, and the inheritance of their present-day descendants.

Moreover, the threat to the southwest wilderness and its caves, and the successful outcome of the Commonwealth's testing of its heritage legislation against the action of the states, makes other potential or actual World Heritage nominations much more secure. One such is also closely associated with the time of very early occupation. Archeological exploration is young in this country, and not well funded; it depends partly on the accessibility of possible sites. Willandra Lakes, in western New South Wales, lie along an ancient and now dry drainage line, which thirty thousand years ago was a series of lakes, but by sixteen thousand years before present was already nearly empty and today is semi-arid, sandy, and eroded by winds. The semi-circular dunes (lunettes) piled up on the lake shores long ago and now eroded into weird white shapes, were called "the walls of China" by early settlers. These fossil lakes and dunes supported, during the Pleistocene, not only a rich freshwater fauna with many fish and mussels, but a human occupation stretching back at least thirty thousand years, and a culture that practiced ritual burial as well as cremation. Ocher has been found in one such burial, which "shows that such rituals go back at least as far in Australia as in other parts of the world such as France, where ochred burials . . . have been found at a similar time."[20]

It is not for their scenic value but for their archeological value that the Willandra Lakes have been nominated as World Heritage; but in spite of the semi-arid landscape based on sedimentary deposits, there may be far more to be discovered from study of the lake chain than the story of human occupation. The now extinct megafauna survived until the end of the last Ice Age ten thousand years ago; giant kangaroos and wombats, *Diprotodon australis,* and huge flightless birds existed then and may have left their fossil bones there, as have the Aborigines themselves. That once-flourishing lakeshore culture, round whose unsuspected remnants the sheep of invading pastoralists grazed tens of thousands of years later, may have much more to tell.

The result of the Franklin Dam case will have its effect also on that other, very different, area, the Great Barrier Reef. For one of the latest additions to the classification of World Heritage is the newly declared Great Barrier Reef Marine Park.

The Great Barrier Reef, a twelve-hundred-mile stretch of corals, sand cays, and isles forms a bastion between the Queensland coast and the open Pacific from Cape York south almost to Fraser Island. It is essentially a submarine mountain chain whose summits are alive and based on the skeletons of myriads of other once-living creatures, the corals that have now formed a limestone rampart. Yet the word "rampart" is misleading, for this is a maze in which reefs and channels and fringing reefs, isles, and isolated rocks—remnants of now sunken mountains—cover about one hundred thousand square miles of shallow offshore continental shelf. The coral reefs themselves form "probably the most extensive series which has ever existed, and almost certainly the largest structure on the face of the earth today created by living organisms."[21]

These are cold words of mere measurement. The reef itself—called by biologists and others simply *the* reef for its size and uniqueness—is beyond measurement; it consists for biologists of its uncountable and stunningly various marine animals. The corals that have built, and continue to build, it, the Anthozoa, (there are two other main classes of marine animals in the phylum to which the reef-builders belong), secrete their own skeletons, picking up from the water the lime with which they clothe themselves and which, as the coral polyps die, becomes the structure of the reef. But the colors—the myriad shades from crimson to green and blue and yellow and purple and indescribable shades between—are in the polyp itself; the dead coral, which breaks up into branches, twigs, and lumps and finally becomes the dazzling sand of the beaches, is white only. Not only are its colors so immensely various, but the shapes of the corals that the polyps build—like trees, like flowers, like mushrooms or leaves or ferns or mosses, but only "like" insofar as we have no words to fit them.

Among these corals, on the reef surfaces and the sandy shallows and the undersea coral cliffs and rocks, live equally uncountable species of marine animals and their larvae which in the free-swimming stages make the plankton that is a food base for creatures as small as the coral polyps themselves and for many larger. Almost all the reef's creatures are intricately colored and shaped—some so amazing that one can only stare wordlessly. Scientists have not yet completed even the taxonomy of all the reef's species, while its ecology is almost unknown. For writers, the task of description is frankly impossible. As a poet recently wrote:[22]

> English is a fine instrument for celebrating snowdrops or daffodils or skylarks and other creatures that have gained a traditional literary meaning over the centuries—but it is tongue-tied when faced with some polyp or reef fish that is a dozen times more beautiful and intricate, but has only a jaw-rattling Latin name.

The reef is probably the greatest reservoir of marine species in the world, with a vast community of mutually interdependent organisms and seabirds: a climax ecosystem, as the ecological jargon has it, unrivaled anywhere except in the tropical rainforests. Its status as "world heritage" is unquestionable. Yet in the late 1960s, at the time when Australia became the target of multinational oil and mineral exploration companies, it was the cause of one of the longest and most stubborn battles between conservationists (and, for that matter, most of Australia) and the Queensland state government, backed by international interests. It was rescued by a combination of factors—determination, resource, popular support, and sheer luck—and in 1975 the Whitlam government, without waiting for a High Court judgment on its offshore authority as against the states, passed a special act, the Great Barrier Reef Marine Park Act, to protect it. Under the act, the Great Barrier Reef Marine Park Authority, with the participation of Queensland's National Parks and Wildlife Service, has finally declared almost the whole of its extent a marine park.

Opposing interests argued that so large an area could surely support *some* industrial exploitation and that to declare the whole area a marine park was unnecessary. They still do so. But the reef is not like a land-based park; it is washed everywhere by intricate communicating currents that bear the lifeline of the reef itself—the plankton that contains the coral larvae—and it has already been clearly shown that the whole area is vulnerable to interference. At the same time as the battle against the government was being carried on, a plague of coral-eating starfish—the Crown of Thorns—was reported to be spreading across the reefs and leaving behind it acres of dead and crumbling corals hung with gray curtains of algae and almost deserted by other organisms. The plague appeared to slacken; the governments, which had declined to fund any attempt to halt it by collecting and killing the starfish, have still done little or nothing towards research or control; now, in 1984, the scientist who first raised the alarm, Dr. Robert Endean, reports that another and even more devastating increase in the numbers of the Crown of Thorns is under way. Clearly, the reef can be, and perhaps is being, destroyed; the factors behind the increase in the Crown of Thorns are still not completely clear, but collection of the predators of the starfish larvae and probably pollution from onshore have been named as among them. Since the reef probably influences through its plankton production many of the other coral areas of the Pacific, such disasters may have much more widespread effects than we yet know.

There has been no lovelier and no more significant gift to the world's inheritance than the nomination of the reef as World

Heritage and the declaration of the Marine National Park. How long it will continue to exist in all that vibrating complexity of life and color depends probably on the way the world goes. Great oil-tankers feel their way through the dangerous shipping channel between reef and mainland, where cyclones are frequent and the bones of many ships lie; industry and farming enterprises pour chemicals and wastes, almost without control, into offshore waters; tourists spearfish, collect shells and corals, legally or illegally; where fifty years ago the reef was almost unknown and disregarded, its new resorts are now swarming with sightseers and tourist operators. No park authority with as little funding as the GBRMP now has can really hope to control what happens in its waters. It is not the explosion of the Crown of Thorns population, but that of the human species and its wants, that will destroy the reef.

Inland from reef waters, the Dividing Range runs north into Cape York, and here are its highest mountains, Bartle Frere and the rest of the Bellenden Ker Range. The Dividing Range is an inheritance from a Tertiary age uplift, running like a long wave along the whole of the east coast above the coastal shelf. Australia has no active volcanoes, but volcanic action played a part in the uplift of the Dividing Range and basalt flows from it provide some of the few patches of really rich soil in Australia. The Border Ranges in the south, and some high mountains from the Burdekin River north to beyond Cairns are a remnant of such volcanoes, and on them Australia's most spectacular rainforests grow. (We called them "jungle" until recently, much as we called the Aborigines "niggers.") Rainforests have been, and are, heavily exploited, cleared wherever slopes are feasible for farming, and the subject of deeply unsympathetic logging operations by State Forestry Commissions both in New South Wales and Queensland; but a few national parks, including the first Queensland parks declared, still hold samples of their original associations, and the Bellenden Ker Range and a few other mountains are somewhat too steep and inaccessible to be seriously depleted as yet. Fires from the lower farming slopes eat back into them and they, like the reef, have become "tourist attractions"; but a growing strength and dedication in the conservation movement has helped to protect some areas even where obstinacy on the part of state governments has been difficult to overcome.

The Report of the National Estate in 1974 said:

The remaining forests of Australia are of international significance as ancient and isolated reservoirs of a great variety of plant and animal species which, especially in northern tropical areas, have yet been little studied by science. They are a non-renewable resource, being unable to regenerate under present land-use practices. The sustained productivity of their soils for agricultural or pastoral use is in doubt; the high rainfall causes them to become infertile or eroded once the forest is removed . . . These changes represent a loss of world heritage of genetic resources, and indeed a loss of the biological perspective for the evolution of man himself.[23]

There are many variations in type, height, dominant species, and species distribution within the wide classification "rainforest." The northern mountain forests are perhaps the most spectacular; their effect on even unthinking tourists is always notable. Tall and low tree species in association spread a canopy or series of canopies that close off the sky and change the light into a depth of green; ferns and vines occupy the lower spaces and scramble up the trunks of the trees: often one can only tell the tree species from the flowers and berries they drop through all this vegetative luxury to the forest floor. The broad-leafed softwoods that characterize most rainforests are interspersed here and there, where the timber-getters have not reached them, by araucarias that push through the canopy. These forests fluctuated in distribution and extent throughout the Pleistocene epoch, with its great climatic changes, and pollen-dating studies done so far appear to indicate that over the past ten thousand or more years, Aboriginal fires have been one factor in their distributional alterations; the eucalypt forest that borders them is favored by fire, while rainforest species do not regenerate once burned.

Where the basaltic flows and granite blocks of the high northern range cease, beyond Cooktown, the Dividing Range lowers, and mazes and plateaus of sandstone partly take the place of the harder rocks. Here are Queensland's great art galleries, where sandstone shelters and overhangs are decorated with an amazing profusion of engraved and painted images left by Aborigines who have now, for the most part, been hunted and collected into reserves that they do not own and that are not "their country." Rugged, steep, hot, bare, and guarded by monsoon rainfall in the Wet, lack of water in the Dry, and the stinging green ants that are legendary even in Australia, home of hundreds of ant species, they were unknown to Europeans until the 1960s. Then Captain Percy Trezise, accompanied by Aboriginal friends, began exploring the area. His book *Quinkan Country*[24] first introduced these galleries to the public; fortunately, they are still difficult to reach. More such galleries have now been found in the sandstone plateaus and gorges of the Dividing Range west of Rockhampton; their extent and importance, and their age, have not yet been publicized.

It has been in the north of Australia that Aboriginal art seems to have flourished most. In Arnhem Land, that other sandstone region whose east coast faces Cape York across the two-hundred-mile width of the Gulf of Carpentaria, and whose north coast borders the Arafura Sea, there are already artifact datings extending back to 33,000 years ago.[25] The region, with its very ancient rocks, "contains the most complex and prolific rock art not only in Australia but also in the world,"[26] and these are still being explored and recorded. But Arnhem Land, like Cape York, is now under heavy pressures by mining developments, and indeed the whole of Australia's northern coastline may be said to have jumped into the realm of controversy and conflict over the past couple of decades.

These northern coasts of Australia were judged very inauspicious for European habitation. A few ill-fated attempts at setting up a port early in the nineteenth century convinced the British that they were best left alone. Later, the port of Darwin became the coastal link between the Overland Telegraph Line and the submarine cable that joined Australia to the world; but it lies in monsoon influences. From Gove in Arnhem Land to the Cambridge Gulf, the Wet season between November and March brings cyclones and storms that can leave ruin in their wake; between the Wet seasons the Dry brings burning heat and a thirst for which the North is renowned. The monsoon rains cover the low-lying land and the floodplains of the north-running rivers—Victoria, Ord, Adelaide, and the two Alligator Rivers. These flow from the great rock outcrops of King Leopold and Durack Ranges and the Arnhem Land Plateau—center of one of the most divisive controversies in Australia today. In the plateau and the wetland plains of the East and South Alligator Rivers lie two conflicting elements—deposits of uranium, and another World Heritage nomination, the Kakadu National Park. At present, even the park itself contains a uranium mine, and this is trouble.

The main uranium deposits now being mined lie in the catchments of the East and South Alligator Rivers, which rise in the Arnhem

Land Plateau. The vast level floodplain is backed by a long sweep of rockwall, the escarpment of the plateau, incised by gorges and in the Wet laced with streams, pools, and waterfalls. The whole region, for many decades after the arrival of Europeans in the south, lay practically undisturbed. Mineral exploration forced on a scientific study in 1972–73—the Environmental Fact-Finding Study—and scientists were for the first time made aware that the region contained many endemic species. The low-lying plains are flooded during most of the Wet, and form breeding and feeding areas for myriads of waterfowl, fish, frogs, watersnakes, and insects; waterfowl in particular breed there in countless millions. The plateau's sandstones, soaked by rains, continue to hold and to release water for months after the Dry begins; the larger streams are permanent and there are always pools and springs in sheltered gorges even when heat has parched the surrounding country to a cinder. Two hundred and fifty species of birds have been reported, fifty mammal species, seventy-five reptiles, and many endemic plants and animals. Even now, species are being discovered that are unknown elsewhere. All this lies within and near the boundaries of Kakadu National Park.

Much of the park was Aboriginal reserve, and the passage of the Aboriginal Land Rights (Northern Territory) Act in 1976 provided for Aboriginal ownership of the reserves in the Northern Territory. Though the Aboriginal owners agreed to allow Kakadu National Park to be declared (with certain of their own conditions), the interests of uranium mining companies, of Northern Territory tourism, of governments, and of Aborigines continue to clash, with even conservationists attempting to intervene. This is not new; during the early 1970s, Stanley and Kay Breeden wrote: "Change is so rapid that what seemed a secure wilderness area a few years ago is an embattled area today. The forces of man-made destruction are poised to despoil the north's and Australia's last major unspoilt regions."[27]

It seems ironic that Aborigines themselves, over many centuries, have contributed one of the most important factors to the "tourist attractions" that bring much of that destruction to their ancient land and its traditions. The escarpment and plateau of Arnhem Land contain one of the greatest art galleries of the world. Its rock shelters and cliffs have been sacred for countless years, and the painted images are various, remarkable, and probably very aged. It has been estimated that some at least date back to eighteen thousand years ago and beyond; and four successive styles of painting have been distinguished.[28] Some paintings seem to document the existence in the region of animals long extinct, or locally extinct.

It is always difficult to have areas reserved as national parks, and sometimes the very reservation puts the survival of the areas at risk. Little can be done about the destructiveness of the ignorant, except to attempt to educate them; and not much funding is ever given to such enterprises, or to policing the regulations that do exist. Kakadu's importance should have warranted proper planning years ago; as it is, the roads that give access to most of it were made with the convenience of mining companies in mind.

In the Kimberley Ranges of Western Australia, where the remarkable Mimi spirit paintings loom and the lively "Bradshaw" figures dance on the rocks, there is no such great park proposal; but the Kimberleys are mountains of great splendor. Even from the air, the ruggedness of the coast from Wyndham to Broome is awesome. Deep sounds and inlets break the coastline, where it is thought that rivers running from the Kimberley high country have worn precipitously walled channels in this area of high wet-season rainfall. Most of the sounds and inlets are nearly inaccessible even by sea; their cliffs rise from mostly unexplored depths of water, and offshore a shallow reef-studded and island-dotted sea defends them. King Sound, the largest and most western stretch of water, with the only developed port and town, is itself scattered with islands. The tremendous tides of the region make Derby a dangerous port, but it has served for years to export cattle and wool, and now ships ply in and out with exported iron-ore from Yampi.

From the air, Derby's main characteristic at low tide seems to be a fan-shaped network of channels dragged by those thirty-five-foot tides through mud and mangroves. The Kimberley Plateau above is part of another most ancient land mass, Stuartiana; it looks down westward on the sand plains that were once laid down under the sea invasions and where the Fitzroy River, which drains the Plateau and the King Leopold Ranges, now runs into King Sound. The Fitzroy and its tributaries, the Margaret and Leopold Rivers, run for part of their length through deep and nearly inaccessible gorges, and in the Wet can be terrifyingly forceful; the Margaret River's course through the King Leopold Range is like a knife cut deeply incised into the ancient sandstone. On the Fitzroy below the plateau, the name of

Fossil Downs Station indicates how rich the limestones from the Devonian Seas are, in corals and many other marine fossils.

The Kimberleys, east and west, their rocks and gorges alternately scoured by monsoon and cyclonic rains and parched by the heat of the Dry, support practically no settlement; but they are the site of one of Australia's most ambitious and expensive nightmares, the Ord Dam. Here, in a fertile valley-plain below the plateau, where the Ord River debouches from the ranges, a huge dam and irrigation project, whose initiation was more political than practical, has struggled for years to find a raison d'être. The "unpeopled North" is a recurrent alarm to Australians; those who declare a new project to turn these almost unpeopled lands into smiling and profitable farmland and provide a population to defend them from imagined invasions can always win votes. In fact, however, the North has always won the battle; only mining (and the Argyle diamond project is now the new dream) ever seems to thrive. Ironically, it seems likely that the Ord Dam drowns much of the diamond-bearing kimberlite country. And the cattle industry that preceded it has resulted in very serious erosion that is silting the dam and will take years and much money to control.

Between Derby and Broome there is scarcely any settlement; west of Broome itself, the Eighty-Mile Beach sweeps in a long curve of dazzling white to mark the northern edge of the Great Sandy Desert. The map shows clearly the path of the ancient sea invasion, from the beach south to the Nullarbor; salt lakes with names like Disappointment mark the map everywhere, west of the Petermann Ranges and north of the Great Australian Bight and the Nullarbor that fringes it. There is no town between Broome and the Transcontinental Railway to the south, and the iron-ore port, Port Hedland, to the west, or between Alice Springs and Laverton, a tiny railhead settlement north of Kalgoorlie—thousands of square miles of nothing. No "civilized" road crosses those flat, sandy, salty hundreds of miles from Geraldton on the western Australian coast to Alice Springs. The Gunbarrel Highway, a track through the spinifex and sand named for its straightness, is traversed only by the very hardy equipped with water and petrol for their four-wheeled drives; and though not long ago a woman crossed it with camels, and alone, it is for us virtually without either food or water.

Yet this desert plain, with the Musgrave and Petermann Ranges, Ayers Rock and Mount Olga and Mount Conner and the country surrounding them and the western Macdonnell Ranges—the central core of Australia—is the home country and has for thousands of years been the sacred origin and life support of the Pitjantjajara people, and the peoples who are their neighbors. They know more of the so-called desert, its mainly nocturnal fauna, its hidden waters, its plants and their uses, than we will ever know, but from a very different point of view. We Europeans for long had no use for this country; now it is in demand for prospecting and possible mining, but the Central Reserve, into which the Aborigines have been huddled, has now passed or is passing into the European-recognized ownership of the Aborigines who live there and who will have a veto over mining if they do not wish it. The Central Reserve, almost four hundred miles from north to south and three hundred miles wide, is unforgettable country. Those tourists who go to the Center have seldom seen the far western ranges, the Petermanns and the western Macdonnells, or the great salt lake, Lake Amadeus, beyond Mount Olga, Mount Conner, and Ayers Rock. The Musgraves, southwest of Ayers Rock, are nearly as inaccessibly waterless and roadless.

This is as well, since to the people of the Central Reserve all are sacred and ceremonial places. The glowing bluish quartzite, the red granites and gneisses, the isolated and fantastic shapes of the three island mountains between the ranges, the undulating red sandhills even seen from the air alone are hauntingly strange. In the ranges lie chasms, overhangs, and gorges, where shade and protection from hot winds keep a few pools of water as almost permanent resources. The white stems and green leaves of ghost-gums, thorny low shrubs, and the mulga and spinifex that thrive even in such low-rainfall areas, make a ground cover for quite a varied fauna. What we call desert is, and has for unknown time, been home, beloved and intimate basis of all of life, to the original people of the Center.

Those deserts terrified the Europeans who first tried to cross them. Almost everywhere, it seemed, the northern coasts were cut off from the more hospitable southern and eastern arc by country apparently uninhabitable. During most of the late nineteenth century, European venturers were lost, or came staggering back with miserable reports. The poet Kendall was haunted by a kind of horror in even thinking of those apparently-blighted hopes and regions—where Ludwig Leichhardt had perished

On the tracts of thirst and furnace—on the
dumb blind burning plain
Where the red earth gapes for moisture and the
wan leaves hiss for rain.[29]

The writer Marcus Clarke, in his preface to Adam Lindsay Gordon's poems, was equally rhetorically distressed by those explorations:

Hopeless explorers have named [the mountains] out of their suffering—Mount Misery, Mount Dreadful, Mount Despair . . . The soul, placed before the frightful grandeur of these barren hills, drinks in their sentiment of defiant ferocity, and is steeped in bitterness.[30]

This central core of a country where early arrivals had hoped to find an inland sea—which had dried to salt and sand aeons before they went to look for it—came as a shock and frustration that may have darkened all our view. We came first as exiles, later as predators; love has come late, if ever, and by the time we began to understand a little of the land, we had already set a pattern of destruction. How to turn the more fertile areas, at least, into an imitation Europe was our early preoccupation. The network of roads, fences, and surveyed boundaries that overlies the Aboriginal ancestral spirit tracks that once connected one side of the continent with another in legend and enactment of ceremonies and trading exchanges; the foreign plants and animals we imported to make us feel at home as well as to support us, do not for Aborigines either justify our invasion or make the country ours. They have never agreed to tolerate us, nor bargained with us over land. In their view, they own the continent, and the land will look after them beyond our time. After all, they have survived all the changes of the Pleistocene, and their way of life, it seems, has persisted perhaps with little change since their Dreaming was laid down. There is little we can say to that.

But there has been some recent and more or less reluctant change in the situation Europeans have forced on them. There had never been any meaningful admission of their prior ownership of the land. The claim, under the now internationally discredited *terra nullius* principle, made by Cook and confirmed by Governor Phillip at Sydney Cove on January 26, 1788, was not ameliorated later in favor of the Aboriginal occupants, whose rights in land were never acknowledged. Such reserves as were later made in the various colonies carried no title but remained in the hands of the crown, and under government administration. Their land was taken progressively, by a sequence described by W.E.H. Stanner as "meeting, sporadic violence, a general struggle, and the imposition of terms by the stronger," which "always appeared wherever settlement went."[31] Some attempts were made by the authorities to intervene in the process, but they foundered on the realities of the situation. Aborigines were, by the operation of the *terra nullius* principle, without rights to the land that Europeans wanted.

After decades of relegation to the reserves as a dying race, the late 1960s and 1970s saw an Aboriginal revival, and their protests met white sympathy. The federal government in the first years of the 1970s drafted legislation on Aboriginal land rights, to be applied in the Northern Territory, which was then administered by the Commonwealth, leaving it to the separate state governments to decide on the application of the principle within the states. Passed in 1976 with some weakening amendments, the Aboriginal Land Rights (Northern Territory) Act provided for Aboriginal reserves to be transferred to Aboriginal ownership, and for other areas outside the reserves to be claimed by Aborigines with provable and traditional links of "ownership." (Aboriginal responsibilities for and rights in land do not in fact correspond to European notions of ownership.)

With the help of interpreters and anthropologists, claims are now being established to land outside reserves, and it has been optimistically estimated that up to 50 percent of the territory may eventually become Aboriginal land.[32] However, much of this was formerly reserve land in any case, and a very small percentage of the remainder is actually productive and supportive, much being desert or, in the Wet, swampland. Meanwhile, some Northern Territory Aborigines whose land is now being mined are receiving mining royalties distributed through an Aboriginal Benefit Trust Account.

The Northern Territory, and, to a limited extent, South Australia, were in 1983–84 the only areas where land rights legislation was operative, though some of the states were engaged in drafting legislation. However, the federal government promised in 1983 to introduce overall land-rights legislation that would override that of states. But in some states, notably Queensland and Tasmania, there is a very strong resistance to Aboriginal land ownership. In both, and elsewhere, a long-standing program of displacement, "relocation," and attempts at "assimilation" has resulted in widespread loss of traditional links with land such as the Northern Territory act requires for title to be granted. An adamant, and adroit, state government in Queensland has preserved a situation in which the only land title achieved by or for Aborigines is a small amount of mainly rural land purchases against state opposition by a Commonwealth fund administered by specially created authorities.

A referendum in 1967, passed by a remarkably high majority, had finally empowered the Commonwealth to pass legislation for Aborigines (who had formerly been under the control of states alone). However, except in the Northern Territory, this had scarcely been applied until 1984, the federal government being reluctant to challenge the powers of intransigent states, and fearful (so its ministers implied) that the powers were insufficient for the purpose. Since 1980, however, two High Court cases[33] have established beyond doubt that the Commonwealth has overriding powers in matters connected with its "external affairs" power, under which Australia has ratified three international covenants on human rights, and another—the World Heritage Convention—that provided the power to protect the archeological as well as the environmental value of the area destined to be flooded in Southwest Tasmania. There can be no question that the land-rights legislation proposed for 1984 is a legitimate use of the power; but there are other moves that state governments can make, and the issue is unlikely to be settled without problems.

Nevertheless, remarkable gains, in a comparative sense, were made during the 1970s and 1980s, many of them prompted by Aborigines' own activism. The shift in interest by the United Nations Human Rights Commission during the 1980s—its postwar decolonization program drawing to an end—towards the plight of indigenous enclave peoples allowed them further hope. Though full self-determination as defined by the United Nations seemed still a difficult goal to reach, their depth of relationship with the land and their influence on its aspect before the arrival of Europeans is now well recognized, and their rights to land and to compensation for the loss of land and of their former way of life have been emphasized in the federal Parliament by ministers and others, and are part of the national debate. Australia has hitherto been isolated from international pressures and many European-Australians have not yet realized that our ratification of the international treaties has put on us a responsibility we are not yet meeting. However, the influence of international law may finally be decisive in the clearing of our own consciences on the Aboriginal question.

The land we occupied less than two hundred years ago has been decisively and immensely altered during that time. Australians of European or Asian descent may never attain the kind of intimate relationship with it that so many millennia have given to its Aboriginal inhabitants. But a growth of attachment on grounds not wholly economic is perceptible already, and may finally bring the two viewpoints a little closer if real action is taken to heal the wounds we have dealt both to the land and its original owners.

ENDNOTES

[1]"Proposal for Establishing a Settlement in New South Wales," August 23, 1783, *Historical Records of New South Wales,* vol. 1, part 2, reproduced in Ged Martin, ed., *The Founding of Australia* (Sydney: Hale and Iremonger, 1978), p. 9.

[2]S. Macarthur Onslow, *Some Early Records of the Macarthurs* (Sydney: 1914), p. 48.

[3]Eric Rolls, *A Million Wild Acres* (Melbourne: Nelson, 1981), pp. 28–9.

[4]See for example R.J. Stanley, "Soils and Vegetation: An Assessment of Current Status," in *What Future for Australia's Arid Lands?,* edited by John Messer and Geoff Mosley (Melbourne: Australian Conservation Foundation, 1983), and Eric Rolls, *They All Ran Wild* (Sydney: Angus and Robertson, 1969).

[5]Josephine Flood, *Archaeology of the Dreamtime* (Melbourne: Collins, 1983), pp. 170–71, 205–6.

[6]From "Lalai (Dreamtime)," recounted by Sam Woolagoodjah, in Colin Bourke, Colin Johnson, and Isobel White, *Before the Invasion: Aboriginal Life to 1788* (Melbourne: Oxford University Press, 1980), p. 51.

[7]A.D. Wilson and R.D. Graetz, "Management of Semi-Arid and Arid Rangelands of Australia," in B.H. Walker, ed., *Management of Semi-Arid Ecosystems* (Elsevier Scientific Publishing Co.) quoted in Messer and Mosley, eds., *What Future for Australia's Arid Lands?,* pp. 1 and 2 (figure).

[8]Charles Laseron, *Ancient Australia,* third edition, revised by Rudolf Oskar Brunnschweiler (Sydney: Angus and Robertson, 1984) p. 166.

[9]Ibid., pp. 37–38.

[10]Ibid., p. 231.

[11]Laseron, *The Face of Australia,* revised by J.N. Jennings (Sydney: Angus and Robertson, 1972), p. 39.

[12]Rolls, *They All Ran Wild,* p. 50.

[13]Ibid., p. 184.

[14]For detail, see R.J. Stanley, in *What Future for Australia's Arid Lands?*, p. 17, table 5; and J.S. Turner, "The Decline of the Plants," in A.J. Marshall, ed., *The Great Extermination* (Melbourne: Heinemann, 1966), pp. 134–53.

[15]Queensland National Parks and Wildlife Service, Eighth Annual Report, 1982–83 (Brisbane: Government Printer, 1983), p. 28.

[16]L.J. Webb, "The Rape of the Forests," in Marshall, ed., *The Great Extermination*, p. 158.

[17]Ibid., p. 156.

[18]*Report of the National Estate,* part II, chapter 3, paras. 3.15 to 3.17 (Canberra: Commonwealth Government, 1974).

[19]Flood, *Archaeology of the Dreamtime,* p. 107.

[20]Ibid., p. 46.

[21]Isobel Bennett, *The Great Barrier Reef* (Melbourne: Lansdowne, 1971), p. 14.

[22]Mark O'Connor, "Putting the Reef into Words," *Reeflections,* no. 11 (Townsville: Great Barrier Reef Marine Park Authority, n.d.), p. 1.

[23]*Report of the National Estate,* para. 3.58, p. 55.

[24]P.J. Trezise, *Quinkan Country* (Sydney: A.H. and A.W. Reed, 1969).

[25]Flood, *Archaeology of the Dreamtime,* p. 90.

[26]Ibid., p. 127.

[27]S. and K. Breeden, *Australia's North: A Natural History of Australia* (Sydney: Collins, 1975), vol. 3, p. 199.

[28]Flood, *Archaeology of the Dreamtime,* p. 128.

[29]"Leichhardt," *The Poems of Henry Kendall* (Sydney: Angus and Robertson, 1920).

[30]*Poems of the Late Adam Lindsay Gordon* (Melbourne: A.H. Massina, 1877) and later editions.

[31]*Aboriginal History,* 1:1, p. 20 (Canberra: Australian Institute of Aboriginal Studies, 1977).

[32]Constance Hunt, "The Aboriginal Land Rights (Northern Territory) Act 1976: an Outsider's Perspective," in N. Peterson and M. Langton, eds., *Aborigines, Land and Land Rights* (Canberra: Australian Institute of Aboriginal Studies, 1983), p. 457.

[33]*Koowarta* v. *Bjelke-Petersen* (1982) 39 *Australian Law Reports* 417, and the Franklin Dam case *Commonwealth* v. *Tasmania* (1983) 46 *Australian Law Reports* 625.

Manning Clark

Heroes

AT THE BEGINNING OF HUMAN HISTORY in Australia, the first inhabitants of the continent had heroes similar to the heroes of Greek and Roman antiquity. The heroes of the Aborigines were animals and mythical human beings who had the qualities and virtues of the gods in the creation stories of other people. Each tribe had its own stories of creation which performed what Hesiod had identified as the function of all stories of creation: to tell how the earth, the sky, the animals, the trees, the plants, the flowers, the fowls of the air, and the fishes of the sea and human beings had come to be. Every tribe had its own collection of stories that were handed down orally from generation to generation by a people who took no interest in the passage of time.[1]

By one of the paradoxes of human history, the European—who had listened with awe to the stories of the heroic behavior of the God of the Old Testament, of how Jahweh expelled two one-time innocents from the Paradise Garden, or of the punishments Jahweh urged the Israelites to inflict on the inhabitants of Babylon for worshipping strange gods—condemned as barbarous superstitions the stories of the Aborigines about the origin of the world. Within a few years of contact with the Aborigine, the European condemned his nomadic way of life, his material backwardness, and his apparent failure to advance beyond the stone age. He also condemned the Aboriginal beliefs. It never occurred to the European that the Aborigine could teach him anything about how to live in the country of the "weird scribblings of nature." So the European did not incorporate into his own portals of renown the heroes of the Aborigines.[2]

When the "colony of thieves" began at Sydney Cove in January 1788, the Europeans were divided on questions of the meaning of life. The Christians, both Protestant and Catholic, were taught by their parsons and their priests to look with horror and contempt on all religious views of the world other than their own. The followers of the Enlightenment were skeptical of all metaphysical explanations of the world. They thought of Christianity as "moral infamy." They thought of the Aborigine's account of the creation of the world and his heroes as superstitions that must be erased from his mind as a condition of his introduction to higher civilization.[3]

In a secular age, the European gradually lost all but intellectual curiosity in the heroes of Greek and Roman antiquity and of primitive people. The heroes of the Europeans in Australia ceased to be the men of super-human strength and dimension, of a god-like or semi-god-like courage or ability. The Europeans never invented tales of a Zeus in Australia making love to a Leda in the guise of a swan. The Europeans had human heroes, not superhuman or divine heroes. Their heroes were the men who did brave or noble deeds, who exhibited extraordinary bravery, firmness or greatness of soul, men fit to be the subjects of epics.

The British in 1788 and in the early years of settlement had their own myth—the myth of the benevolent influence of British civilization. They believed that British political institutions and the Protestant religion were for the men of heroic ingredients. They believed that wherever there was a society with division of power between the king, the lords, and the commons, with an independent judiciary and the rule of the common law, such a society would enjoy a higher material standard of living and a greater degree of individual liberty than any other kind of society. The believers in this myth had their own heroes, who had made possible the victories of England over the world power of Spain and France, and more recently over Napoleon. These heroes had saved the English from the fate of becoming enslaved to a religious or a political tyrant.[4]

The early settlers of Australia carried with them from the mother country the inhabitants of its portals of renown. They adopted as their own the heroes of the British wars against Spanish absolutism and the Catholic menace to individual liberty. There were the English sea-dogs, Drake and Hawkins. There was *Grenville of the Revenge:* there were Cranmer, Latimer, and Ridley: there were William Shakespeare and John Milton: there was the King James Bible, with its heroes and villains. There were the heroes of the wars against the French in the eighteenth century: there was Wolfe, who with other brave men had scaled the heights of Abraham on the bank of the St. Lawrence River: there were the unsung heroes who had pioneered British civilization in the forests of North America against the agents of French and Catholic absolutism and the barbarous and superstitious practices of the indigenous Indians.

There were the heroes who had won the victory against a world conqueror: there was Horatio Nelson, he of the one arm, one eye, and the heroic statements; there was Arthur Wellesley, later Duke of Wellington, the quintessence of the English gentleman who had won the decisive battle at Waterloo against a cad and a usurper. There were the lesser heroes of that titanic struggle between liberty and despotism: there was Sir John Moore, who had fallen at Corunna in Spain and had been buried there—a hero, fit not for a short story, but for poetry, poetry that will be recited for generations in Australia as a fitting tribute to an English hero:

> Not a drum was heard, not a funeral note,
> As his corse to the rampart we hurried;
> Not a soldier discharged his funeral shot
> O'er the grass where our hero was buried.

The early public ceremonies in the first settlements became occasions when public orators and reciters of poetry acknowledged these British heroes. At the dinner held in Sydney each year on the night of January 26 to mark the anniversary of the foundation of the colony, toasts were proposed to such heroes. There were the formal toasts to those who symbolized the myth to which they assented; the toast to the king, the toast to the houses of Parliament, the toast to the judges. There were toasts to the immortal memory of the Right Honourable William Pitt, a defender of British institutions and the Protestant religion. There were toasts to Lord Nelson and Lord Wellington.[5] By the time of Governor Macquarie (1809–1821), a new, and initially rather shy hero was first mentioned at such gatherings. At the beginning of the Macquarie era, on January 26, 1810, the Sydney poetaster Michael Massey Robinson referred to a new object of their veneration and respect. In a poem specially written for the occasion, he referred to "Australasia," which in his mind was linked with the spread of British civilization over the whole world. By the end of the Macquarie era, Robinson sharpened the identification of this new hero of the people. For him, the hero was the country. He wrote the memorable line: "The land, boys, we live in."[6]

In the beginning, the land distinguished Australia from other countries. From the time when the first European—the Dutch seaman Willem Jansz—wrote his first impressions of the country, through Jan Carstensz, Abel Tasman, Willem de Vlamingh and Captain Cook, Captain Vancouver and the French explorers it was the land that caught their eye. The land was forbidding: there was, as Willem Jansz put it so succinctly in 1606, "no good to be done there," or, as Carstensz put it in 1623, the country sustained "savage, cruel, black barbarians." The land was harsh and inhospitable.

The first Europeans who either saw it from the sea, or, taking the advice of the High and Mighty members of the Dutch East India Company, attempted to walk over it, came to the melancholy conclusion that much of it was not suitable for the purposes of civilized human beings. The land could not be metamorphosed into a hero of the people. It seemed designed by nature or possibly by an otherwise inscrutable providence, as a testing place for heroes. The land was a natural setting for an epic of human courage, intelligence, and the will to endure. The question was whether the Europeans were capable of performing the feats of heroes.[7]

By the 1820s in New South Wales, some were asserting there already were such heroes: there were Australian heroes. The question of capacity was debated first in an amusing exchange in the *Sydney Gazette* in October 1823. In that month, one Fanny Flirt wrote to the paper some condescending remarks about Australia and Australians, in the course of which she told her readers that riding through rows of gum trees was not to her taste. As for conversation, Fanny Flirt found Australian talk far too "sheepish." She added that if one were so foolish as to ask for a song in Sydney Town, the man behind the counter would almost certainly chant over an invoice, "Money is your friend, is it not?" The native-born were not amused.

Three weeks later, one Betsey Bandicoot replied to Fanny Flirt in defence of the native-born: ". . . . our Bill (a currency lad, i.e., native-born) can play the flute, hunt the wild cattle, and shoot and swim with the best in the Colony." "Miss Fan Flirt," she went on, "is very much mistaken if she thinks because she has seen 'the lions in Lunnun Tower' that we (the Australian lads and lasses) don't know 'what's What'." Fanny Flirt, she added, had better drop the idea that only English-trained pianists could play "at the pye-anny-fort." A colonial lass could swim further and faster than any of the Fanny Flirts of Sydney Town.

That same decade, a song was first heard in the taverns, around the camp fires, and in other places where men gathered for a drink and a yarn. It was a song about the exploits of a Wild colonial boy, Jack Donahoe or Doolan (there were many variants, but the name was unmistakably Irish). He came from Castlemaine in southwest Ireland. He became a hero for the native-born partly because he was of "poor but honest parents," and partly because he was a man with qualities men and women knew were essential for survival in Australia. He had a heart that knew no danger, he was a stranger to fear, he was prepared to fight against hopeless odds, he was capable of dying with grace and dignity. The native-born Australians had accepted as their hero a man who had the courage to stand up to those who despitefully used him, and the capacity to survive in and subdue the harsh, inhospitable Australian bush.

A bushranger had become the first hero of one section of the Australian people. The convicts and their descendants had raised to the status of a hero a man who had defied the laws of God and man. This bushranger hero was a colonial Ishmael, a man whose hand was raised against every man because every man's hand was raised against him. He was also a colonial Cain, a man who did not accept that he was subject to either the laws of God or the laws of man. As Jim Jones put it in a ballad written in his name:

> And some dark night when everything is silent in the town
> I'll kill the tyrants one and all and shoot the floggers down:
> I'll give the law a little shock: remember what I say,
> They'll yet regret they sent Jim Jones in chains to Botany Bay.[9]

The explorer was a different kind of hero. Much about the explorers' lives was not the stuff out of which, in the popular mind, heroes were made. Charles Sturt was a fusspot and a bit of an old woman; Edward Giles and McDouall Stuart suffered from the same infirmity that almost cut short the life of Michael Cassio in Shakespeare's *Othello*; Robert O'Hara Burke had a reputation for losing his way in the bush, and often had attacks of the "sillies"; Ludwig Leichhardt had extravagant metaphysical longings, a conviction that he would find fulfilment in death's embrace, and a temptation to indulge himself in the sugar bowl and other luxuries in the stores. John Forrest was a clockwork man; Edward Eyre had a touch of the poet; Hume and Hovell walked from Gunning in southern New South Wales to Port Phillip and back, (a journey of eight hundred miles) in 1824, loathing and distrusting each other.[10]

Yet contemporaries and posterity elevated most of these explorers to the rank of heroes. Poems were written in praise of their achievements: the exploits of the explorers became the staple fare of Australian history. Ballads were sung in their honor: the highway from Sydney to Melbourne was named the Hume Highway, the highway from Port Augusta to Darwin the Stuart Highway, the highway from just south of Gundagai to Adelaide the Sturt Highway, and the highway from Port Augusta to Kalgoorlie the Eyre Highway. Federal electorates were named in their honor: Leichhardt and Kennedy in Queensland, Forrest in Western Australia, Mitchell and Cook in New South Wales, Wills in Victoria, and Sturt in South Australia: the state of Tasmania was named after Abel Tasman: many argued Queensland should be called Cooksland; suburbs were named after them, such as Hume in Canberra and Leichhardt in Sydney: their names were sprinkled liberally over streets in the capital cities: statues were erected in the cities and cairns put up along the routes they had traversed.

They were raised to the status of heroes because they had shown that it was possible to subdue the Australian wilderness. They had both the manly virtue of physical courage, and the will to endure. They were the pathfinders for all those who essayed the task of planting European civilization in the Australian bush. As Henry Lawson put it later in one of his stories, "Hungerford," ". . . if I ever stand by the graves of the men who first travelled through this country, when there were neither roads nor stations, nor tanks, nor bores, nor pubs, I'll—I'll take my hat off. There were brave men in the land in those days." "Dipping the lid" was the greatest compliment an Australian bushman could pay.[11]

At the end of the nineteenth century, one section of Australian society swung against veneration of the explorers as national heroes. The introduction of free, compulsory, and secular education in the 1870s, together with the native-born outnumbering the immigrants in the 1860s, created a reading public with an interest in national sentiment. The federation movement, fear of the French, the Germans, the Russians, the Chinese, and the Japanese, and the development of secondary industries strengthened the nationalist movement. Inferiority had become offensive: groveling to the English must cease.[12] This nationalist temper was summed up in the words Joseph Furphy used in the letter he sent to *The Bulletin* in 1897 asking them to publish his novel *Such Is Life*: "... temper, democratic; bias, offensively Australian." Those brave men who had endured the hardships of the Australian wilderness were put up for examination and found wanting. Many of the explorers were not democratic. Some of them, such as Thomas Mitchell and Charles Sturt, were army officers: some, like Edward Eyre and Ludwig Leichhardt, believed that their mission in life was to protect the culture of the few from the barbarizing influence of the masses. The Australian was the man of brawn: Australia belonged to the ruthless and the cunning. Australia belonged to the competent, to those who, as Betsey Bandicoot put it, knew what was what. In the eyes of the nationalists, some of the explorers had committed the Australian sin against the Holy Ghost. They had modeled themselves on the English governing classes: they had put on airs, affected a la-di-da manner, and spoken in a prissy way. Joseph Furphy rubbished Robert O'Hara Burke as a gentleman who took "swell toggery" on that ill-fated expedition out into the Never-Never in 1860–61. The Australian was the innocent: the Englishman, the Irishman, and the Scotsman were the corrupters. The Australian must find heroes from his own people. Colonial governments had given a lot of credit to men like Burke and Wills for "dyin' in the open," but had taken no notice of all the men of the people, all those "thousands o' pore that's died of thirst and hardship in the back country."[12]

The bush, the nursery of all that was different from other lands, was the cradle of the "dinkum Aussie" heroes. Those years when the nationalists were becoming vocal coincided with a revival of bushranging. The bushrangers embodied the sentiments, values, and aspirations of those who resented British condescension towards colonials, and the arrogance of the British governing classes. Ned Kelly (1854–80), who had three glorious years of defiance of law and order, put into his words and his actions what some of the nationalists believed they were striving for. He was so brave that within a decade of his passing a new idiom had been added to the language of the bush people—"as game as Ned Kelly." He talked of being "fearless, free and bold" as the mark of a man. He ranted against blacks, Chinese, Jews, policemen, and effeminate Englishmen, with all the malicious rancor of the original mockers of Botany Bay. For the traditional enemies of his people—he being native-born of Irish Catholic parents—he harbored a hatred worthy of a people who nurtured in their bosoms seven hundred years of hatred of the Anglo-Saxon. He had compassion for the victims of English and Australian land laws. He spoke like a man who proposed to take down the mighty from their seats, send the rich empty away, and fill the hungry with good things. The men of property, the Anglophiles, and the defenders of private property and British institutions took fright. The bush people, the descendants of the bush barbarians of the early days of settlement had carried on the traditions of their ancestors. They had made a folk hero of a man who had placed himself outside the pale of bourgeois society.[13]

While Ned Kelly was making his stand against British philistinism in Victoria, over in the northwest of the continent the Aborigines were acquiring a new kind of hero. In the area of the Kimberleys near Derby in Western Australia, "Pigeon," as he was known to the white man, or Sandamara to his own people, took up arms against the white settlers, their police, and their magistrates. For a few months he lived like a Robin Hood of the Australian bush: he slept in the hollow boles of baobab trees; a rifle replaced the primitive spear and boomerang and bull-roarer with which his ancestors had tried in vain to stem the white man's invasion of his country. He was shot down. In the twentieth century, when the Aboriginal leaders and their European sympathizers were looking for heroes, he was rescued from the obscurity to which the white man believed he had been relegated at the end of the nineteenth century.[14]

At the same time, Australia's favorite bush writer Henry Lawson was conferring the mantle of heroism on his bush people. They were not historic figures: the people of the bush had no memorial. They were the creatures of his imagination, but the words he placed in their mouths, the deeds he described, conferred immortality on them. They were unmistakably Australian. Jack Mitchell knew a thing or two; he had been around. He had the sardonic wit; he expected little from life; he expected nothing but brief pleasure and then never-ending pain from a woman; he knew only one real pleasure in life, in which he let them see how the bushman could "one-up" all comers; he let slip hints of his melancholy, and his conviction that things would never be any different.

There were the men and women who lived out the principles of the bushman's creed of "kindness in another's trouble, courage in your own." There were the men and women who knew, as one character put it, that "there's no God in the Australian outback," that there was no benevolent transcendent being who cared what happened to human beings, that men and women must endure as best they could, with the pitifully inadequate knowledge they had, their coming hither as well as their going hence, that loving-kindness of their fellow human beings was the only comforter that could sustain them through all the changing scenes of life.

The balladist A.B. ("Banjo") Paterson singled out the same qualities in his heroes of the bush. In "The Man From Snowy River," there was Harrison, the old man with his hair as white as snow. Few "could ride beside him when his blood was fairly up." There was Clancy of the Overflow, who "came down to lend a hand." No better horseman ever held the reins. There was also the Man from Snowy River: "And one was there, a stripling on a small and weedy beast." There was the bush pony, the one with all the qualities of a bush hero:

> There was courage in his quick, impatient tread;
> And he bore the badge of gameness in his bright and fiery eye
> And the proud and lofty carriage of his head.

The "Banjo" admired the same qualities as Henry Lawson. Pluck was the stuff out of which heroes were made—pluck and cunning and skill:

> I'm handy with the ropin' pole, I'm handy with the brand,
> And I can ride a rowdy colt, or swing the arm all day.

But, unlike Lawson, Paterson had his faith:

That all things yet shall be for good,
And teach the world at length to be
One vast united brotherhood.

For him there was also the consolation of a meeting beyond the grave:

That when we come to the final change,
We shall meet with our loved one gone before.

For Lawson there were two destroyers of heroes—women and booze. For Paterson there were three—women, cards, and the horses. For both, it was a man's world.[15]

The unsung heroes of the bush became the unsung heroes of the First World War. The bushman's creed—courage, pluck, loyalty, resource—became the criteria for a hero. The men at the top were eyed with suspicion and resentment. Authority and putting on side were just as odious to the Australian soldiers as they had been to the bushman. When the time came to erect statues and memorials to the men of renown in the war, the generals and the admirals were very rarely chosen.

The high-ranking officers in the army associated with right-wing political movements after the war. Within five years of the armistice, Brudenell White gave his name to the White Guard in Melbourne. John Monash was identified with sinister movements. During the Great Depression, Monash was suggested as a possible savior of Australia from anarchy, the threat of social revolution, and the disgrace of repudiating debts. The members of the labor movement, who were traditionally suspicious of war as an imperialist conspiracy against the working classes, did not accept high-ranking military officers as heroes of the people. In every settled district of Australia, the most common monument was a stone statue of the little digger, a common Australian soldier standing with rifle reversed, the digger hat on his head, and the face of a simple bush boy, whose way of life had taught him about pluck and courage and sticking to his mates and survival, and what to think of the big brass who had presided over death and destruction. Yet the war that gave a new lease of life to the values of the old bush culture also sped up the transition from bush heroism to suburban philistinism. In the bush, the way of life—the ever-present dangers, the material hardships, and the loneliness—

had encouraged respect for the men of heroic ingredients. In the cities, the way of life—the ever-increasing creature comforts and hours of leisure—encouraged the growth of philistinism. By 1900, the cities of Australia and New Zealand were known to observers as "giants of British Philistinism." In the last quarter of the nineteenth century, revolutions in transport and communications gradually removed the difference between the bush and city life. The telegraph, the railway, and the telephone "tethered" the mighty bush to the world. These changes gradually removed the main causes of Australian inferiority—the material backwardness and the isolation.[16]

In the period immediately after the war these developments were sped up. Wireless broadcasting annihilated distance. So did the Australian airmen. Keith and Ross Smith flew from England to Sydney in 1919, Charles Kingsford Smith flew across the Pacific from the United States to Sydney in 1928. Once again, their achievements, together with those of Bert Hinkler, were hailed with enthusiasm as evidence that in the air Australians still had the heroic qualities of the bushman: courage, resource, determination, audacity, and the strength to endure hardships without protest. But as with the generals in the army, the aviators blotted their copybooks in the minds of the people by flirting with political movements opposed to the people's belief in equality. They spoke and acted like followers of the Australian versions of Vitalism and Nietzschism. Songs composed to celebrate their triumphs did not live on as did the songs about heroes of the mighty bush.[17]

The motor car, reinforced concrete, the skyscraper, the wheat silo, films, vaudeville, musical comedies, tabloid newspapers, colored comic strips, children's magazines, women's weekly journals, and the wireless created the age of the masses. The question was: assuming that God was dead, assuming that heaven and hell were priests' inventions, then what were the values of the masses in Australia? Now that machines have subdued the bush that had cradled the heroes of old, would there ever again be heroes? If so, who were these heroes of suburbia?

Politics, culture, and sport became the breeding grounds for the new race of heroes. In politics, the choice of a hero depended on political beliefs. Society was divided into two groups. One, the conservative party, which often changed its name but never its fundamental beliefs, was composed of the British Australians, or the Australian Britons, drawn mainly from the propertied classes in land, industry, and commerce; those who either held a stake in the country, or believed that by their industry and talent they would acquire such a stake. They believed in private property, free enterprise, the family, one indissoluble federal Commonwealth under the Crown, and British political institutions. The other, the Australian Labor party, was radical. Its members believed in the cultivation of Australian national sentiment, in equality of opportunity for all, in the use of the institutions of the state to achieve material well-being for all. On the surface, one was conservative, tying Australians to the past. The other was radical, believing in Paterson's "one vast human brotherhood" and the capacity of human beings, especially Australians, to create a better society.[18]

Both groups had their heroes. The first to acquire such a status among the conservatives was Alfred Deakin (1856–1919) who, ironically, winced at the idea of being bracketed with the conservatives. He was prime minister of Australia three times in the years between 1902 and 1910. Deakin, like all the heroes of Australian conservatism, believed in the occupation of the "middle ground" as the key to political power in Australia. He was the political pragmatist, the man who steered Australia along the middle way, between the moral infamies and inhumanity of uncontrolled free enterprise, and the tyrannies and conformism of excessive state interference. Deakin was also an Australian Briton—a man who shared the W.C. Wentworth version of Australia as "a new Britannia in another world." Deakin was the colonial David who stood up to the imperial Goliath. At the Colonial Conference in London in 1887, at which the delegates were expected to display their humility by "whispering humbleness," Deakin objected to the "aristocratic condescension of an (imperial) Minister who spoke as though he were giving them instructions," rather than engaging in an exchange between equals.[19]

Deakin was also a hero because he believed that a Don Quixote of the Melbourne suburbs could overcome the evils of capitalist society. By wise and judicious use of state interference with the economy, a society would be created in Australia that would fulfill the Australian dream of equality of opportunity, the chance for everyone to rise by talent and industry from rags to riches. Deakin was a hero because he had struggled to find an answer to the meaning of life; he had had the courage to face the question: if God is dead, what then? He had had the courage to face up to the "kingdom of nothingness." So Deakin was the hero of the intellectuals, the artists, and professional classes, as well as the men of the stock exchanges and director's rooms. To the men and women outside such groups Deakin was an object of mockery and derision. They called him the "spook man," a Sunday-school teacher who had a remarkable past in front of him, the unwitting spokesman for a reactionary minority in Australia, a hero of ladies' tea parties in the drawing rooms of the suburbs.[20]

By contrast, Robert Gordon Menzies (1894–1977), the most distinguished apologist for British civilization in Australia in the twentieth century, was by birth a man of the people. Yet his early career threatened to deprive him of a permanent place in the portals of renown. Born in 1894 in Jeparit, a tiny settlement on the edge of the arid Mallee wilderness, he rose by the exercise of talents and industry and ambition to a position of prominence as a barrister and politician in the state of Victoria. His early career was haunted by his behavior during the First World War when he did not volunteer for overseas service. He became the butt of cruel jokes and jibes from his enemies. Beneath the impressive, confident exterior there lived this never-healing wound, which put him on the defensive, made him disparage himself, made him behave like a boxer who was up against the ropes. Success at the Bar, in the Victorian Legislative Council, and as a public orator, accentuated his natural arrogance: he began to use his vast gifts as an orator and an exponent of repartee to wound the men and women who dared to oppose him. It was a self-indulgence he seemed either unwilling or unable to deny himself. The price was high: in August 1941 his colleagues in the Commonwealth Parliament asked him to resign as prime minister. He walked out of Parliament House in Canberra a lonely, tragic figure, cut down by little men who were quite incapable of comprehending the lofty vision he had entertained for the future of British civilization in Australia. After the humiliation of August 1941, he came back a chastened man, a man who had acquired wisdom and understanding. From 1949 until his retirement from public life in 1966, he was the hero of bourgeois Australia. He had something to say, and he said it in memorable words. He saw himself as an apologist for the middle classes. Like Deakin before him, he was a middle-of-the-road man. In 1943, he called his section of the Australian people "the Forgotten

People." For him, the middle class was the "salt of the earth." Like Alfred Deakin, he believed in the *via media* between what he called "each for himself and the corroding effect of governmental paternalism," and all that "dry rot of political doctrines" that encouraged the citizen to lean on the state. Like Deakin, he believed in the imperial connection. Australians were unmistakably British. "I am," he said, "a dyed-in-the-wool Britisher." He was for the thrifty and independent people who had contributed so much to the progress and solidity of Australia. He loathed the socialist idea of making a man a pensioner of the state from the cradle to the grave. In every man, he believed, there was a spark of the divine: the souls of men stood equal in the sight of God.

He put into words the hopes, aspirations, and values of bourgeois Australia. By the time he became a political force, the welfare state had drawn the teeth of radicalism and social revolution in Australia. The economic changes during the 1920s had led to the spread of middle-class affluence. Immigrants had their own reasons for accepting the bourgeois idea of private property and the family. The working classes had been influenced—some would say corrupted—by bourgeois ideas of home ownership and the gadgets to relieve women of domestic drudgery. Menzies had a huge constituency. So, for just on twenty years he was the hero of bourgeois Australia. He was extravagant in the language he used to express his veneration for the British monarchy: he accepted the honors bestowed on him by a grateful queen. But these lapses from Australian nationalism were forgiven, or regarded as minor peccadilloes, indulgences pardonable in a man who was presiding over the greatest material bonanza Australia had ever known.

As with Deakin, the radicals were never prepared to confer on Menzies the distinction of being a hero. They saw him as a man who had prostituted his vast talents to the service of an infamous society: they saw him as the lackey of capitalism, the man who was endeavoring to ensure that there would always be a B.H.P. Company and a Bank of New South Wales in Australia. They never lost their suspicion of him as a friend of the Axis powers, as a man who, according to them, had seen a role for Hitler as a savior of Europe from Bolshevism, and a role for the Japanese as the law-and-order men of the western Pacific. For his role on the latter issue, he had been branded "Pig-Iron Bob"—the man who before the Second World

War used the powers of the Commonwealth government to make possible the export of pig-iron to Japan. Australia was too divided for a man of the talents of Menzies to transcend class consciousness and class loyalty and become a hero to all Australians. One measure of his achievement between 1949 and 1966 was that he turned the hatreds of 1939–41 into affection and respect during his long period in office after 1949.[21]

Conversely, a political radical never became for long the hero of bourgeois Australia. As opposed to what occurred in Germany, Italy, and France, the Communist party in Australia did not become a mass movement. The working classes were "ten-bob-a-day" socialists: they never developed a revolutionary consciousness.

The heads of the churches, the priests, ministers, and prominent laymen also never became the heroes of the people at large. Daniel Mannix, coadjutor bishop and later Roman Catholic archbishop of Melbourne, was for a brief period during the First World War the hero of the Irish Catholics. Exploiting skillfully the Irish anger against the British executions of the participants in the Easter Rising, to their delight he called the war "a sordid trade war." With an engaging cheek and charm he declared he was not going to convert his pulpit into a recruiting platform. He gave Irish Catholics the subterranean satisfaction they seemed to crave, by prophesying that the Protestants might win the prizes in this world, but the Irish Catholics would win the prizes in the life of the world to come.

During the First World War, Mannix had about him the magnificent confidence of a man serving a righteous cause. Tens of thousands flocked to hear him whenever he spoke. He wore on his face the mien of a Prince of Christ's Church, and the grace of a man who, like Mary, was mindful of the one big thing. But in 1921, he had an audience with the pope in Rome. His holiness counseled him, for the love of Christ, to refrain from public utterances that might incite the masses to the mortal sin of rebellion against lawfully constituted authority. Christ had assumed the likeness of man to save all men, not just Irish Catholics. A great sadness began to spread over the face of Dr. Mannix, as he came to realize that he had possibly loved the Irish cause more than he had loved Christ and the faith.[22]

The teachings of the priests and the parsons were alien both to the spirit of the age and the spirit of place in Australia. The parsons preached "that-sidedness," the promise of human perfectibility and happiness in some future time and place: the people were becoming more and more "this-sided." The priests and the parsons frowned on pleasure, and the equation of material well-being with happiness: Australians were committed to the pursuit of happiness. The priests and the parsons preached the laws of God few human beings could observe: they asked human beings to love a Being who sentenced the transgressors against such laws to eternal torment. Australians, in the words of a popular ballad, could not and did not "believe in such a place." The parsons traditionally were defenders of the established social order. The priests warned the faithful against the evils of atheistical socialism which threatened the foundations of human society—private property, the family, and belief in God. The parsons alienated themselves from the spirit of the age by denouncing travel on Sundays, drinking, gambling, dancing, and mixed bathing—Australia experienced in the nineteenth century the migration of evangelical puritanism from England and Scotland and Jansenist puritanism from Catholic Ireland. The country of the "bright light of the sun" had adopted the religion and the morality of countries of "darkness." The heroes of the people were those who, unknown to the pages of history, liberated Australia from the straiteners and the life deniers.

But before religious faith dropped from a roar to a whisper, members of each religious denomination had their own heroes. The Catholics venerated priests such as Father J.J. Therry, who had shown a Christ-like compassion to Irish convicts during the 1820s and the 1830s. They gloried in Patrick, Cardinal Moran, the Cardinal Archbishop of Sydney, and Archbishop Mannix of Melbourne, for presenting an alternative to the Protestantism of Australia. The Church of England evangelicals for a time elevated to the status of a hero Charles Perry, bishop of Melbourne during the gold decades of 1853–73, for his defense of Sunday observance and the puritan moral code. The high-minded Anglicans revered E.H. Burgmann, bishop of Canberra and Goulburn in the years after the Second World War, and John Hope, the rector of Christ Church St. Laurence in Sydney, for their contribution towards the victims of capitalist society. The Presbyterian missions warmed to John Flynn, the clergyman working for the Presbyterian Inland Mission, for his heroic efforts to bring the comforts of civilization to the white inhabitants of the inland. The Methodists were proud of the campaign conducted by William Henry Judkins against gambling, and of George Alfred Judkins for his insistence on moral uprightness, and for his warning to a wicked and adulterous generation not to dance their way to damnation. But the greater the spread of material well-being, the more drudgery eliminated from the workplace and the home, the longer the hours of leisure, the more accessible the means of titillation and pleasure, the more the people at large lost interest in a life in the world to come. They wanted their happiness here and now. By the end of the Second World War, most Australians belonged to the "God is dead" generation.[23]

The labor movement held out the promise of creating a society in which all Australians would be able to pursue such happiness. The pioneers of this movement staked a claim to the title of heroes of the people. First there were the Davids who inspired and led the people in the early battle against the Goliath of capitalist society. The inauguration of the Commonwealth of Australia on January 1, 1901 gave such leaders the opportunity to be heroes of the whole of Australia, not just to the people of one state. William Morris Hughes had a chance to know such glory. Between 1890 and 1914, he wrote and spoke like a friend of the people, the man who, with his colleagues in the political labor movement, would lead the people out of bondage and misery into a life better than any they had previously known. By May of 1916, the Australian soldiers nicknamed him "the little digger," the soldiers' hero.

But by then Hughes had made a bargain with the traditional enemies of the Australian working classes. He had promised some members of the English governing classes to introduce military conscription in Australia. The "little digger" was transformed into a Judas. From that time on, the supporters of and believers in Labor as the hope of the world must live with the fear that their leaders will fall into corruption. Labor must find an answer to prevent the heroes of their band of idealists from degenerating into a corrupt oligarchy concerned primarily with the capture of political power, or susceptible to offers from the enemies of the workers to "rat on their mates." Labor in its infancy was proud of being cast in the role of a Christ figure to the people of Australia:

My true name is Labour (sic)
Though priests call me Christ.

In the mature years of the Labor party, its supporters learned to live with the Judas figures in their midst. Bitter experience taught them that Labor heroes were more vulnerable than the rank and file to the thirty pieces of silver from "Mr. Money Bags."

The price of Hughes's act of betrayal for Labor was thirteen years in the political wilderness in national politics. During that period, Queensland, New South Wales, and Tasmania became almost exclusively Labor states. It was the decade when state enterprise, old-age and invalid pensions were Labor's panacea for the ills and moral infamies of capitalist society. Radicals, militants, Marxists, Wobblies, and communists raved on about betrayal. But in the three Labor states, a majority entertained a hope that a blend of state enterprise, state control, and private enterprise would bring material well-being for all, and equality of opportunity without the conformism and spiritual bullying that the communist leaders in the Soviet Union were employing with such barbarity and inhumanity. Right-wing Labor was the Australian answer. Right-wing Labor would make life cozy and comfortable for everyone.

Coziness and convenience were not the stuff out of which heroes were fashioned. The Labor heroes in the states were the leaders who promised to lead the people to victory against their traditional or mythical enemies—the unidentified Mr. Money Bags in the Australian cities and the moneylenders in London who were sucking the lifeblood out of Australians in interest payments on overseas loans. Labor leaders in the states were delightfully vague on how this victory was to be achieved, and what sort of society would emerge after the people had been liberated from the Scrooges of London. Like the Jewish people of the Old Testament, the people needed a leader to rescue them from their own captivity.

John Thomas Lang (1876–1975) assumed the role of such a hero for the people of New South Wales between 1925 and 1932. He was a man of the people who had made good. He or his backers coined slogans that cast him in a role of greatness: "Lang is greater than Lenin." He held up to ridicule and hatred the imaginary enemies of the people—the Jewish overseas bankers, especially in London, the colored peoples of the western Pacific, and all effeminate Englishmen.

He prophesied a day would come when the little people of this world would come into their own, when they would be liberated from being enslaved to their creditors. Then they would own their own block of land, on which they would build their own house, and rear their own families. Lang wanted the virtues of suburbia, the peace and quiet, the coziness, the absence of fuss, to spread over the whole of Australia. It was a vision for those who had abandoned the idea of Australia as a country where only eagles flew in the sky. It was a vision for those who had enshrined coziness and convenience as the gods of suburbia. It was a little man's vision: it was a sketch of what might happen after Lang, like Christ, had whipped the money changers out of the new temple of Australia—the home in the suburbs.[25]

On the national level, the hero of Labor was John Curtin (1885–1945). Like Menzies, he was by birth a bush boy: like Menzies, he moved in boyhood from the innocence and cunning of country life into the city of Melbourne, where he fell into an uproar and excitement that for a time nourished a weakness inside him. He used alcohol to make bearable the sufferings of a sensitive man in the bear-pit of Australian public life. Like Menzies, Curtin did not volunteer for service overseas during the First World War.

But there the similarity ended. Menzies, the bush boy, became the apologist for British civilization and the defense of the existing social order in Australia. Curtin, another bush boy, became an evangelist for a heaven on earth to replace the life of the world to come. Menzies retained his faith in Christ's teaching of a kingdom of God both in this world and in the world to come. Curtin, after rejecting the Catholic faith of his fathers, became for a time a believer in a socialist society as a cure for poverty, war, and all forms of exploitation. Both were lonely men. Menzies looked to ambition to stifle the sorrow in his own heart: Curtin looked to a better society to help him to forget that he had been alienated from the world of lovers and believers. Behind the mask either of worldly grandeur or the universal embrace, both longed to win a victory in the heart of another human being.[26]

Curtin was to know briefly a victory in the hearts of the people at large. Recognition came late for him. The First World War soured him. The Second World War gave him the opportunity to rise to the status of a national hero. In the First World War, he had become a minor hero with the people opposed to conscription for military service overseas. But dependency on alcohol to make life bearable had come between him and public recognition of his qualities, and his chance to fulfill what he believed to be his destiny. By 1935, the victory over that monster had been won. Then by another odd irony in human affairs, the fatal flaw in Menzies, the overweening arrogance, gave Curtin in October 1941 the chance to walk on to the stage of public life as a man of heroic proportions, when he became prime minister of the Commonwealth of Australia.

Like the explorers and the pioneers of civilization in the mighty bush, he had in abundance courage in the face of great odds. The explorers and the pioneers went into the mighty bush as subduers and dominators over a malign foe—the Australian wilderness. Curtin led his people against an equally formidable foe—the Japanese imperialists and war mongers. To achieve victory, he stood up to Churchill on the issue of the disposition of the Australian Imperial Force. He educated the members of the Labor movement to accept a reversal of the stand against conscription adopted during the First World War. He persuaded Labor to abandon its traditional belief that conscription for overseas service threatened alike the liberty of the people, and those "sacred cows" of Labor politics, the standard of living of the workers, and the maintenance of a White Australia. He persuaded Australians to abandon their traditional dependence on British naval power to save them from invasion by a foreign power. In the dark months of late 1941 and early 1942, he was like a theologian who believed he had a mission to delete some clauses from the Nicene Creed.

Curtin also had the courage and the vision to speak up for the cultivation of Australian sentiment. Australians, as he saw it, had accepted all too willingly the role of second-rate Europeans rather than Australians. The Australian Broadcasting Commission, the commercial broadcasting stations, the press, the universities, the churches, the schools, and the journals assumed that British middlebrow culture and the American pop culture answered the intellectual and artistic needs of the Australian people. Curtin suggested an increase in the Australian content, he being a traditional Labor believer in the proposition that Australian education and culture should be Australian-centered. Australia should cease to be a second-rate branch of British culture. Australia was no longer a colony, but a province of the English-speaking world, with a distinctive culture and character of its own. But Curtin was not a Boston Tea Party man: he dropped his sword before the giant of British philistinism. That battle was left for future generations to wage. The Curtin deeds of heroism in politics and culture were followed by an Indian summer for British philistinism under Menzies, who was rewarded for his loyalty with such British titles as Knight of the Thistle and Lord Warden of the Cinque Ports.[27]

Comedians, rather than historians, taught Australians who they were. From the time of the convict era, Australian humor always had the sardonic, savage flavor of a disenchanted, embittered people, a people who knew the one certain thing in life was defeat and failure. New South Wales was not just a colony of thieves: it was a society of mockers and melancholics, the victims of the "Botany Bay disease." The early ballads had given expression to this subterranean satisfaction in mocking at all human endeavor, this pleasure in discomfiting the pretentious, those who put on airs and all who crooked the knee or groveled to people in high places. In the Middle East, as Herman Melville pointed out, a "ghastly country" had produced a "ghastly theology": in Australia a "ghastly country," a country that knew more dry places than green, produced a ghastly, savage humor.

In the flowering time of the bush culture, when mateship and equality became the standards of a man's worth in Australia, comedy had been the medium by which men and women were reconciled to the vagaries and inhospitality of the physical environment, and to being treated as inferior to the representatives of the British governing classes. In *The Buln Buln and the Brolga,* Joseph Furphy began to do for Australians what American writers of earlier decades had done for the consolation of Americans, to stiffen their resistance to British condescension and arrogance towards their material backwardness, their isolation and their cultural inferiority. Furphy told a comic story of an encounter between an Englishman (a liar, a corrupter, an ineffectual, effeminate man) and an Australian (an innocent, a natural speaker of the truth, and a virtuous man). The puritan morality on questions of sexual behavior lingered on in Australia as in America, New Zealand, and Canada long after the faith that first defined that morality had dropped to a whisper in the mind, and a shy hope in the heart. The heroes of Australia observed the puritan morality, and made a token nod towards belief in God—like a sotto voce "amen" after a parson or a priest recited the Lord's Prayer.

The life-affirmers received enlightenment and encouragement from the comedians on the stage. "Roy Rene," also known by his stage name of "Mo," established in the 1920s the right to refer on the stage, if only by spelling the word, to a central fact in human life. "Roy Rene" became a hero of the Australian emancipation from a taboo on all public references to certain parts of the body. In the early 1930s, he presented to mass audiences the idea of the Australian man and woman as innocents of the bush, tempted from time to time by the English corrupters but always possessing the moral courage and strength to resist the temptation of a walk down the primrose path of English decadence to the eternal bonfire.[28]

The heroes of the world of sport played a similar role. In cricket, the great trial of strength was in the biennial test matches between England and Australia. The men who participated in these encounters before the First World War were like demigods who roamed the earth in Greek mythology: they were the men who performed the god-like feats. There were the demon bowlers, said to bowl so fast that the ball traveled like "greased lightning." According to legend, these heroes with the ball had the power to defy the laws of gravity. There were batsmen like Victor Trumper, a man of such beauty and grace and distinction that, whereas ordinary mortals leg-glanced the ball to the boundary outside their legs, he glanced it between his legs and his bat. He had such skill, such success, that it became a popular boast to say in a bar: "Did I ever tell you about the day I bowled Victor Trumper for a duck?"

The horrors and the casualties of the First World War had conferred on the heroes of the cricket field the role of taking revenge on the English for their alleged indifference to the lives of Australian soldiers during the war. Experiences at Gallipoli, the Somme, Pozières, Ypres, and Passchendaele had planted the idea in some Australian minds that the English upper classes were prepared to use Australians as cannon fodder to preserve their own privileged position in the world. Australians had more than a suspicion that their own soldiers were vastly superior to the English, that the Digger had the courage, the resource, and the initiative so lacking in the Tommy. There were jokes; there were oaths; there was anger. The first cricket test series in Australia in the summer of 1920–21 degenerated from a trial of strength and skill into an occasion for settling such scores. The Australians won the series easily. The captain of the Australian eleven, Warwick Armstrong, became a national hero.

Armstrong had the appearance and strength of a hero endowed with superhuman powers. He was a giant in height, standing over six-and-a-half feet: he was a giant in size, being eighteen stone in weight, and of a girth so massive no standard-size belt encircled him. He was a man of few words. Off the field, he had the social graces of a gentleman. He was an odd man out in the Australian portals of heroes, reveling as he did in wearing the striped blazers, the gaudy caps of social privilege, and frequenting the clubs reserved for those occupying high places in society.

But on what mattered to an Australian, he was a win-at-any-cost-and-by-any-method man. To the delight of the Australians, he was just as successful in England on the tour of 1922. To the English, he displayed on the field many of the features they despised in Australians. He was the man of brawn, the man who sulked when not on top or in a position of prominence. The English complained that it "wasn't cricket," that Armstrong was not a "play up, play up and play the game" man, that he was a victory-no-matter-how man, a vulgarian, a barbarian who had been spawned in the uncultivated societies of the new world. But Armstrong knew what was what. For that alone, he became for a season a national hero, a rank he enjoyed until a true genius of the cricket field reduced him to one of those giants who had batted and bowled in the days before the leveling flood of mass civilization. By yet another old irony, Armstrong held a shy hope of a world to come. He was a bit of a metaphysician in a society that had turned to sport in part because it knew this life was all there was, that the rest was silence.[29]

Donald George Bradman had all the ingredients to become a hero of the world of sporting men. He was a bush boy. While other bush boys idled away their time trapping rabbits, catching yabbies, swimming in the local water hole, or yarning, the young Bradman worked out a contrivance with bat and golf ball to teach him speed in deciding the direction of a ball, and skill in hitting it in any direction he chose. As a youth, he performed such prodigious feats with the bat that he had created a legend for himself as the boy from Bowral before he tested his powers at the mecca of cricket lovers—the Sydney Cricket Ground.

Bradman aimed high. Lesser mortals were content with making a century. When Bradman reached a hundred, he took block, played a maiden over, then set out for his second century. Not content with that, he set out ruthlessly to compile the third century. He took no risks, rarely lifting the ball in the air until he was well into his second century. Yet he had the daring and the pluck of the bushrangers and the explorers. He flouted successfully many of the traditional canons on how to bat; he exposed all his stumps and still succeeded in hitting the ball to the boundary; he was a machine man in the age of the masses. He was successful: he tickled the madness in his admirers by the magnitude of his success in the test matches against the Englishmen in 1930. The man himself remained the subject of many stories. No one could provoke him into uncovering the inner man. No one was permitted to pluck at the heart of his mystery. It was like the remark in *Peer Gynt* about peeling the onion. Bradman never permitted anyone to peel off the outer casing, let alone peer at what was going on at the center.[30]

Australians were not concerned to probe what held a man together in his innermost parts. They were not ideologues, metaphysicians, or listeners to "what the heart doth say." They admired skill; they admired success; they loved it when their heroes ground their opponents into the dust. The spiritual descendants of the mockers of Botany Bay had very satisfying emotional bouts roaring and yelling at the Wagnerian godlings of Australian rules football in Melbourne, Adelaide, Perth, and Hobart. As with cricket, there were the demigods of the early years, the men who had performed the prodigious feats. Conversations in the bars of hotels and in men's clubs and on the beaches in the time of year when the days grow hot in the modern Babylon handed on the wondrous deeds of these mighty men of renown. There was Dave McNamara who, according to legend, once place-kicked a ball ninety-seven yards: there was Roy Cazaly who leaped so high off the ground to take a mark that his deeds became part of the language of sporting men—"Up there, Cazaly" has entered the language; "Up There, Cazaly" eventually became a song. The heroes become the occasion for those sporting arguments that are never-ending because there is no criterion for a decision. For a generation, men and sometimes women (for by the 1930s they have invaded yet another male sanctuary) argued for hours whether Duncan, Brown, and Clark of Carlton were a better halfback line than Lucas, Kingston, and Tuck of Collingwood.[31]

* * *

Just as, according to the hymn, time like an ever-rolling stream bears all its sons away, so the heroes of public life, the heroes of the battlefield, the heroes of the air, and the heroes of the sporting field rarely survived more than one or two generations. The public monuments of Australia became in time the graveyard of dead heroes. Every generation writes its own history in its own image: every generation admits into the portals of the heroes men fashioned in their own image. One generation, we are told, cometh, and another passeth: the earth abideth for ever. Perhaps the earth was the only permanent hero the Aborigine and the European were to know and, in time, to accept.

Perhaps the children of this generation have already begun to prove wiser than the children of Christendom and the Enlightenment. They have already taken up the burden of ending all forms of domination, of man over woman, parent over child, white man over the Aborigine, man over the environment. They have begun to discover the heroes of the past relevant to their own image of the world. Some of the fathers of the new generation have already taken their seats on the penitents' stools. The children have burrowed around in the past to find heroes who were pleasing in their sight. The men who wanted women to have life and have it more abundantly, the men who wanted to make amends for male domination in Australia have been up for examination as potential heroes. Aborigines who resisted the white man's domination have already appeared in the history books. White men have resurrected from the past the representatives of their people who had the courage and the daring to denounce the white man's deeds of abomination against the Aborigine. Historians have discovered that the Rev. Mr. Gribble not only had the courage to stand up to Ned Kelly. He was also, as the simple words on his tombstone in Waverley Cemetery so eloquently testified: "The friend of the blackfellow."

The people, not the mighty men of renown, have become the heroes of the new generation of historians. So far, the people have not appeared in their books and articles as recognizable human beings. Commodities have pushed human beings off the pages of Australian history. But in time these "new men" will probably discover the comic, the epic, and the tragic figures in the history of the common people. The discerning ones amongst the "new men" have already perceived why those of fine sensibilities in previous generations have always understood the words of the psalmist conceived in another dry land: "For I am a sojourner here, as all my fathers were." The heroes of the people are now those who have learned to endure, with dignity and courage, the fate of being a human being in Australia.

ENDNOTES

[1]Ronald M. Berndt and Catherine H. Berndt, *The World of the First Australians* (Sydney: Ure Smith, 1964) chap. XI; Jennifer Isaacs, ed., *Australian Dreaming* (Sydney: Lansdowne Press, 1980).

[2]Henry Reynolds, *The Other Side of the Frontier* (Ringwood, Victoria: Penguin, 1981) chap. 1.

[3]Henry Reynolds, *Other Side of the Frontier,* chap. 1; C.M.H. Clark, *A History of Australia,* vol. 1 (Melbourne: Melbourne University Press, 1962), pp. 4–5.

[4]Clark, *A History of Australia,* vol. 1, chaps. 2 and 3.

[5]Clark, *A History of Australia,* vol. 1, p. 255.

[6]Ibid, pp. 327–9.

[7]J.E. Heeres, *The Part Borne By The Dutch In The Discovery Of Australia* (London: Luzac and Co., 1889), pp. 4–6.

[8]Clark, *A History of Australia,* vol. 2 (Melbourne: Melbourne University Press, 1968), pp. 157–8.

[9]Thérèse Radic, *A Treasury of Favourite Australian Songs* (Melbourne: Currey O'Neil, 1983).

[10]Ernest Favenc, *A History Of Australian Exploration* (Sydney: Turner and Henderson, 1888); G. Dutton, *The Hero As Murderer* (Sydney: Collins-Cheshire, 1967); Patrick White, *Voss* (London: Eyre and Spottiswoode, 1957); E.M. Webster, *Whirlwinds In The Plain* (Melbourne: Melbourne University Press, 1980).

[11]Henry Lawson, "Hungerford," in Henry Lawson, *While The Billy Boils* (Sydney: Angus and Robertson, 1893).

[12]Joseph Furphy, *Such Is Life* (Sydney: Angus and Robertson, 1945), publisher's note and pp. 32–3; Joseph Furphy, *The Buln Buln and the Brolga,* (Sydney: Angus and Robertson , 1948); K.S. Inglis, *The Australian Colonists* (Melbourne: Melbourne University Press, 1974); Humphrey McQueen, *A New Britannia* (Ringwood: Penguin, 1970).

[13]J.N. Molony, *I Am Ned Kelly* (Ringwood: Allen Lane, 1980); Ned Kelly (?), "The Jerilderie Letter," quoted in M. Brown, *Australian Son* (Melbourne: Georgian House, 1948), pp. 271–82; Clark, *A History of Australia,* vol. 4 (Melbourne: Melbourne University Press, 1978), pp. 324–36; Douglas Stewart, *Ned Kelly* (Sydney: Angus and Robertson, 1943).

[14]Henry Reynolds, *The Other Side Of The Frontier* (Ringwood: Penguin, 1981); oral tradition in Derby area of Western Australia.

[15]Henry Lawson, "The Union Buries Its Dead," in his *Short Stories In Prose And Verse* (Sydney: Angus and Robertson, 1893 and 1894); Lawson, "Water Them Geraniums," in his *Joe Wilson And His Mates,* (London: Blackwood, 1900); Lawson, "Brighten's Sister-In-Law," in *Joe Wilson And His Mates* ; "Mitchell on Women" in Lawson's *On The Track and Over The Sliprails* (Sydney: Angus and Robertson, 1900); *The Collected Verse Of A.B. Paterson* (Sydney: Angus and Robertson, 1946); Clement Semmler, *The Banjo Of The Bush* (Sydney: Angus and Robertson, 1966).

[16]For a discussion of these issues see P.R. Stephensen, *The Foundations Of Culture In Australia* (Sydney: W.J. Miles, 1936), and D.H. Lawrence, *Kangaroo* (London: Heinemann, 1923).

[17]Sir Charles Kingsford Smith and C.T.P. Ulm, *Story of* Southern Cross *Trans-Pacific Flight* (Sydney: Penlington and Somerville, 1928); Geoffrey Blainey, *The Tyranny of Distance* (Melbourne: Macmillan, 1968).

[18]R.G. Menzies, *The Forgotten People* (Melbourne: Angus and Robertson, 1943); Platform of the Australian Labor party in 1905.

[19]Alfred Deakin, *The Federal Story* (Melbourne: Robertson and Mullens, 1944) chap. 3.

[20]For two opinions on Alfred Deakin see J.A. La Nauze, *Alfred Deakin* 2 vols., (Melbourne: Melbourne University Press, 1965) and Clark, *A History Of Australia,* vol. 5 (Melbourne: Melbourne University Press, 1981).

[21]Menzies, *The Forgotten People* (Melbourne: George Allen and Unwin, 1943); Cameron Hazlehurst, *Menzies Observed* (Sydney: George Allen and Unwin, 1979).

[22]Michael Gilchrist, *Daniel Mannix, Priest and Patriot* (Blackburn: Dove Communications, 1982), pp. 66–68 and 97–101.

[23]K. Dunstan, *Wowsers* (Melbourne: Cassell, 1968); W.S. McPheat, *John Flynn, Apostle To The Inland* (London: Hodder and Stoughton, 1963); T.L. Suttor, *Hierarchy And Democracy In Australia* (Melbourne: Melbourne University Press, 1963); L.C. Rodd, *John Hope* (Sydney: Alpha Books, 1972).

[24]V.G. Childe, *How Labor Governs* (London: Labour Publishing Co., 1923); R.N. Ebbels, ed., *The Australian Labor Movement* (Sydney: Australasian Book Society, 1960); L.F. Fitzhardinge, *William Morris Hughes,* 2 vols. (Sydney: Angus and Robertson, 1964 and 1979); Donald Horne, *In Search Of Billy Hughes* (Melbourne: Macmillan, 1979).

[25]Miriam Dixson, *Greater Than Lenin* (Melbourne: politics monograph, 1977); J.T. Lang, *I Remember* (Sydney: McNamara Books, 1956); Heather Radi and Peter Spearritt, eds., *Jack Lang* (Sydney: Hale and Ironmonger, 1977).

[26]R.G. Menzies, *Afternoon Light* (Melbourne: Cassell, 1967); Lloyd Ross, *John Curtin* (Melbourne: Macmillan, 1977); L.F. Crisp, *Ben Chifley* (London: Longman, 1961).

[27]Ross, *John Curtin*; Paul Hasluck, *The Government And The People 1942–1945* (Canberra: Government Printer, 1970).

[28]Furphy, *Buln Buln and Brolga*; A.E. Davis ("Steele Rudd") in *On Our Selection* (Brisbane: University of Queensland Press, 1899; rep. 1970); C.J. Dennis, *The Songs Of A Sentimental Bloke* (Sydney: Angus and Robertson, 1915).

[29]Radcliffe Grace, *Warwick Armstrong* (Camberwell: privately published, 1975); Laurence Le Quesne, *The Bodyline Controversy* (London: Secker and Warburg, 1983).

[30]Michael Page, *Bradman* (Melbourne: Macmillan, 1983).

[31]I.A.H. Turner and Leonie Sandercock, *Up Where, Cazaly?* (Sydney: Granada, 1981).

K.S. Inglis

Ceremonies in a Capital Landscape: Scenes in the Making of Canberra

12 March 1913

THE MEN STOOD ON A DAIS open to the autumn sun, on a hill freshly named Capitol. The British Empire was embodied in Lord Denman, representative of the king, wearing plumed hat and epaulettes. Scotland was audible in the voice of the prime minister. The American accent of the minister for home affairs reminded his hearers, if they needed reminding, that the creation of a capital city for a federal and democratic nation had been accomplished once before.

Even more than the United States at its beginning, the Commonwealth of Australia was composed of British immigrants and their descendants. By 1913, though, the great English-speaking republic had rich meaning for Australians as model, influence, and potential ally. Between the poles of Westminster and Washington, notions and sentiments of Australian nationality were to form shifting patterns during the twentieth century. The federal capital has been a theater for this interaction of empire, Pacific neighbor, and nation. Slicing into its history at a series of ceremonial moments, we may halt the shifts, inspect the pattern at each chosen interval, and hope to gain some insight into the people who were building and inhabiting this city on the limestone plains.

From newly planted poles flew Union Jacks and flags of federal Australia—one-quarter Union Jack, with the five stars of the Southern Cross, and a seven-pointed star representing the Commonwealth of Australia, its six states and territories. The guests seated in temporary grandstands had made long journeys from centers of civilization, for the constitution enacted in 1900 required that the capital territory be within the state of New South Wales but at least a hundred miles from Sydney, and that Melbourne be the capital until the federal city was ready. They had spent the night under canvas—even the vice-regal party, one of whose tents was left over from the Delhi durbar of 1911. With trowels made of Australian gold, the governor-general and each minister tapped foundation stones on the base of the Commencement Column. At noon, Lady Denman took a piece of paper from a gold case. Only members of the federal cabinet knew the word she was about to speak, and not even they knew how she would pronounce it.

Giving a name to the federal capital had proved more difficult for Australians than for Americans, for we had no George Washington. The politicians had rejected more than seven hundred proposals: floral and faunal (Eucalypta, Kangaremu), abstract (Democratia, Federata, Pacifica), imperial (New London, Empire City), and miscellaneous, including one made up of first syllables from each state capital: Sydmeladelperbrisho. Those six had all been imperial in origin: Sydney, Hobart, Perth, and Brisbane for British officials; Melbourne for a prime minister; Adelaide for a queen. Names like those, unquestioned as fit for colonies, were not on the short list for the nation. Finally, the ministers picked a word with some history but with diverse spellings and no agreed meaning, a word in use since the 1820s for part of the rural landscape now visible to Lady Denman. Around the cabinet table some (probably the native-born) gave it three syllables, saying *Can/berr/a,* and others (probably the immigrants) clipped it to *Can/b'ra.* Lady Denman looked at the paper and said: "I name the capital of Australia Can/b'ra."

Most people with an opinion on the matter believed that Canberra was an Aboriginal word, though they differed over whether it meant women's breasts—after two rounded hills, Black Mountain and Mount Ainslie, in the middle distance from today's ceremony—or meeting place, or something else again. Aboriginal inhabitants of the region could no longer be asked for a ruling. Their absence was noted as significant by the attorney-general, William Morris Hughes, when he spoke at the official luncheon. "We are engaged in the first historic event in the history of the Commonwealth today," Hughes declared, "without the slightest trace of that race we have banished from the face of the earth." He contemplated their extinction not with regret but with white Australian resolve. "We must not be too proud lest we should, too, in time disappear. We must take steps to safeguard that foothold we now have."

For the politicians this was a happy day. Andrew Fisher, prime minister, Hughes, attorney-general, and King O'Malley, minister for home affairs, had come to Australia as immigrants in the 1880s: Fisher, from the coal mines of Scotland; Hughes, from dank classrooms in London; O'Malley, from living on his wits in North America. They had entered Parliament as Labor members, they had taken over the federal government, and today they were inaugurating its capital—in Hughes's phrase at lunch, its "symbol of nationality." For Lord and Lady Denman, the event was less tedious than most of their vice-regal chores. He was a soldier and a Liberal politician before becoming the fifth British peer to represent the monarch in federated Australia, and he would go home two years short of the five for which he was appointed; among other troubles, his hay fever exploded whenever he was close to pollen from the wattle that was coming into fashion as Australia's national flower. In their speeches at lunch, Lord Denman and the ministers said much about the future. As Oscar Wilde remarked of America's youth: the future was Australia's oldest tradition. "She is not yet," wrote the author of *The Dominion of Australia: a Forecast* (1877) in verses learned by schoolchildren. For orators in a tent on the site of an unbuilt capital, the theme was irresistible. Their listeners heard prophecies of imperial unity, national grandeur, and—from O'Malley—accord with the United States; "The federation of English-speaking peoples," he said, ". . . should be the pre-eminent aspiration of all thinking Australians."

That view of Australian-American relations was well received at political gatherings as long as "federation" was not meant literally. The visit of the Great White Fleet to Australian ports in 1908, three years after the Japanese sank the Russian fleet, had occasioned cordial statements about trans-Pacific fraternity. The constitution-makers in the 1890s had taken almost all they could from United States practice consistent with having a monarch and a parliament. In Melbourne, the chambers lent to the federal government were now called the House of Representatives and the Senate—not, as in colonial days, the Legislative Assembly and the Legislative Council. The idea of creating a federal district for the capital, away from contending cities, was American; and the years just after 1900 were a good time to learn from the experience of Washington where the McMillan commission had exposed the muddle and expense caused by uncalculated departures from Pierre L'Enfant's plan and by failure to anticipate the consequences of growth. One way and another, Canberra would owe a good deal to Washington.

The Australian capital was given much more land. Where the Americans, fearing big government, decreed in their constitution that the federal district be no more than ten miles square, the Australians provided for not *less* than that area: in a drought-prone continent they thought it wise to guarantee the capital an adequate catchment area for water, and they wanted the Commonwealth, not private citizens, to benefit when the creation of the federal city increased the value of surrounding land. Their divergence from the American model had an American inspiration, for it was Henry George who had made Australian reformers sensitive to the value of land as a public resource. On the initiative of King O'Malley, the Parliament resolved in 1901 both that the federal territory have plenty of land and that the land be leased, not sold. (Regard for American radicals was expressed also in spelling the name of the Australian reformers' party. The force of production, the activity of work, was spelt *labour* in Australia as in Great Britain; but the party holding office in 1913 was *Labor*.) In the event, the federal capital territory covered some nine hundred square miles of mountains and plains. The site reserved for the city was a rectangle of twenty square miles. From Capitol Hill you saw the distant ranges, local mountains, lower hills within a basin, the Molonglo River flowing or trickling across its flood plain, and undulating grasslands some eighteen hundred feet above sea level. At that height, the region had cooler nights in summer than the coastal cities, and in winter frosty nights were usually followed by crisp sunny days. Fewer than two thousand people lived in the whole territory, most of them on pastoral stations and farms. Sheep grazed in the future city. From Capitol Hill, the oldest human-made object visible in the landscape, and the only vertical one, was the spire of St. John's Church of England. The Commencement Column was designed to proclaim this city as federal, national, and imperial. The hexagonal base in which stones had been laid represented the states; a shaft rising from the base would stand for the Commonwealth of Australia; higher yet would be an obelisk of British granite, signifying the Empire.

No speaker at the ceremony mentioned Walter Burley Griffin, the American architect who less than a year ago had won first-prize in a competition to design the federal city. To bring up his name would have been to remind the guests that the capital territory had already been the subject of two large fusses. First, British professional bodies of architects and engineers had advised their members at home and in Australia and elsewhere in the empire not to enter the competition because a layman, O'Malley, was to be the adjudicator. That boycott may have saved Canberra from being a monument to Edwardian imperialism like the new Delhi, planned in 1912–1913. In fact, O'Malley as minister accepted the verdict of two out of three professional assessors and gave the prize to Griffin in Chicago. The second fuss happened when O'Malley decided not to use Griffin's design but to have a plan drawn up by three public servants that would incorporate some of Griffin's ideas with ideas from other competitors, and save money. In May 1913, Labor lost an election. A new minister for home affairs set aside the public servants' design and invited Griffin to Australia. The mercurial O'Malley declared that he had really preferred his fellow American's plan, but "had not courage to bring Mr. Griffin to this country because people would immediately have said that one Yankee was bringing out another."

The surveyor who recommended the Canberra site had been instructed to find a place fit for "a beautiful city," a location to accommodate "a design worthy of the object, not only for the present, but for all time . . . ." Such a vision was deeply congenial to Walter Griffin, working as he did in Chicago, home of the City Beautiful movement, and attracted as he was to modern notions of utopia. He and his wife Marion, who did the superb drawings for his entry, were both vegetarians and theosophists. When they set off for Australia, he was thirty-six, she forty-one, and they had been married two years. They had studied at the country's two oldest schools of architecture, Walter Griffin graduating from the University of Illinois in 1899 and Marion Mahony becoming in 1894 the second woman to graduate in architecture at the Massachusetts Institute of Technology. Both had worked closely with Frank Lloyd Wright, though Walter Griffin offered more homage to Wright's mentor, Louis Sullivan. Chicago had been one of ten cities around the world (New York and Washington were others) to which models of the federal city site were sent for potential competitors to inspect. It was a good vantage point for contemplating Australia. The Illinois Territory had been established soon after the first settlement of Australia; Chicago, like Melbourne and Adelaide, was a city of the 1830s; and the cycloramic paintings that accompanied the model showed that the southern tablelands of the federal territory were similar to the prairies of the American Midwest. The rhetoric of Chicago planners, egalitarian and anti-metropolitan, sounded sweet to Australian ears. Griffin was determined "to treat architecture as a democratic language of everyday life."

The Griffins' drawings showed a city and suburbs composed of interlocking circles and hexagons. At the center lay two axes at right angles, a land axis running northeast from Capitol Hill to Mount Ainslie, and a water axis running southeast from Black Mountain along the river. The Molonglo would be transformed into a chain of lakes and basins accessible to the people. From Capitol Hill would run two principal avenues, one to the north of the land axis and one to its east, intersecting with the water axis to form a triangle occupied by national institutions. The northern avenue would continue to a hill where municipal activities would cluster, and from there to suburbs of radial layout; the eastern avenue would lead to a commercial center and railway station. The avenues and waters, the placing of national and municipal and commercial activities, all bore an orderly relationship to Griffin's two axes; the axes, he declared, delighted at the harmony of geometry with nature, were "determined by the most important natural features of the site." It was his tender reading of the landscape that appealed most to the assessors.

Griffin's proposals for both the location and the style of national institutions were tentative, though sometimes elaborate. The national university, for example, was to be set in concentric circles, with pure studies such as philosophy and mathematics in the middle, surrounded by the less abstract sciences and arts, and on the rim, engineering, commerce, and other applied disciplines, sharing a frontier with the municipal center. Buildings should have plenty of space between them, not—the phrase has a Jeffersonian ring—"stand on end as in the congested American cities." On the question of style, his starting-point was a doctrinaire disapproval of imitating the past: to adapt any historical style would be to perpetrate "a caricature instead of a reminiscence of its own proper grandeur." Here spoke the follower of Sullivan and Wright, sharing their vision of a totally indigenous architecture arising from the soil and spirit of the Midwest, and hoping that a similar miracle could be made to happen in Australia—helped to birth, perhaps, by the very insularity of the country.

The highest structure in the city was to be the Capitol, on Capitol Hill, which might have a "stepped pinnacle treatment in lieu of the inevitable dome." That would give the Capitol the air of an Eastern temple, and possibly Griffin's attachment to theosophy affected his thinking about the function as well as the form of the building. Despite its name, the Capitol was not the legislature. The brief for competitors had specified a "statehouse" to hold historical records and provide a venue for ceremonies. To Australians, that term did not signify a legislature; indeed, its use would baffle them unless they happened to remember a scheme for a pantheon of that name, proposed and abandoned when the senior colony, New South Wales, was about to celebrate its centenary in 1888. The statehouse took Griffin's fancy, and as the Capitol it would dominate his landscape. Like Pierre L'Enfant perceiving the eminence called Jenkins's hill, Griffin saw Kurrajong Hill as a pedestal waiting for a great monument. Why did he not put parliament there, instead of giving the lawmakers a site below and in front? There may be a clue in his description of the Capitol as "the sentimental and spiritual head" of the nation, as distinguished from "the actual working mechanism of the Government of the Federation." Parliament was mundane, material, a place of division and contention, and therefore not for the heights; the Capitol was a temple of humanity, to which citizens and legislators would look up. Precisely what achievements the Capitol would celebrate was a question for the clients; and in 1913, as we have seen, they were still inclined to scan the future for answers.

Griffin found Canberra, and Australia, less somber, more beautiful than he had been led to expect. "Australians do not paint their country as they should," he told them. "The gum tree instead of being one continual monotony has strongly appealed to me. It is a poet's tree, and ought to have a more dignified name." Even the politicians were a pleasant surprise. "I have planned a city like no other city in the world," he said. "I have not planned it in a way that I expected any governmental authorities in the world would accept." Yet, in October 1913, the Commonwealth of Australia appointed Walter

Burley Griffin to be its federal capital director of design and construction.

Many years later, when Canberra had a past as well as a future, a gathering of residents resolved that people could call themselves "pioneers" if they had been living in the district on 12 March 1913.

9 May 1927

The Duke of York, second son of King George V, had cruised out with the Duchess in HMS *Renown* to open the first sitting in Canberra of the Commonwealth Parliament, just as his father, also as Duke of York, had come to inaugurate the parliament in Melbourne, twenty-six years ago to this day.

The royal couple were guests at Yarralumla, a pastoral homestead three miles west of Capitol Hill, which had been bought by the federal government and was used now as a temporary residence for the governor-general. Their host was Lord Stonehaven, formerly a British diplomat and Conservative politician. From Yarralumla, Canberra's approximation to Buckingham Palace, they were driven this morning by car to the Lodge, a modest new villa close to Capitol Hill, Australia's version of 10 Downing Street. Here the duke and duchess climbed into a state coach drawn by four horses and proceeded downhill for a few minutes to the new Parliament House, a plain building, long and low, its white painted stucco gleaming in the sunlight, standing on a rise between Capitol Hill and the river, and facing a landscape as pastoral as in 1913. Lord Stonehaven was waiting on the steps to greet the duke and duchess, watched by five hundred official guests and from farther off by thousands who had made their own way. Military bands played "God Save the King," and when the duke and duchess reached the top of the steps, the anthem was heard again, this time sung by Nellie Melba, Dame of the British Empire and about to be promoted to Dame Grand Cross for today's performance. The most famous of Australian voices was heard, more or less, by listeners to primitive wireless sets elsewhere in Australia, and so were the speeches from the portico and inside the House.

The prime minister, Stanley Melbourne Bruce, in silk top hat and morning suit, spoke first, followed by the duke. Bruce was Australian-born, unlike the Labor men of 1913 and like all prime ministers from now on; but he looked and sounded an English gentleman, and he liked to affirm the imperial presence in Australia. On his initiative, the public hall being constructed in Canberra was called Albert, after London's and because that was the duke of York's name; and when he opened a block of shops and offices at the new Civic Centre later in 1927, Bruce insisted that the road around City Hill be called, not the Hexagon, as in Griffin's plan, but London Circuit. Like the speech-makers of 1913, the prime minister and the duke had much to say about the future. But in 1927, the orators spoke also of an achievement. At the new Parliament House, as now on every respectable public platform, the deeds of Australian soldiers at Gallipoli, on the Western Front, and in the Middle East, were recalled with pride. The anniversary of the landing at Gallipoli on April 25, 1915 had become, within a decade, the most solemn day in the national calendar. Few people responded to the idea that Australians should celebrate their nationality on May 9, commemorating the opening of the federal parliament. Each January 26 they gave tepid recognition to the landing of convicts at Sydney Cove on that day in 1788. The one day really sacred to the nation was Anzac Day, as Australians called it, sometimes remembering and sometimes forgetting that their kinsmen across the Tasman Sea had also belonged to the Australian and New Zealand Army Corps. Bruce and the duke both offered tributes to the soldiers. Next morning the duke dropped in on the federal executive of the Returned Sailors' and Soldiers' Imperial League of Australia—in common speech RSL—that had been allowed to use the dining room of Parliament House in recognition of its having an access to government and a place in society accorded to no other voluntary organization.

After the speeches on the portico, the duke unlocked glass doors and entered King's Hall, followed by official guests who saw him unveil an object as imperial in provenance as a monument could be. In London, a sculptor from Australia, Sir Bertram Mackennal, had executed a bronze statue of the king for the Viceroy's palace in New Delhi, occupied in 1927; this was a replica.

Guests were packed into the galleries around the Senate chamber while the thirty-six senators (six from each state) waited for the seventy-five members of the House of Representatives to be summoned from their own chamber by the Usher of the Black Rod. In the House of Representatives, the Speaker's canopied chair was a replica of the one in the House of Commons, and contained wood from

Nelson's *Victory* and from the old Westminster Hall. The House had green furnishings, like the Commons; the Senate, red like the Lords. The carpets were artifacts of the imperial economy, made in the motherland from Australian wool. The seats in each house, though, were arranged in the shape of a horseshoe, as in Washington and not in London. The Senate's galleries were jammed as members of both chambers assembled to hear the duke read out the king's message empowering him to inaugurate this sitting of parliament. Up in the eastern gallery sat Walter and Marion Griffin. Their invitations had come late, after suggestions in the papers that they were being snubbed. It was widely known that Griffin had nothing to do with the design of this building, and disapproved of both its character and its location.

Participants and guests attended a luncheon in the parliamentary dining room and an evening reception in King's Hall. Ordinary citizens watched in the afternoon the first mass fly-past staged by the Royal Australian Air Force. Next morning they could file past the House as the duke and duchess stood on the steps. A few pioneers of the district were presented to the royal visitors. One Aboriginal had turned up from somewhere to walk in the procession: an old man with straggling hair and beard, dressed in white men's cast-offs and answering to the whimsical name Marvellous. He was not presented to the duke and duchess.

Walter Griffin had withdrawn from the planning of Canberra after seven tempestuous years. In 1914, he made arrangements for a worldwide competition to design the Parliament House. During the war the contest was postponed, never to be revived. Many people believed that the whole Canberra enterprise should be deferred until the war was over, and although that never became official policy, conflicts between Griffin and public servants prevented nearly all progress except the planting of trees. Griffin could never have worked comfortably with men whose guiding principles were practicality, economy, and punctuality. Like many a vegetarian, Griffin was both gentle and stubborn; like many an architect, he drew more clearly than he wrote or spoke. Griffin took until 1918, after years of demands from ministers, to produce his final plan for the city. In 1920, the government, convinced that he could not carry the executive responsibility required for building the city, established a Federal Capital Advisory Committee and offered him a place on it. He refused, and that was the end of Griffin's connection with Canberra. His appointment as director of design and construction had been half-time, allowing private practice. The Griffins were given many commissions, the most ambitious being Newman College in the University of Melbourne. After 1920, they lived in Sydney; from 1925 on, in the suburb of Castlecrag, a residential estate developed by Griffin. He did plans for Leeton and Griffith, new towns in New South Wales. In Melbourne, a dazzling cinema and the tall office block on top of it bore the name Capitol which he had brought to Australia. In Canberra, the only structure to show for his years in government service was a general's grave, which tourists would visit without knowing that its designer was the creator of the city. Marion Griffin, looking back over life and work in both hemispheres with the man she venerated as the world's greatest architect and town planner, reflected that the magic of America was creative individualism, which she contrasted with the obstructive collectivism of Australia.

In gray collectivist prose, the committee Griffin had declined to join recommended in 1921 that "utilitarian development and economy should be the aim in the first stage, leaving to future decades—perhaps generations—the evolution of the National Capital on lines that are architecturally monumental." The future, in short, could be left to the future. In the meantime, Canberra would be "a garden town, with simple, pleasing but unpretentious buildings, mostly single story, planned nevertheless to afford adequate comfort and reasonable convenience. . . ." Cabinet approved the committee's parsimonious proposals, and building began. All those words appeared dismally significant to Keith Hancock, a young professor of history who had returned to his native land after studying at Oxford. Hancock's *Australia,* published in 1930, shaped his compatriots' thinking more than any other book of its time, not least for the pages in which he convicted Australians of having settled for that "middling standard," that democratic tyranny of the multitude that Tocqueville had discerned a century earlier in America. Canberra was a central exhibit for Hancock's case—the City Beautiful trimmed down to what Australians thought they could afford. Not that Griffin's own vision attracted Hancock. The American had won "a competition for foreigners judged by mediocrities"; his design was "elaborately formal," "a cast-iron scheme to which Canberra must be fitted." Living in Adelaide, Hancock was repelled by the distant prospect of a capital that combined petty-bourgeois suburbia with a dogmatic and alien plan.

As a blueprint for posterity, that plan had survived Griffin's departure. The Federal Capital Advisory Committee was instructed by the government to make sure that public servants did not depart from it. In 1924, an act replaced the advisory body with a Federal Capital Commission that had executive powers; it also said that Griffin's 1918 design for the city was to be published in the *Commonwealth Gazette* and that no alterations were to be made without the authority of Parliament. The idea of a statutory commission, free of political control, to develop the capital, owed something to the example of Washington, though the device was already familiar in Australia (as not yet in England) for running railways, harbors, and other utilities. The gazetting of a master plan was also done with an eye to Washington's experience. But the politicians had made one change affecting their own accommodation before passing this act. In 1923, a parliamentary committee heard conflicting advice on two overlapping questions. First, whether to start on a permanent Parliament House or whether to put up a "provisional" one—that word chosen as a compromise between "permanent" and "temporary," suggesting a life of fifty years or so which would make posterity decide what to do next. Second, whether to place the Parliament on top of Capitol Hill; or whether to use Griffin's site, the lower crest of Camp Hill just below Capitol Hill towards the river; or whether instead to construct a provisional building on the slope of Camp Hill leaving the summits of both hills vacant for the time being. Griffin, appearing as a witness, argued for the nucleus of a permanent building on Camp Hill. The politicians voted for a provisional building lower down, which seemed to Griffin "like filling the front yard with outhouses." The government architect John Murdoch was given the delicate job, as the director-general of works described it, of designing a building "with simple lines and without architectural embellishment," but not so austere or uncomfortable that the politicians would be inclined "to hurriedly leave for a permanent monumental building." The first sod was turned on August 28, 1923 as architects protested about the abandonment of the competition; one predicted that Canberra would become the laughing stock of the British Empire, and Australia's only professor of architecture asked: "To what purpose could such a specially planned temporary structure be usefully put after the permanent building is erected?" Half a century on, that question would become pressing. By that time, other professors of architecture, looking back at what public clients got in the 1920s when they asked for monuments, were inclined to think that Canberra was lucky to be given a Parliament House of such pleasing simplicity.

Public servants selected for transfer to Canberra called the trains that carried them and their families from Melbourne the first fleet, comparing themselves with the convict immigrants of 1788. Two office blocks in the provisional style, one west and one east of Parliament House, were put up for them while a permanent and monumental administrative building designed by competition in 1924 was deferred. They lived in sturdy cottages without fences, which looked to an early resident "like toy bricks on the open plain," or in government-built hostels and boarding houses. Frugal urban amenities were ready, or almost ready, for the first fleet: schools, a shopping block, the Albert Hall, the Capitol cinema (Griffin's word coming back to his city from Melbourne), playing fields. When the Federal Capital Commission asked newcomers about their sporting needs, one replied: "Surfing." The word had been hardly known when an inland site was chosen for the capital, but by 1927 the most un-Australian thing about Canberra was that its residents were so far away from the national summer pleasures of the beach. A piece of coast at Jervis Bay, to be sure, had been transferred from New South Wales to the Commonwealth in 1915, but the railway planned from Canberra was never built. Residents had to wait until January 26, 1931 for a swimming pool, and much longer for a road to take them comfortably through the mountains to the sea.

At first, the purchase of alcohol was prohibited to inhabitants of Canberra by an edict from the time of King O'Malley, who abhorred what he called "stagger-juice"; traffic across the New South Wales border to the town of Queanbeyan thinned when prohibition was repealed in 1928. Canberrans lacked political rights. Like the people of Washington, the seven thousand citizens of the territory in 1927 were not represented in the legislature that met among them, and they had no say in municipal affairs. They were compelled, however, to vote for the election of members to an Advisory Council, established in 1930, which had no executive or administrative functions. City Hill, across the river from Capitol Hill on Griffin's plan, still lacked Griffin's City Hall, and there was no haste to complete the avenues that would link his national, municipal, and mercantile areas. The Federal Capitol Commission did give them names, though. Commonwealth and King's Avenues would converge on Capital Hill, and on the other side of the lake, if it was ever made, Constitution Avenue would connect them.

The landscape waiting for its city was becoming a garden. Thousands of trees—within twenty-five years, millions—were planted in the grasslands. Native eucalypt and acacia, fir and pinoak and birch from north America, Mediterranean cypress and Lombardy poplar, English oak and elm and beech, trees from all over the temperate world, grew in parks and streets and on the hills. In the chill of autumn, immigrant leaves turned colors unknown down on the coast, and in spring jacaranda, Japanese cherry, and acacia burst into blossom. Public and domestic planting mingled across the footpaths, except where householders forbidden to build fences demonstrated that the Australian's home was his castle by raising a hedge of the onomatopoeic privet. The Duchess of York planted a candlebark eucalyptus and a cricket-bat willow.

11 November 1941

At the foot of Mount Ainslie, five thousand people stood with bowed heads. The ritual of Armistice Day—two minutes' silence at the eleventh hour of the eleventh month—was being combined with the opening of the Australian War Memorial. Had the builders finished in time, the ceremony would have been arranged for Anzac Day; but November 11 was second only to April 25 as a time to honor and to mourn the soldiers. The governor-general called this gray stone building a shrine; the prime minister described it as a sanctuary that would inspire the parliament. There was nothing quite like it among war memorials anywhere: at once a people's museum, a scholar's library and archive, and a temple. Here, rather than on Capital Hill,* was Australia's pantheon.

The dead heroes lay where they had been killed, on the other side of the world. There were sixty thousand of them from a population of four million—about as many as had died in battle from the United States, with its hundred million. Memorials bearing the names of the

*No longer "Capitol": the "o" signifying Griffin's vision of the hill had been quietly removed.

absent dead were raised in every city and town; and even before November 11, 1918, some people were thinking of a national memorial in the unbuilt federal capital. It began as a vision in the mind of Charles Bean, war correspondent with the Australian Imperial Force and later its historian, who conceived a "solemn, exquisite building" that would hold for all time "the sacred memories of the AIF." The federal government approved the project, and in 1923 the Federal Capital Advisory Committee chose a site on Griffin's land axis, opposite Parliament House, noting that the two buildings could face each other, as the All-India Memorial and the Viceroy's Palace did in New Delhi, at ends of a ceremonial avenue. A competition was announced, limited to British subjects resident in Australia or born here and living abroad. In 1911, it seemed right to invite the architects of the world to submit plans for the capital; but the designer of this shrine had to be Australian and imperial, like the army it honored. The politicians imposed a limit of $250,000—$80,000 more than the budget for the provisional Parliament House, but still only enough, the adjudicators observed, for "a building of exceedingly simple character, and of smallest possible dimensions." In the 1920s, even the cathedral of Australia's civil religion must conform to the middling standard.

Only one of the sixty-nine competitors managed to keep within the limit while fulfilling a condition that the names of the dead must be recorded around the walls of a Hall of Memory. The author of that design was then invited to collaborate with another entrant who had kept the Hall of Memory economically small by putting the names along colonnades outside it. Their joint plan, accepted by cabinet in 1928, combined long, low, plain, modern lines with a dome recalling Santa Sophia in Constantinople. Walter Griffin, invited by the politicians to give an opinion, approved both the site and the design. One of the architects expressed the hope after visiting Washington that one day the approach to the Memorial might resemble the Mall.

On Anzac Day in 1929, when Lord Stonehaven unveiled a stone, it seemed safe to announce that the Memorial would be ready in three years; but the project was deferred by a government struggling to administer the Depression. On Capital Hill, the unfinished Commencement Column became a symbol of the national economy, its foundation stones "covered with rotten timber, riddled by white ants," as old King O'Malley observed in 1932, deploring the "desecration of this National Monument." Pressed by returned soldiers, the government authorized a start on the War Memorial in 1933. Next year, the Duke of Gloucester, the King's third son, visited Canberra after opening shrines to the war dead in Melbourne and Sydney and added one more tree to the landscape—a pine, planted near the foundations of the War Memorial, sacred because grown from seed carried off Gallipoli by an Australian soldier in 1915.

The War Memorial was the only monumental public building in Canberra. The name of National Library had been given to a structure east of Parliament House adequate for the readers of a small town. A tiny University College, remotely controlled from the University of Melbourne as an evening school for public servants, had no accommodation of its own. Substantial churches were constructed, and from 1936 the old graveyard of St. John's church was no longer the only burial ground in the territory: a civic cemetery received the bones, and later the ashes, of the increasing number of people who stayed in Canberra to die.

The living in 1941 numbered eleven thousand, four thousand more than in 1927. Most federal departments had moved their headquarters to Canberra. Their members were accommodated at work and at home without damage to Griffin's plan, though it had some narrow escapes. The Federal Capital Commission, created in 1925, was abolished in 1930 by a Labor government that mistrusted independent corporations. Labor's successors did not bother to restore it, leaving Canberra under direct ministerial control. In 1938, Parliament responded to criticisms that piecemeal decisions were eroding the plan, and a National Capital Planning and Development Committee was established, whose members were to include three experts not in government service. The committee advised successfully against the construction of two more provisional administrative blocks inconsistent with Griffin's design, and against putting a permanent hospital on his university site.

Like other architects in private practice, Walter and Marion Griffin struggled for commissions during the Depression, and in 1935 they left Australia for a project in India, where Walter died of peritonitis in 1937. He had remained mystically confident about Canberra, expressing in 1934 his faith that "an unorganized, incoherent, unvoiced Australian sentiment" would eventually prevail in the making of the city. The only structure of his own design to survive

Griffin in Canberra, apart from the general's grave, was a garbage incinerator.

War made Canberra a busier place by enlarging the activities of the federal government, but much of the expansion was centered in Melbourne, where the defense department had remained, and in Sydney. As cabinet normally met in Canberra, ministers and senior public servants did punishing amounts of travel by rail, road, and air. Three ministers and the chief of the general staff were killed when an airplane carrying them from Melbourne crashed close to Canberra on August 13, 1940. A monument marks the spot. At the center of the city, however, you might still run into a mob of sheep. Over to the east, the War Memorial sat like a lion in open grassland.

Its opening day was rich in ironies. The Second World War had overtaken Australia during the making of this monument to the first; three divisions of a Second Australian Imperial Force were in the Middle East, and a fourth had been sent to Malaya in case the Japanese entered the war. The prime minister, five weeks in office at the head of a new Labor government, was John Curtin, who had been imprisoned briefly in the First World War after failing to enlist for military service.

The governor-general, Lord Gowrie, was apprehensive about his new advisers. In 1931, a Labor government had appointed as governor-general Sir Isaac Isaacs—an Australian, a retired politician (though not of the Labor persuasion), a septuagenarian, and a Jew. King George V announced not, as is usually done, that he had been pleased to appoint Isaacs, but just that he had appointed him. The monarch was not at all pleased, believing that a "local man" could not represent him properly and angry that the Australians had not consulted before putting up Isaacs's name. Not long before he died in 1936, the king had the satisfaction of knowing that his next representative would be Lord Gowrie, a British professional soldier wounded at Gallipoli, who had served already as governor of South Australia and who was to stay at Yarralumla longer than any other occupant. Gowrie saw it as his task to "try and re-establish the dignity of that office." His job became more challenging when he had to swear in as prime minister the son of an Irish Catholic policeman.

At the end of 1941, the anti-conscriptionist agitator of 1916 was leader of an embattled nation. Curtin issued a New Year statement to the people saying: "Australia looks to America, free of any pangs as to our traditional links or kinship with the United Kingdom." Imperially minded critics in Australia and England, slow to realize what was happening to the north, accused Curtin of disloyalty. Early in 1942, he refused Winston Churchill's pressing request to divert to Burma the men of two Australian divisions recalled from the Middle East. On March 26, General Douglas MacArthur, having been ordered by President Roosevelt to escape from Corregidor, met Curtin in Canberra. He drove up from Melbourne, as his subsequent *Reminiscences* described, "through prairie grasslands and groves of native trees." In the cabinet room of Parliament House, MacArthur attended a meeting of the Advisory War Council. As a guest on the floor of the House of Representatives, he listened to an hour of proceedings, thanked the Speaker for the courtesy, and said, "If the Australians can fight as well as they can argue we are certain of victory." In the parliamentary dining room he told members that he felt at home already, thanks to an "indescribable consanguinity of race." Curtin appeared in MacArthur's *Reminiscences* as "the kind of a man the Australians called 'fair dinkum.' As I rose to leave, I put my arm about his strong shoulder. 'Mr. Prime Minister,' I said, 'we two, you and I, will see this thing through together. You take care of the rear and I will handle the front.' He shook me by both my hands and said, 'I know I was not wrong in selecting you as Supreme Commander.' " The selection of MacArthur to command Allied operations in the southwest Pacific had been Roosevelt's, the Australian government merely assenting; but it suited both parties to say that Australian servicemen had been put under United States command on the initiative of their own government, and to encourage the myth that first MacArthur and then massive American forces had arrived in response to Curtin's New Year appeal.

That cry for help was no declaration of independence. Lord Gowrie and Curtin quickly became friends, even intimates. During MacArthur's visit, and again when Eleanor Roosevelt came to Canberra in 1942, Gowrie was invited to take part in briefing the Americans. In 1944, when MacArthur was Curtin's guest at the Lodge to celebrate the second anniversary of his coming to Australia, Gowrie had the supreme commander out to Yarralumla to invest him honorarily with the insignia of the Knight Grand Cross of the Most Honourable Order of the Bath. Gowrie, aged seventy-two, left for home six months later, to be replaced on Curtin's personal recommendation not by an Australian but by the Duke of Gloucester. The wartime American presence was nevertheless of momentous significance to Australia. In 1939, Australia's formal international relations were colonial: the government dealt with the rest of the world, including the empire, through Great Britain, and Canberra's only diplomatic residence belonged to the British High Commissioner. A Canadian representative arrived in 1940, and so did a minister for the United States. Close to the Lodge, the Americans began in 1941 to put up an embassy (until 1946 called a legation) designed in the style of Williamsburg. For a decade it was the only building in Canberra put up by a foreign government, and long after that it remained the largest.

Towards the end of the war, heart disease confined Curtin for spells in the Canberra hospital, and on July 5, 1945 he became the first prime minister to die in Canberra. His body lay in state in King's Hall, the coffin draped with an Australian flag and guarded by a sailor, an airman, and two soldiers.

15 February 1954

The mace, symbol of royal authority, carried on the shoulder of the sergeant-at-arms as he led members of the House of Representatives into the Senate chamber, was a gift from the House of Commons to commemorate fifty years of federation. The chamber was even more crowded than on May 9, 1927, for in 1949 the number of senators had been increased from thirty-six to sixty, and the House of Representatives enlarged from 75 to 123. The galleries were full of guests who were to see Parliament opened by the monarch herself. Queen Elizabeth II and the Duke of Edinburgh, touring the empire and Commonwealth, were in Canberra for five days. The speech setting out what her government—"my ministers"—had in store for the session was heard by listeners to radio, as her father's was in 1927, but by no special arrangement, for since 1946 the proceedings of Parliament had been broadcast regularly. Her ascent of the steps with the prime minister, Robert Gordon Menzies, and her passage through King's Hall, were described by a team of commentators led by three from the British Broadcasting Corporation who were old hands at fluent and reverent reporting of royalty. Radio covered every public moment of the tour, and the front pages of newspapers were filled with photographs of the phenomenon at which Australians marveled: the face on the money, smiling in their own streets. As she entered the Senate, one paper reported "a gasp of admiration spontaneous and uncontrollable." "THE QUEEN IS IN AUSTRALIA!" said the title on a movie newsreel.

In front of Parliament House flew Union Jacks alongside Australian flags with a newly official status. The politicians had discovered that the design and dimensions of the flag with Union Jack and stars had never been properly defined, and they put that right by an act just in time for the visit. Between the flagpoles stood a solid stone memorial to the queen's grandfather King George V, commissioned by the federal government soon after he died but delayed by war and the death of two sculptors until it became Australia's last traditional imperial monument. A statue of the king faced Parliament House, back to back with a crusading St. George on horseback looking towards the War Memorial, and accompanied by inscriptions and medallions recording the king's opening of the first parliament and the two foremost official national achievements: the federal movement, and the engagement of military and naval forces in the Great War.

On February 16, the queen unveiled the inscription on a monument more contemporary in style and message. On Russell Hill, north of the Molonglo, close to the point where King's and Constitution Avenue met, an aluminium American eagle rested on an aluminium-sheeted column 220 feet high. The words on the base, unveiled by the queen, told posterity that John Curtin's plea had been answered: "In grateful remembrance of the vital help given by the United States of America during the war in the Pacific, 1941–1945." The Australian-American Memorial had been created on the initiative of the Australian-American Association, a body of wartime origin and with commercial, political, and social purposes, which held a competition, opened a public subscription, and secured a grant from the federal government. Connoisseurs of the capital landscape welcomed the verticality of Richard Ure's perch for Paul Beadle's bird. Before long it would be surrounded by the offices of the defense department, and that was appropriate. The historian W.J. Hudson sees the strategy of successive Australian foreign ministers after the eclipse of British power in the Pacific as "ensnarement of the United States." That was certainly the policy of Richard Gardiner Casey, minister for external affairs since 1951. The ANZUS treaty of that year, signed while Australian servicemen were fighting in Korea, represented some progress towards the goal, and was historic in having as parties two Commonwealth dominions but not the motherland, even though the British government had wanted to be included. If the American eagle on Russell Hill was not actually ensnared, it looked unlikely to take off.

The queen inspected the Australian War Memorial, escorted by its creator, Charles Bean, and laid a wreath on the Stone of Remembrance. The Duke of Edinburgh opened University House, hall of residence for a new Australian National University—on Griffin's site, but not laid out according to his vision of the map of learning, or to anybody else's in the Australia of 1913. It was to be a cluster of research schools, initially in the physical and social sciences, Pacific studies, and medical research. The founders hoped that generous salaries, study leave, and research budgets would induce eminent Australian scholars working abroad to come home and would attract to Canberra outstanding people from elsewhere. The historian Sir Keith Hancock, Canberra's early critic, became director of social sciences in 1957 after holding professorships in Birmingham, Oxford, and London. Academics teaching in the state universities found it hard to greet the rich newcomer without envy—especially those in huts down the hill at the Canberra University College, most of whose students were still public servants studying part-time for degrees from Melbourne.

At Yarralumla, the queen and the duke stayed with Field Marshal Sir William Slim, who had recently replaced Sir William McKell, Labor premier of New South Wales when appointed on the advice of the federal Labor government in 1947. As leader of the opposition, Menzies deplored that choice; in office he got on well with McKell, had him accept a knighthood though that was against Labor policy, and reverted to the tradition of bringing out an eminent Briton. Slim, a professional soldier, belonged to the imperial freemasonry of men who had fought at Gallipoli. He became the first governor-general to receive an Aboriginal at Yarralumla, when the painter Albert Namatjira was invited to meet the queen. His water colors of Northern Territory landscapes had made Namatjira the most famous of the few Aborigines known for mastery of a European accomplishment. Having attended the royal garden party, he was even more newsworthy later in the year when arrested for drinking alcohol, an offense because the law defined him as a ward, not a citizen.

The prime minister was at the queen's side whenever it was ritually proper for him to be there. Menzies was a lucky politician, and 1954 was his luckiest year. The royal tour gave him much joy. In a country with no tradition of panegyric he was better than any other politician at making flowery speeches. Often he declared himself "British to the bootheels," a resolutely old-fashioned image. He had a conservative lawyer's delight in the mysteries of the British constitution, incarnate in his guest. He loved the role of imperial statesman. Within weeks of playing silver-haired host to the young queen and her consort, Menzies went to the country in a general election, displaying as never before a genial avuncularity. The royal yacht sailed away on April 1. Two days later, Vladimir Petrov defected from the Soviet embassy. He and his wife, MVD agents, were granted political asylum on April 13. On May 3, Menzies's government established a royal commission to inquire into Soviet espionage in Australia, with particular reference to information supplied by the Petrovs, and on May 29 Menzies and his Liberal and Country party coalition won the election. The royal commissioners concluded, not surprisingly, that the Soviet Union had been using its embassy as a cloak for espionage; they found that the only Australians who knowingly assisted Soviet espionage were Communists; they found no evidence to warrant prosecuting anybody. The greatest beneficiary (except possibly for the Petrovs, who changed their names and became clandestine Australian citizens) was Menzies, for a split in the Labor party induced by the episode kept his government in power for as long as he chose to stay.

Most of Canberra's thirty thousand people turned out to see the queen in 1954. The population had doubled since the end of the war as the public service grew larger, more government departments were shifted to the capital, and their transfer generated work, especially in the building industry. The Labor government had embarked on, and Menzies continued, a policy of encouraging "displaced persons" and other settlers from postwar Europe to emigrate here and become "new Australians"—an official term that Arthur Calwell, Labor's minister for immigration, had worked hard at popularizing. Canberra in 1954 was the home of more people born in continental Europe (mainly Poland, Italy, the Netherlands, and Latvia) than of people born in the United Kingdom and Ireland. That was a new fact of Australian life, and its implications for a society traditionally almost a hundred percent British were only beginning to be given serious public discussion. In Canberra, new Australian men were employed on the construction of the first permanent administrative building, in the national triangle. The building had been planned by competition in 1924, stretched from two stories to seven, and ended up a gray semi-classical monster. They worked also at assembling wooden office blocks to accommodate newcomers: these buildings, soon named "the woolsheds," were defined as temporary, not provisional, but they are still there. Away from work, residents of Canberra had few more amenities in 1954 than they did in 1941. As citizens they had made slight gains: the powerless Australian Capital Territory Advisory Council was given a majority of elected members in 1954, and a member from the capital was admitted to the House of Representatives in 1949, though he could not vote except in a limited way on matters affecting his own electorate. The *Washington Post* thought these innovations progressive enough to earn congratulations. Suburban houses went up in whatever style of bungalow vernacular was fashionable in Melbourne and Sydney, except where imported prefabs added a Scandinavian accent. Public transport was almost invisible to people familiar with the systems of Melbourne and Sydney. The railway station was out in a southern suburb, not to the east of City Hill as Griffin had planned. Pedestrians had long hikes, and motorists easily got lost in curving streets signposted, if at all, for horse-and-cart drivers with sharp vision.

Postwar growth had turned the landscape into two barely connected towns, one north of the Molonglo and the other south. "Canberra," wrote a keen student of Australian landscapes, Oskar Spate, a few years later, "reached its nadir about 1954." Washington had been derided for decades after the federal government moved in: "capital of miserable huts," "city of streets without houses," "neither a city, nor a village, nor the country," "a mudhole about equal to the Great Serbonian bog." Similarly, the Canberra visited by the queen was "a good sheep-station spoiled," "a garden without a city," "seven suburbs in search of a city," and "the best lit cemetery between Sydney and Melbourne." The Duke of Edinburgh liked especially the term "a city without a soul."

Menzies pressed the queen to come again, and she did. The popular welcomes were always enthusiastic, but never again quite ecstatic. We must not let daylight in upon magic, Walter Bagehot had said of monarchy, and every time she was exposed to Australian sun the queen lost a little of her quasi-divinity. An English planner contemplating the problem of Capital Hill proposed in 1957 that it be crowned by a royal pavilion and apartments that the queen could make her Australian lodge. Republicans and monarchists could agree that this would be a mistake. Menzies, however, indulged in even more effusive sentimentality on the second royal visit in 1963 than on the first. At a banquet in King's Hall, the queen sitting beside him, Menzies spoke of her in verse from the reign of Elizabeth I:

> I did but see her passing by
> and yet I love her till I die.

Elizabeth II blushed. Later she dubbed him Sir Robert, and not merely, like many colleagues and supporters, a knight in an order created to honor colonials, but one of the Most Ancient and Noble Order of the Thistle, a company limited to sixteen men chosen personally by the sovereign. Cartoonists loved the thistle. Archaic symbols of empire gave Menzies more and more delight. In 1965, when his government accepted advice to make the currency decimal, he wanted to put the name "royal" on the unit that would replace the pound. He yielded to a public opinion that preferred "dollar," recognizing reluctantly that culture, commerce, and strategic interest made it more rational to choose a familiar American term than a manufactured British one. Australian faces replaced the queen's on the notes, but her profile remained on the coins produced in Canberra's new mint.

20 October 1966

Air Force One touched down in the dusk. Another Boeing 707 carrying the bullet-proof bubble-top Lincoln and Secret Service Cadillac had landed already, and two more, full of reporters, were making their descent across the paddocks. From his personal podium with its presidential seal, beside a pole flying the stars and stripes, Lyndon B. Johnson thanked his hosts for a beautiful Texan sunset and a wonderful American rainbow. To his right, as a band played "God Save the Queen" and "The Star-Spangled Banner," stood the prime minister, the governor-general, and the United States ambassador. Close to his left, Rufus Youngblood—familiar here as in every land with television for his presence at Dallas on November 22, 1963—scanned the crowd of Canberra people who had come out to the airport to see the first moments of the first visit to Australia by an American president.

This was also Johnson's first overseas journey as president. After three days he would fly to Manila for a conference with leaders of the six nations, Australia among them, who were involved alongside the United States in Vietnam. Midterm elections were due the week after the president returned to Washington, and allies in Vietnam were all the more precious as opposition to the war gathered at home. Sir Robert Menzies had committed Australian soldiers in 1965, the year the queen appointed him to succeed Sir Winston Churchill as Lord Warden of the Cinque Ports. After Menzies's retirement early in 1966 at the age of seventy-one, his affable successor Harold Holt sent more troops to the war. There were now about forty-five hundred.

In June, the new prime minister had visited London, where he found people lamentably uninterested in Asia, and Washington, where he addressed the National Press Club as American bombs began to fall on oil installations in Hanoi, and said that Australia would go "all the way with L.B.J." This was referred to as Holt's "Declaration of Dependence" by the Washington correspondent of one Australian newspaper. Holt's colleagues in cabinet thoroughly agreed with the sentiment, wince though some might at his expressing it in the form of a jingle. In conservative thinking, the more thoroughly the United States was embroiled against communist forces in Asia, the better for the security of Australia. It was not easy to say who was keener to lead whom into the quagmire of Vietnam. Johnson was touched by Holt's pledge, and it may well have decided him to make the long flight down under. He had been to this country in 1942, as he said at the airport, and found the land, the cattle, the sheep, and the people so like those of Texas that he thought of Australia as his second home. American reporters noted that his exploits in the Pacific war became more Mittyesque with every Australian telling, until the former naval lieutenant remembered fighting side by side with the Aussies in the trenches.

Holt joined the Johnsons in the presidential limousine for the drive across Canberra and out to Yarralumla, where the governor-general had gone ahead to receive them. He had a long wait, for time and again the president made the car stop so that he could wade into the crowd, grasping hands, praising Australia through a megaphone, thanking a man with a placard bearing Holt's Washington ode, presenting a bewildered Holt to spectators. The governor-general was an Australian, though no American would have guessed it from his name, bearing, or voice. Mrs. Johnson in her diary described Lord Casey and his wife as "the sort of people who have made England great." Casey had been made a British peer in 1960 after nearly thirty years in Australian politics, the last ten as Menzies's minister for external affairs. His accent remained as upper-class English as when he graduated from Cambridge before the Great War—in which he, too, served at Gallipoli. Menzies's choice of him as governor-general in 1965, happily accepted by the queen, put an end to the custom of importing Englishmen. Shaking the president's hand at Yarralumla was a gratifying experience for Casey: a ritual sealing of the Pacific alliance.

Two thousand people were waiting with friendly and hostile intentions outside the Canberra Rex Hotel on Northbourne Avenue, north of Civic Centre, where the Johnsons were supposed to be spending a free evening. A band played songs from "My Fair Lady." Demonstrators waved and chanted slogans some of which were familiar to the American reporters, some new: "Allies yes, satellites no." "We're not cattle and this isn't your ranch." "Go away, L.B.J." The deeply American message "Make love not war," printed on the tight-fitting T-shirt of a pretty young blonde, was reproduced all over the United States. The president never saw or heard these statements. He and Lady Bird Johnson dined with the Holts at the Lodge and were smuggled into the hotel by a back door.

Next morning, the president laid a wreath at the Australian War Memorial on a Stone of Remembrance guarded by four soldiers back from Vietnam who stood stiff as statues, heads bowed, as he murmured gratitude and admiration to each man. He stopped at the American-Australian eagle, read the message of appreciation at its base, and declared himself deeply pleased before taking off for Parliament House. A forest of poles carried equal numbers of American and Australian flags. In the cabinet room, Johnson talked with Holt and senior ministers, and in the dining room he and party leaders made speeches over lunch. Arthur Calwell's, for Labor, had the guest frowning. The seventy-year-old Labor leader had a well-informed reverence for the founders of the United States, especially

Jefferson, possibly imbibed from an American grandfather; and he paid tribute now to the revolution that gave the world the Declaration of Independence. On the other hand, he had a social democrat's conviction that the modern American parties were Tweedledum and Tweedledee, and he quoted at the president a description of them as two identical bottles bearing different labels and both empty. More seriously, he spoke of Vietnam in terms sure to make Johnson bristle, invoking the names of Americans—Fulbright, Robert Kennedy, Wayne Morse—who were, he said, "not prepared to go all the way with L.B.J." That goaded the visitor to throw the words back in terms suggesting that Calwell was not only anti-American but un-Australian. "Americans know that when freedom is at stake and honorable men stand in battle shoulder to shoulder, Australians will go all the way until liberty and freedom are won." Liberal and Country party members stood up to applaud; Labor men remained seated, and not all put their hands together.

On the third day, after visits to Melbourne and Sydney, the president turned out in cowboy boots and Stetson, rancher's gear for a Texan-Australian barbecue at Lanyon, one of the territory's old pastoral stations. The guests came in suits and dresses as for an Anglo-Australian garden party. Australian cattle and sheep died to make (by *Time*'s count) twelve hundred pounds of steak and eight hundred double lamb chops; strawberry ice cream was served in the shape of kangaroos, and a live kangaroo was photographed taking a biscuit from the president's hand. The host was the Texan ambassador, Ed Clark, a buddy of Johnson's who wore a yellow rose everywhere and who knew by heart the president's telephone number.

In the November elections, the Democrats fared badly; in Australian elections the same month, Holt reduced Calwell's followers to 41 out of 123 in the House of Representatives. (Though it was no practical help to Calwell, full voting rights were now given to the member for the Australian Capital Territory, a Labor man). Johnson sent Holt a message of congratulations that Calwell denounced as reeking of patronage, interference, and arrogance. The presidential visit had been a bonus for Holt, and hastened the day Calwell would step down for Gough Whitlam. A year later, Johnson again flew all the way to Australia, to attend a memorial service in Melbourne for Harold Holt after the prime minister disappeared in the surf. From

London came the prime minister and the Prince of Wales, but not the queen.

"Do you think it is possible to love two people at once?" the queen asked the duke in a *Canberra Times* cartoon the day the American president swept in. "Good morning fellow Americans!" a columnist greeted readers next day. The crowds in every city were larger than at any royal progress, and reporters who had covered tours by the queen marveled at the difference of style. "Prince Philip never stopped the car at a street corner," wrote one old hand. "When did he kiss a baby? When did he call out 'I love ya, Australia'?" When, for that matter, did a royal visitor actually breach protocol by chatting to soldiers in a posture of mourning, as this exuberant and democratic foreigner dared to do at the War Memorial? A president was not hedged with divinity, but it was quite as wonderful for Australians to see him, and they saw more of him. He inspired, moreover, another kind of awe. *Pravda* called Johnson's journey a Hollywood panorama; *Time* thought it bore a resemblance to a Bob Hope extravaganza, maybe *The Road to Manila.* Here he really was, not on celluloid but whooping through the streets of Canberra, glowering at Arthur Calwell, possibly the most powerful man in the world. "He's very lifelike, isn't he?" said a woman whose hand he almost shook at Canberra airport. And although he went in for a brand of sentimentality quite foreign to the cool queen, the visit expressed actual strategic and economic relationships, whereas royal visits were essays in nostalgia. This, said the news magazine *The Bulletin* on December 31, 1966, was the year when Australians "admitted being part of Asia, and were committed, finally, to alliance with America instead of Britain." "The Brits," as some Australians now called them with a hint of condescension, were trying to get into the European Economic Community, leaving the countries of the old Commonwealth to look after themselves. The United States had replaced the United Kingdom as the main overseas source of both public loans and private investment, and the proportion of Australians whose families had non-British motherlands was still rising.

In the Canberra barnstormed by Lyndon Johnson, nearly a hundred thousand people occupied a city that was beginning to look like a capital rather than a monument to the impermanence of European settlement. In 1954, the Senate had appointed a select committee to investigate the development of the capital. The McCallum committee reported scathingly that forty years after 1913, the central places in Griffin's plan stood out "not as monumental regions symbolizing the character of a national capital, but more as graveyards where departed spirits await a resurrection of national pride." Ever since Griffin was pushed out in 1920, the task of acting on his blueprint had been assigned to posterity. Now, said the senators, the time had come to "place it firmly and squarely on the shoulders of people alive today." The tabling of this report was among events of the mid-1950s, along with the coming of espresso coffee, motels, television, the Melbourne Olympic Games, Patrick White's novel *The Tree of Man,* and Ray Lawler's play *The Summer of the Seventeenth Doll,* which signaled the end of postwar Australia and a new taste for diversity, enterprise, and affirmation. "Make big plans," the senators exhorted, quoting Daniel H. Burnham, chief designer of the Chicago World's Fair and driving force behind the McMillan commission. The McCallum committee was no less important for the making of Canberra than the McMillan commission had been for the re-making of Washington.

Menzies gave his necessary blessing, having evidently decided that Canberra would be among a few positive achievements (rescuing the universities was another) for which he was remembered. An act of 1957 established the National Planning Development Commission to make big plans. More public servants than ever before were transferred from Melbourne; the planners attracted private builders to put up houses and themselves commissioned unfamiliar blocks of apartments.

For administrators from Melbourne and diplomats from Paris or Athens, Canberra was still a rustic place, but public and private enterprise was enriching the city. Airy and well-equipped schools inspired visiting teachers and parents to go back to their states with new visions of the possible. The *Canberra Times,* long cherished for parochiality and misprints, was enlarged and smartened in 1964 to live with the *Australian,* launched in Canberra by Rupert Murdoch, who owned tabloids in Adelaide and Sydney and who defied the judgment of competitors and sociologists that in federal, continental Australia a nationally circulating daily newspaper would be no more viable than in the United States. Concerts and plays by visiting companies no longer had to be fitted into the Albert Hall. In a new Civic Square on the eastern side of City Hill, Thespis frolicked in a fountain outside the Canberra Theatre Centre within sight of Ethos, a winged female holding aloft the sun; she was meant to stand for the spirit of Canberra and was almost unique among its public monuments in having been paid for by private money, from the chamber of commerce. Official Canberra had traditionally been accused of treating commerce as not much more than a source of litter. In the post-McCallum years as before, billboards (hoardings, as Australians called them) were banned but private investment was given more encouragement. East of Ethos, commerce raised a vast marble-faced box known as the Monaro Mall which turned the shoppers' Canberra from a country town into a city and posed a challenge to designers of monumental public buildings: a visitor from another civilization might well have picked the mall rather than Parliament House or any other structure in sight as the place where these people must conduct their most important business.

The National Capital Development Commission gave the city a series of long, low rectangular buildings striped with light columns or mullions: here the mint, there a complex of courts, police station, and reserve bank. Autonomous institutions added shapes of their own, subject to the commission's approval. The Returned Services League, as the old soldiers' organization was now called, moved its federal headquarters in 1956 from Melbourne, where it had been detained by a president whose strategy was to remain entrenched near the head office of the repatriation department and make sorties to Canberra; now, from a compact structure near the War Memorial, its big guns could be trained on Parliament House. On the edge of the University in 1959, the Australian Academy of Science moved in under a copper-covered dome, designed to harmonize with the surrounding hills, influenced by the Kresge Auditorium at the Massachusetts Institute of Technology, and known popularly as the Martian, or Eskimo, Embassy. Its neighbors the Canberra University College and the Australian National University merged at the direction of the federal government in 1960, and in both parts of the tree-covered campus, building committees settled for a muddled anthology of styles.

The neoclassical outlines of a new national library, faced with white marble from Greece, were reflected in the waters of Lake Burley Griffin. For months of 1963–64, the people of Canberra had the pleasure of watching the dammed waters of the Molonglo inch up the concrete piles of the Commonwealth and King's Avenue bridges and out towards waiting foreshores. The English designers of the lake and its bridges, William Holford and Partners, had departed in some details from Griffin's plan, but they saluted him as "a topographical genius." Their bridges defined his central triangle. At last his city was visible, and it was a happy inspiration to name the lake after him (though the form chosen jarred on people who had known him as Walter Griffin, not Burley). "Already," wrote the poet and journalist Kenneth Slessor in 1966, "it has become difficult to imagine Canberra without the clear blue waters that unify and reflect it." Lady Bird Johnson was taken for a cruise along the seven miles of bays and basins and reaches, in the only motor vessel allowed to disturb the water. Yachts learned to use its winds. Anglers were encouraged to catch officially introduced fish. Sand was spread on peninsulas, and toddlers rode tiny surfboards to rehearse for encounters elsewhere with waves. The waters were not always clear and blue, however, and warnings had sometimes to be issued about effluent from across the border in uncontrollable Queanbeyan. Landscape architects worked on the shores of the central basin, between the bridges, to make on the north a people's park and a grand avenue up to the War Memorial (laid down in 1965 for the fiftieth anniversary of Gallipoli), and on the south a setting fit for the permanent Parliament House.

The McCallum Committee urged an early start on that project. The president of the Senate and the Speaker of the House called in 1957 for a "monumental" building, "a national symbol, manifesting . . . Australian pride in democratic institutions." Where should it be? Up on Capital Hill, said McCallum: "Griffin's nebulous plan for a Pantheon should be discarded and plans prepared with a Parliament House as the dominant feature on Capital Hill." Down by the lake, said Holford and Partners: a democratic Versailles with a forecourt every Australian would have the right to enter. On Camp Hill, just above the present House, said custodians of Griffin's memory. The prospective occupants would have to decide.

26 January 1988

Barring acts of God, great powers, or militant unions, the new Parliament House will be occupied in 1988 on the two-hundredth anniversary of British settlement. It seems likely, though not certain, that the British monarch will be invited to unveil the inscription.

The destiny of Capital Hill was settled by an act of 1974 that prescribed the site for Parliament. Malcolm Fraser, Prime Minister from the end of 1975, committed his Liberal-Country party coalition to cut public expenditure, and did not authorize a start on the project until late in 1978. Since 1927, two wings had been added and the original floor space nearly trebled, but more and more people had to be fitted in. The number of elected members, which increased in 1949 from 111 to 183, rose to 189 in 1975 when the Australian Capital Territory and the Northern Territory were given two senators each, and in the House of Representatives the capital acquired a second member and the north its first. The size of cabinet had doubled. Ministers gave themselves larger personal staffs and allowed private members to have assistants. The press gallery expanded until there were as many journalists working in the building as there had been politicians in 1927. The provisional roof sprang leaks, and provisional floorboards worked loose. The high cost of altering and maintaining the old building became one of the arguments for getting on with the new one.

Early in 1979, the Parliament House Construction Authority was formed and an open competition arranged. When the winner was announced in mid-1980, first reports said that the design was by an Australian, Richard Thorp, a resident of the United States and Italy since 1971 and now employed in the New York office of Mitchell/Giurgola. Later, in official literature, the architects were named as Mitchell/Giurgola and Thorp, and in public discussion Romaldo Guirgola was commonly described as the author. Giurgola was born and graduated in Italy, moved to the United States and became prominent in the 1970s as a practitioner of postmodernist architecture, that umbrella term used of people who identified modernism with austerity and rigid geometry, "boring boxes."

The building in progress on Capital Hill is not at all like a box. It hugs, even burrows into, the circular site. The first bewildering evidence of progress, to people driving south along Commonwealth Avenue, was the crest being scraped away to let the building sit low. The *Canberra Times*' humorist, Ian Warden, professing disappointment that the building was not to be in wedding-cake style, compared it to a pizza, or a cow-pat on a hillock. Some opponents of the Capital

Hill site had said that it was wrong for legislators in a democracy to place themselves above the people. This design will actually allow people to walk over the top of the politicians.

It has severe critics. One, the architect Peter Myers, accuses the building of being laid out according to the male anatomy, like the temple at Luxor and the Eiffel tower, and sees it as a spreadeagled giant, celebrating the power of one man. The space given to the executive has been questioned. The executive wing is built around a central courtyard: a large suite for the prime minister, ministerial suites, and a cabinet room. Graham Freudenberg, who worked for Gough Whitlam when he was prime minister, denounces the new House as a monument to executive power, a capitulation of parliament to government. Certainly it recognizes a spectacular divergence in Canberra from the Westminster model, and one that the old House was not designed to accommodate. In London, ministers work in their departments, the prime minister's base is an office at 10 Downing Street, and cabinet meets there. In Canberra, ministers, including the prime minister, work in Parliament House and have their cabinet meetings there, too. The reason usually given for this departure from British practice is that Canberra's standing orders, unlike Westminster's, require ministers to be within a quick sprint of the legislative chambers whenever the bells ring for a division. How that difference emerged, and why Australian ministers put up with it, is a mystery. There may have been other reasons why ministers went so seldom to their departments. By the time most public servants moved from Melbourne, ministers were well settled in at Parliament House. Having family households in distant electorates and treating Canberra as a camp or a dormitory, ministers liked to huddle with each other and with private members in warmth and security. As for the prime minister, the Lodge was conceived only as a suburban residence in a fairly egalitarian society, with no spaces for staff or cabinet. If the new House were to reverse the history of relations between executive and legislature, then the clients who dictated the brief would have needed to re-think drastically their own ways of life.

High above this building, a huge flag will fly, a signal for tourists and visible twice from below, up through the clear glazed ceiling of the Members' Hall and down into a reflecting pool. Some find this apotheosis of the flag rather American, and they have a point: Old Glory is both more sacred and more popular than either the Union

Jack or the Australian national flag. Australians going to their first game of baseball are not prepared for the ceremony which precedes it, as players and spectators face the flag and stand still for the anthem that celebrates its holy night. Only "God Save the Queen" has had that status at public events in Australia, and where a patriotic icon has been needed to adorn a wall, public and private people have been less inclined to put up a flag than a portrait of the monarch. But that is changing. The great flag on its frame over Capital Hill may be nicely timed to proclaim the triumph of a trend. The queen's face is seen less and less these days, and "God Save the Queen" is not heard so often. The Union Jack, once a common partner to the Australian flag, is a rare sight. As imperial images fade, the idea of a republic becomes steadily less sacrilegious. When Bob Hawke says he sees a republic as inevitable (though not to be campaigned for), scarcely a bulldog barks. Meanwhile, Australian flags proliferate. When *Australia II* won the America's Cup, one was spread across the top of the Sydney harbor bridge; it was described as the world's biggest, but there are at least two other claimants for that Texan title, in Canberra and Melbourne.

But *which* flag will fly over Parliament House in 1988? The architects' sketches properly show the one with Union Jack, Southern Cross, and federal star. That flag, however, is now under challenge by people not otherwise radical. A rich wine maker, Sir James Hardy, flying the Australian flag from the stern of his yacht during races off Florida and the Bahamas, was irritated to be asked again and again what part of Britain he was from. Hardy became chairman of Ausflag 1988, formed to find a more suitable emblem in time for the bicentenary. The campaign was opposed, however, by leaders of the Returned Services League (RSL), bastion of imperial patriotism, who created an Australian National Flag Association to defend tradition. Changing the flag, said their president, would be like burning all the history books; he thought Sir James Hardy should have the decency to hand back his knighthood, and there was talk of removing Hardy's wines from RSL clubs. In old imperial Australia, when beer was the orthodox masculine drink, that might not have sounded a grave threat; but the taste of men who identified themselves as returned soldiers was changing even if their attachment to the Union Jack was not; and Sir James Hardy chose to resign from the campaign.

Meanwhile, Ausflag 1988 received more than five thousand suggestions. Among candidates being waved were the boxing kangaroo that was mascot for the America's Cup team at Newport, and a stylized Southern Cross first flown by rebellious gold diggers in 1854, which was taken up on both the far left and the far right by groups with different perceptions of what the rebellion was about. A koala flag accompanied Australia's legions to the Los Angeles Olympic Games. The boomerang had its supporters. The reformers propose a national plebiscite in 1986. They will be happy with any design that is elegant, identifiably Australian, and does not incorporate the Union Jack. If such an emblem is hoisted on Capital Hill in 1988, it will signify a mild affirmation of independence.

Visitors will enter the new Parliament House through a portico whose facade resembles the front of its predecessor down the hill. Whether the observer picks up the postmodernist allusion will depend a good deal on whether the original is still there; that is problematic. There is one opinion that the provisional building should be knocked down, to stop it blocking the grand view along the axis from Capital Hill to Mount Ainslie. Other people say that the old House should be preserved as part of the national estate, because it is so full of history in a land where that resource is scarce, and because its very plainness, its lack of monumentality, has endeared it to Australians. It sits "comfortable and accessible," wrote an admiring architect in 1977. The building had actually become less accessible by then. In case tourists were terrorists, they had to go in a pokey side entrance instead of walking up the steps, submit to physical and electronic scrutiny, and wear a name-tag if going beyond King's Hall and the public galleries. Such precautions were unknown in Washington's capitol, to the surprise of Australians visiting, as they believed, a land charged with violence. Once the politicians move uphill, however, the building could become again its old welcoming self, perhaps as a conference center, or a national portrait gallery, or a museum in which scholars, artists, and engineers combined to bring people the signs and sounds of the federation. The regular rituals, the high moments, could be displayed, and the interruptions and intrusions, and the astonishing events of November 11, 1975, when out at Yarralumla a governor-general, Sir John Kerr, dismissed a prime minister, Gough Whitlam, who had a majority in the House of Representatives though not in the Senate. Outside

Parliament House, where an angry crowd had gathered, the governor-general's secretary read a proclamation dissolving the Parliament, which ended: "God Save the Queen!" "Well may they say 'God Save the Queen!,'" shouted Whitlam, towering over the hapless official, "for *nothing* will save the governor-general!"

Photographed, filmed, recorded, and re-created years later with archaeological care in a television series *The Dismissal,* this scene is imprinted on millions of minds. Like Americans recalling Dallas on November 22, 1963, Australians remember where they were when they heard what the governor-general had done. (We have been luckier than Americans, so far, in our political cataclysms. Of three prime ministers not to survive office, two have died of illness and one from surfing; none has been close to impeachment.) Civics lessons at school had not prepared people to know that the constitution allowed the dismissal, and they thought there was a convention that whoever had a majority in the House of Representatives governed the country. Kerr's coup, as some people called it, recruited supporters to the cause of writing a new constitution that would specify exactly what the occupant of Yarralumla could and could not do.

Though Whitlam lost the election held on December 13, 1975, he was right about the fate of the governor-general. Sir John Kerr—boilermaker's son, a left-winger when young, chief justice of New South Wales, nominated for the job by Whitlam in 1974—could not count on appearing in public after November 11, 1975, in Canberra or elsewhere, without being the object of a hostile demonstration. The Liberal prime minister Malcolm Fraser got him to resign in July 1977, five months before an election. Whitlam himself bowed out after losing that one, and Bill Hayden led Labor to a narrower loss in 1980. Yarralumla was occupied by two more lawyers, Sir Zelman Cowen and Sir Ninian Stephen, the one an academic and the other a judge, who behaved with tact and grace and were spared any serious constitutional crisis. The homestead originally designated as a temporary Government House, much altered and extended over the years, now appeared likely to remain the governor-general's residence for as long as the office lasted.

A new Labor leader, Bob Hawke, moved into the Lodge in 1983. After a year he appeared set for a long lease, and could well be the first prime minister to occupy the new Lodge, planned for a site closer to Yarralumla, on a ridge over the lake and with a fine view of Black Mountain.

The rural aspect of Canberra's character, once a matter for reproach or apology, was now cherished by people newly sensitive to the environment: "bush capital" was a term used proudly, even possessively. The artificial lake rapidly became part of a natural landscape, to be defended against the planners' highways. The Whitlam government of 1972–75 pleased conservationists by making Canberra the only Australian city with a proper network of cycle paths, and dismayed them by putting a telecommunications tower on the top of Black Mountain. To approaching car travelers, the Telecom tower appears first as an exclamation mark on the horizon: Yes, you are nearly in Canberra! Closer up it has been described by people who do not like it as a concrete parsnip, a thing from Star Wars, and a gigantic hypodermic needle puncturing the sky. Its designer happened to be Richard Ure, architect of the Australian-American Memorial; but the National Capital Development Commission did not want this crowning piece of verticality. The Australian Post Office did, and prevailed over the Committee of Citizens to save Black Mountain, who opposed the tower on ecological, aesthetic, and other grounds, in what their war historian called *The Battle of Black Mountain.* He was Sir Keith Hancock, who had retired in 1965 from the Australian National University and who had come to cherish the city about whose prospects he had once been so skeptical. Canberra, he believed, had become "a truly distinguished architectural achievement" because the planners had followed what now seemed to him the fundamental article of its designer's creed: in Griffin's words, "that the skylines of Canberra's encircling mountains in their near-natural state shall contrast with and complement the intricately patterned manmade landscape of the Molonglo Basin." For Hancock and his allies, Black Mountain became a sacred site. "No other city in the world possesses anything to compare with it," he declared, ". . . For many years past scientists, poets, bushwalkers, teachers with their pupils, parents with their children, have been learning to read Australia's book of nature beneath the mountain's canopy of trees." Now half a million people each year drive to the summit, ascend the tower by elevator to a lookout, and take in the glories created below by nature and Griffin and the planners.

The population passed two hundred thousand in 1976. The National Capital Development Commission extended the city into districts well beyond Griffin's brief, heckled intermittently by a House of Assembly that had replaced the old Advisory Council but had no more teeth. The Fraser government, though committed to public parsimony, allowed monumental projects to proceed, among them a splendid National Sports Centre and a second lake in the new center of Belconnen. Private enterprise added two more malls, the Lakeside Hotel, cinemas, massage parlors, and Vietnamese restaurants that were reminders of a lost cause.

Canberra became the best place to see new Australian architecture. John Andrews returned from North America, where he had done Scarborough College in Toronto and the new home of the Harvard Graduate School of Design, to plan student residences, a technical college, a bus exchange, and a block of offices in the Belconnen Town Centre. Harry Seidler, a pupil of Gropius's at Harvard, designed a palazzo on King's Avenue for the Department of Trade. Colin Madigan won competitions for the High Court and the Australian National Gallery, white concrete-and-glass neighbors on the southern shore of the lake. The High Court, opened in 1980 by the queen—the queen of Australia, as she was officially styled in 1973—has a nave-like foyer three stories high that enjoins awe and suggests that a case can go no higher than here, unless to heaven. (The judges resolved in 1978 that the court was no longer bound by decisions of the privy council in London.) The chunky and angular National Gallery is described by its maker as a warehouse for art, and by one critic as a "wham, bang and thank you ma'am machine for processing the masses with culture." Resting on their way through the gallery, visitors get a fine view of two objects in the lake which are actually British but do not appear so: as monuments created in the twilight of empire they are reticent about their character. A carillon was installed in 1970 on a little island connected to the shore, after years of Anglo-Australian discussion about a suitable gift from the people of Great Britain to mark the capital's jubilee in 1963. A jet of water switched on by the queen, also in 1970, commemorated the two-hundredth anniversary of James Cook's putting New South Wales on the map of empire. The attentive tourist discovers that the jet is accompanied on the shore by a globe recording Cook's voyages, and may notice that the carillon's repertoire includes the sounds of

Big Ben. To the casual eye or ear, they are no more than pleasing devices putting vertical elements into Griffin's triangle. The one British monument within that area that did proclaim its meaning—the King George V memorial, square in front of Parliament House—now struck its custodians as an ugly interruption to the vista, and was quietly moved to one side. The statue of the same monarch in King's Hall awaits its fate, the twin in New Delhi having long since been removed from what used to be the Viceroy's Palace.

Compared with Washington, Canberra is still bare of public monuments. True, those in the American capital took a long time. The memorial to George Washington was not finished until the 1880s, and those to Jefferson, Grant, and Lincoln are works of the present century. But Canberra will never have monuments on the scale of Washington's huge obelisk or the mighty figure of Lincoln sitting in his temple: these objects make statements of a grandeur that no Australian would think seriously of attempting. They honor achievements, in revolution and civil war, of a kind never so far demanded from an Australian leader. As the history of the Commencement Column testifies, the mild accomplishment of federation did not call eloquently for celebration in stone. Nor did it yield any sacred text. The Australian Archives will soon move to a permanent home by the lake, but it will not have the religiosity of Washington's, where the original Declaration of Independence and Constitution are displayed as holy relics. Our constitution is an act of the imperial Parliament, and the dusty original lies in London unsought by any Australian government. No words from the speeches of great men are carved in stone around Canberra, like those statements by Lincoln, Jefferson, and others on walls in Washington. Within the legislature we have little to compare with the visual history packed into the Capitol on fresco, canvas, and frieze; in statue, bust, and medallion. A provisional building, to be sure, was not the place for ambitious decoration. Even in a permanent parliament, though, our politicians would not have thought to invoke any past beyond that of the British empire. One large difference between American democracy and ours is evident to any Australian who contemplates the medallions of lawmakers around Washington's House of Representatives, from Moses and Solon to Blackstone and Napoleon, declaring that the politicians who deliberate in their presence are heirs to the wisdom of all ages and all Europe.

Australian history and nature are quietly recorded in the naming of Canberra's parts. The first suburbs were called after fathers of federation except where tradition had planted names already. For streets, the early planners considered Washington's system of letters and numbers but preferred a nomenclature derived from "Australian men of fame"—explorers, governors, politicians, soldiers, scholars, writers, artists. For decades, the catalogue was confined to worthies who were male and white. Some women have now been admitted. The names of individual Aborigines are rare, since so few are known to white history; but botanists supplied many names of native flora. The present writer lives in Nardoo Crescent, O'Connor; the suburb is named after a politician active in the cause of federation who became one of the first High Court judges, and the street after a plant used by Aborigines for food. Alert schoolteachers make pupils aware that their addresses are laden with national history. By 1990, teachers will be taking their classes to the Museum of Australia, which is to be created around the three overlapping themes of Aboriginal Australia, European Australia, and the interaction of humanity with the Australian environment. The museum will occupy a complex of galleries and outdoor areas at the rural western end of Lake Burley Griffin.

Griffin's name is highly honored. Professional interest in his work intensified in the 1950s as architects tired of the international style and town planners looked around for inspiration. In 1952, Robin Boyd, who opened the eyes of a generation to their built environment, wrote with excitement of Griffin's houses in Sydney and Melbourne and judged the plan for Canberra "as imaginative and spectacular as that of any town in the old or new worlds." In 1964, a young architect, James Birrell, wrote the first book about him. In the 1960s, the National Capital Development Commission appointed as chief town planner Peter Harrison, who had made a close study of Griffin's life and work. In 1977, Donald Leslie Johnson, an American teaching in Australia, published *The Architecture of Walter Burley Griffin,* an admiring analysis of his work in America, Australia, and India. Official regard was secured when the McCallum Committee endorsed "the true worth of Griffin's vast conceptions." In 1963, Canberra's jubilee year, his face appeared on a stamp issued to celebrate the making of Lake Burley Griffin. Beside the lake, in a permanent planning exhibition, an audiovisual presentation offers veneration: as the lights go down, the theatrette becomes a shrine.

What would Walter Griffin think of Canberra? Its makers invoke his blessing with more or less justification, as builders of Washington have long declared that they are executing the will of L'Enfant. We can be sure that he would not have approved the lakeside sites of the gallery and the court and the library, believing as he did that the contours of the basin should be preserved and monumental structures placed uphill. The neoclassical facade of the library would not have pleased him, and that probably goes for the rectangular striped public buildings of the 1960s. The lake transforms the landscape as he meant it to, though he intended people to work and shop and dine and sleep beside it as people do beside, say, Lake Como, not to be cordoned off from it, as they now are, except as motorists, ramblers, or patients in the Canberra Hospital. His central inspiration, the national triangle, is triümphantly in place.

And Capital Hill? Griffin might lament the lost Capitol, though he could not say more clearly than anybody else how it would work, and he might welcome the Museum of Australia as serving some of its purposes. Whatever he thought of the new Parliament House, he would surely recognize the designers' respect for his vision.

Griffin, his successors, and their clients the politicians have given Australia a capital city that delights many a foreigner (to go from Canberra to New Delhi, Mark Girouard observes, is to go from success to failure); that is congenial to most of its residents; that can move an intellectual to pride ("a grand national capital," writes Bruce Grant in *The Australian Dilemma*, ". . . more habitable than the cityscape of Brasilia, more coherent than New Delhi, less formal than Washington"); and that is visited each year by about a million other Australians, coming to see what they have paid for. They make laconic jokes about the curves they get lost in, the politicians they watch from the public galleries, Jackson Pollock's *Blue Poles* in the gallery, and other costly objects in the landscape. They vote the War Memorial the best place for tourists. They come again. "We have a right to enjoy it," remarks a citizen from Newcastle, a botched city on the coast. The most popular time is January, month of summer holidays, and there should be a fine crowd when the flag goes up over Capital Hill.

REFERENCES

The story of Canberra is recorded extensively in Commonwealth parliamentary papers. I have drawn substantially on Lionel Wigmore, *The Long View: A History of Canberra* (Melbourne: Cheshire, 1963) and Harold L. White, ed., *Canberra: A Nation's Capital* (Canberra: Australian and New Zealand Association for the Advancement of Science, 1954). Hank Nelson has let me use an unpublished study of John Curtin and Douglas MacArthur.

The *Australian Dictionary of Biography* (Melbourne: Melbourne University Press, 1966), vol. 9, has a fine entry on Walter Burley Griffin by Peter Harrison. He and Marion Mahony Griffin await thorough study. A valuable reference work is Donald L. Johnson, *Canberra and Walter Burley Griffin: A Bibliography of 1876 to 1976 and a Guide to Published Sources* (Melbourne: Oxford University Press, 1980). There are riches to be quarried from Marion Mahony Griffin, "The Magic of America: A Biography of Walter Burley Griffin," a vast unpublished collage of materials relating to the Griffins' life and work. The original is held by the New York Historical Society; the National Library of Australia has microfilm. Jill Roe has made a start on this material, and I have used her "Paradigms of the City," *Sydney Gazette*, 5, December 1982, p. 15.

Zelman Cowen

The Office of Governor-General

IN THE SECOND WEEK OF NOVEMBER 1975, I was attending a meeting in Boston. I switched on the television set in my hotel room for a news bulletin. Among the items was a report that the governor-general of Australia had dismissed the prime minister, Mr. Whitlam, and his government. News items from Australia rarely capture such attention in the United States, but this one, however imperfectly understood, in a very different political and constitutional environment, was seen as sufficiently unusual and dramatic to command a place.

I had left Australia as the political crisis was mounting. The Australian Senate was persisting in a refusal to pass the supply bills of the Whitlam Labor government which had been carried in the House of Representatives. This Senate action was made possible by the fact that the government did not command a majority there; the opposition was avowedly using its numbers to force the government to resignation and to a general election in times that were not propitious for it. The use of Senate power to deny supply to the government in order to achieve this end was bitterly attacked by the government, which refused to resign, so that the danger that supply for the services of government would dry up became increasingly urgent. It was in these circumstances that the governor-general of Australia, Sir John Kerr, after ascertaining that the prime minister would neither resign nor advise a dissolution of both houses of the Parliament or the lower house, withdrew his commission on November 11. He then commissioned the leader of the opposition, Mr. Malcolm Fraser, on terms that he would secure the passage of the supply bills through the

Senate, advise a dissolution of both houses of the Commonwealth Parliament, and proceed to a general election. Mr. Fraser complied, and the ensuing election in mid-December gave him a massive victory. He remained in government, with further elections in 1977 and 1980, until he lost office in the election of March 1983.

The action of Sir John Kerr was unprecedented in Australian constitutional history. In 1932, the governor of the state of New South Wales had dismissed the ministry on the grounds of illegal conduct. In 1975, there was no suggestion of any illegality on the part of the Whitlam government; the basis was his failure to secure supply and his refusal to resign and recommend a dissolution. The report of the event on Boston television was a distant echo of the storm that swept Australia. While the governor-general had and has his staunch supporters, there was widespread shock and criticism, and his action was vehemently attacked by Mr. Whitlam and his supporters. In the immediate aftermath, the dispossessed prime minister called on the Australian people to maintain their rage; nothing, he said, could save the governor-general. Donald Horne, writing some time later, while Sir John Kerr was still in office, said that it was a consequence of what was done in November 1975 that the position of the governor-general, far from being "above politics," had been shown to be one that could be used to the advantage of one political party over the others; that it could be seen as the destroyer of political consensus, a cause of civil discord, and the principal enemy of political democracy. In some places, it was claimed that there was a wider conspiracy, and that there was evidence of foreign meddling intended to bring about the destruction of the Whitlam government. The "rage" expressed itself in ugly demonstrations against the governor-general as he went about the business of his office, particularly in 1976. The event also called forth a spate of books, many hostile to the governor-general and arguing the case for constitutional change. Some argued for an Australian republic.

Scholars like Geoffrey Sawer, who was critical of the governor-general's act, called for a sense of proportion in judging the action of Sir John Kerr. He said that it was ludicrous "to make him appear as some monster carrying out a coup d'etat," that the crisis had its origin in the dispute between the two houses of Parliament and that the governor-general had sought to end it in a way that had the sole effect of leaving the final decision to the electorate. Sawer also judged that, while immense in its immediate impact, the event would very soon pass quietly into history.

> Constitutional crises such as . . . the Kerr-Whitlam case of 1975 have always aroused passionate denunciations and defences, and the denouncers have usually announced that the end of constitutional government is now at hand. The record shows that while such instances have indeed had important constitutional consequences . . . the more extreme convulsions or revolutions have not occurred and the Kerr-Whitlam case may well turn out but a stone in the pond of history.
>
> The electoral verdict (of December 1975) was such as to suggest, unless the Fraser Government turns out exceptionally incompetent or unlucky, that a period of six years will elapse before the Australian Labor Party again assumes power. In that time Sir John Kerr is likely to have vacated office and memories of his action will be dim.

If what was done in November 1975 is judged to be but a stone in the pond of history, the ripples remain plainly visible. Some, like Donald Horne, have claimed that since November 1975 Australia is faced with the prospect of a "governor-generalate," by which is meant either a general supervision of the policy of the federal parliament and government by the governor-general, or a capricious intervention in policy and administration by him. Sawer has very effectively pointed out that there is poor warrant for this in Kerr's own action. There is no doubt, however, that Sir John Kerr's action in November 1975 created deep division in the Australian community. It is in the nature of the exercise of such power that it does so; in the early years of the reign of King George V, when controversial constitutional issues arose, particularly over Irish Home Rule in 1912–1914, the British prime minister warned of the dangers of independent action (independent, that is to say, of the advice of ministers) by the king. Mr. Asquith said that the king "would, whether he wished it or not, be dragged into the arena of party politics, and, at a dissolution following such a dismissal of Ministers . . . it is no exaggeration to say that the Crown would become the football of contending factions." In Sir John Kerr's memoirs, *Matters for Judgment*, published in 1978 after his retirement, he tells of his consideration of a *personal* course of conduct at the time of the crisis. He says that he considered the desirability of resigning forthwith, to remove himself as a personal factor from the bitter controversy that followed his action. He judged at the time that the interests of the country and the polity were better served by his remaining in office and suffering the personal consequences and discomforts.

At an earlier stage in the book, he says that when Mr. Whitlam approached him to invite him to accept appointment as governor-general, there was some discussion of the length of the term of office. While the governor-generalship has no fixed term, and is held at the queen's pleasure, there was some indication that Sir John might expect to continue in office for double the "conventional" period, that is, for some ten years.

The events of 1975 changed all that. Even though Sir John continued in office for two years thereafter, he says that by early 1977 he reached the conclusion that the best interests of national unity in Australia would be served by his resignation. This was not known publicly (or by me) when in April 1977 I was asked to come to Canberra to meet the prime minister at dinner. I thought it was unlikely that the intent was purely social, but I had no specific idea of his purpose. After dinner we went into the prime minister's study. He told me that Sir John Kerr proposed to resign and that he wished to propose my name to the queen as his successor. It was a dizzying moment; I said that I must consult with my wife and that, of course, was agreed. A senior officer of the prime minister's department then came in to give some account of matters associated with the office. I returned home and, after consultation, I said to the prime minister that if he was of a mind to place my name before the queen for the appointment I should be greatly honored. Confidentiality was well, almost miraculously, preserved; it was only a few days before the day set for the announcement, July 14, 1977, that Sir John's intention to resign was reported in the press. That immediately led to speculation about a successor, and of the problems he might face. In the speculation my name was not mentioned; indeed, on July 14, 1977, when it was known that an announcement was to be made later in the day, I received an American visitor, a distinguished constitutional lawyer, who came to see me in company with an Australian colleague. There was some discussion, not introduced by me, about the expected announcement, and the American visitor, with some general knowledge of earlier troubles and tumults, asked what foolish fellow (his actual words were even less comforting) would wish for that appointment. A day or two later he offered some rather uncomfortable apologies. I said that this was unnecessary, that he probably expressed a not uncommon opinion, and that he had really been a little unlucky in encountering the one man in Australia least likely to be encouraged by the expression of such a point of view.

At the due time, the announcement was made. Some arrangements had been made with the prime minister's department to deal with what followed. The telephone began to ring. Within minutes, Commonwealth security officers were in position, and they did not depart until the day I left office. Soon afterwards, surprised representatives of the Australian media poured into the house, and next day a national media conference was set up and held there.

The events of November 1975 gave the governor-generalship a prominence in Australian debate that it had never previously occupied, and that concern with the office and its role persists. It is not likely that before 1975 such a volume as this would have included an essay on the governor-generalship. Now, the situation is different. This is an account by one who has long studied the office and has also served in it, as successor to Sir John Kerr.

II

An understanding of the office of governor-general requires some reference to history and to Australian constitutional arrangements. British and American influences are reflected in the constitution of the Commonwealth of Australia. The founding fathers were representatives of the Australian colonies that sought national association in a federation, and for that the United States provided a powerful influence and model. The greatest of Australian lawyers, Sir Owen Dixon, wrote that they found the American instrument of government an incomparable model. They could not escape from its fascination; its contemplation damped the smoldering fires of their originality. Be it so, the American influence did not wholly dominate. The federating units were British colonies that had evolved institutions of internal self-government under the Crown, represented in the colony by a governor, and they had fashioned institutions of responsible self-government on the British model. The new Commonwealth of Australia was formally constituted by a United Kingdom act of Parliament, though the substance of the constitution was debated, drafted, and approved of at home. The constitution was not then fashioned for a wholly independent Australia, but over time, it has proved to be a generally workable instrument of government for an independent nation. Australia was born as a colonial Commonwealth, later to be styled and to become a self-governing dominion, and later still an independent state and member of the Commonwealth of Nations. The Commonwealth constitution recognized the queen as head of state and the governor-general as her representative, charged with the performance of a variety of functions assigned by her. The constitution, however, vested important functions in the governor-general *without* reference to the queen, and these included powers to appoint and dismiss ministers, to summon, prorogue, and dissolve Parliament, and to appoint judges. The command-in-chief of the armed forces was vested in the governor-general as the queen's representative. Some uncertainty arose out of the conferring of powers on the governor-general by reference to varying formulae, some on the governor-general-in-council, others on him directly. By the time the constitution came into operation it was clearly established, in accordance with Westminster principles, that the governor-general normally acted on ministerial advice and that this did not necessarily depend on whether the function was assigned in terms to the governor-general-in-council. It is clear, however, that there are powers which, in law, may be exercised by the governor-general in his own independent discretion. This was established in the first decade of the Commonwealth, when governor-generals rejected the advice of prime ministers to dissolve the House of Representatives. The conspicuous case of independent action was, of course, the exercise of the power of dismissal by Sir John Kerr in November 1975.

That was, moreover, an exercise of an independent discretion under authority of a constitutional provision that vested power specifically in the governor-general; Sir John Kerr acted without reference to the queen. On November 12, 1975, the Speaker of the House of Representatives, which had been dissolved the previous day, made an approach to the queen as head of state of Australia. The Speaker asked her to take action to restore Mr. Whitlam to office as prime minister. The private secretary to the queen answered that this was not constitutionally appropriate. He wrote:

As we understand the situation here the Australian Constitution firmly places the prerogative powers of the Crown in the hands of the Governor-

> General as the representative of the Queen of Australia. The only person competent to commission an Australian Prime Minister is the Governor-General, and the Queen has no part in decisions which the Governor-General must take in accordance with the Constitution. Her Majesty, as Queen of Australia, is watching events in Canberra with close interest and attention, but it would not be proper for her to intervene in person in matters which are so clearly placed within the jurisdiction of the Governor-General by the Constitution Act.

While the queen is unquestionably head of state and the governor-general her representative, the power to dismiss ministers is one which, by the constitution, is specifically vested in the governor-general. So, as Professor Geoffrey Sawer says, "the petitions to the Queen asking her to give directions to Sir John Kerr as to his exercise of the power to dismiss Ministers ... were ... futile as well as demeaning; on that matter, the Queen had no power to give any direction." Sir John Kerr in his book *Matters of Judgment* stressed that his actions in the constitutional crisis were his own, that at no stage did he consult with the queen before taking action, and that he advised her immediately after the fact of what he had done.

> I did not tell the Queen in advance that I intended to exercise these powers on November 11. I did not ask her approval. The decisions I took were without the Queen's advance knowledge. The reason for this was that I believed, if dismissal action were to be taken, that it could be taken only by me and that it must be done on my sole responsibility. My view was that to inform Her Majesty in advance of what I intended to do, and when, would be to risk involving her in an Australian political and constitutional crisis in relation to which she had no legal powers; and I must not take such a risk.

III

The office of governor-general made its appearance within a federal constitutional structure in which there were already six governors of the federating colonies that became the states. In the debates preceding federation, the possibility of dispensing with state governors was canvassed, but state wishes to preserve these offices prevailed. So it was that the relationship of the governor-general to state governors had to be determined. The title "governor-general" suggests a supervisory or superior authority, and when the first governor-general of Australia (who had earlier been a governor of Victoria) sought to establish this by requiring state governors to report to the United Kingdom authorities through him, he met strong resistance on the part of state governors, and they sustained their positions. So it is established that state governors do not answer to the governor-general. In practical terms, then, the title of governor-general matters primarily for purposes of ceremony and precedence. There are cases when state governors inform the governor-general of state action, but this is for convenience, and as a matter of courtesy, not of obligation.

The early governor-generals saw themselves, and were seen by the British and the Australian governments, as charged with dual responsibilities. A historian of the office describes the first governor-general, Lord Hopetoun, as "both local constitutional monarch and imperial diplomat." The discharge of these two roles was not always easy; a governor-general of Canada explained—it may be complained—that "a colonial governor is like a man riding two horses in a circus." In one aspect, the governor-general performed the role prescribed by the law and custom of the constitution; in the other he was the principal representative of the British government in Australia and, as such, was a protector of British and imperial interests. Thus, such matters as immigration and tariff policies were of special concern to the United Kingdom government and so too were defense and foreign affairs issues. The governor-general reported to the United Kingdom government and communications between the Australian and the United Kingdom governments were passed through the office of the governor-general.

These arrangements came under increasing pressure. As Australian ministers met with United Kingdom counterparts at colonial and then at imperial conferences, as negotiations on defense progressed, there was an increasing measure of direct communication between ministers and governments. The appointment of an Australian high commissioner to the United Kingdom in 1910 also raised questions about these channels. More generally, as Australia moved from colonial dependence, it became more difficult for the governor-general to maintain his two roles. During the term of Sir Ronald Munro-Ferguson, an able and active governor-general, which spanned the years of the First World War, there were many issues in contention between a strong governor-general and strong prime minister. While the governor-general strove to assert a general supervisory role and to maintain control of the channels of intergovernmental communication, Hughes as prime minister pressed insistently for the right of direct communication between his office and the British government. Hughes not only communicated directly, but sought a formal change in arrangements that the governor-general saw as "lowering his status and restricting his sphere." The governor-general was opposed to "a change which transforms the representative of the Crown into a social figurehead having less than ambassadorial responsibility . . . which must necessarily diminish his power of usefulness, both as the official head of the government in Australia and as a factor in maintaining the unity of the Empire."

Between the wars, a comprehensive redefinition of the relationship between the United Kingdom and the self-governing dominions was undertaken, and a new and comparatively detailed reformulation of the Commonwealth structure was effected. As part of this, the role of the governor-general was reformulated. Expressed in terms of an agreed convention, it was declared that governor-generals of the self-governing dominions occupied in relation to their governments the same position "in all essential respects" as did the king in relation to the United Kingdom government. No attempt was made to spell out the position of the king. From this redefinition, however, it followed that a governor-general could no longer be seen as representing United Kingdom or general imperial interests. The United Kingdom government should be represented by officers specifically appointed for the purpose and so it came about, although it took some years to put in place, that a British high commissioner represents the United Kingdom in Australia, as in other Commonwealth countries. There was also a change in channels of communication; henceforth direct communication between governments was the regular procedure and the governor-general ceased to be the channel for communication between the Australian and the United Kingdom governments.

A matter of great importance was the source of appointment of the governor-general. The first governor-general, Hopetoun, was necessarily appointed by the king on the advice of United Kingdom ministers; there was, as yet, no Australian government. As early as 1902, however, the first prime minister, Edmund Barton, asked that several names be proposed by the United Kingdom government from which the Australian government might choose a governor-general. The British government responded by presenting one name and asking whether it was acceptable. In changing circumstances, in 1919, W.M. Hughes, as prime minister, called not only for consultation between the British and Australian governments on the appointment of a governor-general, but also for a "real and effective" Australian voice in the selection. He proposed that dominion governments be entitled to submit their own nominations that might include local citizens. When the next appointment was to be made in 1920, the British government presented a list of three United Kingdom nominees from which the Australian government chose Lord Forster.

The Imperial Conference of 1926, in redefining the role of the governor-general, did not deal specifically with this matter. It came to a head, however, in 1930, when on the retirement of Lord Stonehaven, the Australian Labor government of J.H. Scullin resolved to recommend the appointment of an Australian born citizen, Sir Isaac Isaacs.

Isaacs had had a most distinguished career. Born in 1855 in humble circumstances, the son of newly arrived migrant parents in Melbourne, he grew up in rural Victoria, became a barrister and a leading member of the bar, a colonial politician and minister, an active member of the federal constitutional convention of 1897–98 that drafted the Commonwealth constitution, a foundation member of the Commonwealth Parliament and later attorney-general, and then a justice of the High Court of Australia. He served as a member of that court with distinction for a quarter century from 1906, and in 1930 he was appointed chief justice, when he was already in his mid-seventies.

When the intention of the Australian government to recommend Isaacs became known, as it did in advance of the appointment, there was controversy and division in Australia. There were questions of the propriety of appointing a "local" man, and about the role of the Australian government in making a recommendation to the king. In the United Kingdom, attempts were made to dissuade the Australian prime minister from persisting in this course. The king, George V, was strongly opposed. Specifically, the king desired the appointment of Lord Birdwood, who had commanded Australian troops in the First World War. He was also opposed to the appointment of Isaacs on a variety of stated grounds: Isaacs was too old; he was a "local" man and therefore too close to the local scene; and the king's personal representative should be personally known to him.

Scullin and his government stood their ground, and it was apparent that there was need for a definition of the principles and procedures for the appointment of a governor-general. It was agreed at the Imperial Conference of 1930 that the governor-general should be appointed by the king on the advice of the dominion government concerned, such advice to be formally tendered after informal consultation with the king so that he had an opportunity to express his views before being presented with formal advice. The United Kingdom government should play no part in these procedures. In accordance with these procedures, save that in this case there had been no informal consultation, Isaacs was appointed. In face of Scullin's persistent advice, the king agreed, though not very happily, to the appointment.

Isaacs served as governor-general with total dedication and with great competence in difficult depression years. His age did not diminish his appetite for hard work or his capacity, and the fears of "local" entanglements proved to be unfounded. He was a preeminent Australian who served with great distinction in the office. In 1936, he was succeeded by a non-Australian, Lord Gowrie, who had served as a state governor, and he, in turn, was succeeded by the only royal governor-general of Australia, the Duke of Gloucester. Then in 1947, Mr. (later Sir) William McKell was recommended by the prime minister, Mr. Chifley. At the time Mr. McKell was the serving Labor premier of the state of New South Wales. It appears that no other name was proposed and that there was no informal consultation before advice was tendered to the king. This appointment provoked sharp controversy, particularly because of Mr. McKell's situation at the time.

The three governor-generals who followed all came from the United Kingdom and all were appointed on the advice of Sir Robert Menzies. It appeared to be settled that the prime minister rather than the government (Cabinet) is the source of advice, and Menzies in his book *Afternoon Light* (1967) gives a characteristic account of the steps that led to the appointment of the distinguished soldier, Slim, on the retirement of McKell. Since 1965, there have been five Australian appointees: Lord Casey, Sir Paul Hasluck, Sir John Kerr, myself, and the present incumbent, Sir Ninian Stephen, who though not born in Australia, grew up and made his professional life in Australia and was, at the time of his appointment, a distinguished judge of the High Court of Australia.

Lord Casey's appointment was received with general approval and it is now a little odd to look back only fifty years to recall the divisions that the proposal to appoint a "local man" aroused. There are echoes of old debates: I have recently heard argued, in reference to New Zealand, the case for appointing a man without "local" associations and identification and possible embarrassments. I see little merit in this; Sir Paul Hasluck's view that "the pattern has been clearly laid down for appointing an Australian as Governor-General" has general support and was affirmed by a recent constitutional assembly broadly representative of Australian political life. At one stage, it was suggested by both Menzies and Casey that there might be cross-appointments—for example, of a Canadian to Australia—and that this would strengthen the bonds of Commonwealth. It is imaginative, and it might have been acceptable at an earlier time, but the view that now has general acceptance is that the appropriate appointee is an Australian who has a good understanding of the country, its people, and its institutions and who, in his person and community standing, commands general respect. I say his; Canada has pointed the way to the appointment of a woman governor-general, and I do not think that sex is an issue in Australia at this time. What is more at issue is whether there should be a governor-general at all, and this is bound up with the broader issue of an Australian republic. There is no doubt that the events of November 1975 gave an impetus to the cause of republicanism in Australia. Before I come to that, however, I wish to consider more fully the role of the governor-general in Australian government.

IV

A former minister in the Whitlam government wrote in 1977 that the grievance against Sir John Kerr was that he exceeded the limits of power that British monarchs had long accepted, namely, that under no circumstances could he act on his own personal initiative but only on the advice of freely elected ministers. A monarch or viceroy who acknowledged that his role was "purely ceremonial and divorced from the exercise of real political power" had been broadly acceptable; if the governor-general "had no real power but to open fairs, cut ribbons and the like . . . what would it matter whether we called our system republican or monarchic or anything else?"

The claim that Sir John Kerr exercised a power extending beyond that of the monarch in the United Kingdom is correct in the particular case only. The situation that arose in November 1975 in Australia could not have arisen in the United Kingdom, because the power of the House of Lords to hold up supply voted by the House of Commons has effectively disappeared. There are statements in the books by constitutional writers that there are available to the Crown great discretionary powers to deal with crisis situations, but the Crown has not exercised such powers; mindful, no doubt, of the warning given by Asquith just before the First World War that their exercise would drag the Crown into the arena of party politics and that it would become "the football of contending factions." A hundred and twenty years ago Walter Bagehot wrote in his celebrated *The English Constitution* of a monarchy that, divorced from arbitrary personal power, had become increasingly the symbol of the unity of national life. He saw it as the most intelligible part of the political system for ordinary people who continued to believe that they were governed by the queen, even though her ministers exercised the substantive power and authority. He spoke of effective and dignified roles in government, and of the Crown as performing the dignified role. He saw the monarch, nonetheless, as an effective source of influence, and this he expressed in well-known words: "The sovereign has, under a constitutional monarchy such as ours, three rights—the right to be consulted, the right to encourage, the right to warn." The monarch's effective exercise of these rights depends upon interest, experience, and knowledge. In our day, the queen in the United Kingdom commands great sources of information, through access to government papers, personal knowledge of and association with many people; she enjoys a permanence of place that affords an opportunity to gain much knowledge, and the free and regular flow of discussion with her advisers. To this may also be added Bagehot's "magic."

With the governor-general, this is not the case. He does not have the permanence of place assured to the monarch, but, rather, a limited and comparatively short tenure. The Imperial Conference of 1930 established by agreement that the governor-general is appointed by the monarch on the advice of the Commonwealth prime minister; this carries with it the implication that his appointment will also be terminated on the advice of the prime minister. In the November 1975 case, Sir John Kerr was charged with acting "by stealth" in not warning Mr. Whitlam of his intentions. The point is made in response that the governor-general was vulnerable; that a disclosure of his intent might have led to a "race to the Palace" and recall by the prime minister of the governor-general before he could carry out his intended course of action. It may be that advice to the queen to recall a governor-general does not necessarily oblige her to comply forthwith; that she is entitled to consider the matter and to give the governor-general an opportunity to be heard. There are no certain answers. What is clear is that the position of representative is, in this respect, different from that of the monarch. One of the questions that arises out of the 1975 crisis is whether there is not a case for the provision of some security of tenure for the governor-general, to allow him to exercise his judgment and take a course of action free of such pressures.

This apart, there are differences between the position of governor-general and that of monarch. Experience and observation make it clear that the "magic" Bagehot described attaches to the monarch but not to the governor-general. The latter is certainly accorded respect and courtesy, but he has no comparable aura. The governor-general has available to him dispatches and Cabinet documents, and he meets with ministers, the prime minister, and others who inform him of the business of government. In the Australian case, however, there is the testimony of Sir Paul Hasluck who preceded Sir John Kerr in the office, which my own experience confirms, that the governor-general does not enjoy the same regularity of meeting with the prime minister, as does the monarch with the prime minister of the United Kingdom. Hasluck and I both believe that this is unfortunate, and that it would be better if the British practice prevailed. Sir Paul Hasluck has recently written that

> . . . if there had been more talking and a higher degree of confidence between Governor-General and Prime Minister it is possible that no crisis would have arisen. The role of the Crown (and hence the Governor-General) to be consulted, to encourage and to warn can only be fulfilled if they talk to each other in terms which reflect that they have respect for each other. The clearest way to improvement is not by changing the constitutional role of either office but by establishing more strongly a convention that the Prime

Minister makes regular calls on the Governor-General as a matter of governmental routine.

We cannot know whether this different practice would have averted the crisis of November 1975; Sir John Kerr's account in *Matters for Judgment* states very clearly that Mr. Whitlam was quite inflexible. It cannot be doubted, however, that the establishment of a routine of frequent and regular meetings between prime minister and governor-general is a greater assurance of familiarity and ease of relationship.

Bagehot's three rights of the monarch—to be consulted, to encourage, and to warn—are rights of substantial importance. His point was that, assuming that the monarch would ultimately accept ministerial advice in accordance with constitutional principles, his entitlement to and exercise of these rights gave him an important role, the more substantial as his experience and confidence grew. There is abundant testimony to the effective use of such rights by modern monarchs; the recent *Life of King George V*, grandfather of the present queen, documents this effectively. My own experience as governor-general of Australia reveals clearly that within the context of Bagehot's three rights, such an influence could be brought to bear upon the processes of government. There were many cases to illustrate this. The most obvious illustration was the business of the federal Executive Council over which, week by week, the governor-general presided, advised by ministers. In the council, a great deal of governmental business was undertaken concerning regulations, orders, proclamations, and the making and termination of a wide range of appointments. A variety of organizational matters was also dealt with.

Sir Paul Hasluck has written about the Executive Council and the governor-general's role in it, and much of his experience accords with my own. The governor-general could and did play a significant role by requiring ample and adequate explanations and reasons for what was proposed. I was able to ask questions in advance of the meeting of the council to satisfy myself that I understood what was being done, and that it was done regularly. At council meetings, I would raise questions with the attending ministers so that they could take into account the doubts, questions, and concerns of the governor-general before they tendered advice to him. His experience in questioning proposed actions and procedures and in raising points, as his experience increased, served especially the interests of regularity, which in the press of big, busy, and complex government may not always be assured. Such conduct on his part allows him to play a useful, and it may be an important, role in government, a role consistent with a meticulous respect for the principle that the governor-general acts upon the advice of ministers. A vigilant and inquiring governor-general comes to be recognized as such in the departments that have the responsibility for preparing the business of government.

All of this gives a very different picture of the role of the governor-general from that drawn by the minister, who would have it that "he had no real power but to open fairs, cut ribbons and the like." It may be that such language is designed to state the case against great claims to discretionary power and was framed in terms of caricature. The minister, from his own recent experience of government in the Executive Council and elsewhere, must have known that his reading was not in accord with the facts, events such as those of November 1975 notwithstanding. Sir Paul Hasluck, in an essay *The Office of Governor-General* (first prepared as a lecture in 1972 and reprinted in expanded form in 1979), has said that

> the part played by a Governor-General in Australian government may vary with the personality and qualifications of the Governor-General and on the way each occupant of the office chooses to interpret his role. Conceivably a Governor-General could be a cipher, do whatever he was told to do without question and have little influence on what happened. I have spoken on the assumption that Governor-Generals will be active and I fervently hope that Australia in the future will never have the misfortune to have an inactive one.

I strongly agree with Sir Paul. There is, however, a disposition, particularly in the aftermath of November 1975, to diminish the office, pretty much as the Labor minister has done, to describe the holder as "chief ribbon bestower and chief ribbon cutter" and nothing else, and, in line with this, to question whether an appointee is not "too well qualified"—as if to say that the office calls for no substantial qualities of mind, no particular distinction. My own experience corresponds with that of Sir Paul Hasluck; what was asked of me in the performance of a wide range of duties demanded the highest intellectual and personal resources available to me. When

I spoke to the National Press Club in Canberra in mid-1982 as I was leaving office, I said that it served no useful purpose to characterize the office of governor-general as purely formal and ceremonial. As with the monarch, so too with the governor-general, much time and energy go into the performance of a wide range of non-constitutional, non-political, and in this sense ceremonial activities—what Bagehot described as the discharge of the dignified role of the monarch. If writers are pleased to describe this as ribbon-bestowing and ribbon-cutting, let it be recognized that the bestowing of ribbons is a recognition of significant and diverse community service by individuals, and that is no poor thing. The many ceremonies and openings are associated with a variety of activities in the country's national life, ranging from the broadly national to the local. They took the governor-general to many places in a vast nation continent; they led him to comment upon many significant activities, issues, and occasions. The openings were not infrequently those of national and international conferences; gatherings of professionals, businessmen, specialists; meetings of academic bodies and learned societies.

From the earliest days of the Commonwealth of Australia, governor-generals have recognized and agreed upon the importance of traveling throughout Australia. Lord Hopetoun, the first governor-general, saw such activity as providing a needed national focus in the early days of Australian federation. In an early speech, he promised to demonstrate "to the many that they are living under one central government." Right up to the present day, his successors have followed this course, and for the same reasons of national identification. At an earlier time, it was done, often arduously, by slower means of transport. In our day, jet aircraft annihilate distance, diminishing the rigor, but not the extent of travel.

A governor-general, like the monarch he serves, gives a great part of his time and energy to the discharge of duties of such a character; much of what he does is outside the work of government that is reposed in the hands of those whom Bagehot described as the possessors of "effective" power. I believe that it is the case that, within the polity, the governor-general, like the monarch, makes his greatest contribution through the continuing and committed performance of these duties. It may be well to restate what I said in my farewell speech in Canberra in 1982. I said that I believed that through such work, through travel and participation in such activities, the governor-general offers encouragement and recognition to many of those Australians who may not be very powerful or visible in the course of everyday life, and to the efforts of those individuals and groups who work constructively to improve life in the nation and the community. My experience of the office was that much was demanded and expected of me and I sought to respond as best I could. Sir Paul Hasluck has said that Australians both expect and appreciate statements by a governor-general on matters of current concern at a level different from that of party-political controversy, and I was intellectually stretched and tested in the preparation for speeches, meetings, and activities. Knowledge, experience, and capacity were constantly called on and tested. As did Hopetoun, I also saw that a major role for the governor-general was performed in the discharge of a myriad of functions all over Australia. The response was often quite remarkable and was certainly very moving. I think that it is right to say, as Hasluck did, that the office of governor-general is the highest single expression in the Australian governmental structure of the idea that Australians of all parties and all walks of life belong to the same nation. Recognition of this casts heavy burdens and responsibilities on the Australian who holds the office.

V

The events of November 1975 inevitably brought the governor-generalship into sharp, and for a time violent controversy. Sir John Kerr remained in office for two uncomfortable years thereafter; then he judged that he should go considerably before the normal time. It is fair to say that that decision commanded wide support, and was not only endorsed by critics and opponents. Twenty years earlier, in one of the great Pakistani constitutional cases of the mid-fifties, the chief justice of Pakistan spoke of the possibility of the exercise of comparable power by a governor-general and of the consequences. It would "rivet the attention of the country" to the issues that provoked it, but it could mean that the governor-general "may have to go." Before 1975, however, statements that raised the possibility of such action by a monarch or governor-general passed without much notice or debate. Indeed, in 1972, Sir Paul Hasluck in *The Office of Governor-General* had formulated it in very sweeping terms:

In abnormal times or in case of any attempt to disregard the Constitution or the laws of the Commonwealth, or even the customary usages of Australian government, it would be the Governor-General who could present the crisis to Parliament and, if necessary, to the nation for determination. It is not that the Governor-General (or the Crown) can over-rule the elected representatives of the people but in the ultimate he can check the elected representatives in any extreme attempt by them to disregard the rule of law or the customary usages of Australian government and he could do so by forcing a crisis.

That was a far-reaching statement, given little attention at a time when the office of governor-general was not in the forefront of public attention. That was also a period, Hasluck wrote, when the role of the governor-general seemed to be a matter of unbroken routine. So, indeed, it remained throughout my time, and so it has been very largely since November 1975. Such discretions as holders of the office have been called upon to exercise have been minor in comparison. If, however, the office has, in the years that followed, been seen to be "restored"—to use a word that has recurred in writing and speech about it—it should not be thought that the events of 1975 have been forgotten. One event or another revives the memory and the issues—as the debate on the possibility of the appointment of the Prince of Wales as governor-general reveals—but apart from special events, the action of the governor-general in November 1975 is remembered by supporter and opponent alike. The governor-generalship has a visibility that it did not have before that time; it is now associated in the public mind with political power, or at least with the possibility of such exercises of power. Appointments to the office are now made, I believe, with this in mind and certainly with the recognition that the governor-generalship is a visible and controversial office within the Australian community.

This leads to the point that, since November 1975, there has been continuing discussion of the possibility and desirability of constitutional change to reduce or to prevent the possibility of future crises. The debate, to some extent, has focused on the issue that gave rise to Sir John Kerr's action: the deadlock between the two Houses that led to the perceived threat to supply. More generally, it has been concerned with the possibility of defining and restricting the powers of the governor-general. This is now seen as more urgent, though it is not new; almost fifty years ago, Dr. H.V. Evatt, an eminent

Australian jurist, argued in his book *The King and His Dominion Governors* (1936) for the desirability of defining as precisely as possible the discretionary "reserve" powers of monarch, governor-general, and governor. Thus far, however, the debate has not yielded agreed change in the law.

The argument is carried further: the action of Sir John Kerr gave a renewed impetus to the cause of republicanism in Australia. This also is not new; radical nationalists in the latter part of the nineteenth century associated the claim to independence with an Australian republic. The monarchy was seen as a symbol of British dominance and Australian subordination. As Australia has moved to independence, as the population of the nation has been swelled by large numbers of people who have no British roots and little instinctive feeling for British institutions and history, the cause of republicanism has found more fertile soil. And, as Geoffrey Dutton wrote in *Republican Australia* (1977), the events of November 1975 provided a catalyst. "Those Australians who have stayed awake have had to start thinking seriously about the Constitution, the Queen and the Governor-General." Of course, the monarch played no part in what was done, and the governor-general was appointed on the advice of the prime minister whom he brought down on November 11, 1975. A republic, of itself, would not necessarily dispose of the problem of the exercise of such discretions. But the fact that a governor-general, unelected and the representative of the queen, acted in this way is seen by some—perhaps by a growing number of Australians—as grounds for remaking the constitution without monarchical institutions and representation. The achievement of full independence for Australia, the changing pattern of her relationships in the world, and the changing character and composition of Australian society and the Australian people have all affected our view of the special relationship with Britain and its institutions. It is not enough that the queen, who is monarch in the United Kingdom, now has a quite distinct Australian title. I do not believe, however, that the growth of republican sentiment is strong enough today to produce constitutional change, a change that is very difficult to achieve within the existing constitutional framework. Nor do I believe that the achievement of an Australian republic is seen as a high priority by government leaders who, while they list it on the agenda of change, seem content to leave it on the back burner.

Hugh Collins

Political Ideology in Australia: The Distinctiveness of a Benthamite Society

AUSTRALIA'S POLITICAL LANDSCAPE presents to the American observer a curious mixture of the familiar and the foreign. The familiar elements include a written constitution; a federal polity; a national legislature with chambers called the Senate and the House of Representatives, whose members are elected by different constituencies—state and district—and for different terms; judicial review of legislative competence and executive action; electoral politics conducted within a broadly two-party system; territorial sovereignty that is essentially continental in scope; and a common rhetoric expressing the expectations and exhortations of liberal democracy. Alongside these familiar features, however, are such foreign institutions as a monarchial head of state; cabinet government, with the political executive drawn from and answerable within the legislature; a party system highly disciplined not only by the constant parliamentary confrontation between government and opposition, but also in the internal operation of the party machines (one of which is avowedly socialist); and a professional public bureaucracy, nominally neutral in the competition between political parties and somewhat insulated against immediate intrusions by the legislature. Although foreign in American experience, these elements are recognizably British in derivation. The novelty of the Australian political landscape is thus first revealed as a combination of the Westminster model and a federal framework. In this environment, a British observer, no less than an American, will probably remark that everything looks at once much the same and yet quite different.

The intriguing sense of difference will be heightened once the observer has assimilated the larger features of the landscape into a general pattern, and moves beyond a perception of external appearances to consider the smell and feel of what is actually happening within this environment. In what is argued about, how these disputes are conducted, and upon what assumptions the debates proceed, the distinctiveness of Australia's politics is fully revealed. To explain this matrix of assumptions and these modes of debate is the concern of this paper: it is, in short, an examination of political ideology in Australia. My argument is that the mental universe of Australian politics is essentially Benthamite. Australia's perennial debates and present predicaments may be understood, the differences presented to an American—or British—observer become comprehensible, if one begins by regarding Australia as a Benthamite society.

II

What is meant by "Benthamite society"? Simply, that the dominant ideology of this society conforms to the essential character of Jeremy Bentham's political philosophy. Three aspects of Bentham's thought are crucial here: his utilitarianism, his legalism, and his positivism. Each of these requires a brief discussion before demonstrating that the tensions and tendencies within Bentham's philosophy became the dilemmas and directions of Australian politics.

First, the utilitarianism. The central problem in Bentham's political theory is to reconcile the pursuit of individual interest with the achievement of the sovereign interest or greatest happiness. A rational calculus for accomplishing this reconciliation is provided by the principle of utility. Political institutions and policies are to be assessed in terms of the impact of their operation upon the interests of the majority—and that Bentham conceived not as groups or classes but as the sum of individual interests. Bentham's lengthy account of schemes for representation, legislation, and administration is a detailed exposition of the institutional means of securing that public good which maximizes private interest.

This individualism makes his theory anti-collectivist. Although the agenda of Bentham's utilitarian state includes issues that are now associated with a collectivist age, such as education, health, and welfare, in Bentham's system these tasks are firmly secured to individualist interests.[1] A collectivism that captures utilitarianism's political instruments would always be in conflict with Bentham's commitment to individualism.

Bentham's theory is equally hostile to doctrines of social contract. Although a theory of individual interests, it rejects the notion of natural rights which was central in both the American and the French revolutions. Elie Halévy states Bentham's position succinctly: "Governments were instituted not because man had rights but because he had none. . . ."[2] In an ideology faithful to Bentham's system, natural rights will be an alien tradition.

The rationalist assumptions of Bentham's philosophy signal an approach to politics that is both secular and instrumental. Here is no deistic basis for religious exceptionalism; political institutions are human contrivances, not divinely ordained. The expectations are mundane and unheroic; there is neither a messianic mission nor a return to a classical ideal.[3] Utility imposes its own discipline upon reality and sets its own limits to imagination. (To anticipate a little, as much is signified in Australia's parliamentary architecture, which is markedly utilitarian by contrast with the confident classicism of America's state houses and, supremely, the U.S. Congress.)

The second aspect of Bentham's thought to be noted is its legalism. Both John Stuart Mill and Macaulay, his contemporaries, present Bentham as first and foremost a legal theorist.[4] From his early work, the *Fragment on Government,* to his mature achievement, the *Constitutional Code,* Bentham's concerns are preeminently those of the jurist. Legalism supplies the categories by which his extraordinary classifications of institutional forms and functions are organized. Legislation is at the heart of his theory of government; hence the need of a particular electoral system and for an apparatus of administration that is perfectly compatible with Max Weber's rational-legal form of legitimacy. Bentham is a theorist of law and government rather than of liberty and opposition. The politics he expounds is the operation of interests rather than the functioning of consent.

Positivisim, the third aspect of Bentham's thought, is perhaps a corollary of his rationalist and legalist assumptions. "His was an essentially practical mind," wrote John Stuart Mill.[5] That practical bent; the insistence upon a separation of fact and value which he inherited from David Hume; the habit of dividing and quartering all speculative thought: these elements combine to explain why

Bentham's philosophy is such a fertile seedbed for modern positivism. His surprisingly modern linguistic analysis is evidence alone for this. A Benthamite ideology can therefore be expected to possess a predisposition toward positivism.

III

Benthamism did not reach Australia disembodied, nor was its victory there immediate. To identify it as Australia's dominant ideology is simply to say that those who prevailed in the colonial political struggles of the nineteenth century were, consciously or unwittingly, bearers of these ideas.

Chartism, for example, provided a direct connection. Consider the case of Henry Parkes, a central figure in the nineteenth-century politics of New South Wales and a crucial actor in the achievement of federation. Parkes was a badge-bearing member of the Birmingham Political Union during the agitations that preceded the 1832 Reform Bill; he was present at the great meeting in 1838 when Birmingham accepted the Charter; the following year he was in London while the Chartist Convention met, although—significantly—he left England for Australia before his townsfolk withdrew from the convention signaling the collapse of the alliance between middle and working classes that had formed this artisan's political apprenticeship. Of the democratic movement that Parkes and others organized in New South Wales from the late 1840s, his biographer writes: "They were transferring to a new but remarkably similar situation political ideas and methods they had learnt in their youth, particularly in the work of the Birmingham Political Union and organizations like it."[6]

The theoretical task of justifying the assumptions underlying the Chartist movement—why suffrage should have been the key to reform, why the route to change should follow the path of representation rather than that of revolution, why the reformist middle classes and the disaffected lower orders should have been persuaded to join forces in pursuit of an interest considered common to both—was essentially Bentham's achievement. In John Stuart Mill's words, Bentham "gave voice to those interests and instincts" identified with radical reform.[7]

"Within ten years of the discovery of gold," the Australian historian Sir Keith Hancock observed, "practically the whole political programme of the Chartists is realised in the Australian colonies."[8] That Chartism should have succeeded so completely in Australia by the 1860s, while failing so bitterly in Britain, is doubly significant in any appreciation of the distinctiveness of Australia's political culture. For, as well as marking the point of departure of Australia's political culture from its British background, it also marks the essentially Benthamite character of this antipodean offshoot.

The distinctiveness of the political culture is a product of the novel setting no less than of the transported ideas. After all, the state that was delivered to Australia's colonial democrats was inevitably a stronger, more intrusive, legitimately interventionist instrument than Victoria's Britain: each of the six Australian colonies was centered upon an administrative capital from which governors disposed of land, supervised economic development, and gradually shared power with representative institutions. Furthermore, unlike their reformist cousins in England, nineteenth-century Australian democrats did not have to contend against the traditional restraints of established church, military services, and landed aristocracy.

The transplanted British understood that this new environment altered them and their politics, even as they reproduced the parliamentary procedures and party labels of British politics. The best-educated and most self-conscious of the colonial liberals, C.H. Pearson, acknowledged this when he referred to his first experience of settlement in Australia as having changed him from "a liberal of the English type to a democratic liberal."[9] He drew upon that experience to urge the Australian example in the course of the British campaign to extend the franchise.[10] Pearson's definition of democracy was consistent with his political program and with the tenets of utilitarian liberalism: ". . . self-government by men educated up to a common low level, and trained by the habit of self-government under institutions which secure power to the majority."[11]

The native-born architects of Australia's political institutions and constitutions were no less indebted to a Benthamite utilitarianism. Consider the program outlined in the "concrete definition" Alfred Deakin's biographer gives for the Victorian liberalism of the future Australian prime minister and his contemporaries: ". . . land legislation; protection; free, compulsory and secular education; payment of members of Parliament; factory acts; early closing; anti-sweating legislation."[12] The only item in that program that would have startled an English utilitarian of the same period is protection. Its adoption by the Australians was not so much an act of heresy as a pragmatic adaptation of utilitarian orthodoxy to their new environment. In their setting, the interest of the majority lay in precisely the economic protection that was anathema to Mill and his party—a difference that, incidentally, underscored those calculations of interest that lay behind the exalted "principle" of free trade.

The abstract Benthamite ideas that adhered to these concrete enactments and achievements of the nineteenth century endured as the dominant ideology in the twentieth century, shaping the nation's institutions, images, and ideas. Indeed, so completely has this philosophy captured Australia's public mind that the sporadic appearance of different political ideas, whether of the left or of the right, is better understood as a reaction against this hegemony than as the motion of independent forces. Accordingly, the moral posture of these protests is more typically dissent than defiance, while the characteristic response of the dominant ideology is disdain rather than debate.

IV

The central features of the Australian political system—federalism and cabinet government—exhibit a utilitarian character. Thus, federalism is a product of convenience rather than of conviction. Unlike Switzerland, or French and British Canada, Australian federalism is not a means for preserving the integrity of linguistically distinct communities within a single polity. Nor, as in the American case, is it traceable to the normative assumption that, even within a relatively homogeneous community, power should be divided between levels as well as branches of government. Rather, the constitutional framework chosen in Australia in the 1890s was a practical adjustment to circumstance. Faced with small communities separated by great distances but already endowed with political institutions, those seeking a limited range of cooperative action in matters like defense, trade, and immigration found a federal scheme expedient. There continues to be a lively interest in federalism in Australia, but it remains focused upon the practical working-out of fiscal, constitutional, and administrative arrangements between the states and the Commonwealth. Political appeals to "states' rights," like declarations of "new federalism," are typically and realistically understood as claims to particular shares of the federal pie rather than as articulations of normative principle.

Cabinet government has provoked a perennial debate among Australia's politicians and political scientists about ministerial responsibility.[13] When cabinet ministers may be held responsible, for what, and to whom; whether the parliamentary machinery of accountability and the sanction of resignation are myth or not: such questions have aroused keen interest. The details of these controversies matter less here than the substance of the argument. For surely what is at stake in this debate is a perfectly Benthamite concern with whether and how office-holders can be made constitutionally and practically responsible for the performance of their duties.

In the twentieth century, Australia's political leaders have succeeded, survived, or succumbed largely according to their ability to manipulate the dominant ideology within their own party and against its rivals. Thus, J.B. Chifley, the popular post–Second World War Labor leader, courted defeat for his government when, consistent with socialist doctrine, he sought to entrench and extend in peacetime a range of government controls and activities that during wartime emergency had been accepted as temporarily necessary. R.G. Menzies recovered from defeat within his own coalition and achieved his long ascendancy with an essentially utilitarian program combining the promise of national development with an appeal to individualist interests. Bob Hawke secured the electoral defeat of Malcolm Fraser in 1983 by presenting the latter's government as an instrument of the few at the expense of the many. Hawke offered instead a commitment to "consensus," which translates readily into the greatest happiness of the greatest number.

Just as the dominant ideology could be used to win power, so could it be deployed for defeat. Here the political career of W.A. Holman is instructive.[14] By using the dominant ideology skillfully, Holman won power, losing it when the ideology, in turn, was used against him. Active during the 1890s in the formative period of the Labor party in New South Wales, Holman rose to the state premiership in 1913. Within his party, he was identified as an author of the solidarity pledge by which Labor parliamentarians were bound to vote in accordance with their caucus majority; beyond the party, he was popular as an orator and as a conscientious creator of diverse and successful public enterprises. Socialist objectives, though hardly unimportant to him, were always secondary to reformist proposals sure to gain popular acceptance. Rather than adhering to the strict letter of the party platform, and to the dismay of Labor's left-wing unions, Holman's campaigns were based upon an electorally motivated package he called his "fighting platform." He used the discipline of the pledge to keep parliamentary malcontents in line, and his strategy succeeded. During the First World War, however, he sided with the federal Labor prime minister, W.M. Hughes, in favor of conscription for military service. A majority within the Labor party and also in national referenda disagreed. The pledge was used against him, and Holman, like Hughes, chose to leave the Labor party and to lead a new anti-Labor coalition. Although initially successful, Holman's attempt to preserve a commitment to the public enterprises he had earlier fostered was eventually defeated within his new coalition by conservatives who used methods of electoral expediency similar to those by which he had triumphed against the left as Labor leader.

The habits and institutions of Australian politics provide further evidence of the Benthamite ideology's dominance. In the party system, for example, the two sides can be considered as working out the tensions implicit in the original Chartist compact between employer and artisan. The labels of the non-socialist coalition have changed periodically, but the structure of the competition as well as of alignment within it has remained remarkably stable since the First World War.

Don Aitkin, the analyst of that stability, regretfully concludes that for Australians party alignment is a function of "habit" rather than of "understanding."[15] Surely, partisanship can be habitual because there is so little to understand: the competitors are offering only slightly different brews of the same ideological ingredients. Because the basic values are so similar, the party competition characteristically focuses upon tactics and motives rather than upon strategies and goals. Since in practical operation the parties are so alike, the rhetoric used by each side typically strains to present the rival in the image of its most extreme and impotent faction.

The deregulators of the 1970s and 1980s complain no less than the New Left of the 1960s and 1970s that the purity of their ideal has been polluted by the practices and assumptions of their representatives in the political system. The Benthamite center holds. At the intersection of Australian party politics there is only one street lamp, which becomes the single and simultaneous target for the stones cast, whether by the Hayek push or by the Habermas collective.

The embodiment of the Hawke government's "consensus" policies in a televised national economic summit conference, and a statutory economic planning advisory council of government, business, and union representatives have led some commentators to declare the emergence in Australia of corporatist politics. Yet, quite apart from the structural impediments to a corporatist model in Australian politics,[16] the language and intention of these innovations is perfectly consistent with the utilitarian ideology. In the "wages accord," that reconciliation between master and man that is at the heart of Hawke's policies, there is more of Birmingham than of such corporatist capitals as Bonn, Brussels, or Buenos Aires.

Indeed, the force of the ideology is especially evident in the field of industrial relations. In stark contrast to the competitive bargaining associated with American labor relations, Australian industrial disputes and wage settlements occur within a national system of compulsory arbitration. Employers, unions, and government pursue their claims before a judicial establishment in a highly regulated setting. It is a mark of this society's legalism that most of these actors cannot conceive of justice occurring within any other scheme. Moreover, as in other areas of public policy, the legalism of industrial relations in Australia is exacerbated by federalism, with complicated provisions for separate, conjoint, and overlapping arenas of jurisdiction and activity.

Customary observations on Australia's political habits reflect the distinguishing characteristics of the Benthamite ideology. Thus, from Bryce onwards, observers have remarked on the attachment to interests rather than ideas in Australian politics.[17] The surprise registered in this comment is not that interests are discovered to operate in politics, but that in Australia they do so unashamedly, with little resort to ideals and ideas to clothe their naked intent. Yet what else would one expect in a Benthamite culture? The utilitarian psychology in Australia legitimizes the pursuit of interest, while the dominance of the ideology negates the possibility of a genuine battle of ideas.

Or consider A.F. Davies's celebrated judgment that Australians have a talent for bureaucracy.[18] Federalism, always a breeding-ground for overlapping administrations, partly explains this national trait. But a Benthamite acceptance of public activity in performance of the state's responsibilities suggests that this aptitude has also been fostered by the society's ideological assumptions.

A popular conception of politics as confined to the narrow sphere of electoral and ministerial activity reflects a Benthamite influence. Ask an Australian for a theory of politics and the probable response will be a fragment on government. Not only is the conception of politics tightly circumscribed, there is little demand that political practice conform to doctrinal consistency. For practitioners and observers alike, the compelling proofs for a political proposal in Australia are the twin utilitarian standards of efficacy (will it work?) and plurality (have you got the numbers?).

Australia's intellectual climate has powerfully supported these tendencies in the nation's politics because it, too, has been marked by Benthamite characteristics. The universities, which have codified and certified useful knowledge, have been mostly post-Darwinian creations: the particular scientific paradigm they have enshrined has reinforced the tendencies of utilitarianism. Empiricism has been a natural enemy of speculative thought; positivism has reigned, almost without challenge,[19] in science, law, philosophy, history, economics, and the social sciences. The secular, "engineering" character of Australian tertiary education is nowhere more evident than in the professional separation from humanities and social sciences achieved by law and economics. The autonomy of law and economics faculties has been to the detriment of each and at the cost of all, since they supply the graduates who chiefly govern the nation—the former in the legislatures and the courts, the latter in the bureaucracies, private as well as public.

Religion, too, has been compatible with the dominant ideology rather than resistant toward it. To be sure, the colonial inheritance was Irish Catholic as well as Anglo-Scots Protestant. Yet in matters of faith, the fundamentalism, or theological positivism, of each is more striking than the sectarianism that divided them, while in questions of politics the Irish Liberator and the English Chartist could make common cause.[20] (Did not Daniel O'Connell pay homage to Jeremy Bentham, the friend of Francis Place?)

It should not be surprising that the Benthamite ideology is compatible with Australians' conventional sense of identity—that myth of national character that depicts them as practical, sporting, fair-minded, and egalitarian. For these are a people proud in their pragmatism, skeptical of speculative and abstract schemes, wedded to "common sense." They are passionate about sport, yet legalistic limits are imposed upon competitive zeal: above all else, their sporting ethic demands adherence to the umpire's decision. Australians make much of their sympathy for the underdog, and their expectation that decent public provision should be made for individuals in distress is pure Benthamism. Nevertheless, this is a conformist compassion; they have been notably intolerant of minorities. The history of Australia's treatment of Aboriginals, for example, is a tragic demonstration of the limits to these views: where this history is not simply a record of racism and neglect, its attempted benevolence reveals the shortcomings of Benthamite bureaucracy applied to a culture in which its assumptions are irrelevant.

While the connections between the dominant ideology and the nation's perception of its own identity can be readily sketched, the task of fitting Benthamism into Australia's perceptions of the outside world is more difficult. The difficulty partly arises as a general problem: all liberal political philosophies are uncomfortable in the power-political milieu of international relations, where law and the common good are at the mercy of power and force.[21] More concretely, the difficulty arises because other influences besides the utilitarian ideology have significantly shaped Australia's experience of the external world. Chief among these other influences has been imperialism. The domestic success of Benthamite utilitarianism in Australia occurred behind the shield of Britain's imperial protection, which was regarded as one of the "givens" in this settler society.

Yet if imperialism has drawn the map of Australia's larger world, utilitarianism has provided the formula for operating within it. Australian diplomacy has been essentially an expedient accommodation to a preponderant power. This pattern, developed under Britain, was largely transferred to the United States, whose global primacy was assumed as a condition of Australian security through the 1950s and 1960s. To be sure, with both Britain and America, the utilitarian calculations of the minor ally have at times been blurred by sentimental attachment to the protector, but that sentiment and a utilitarian mental universe have together provided a basis for foreign policy. There has been virtually no tradition of balance-of-power thought, nor of collective security in the strict sense. Even the critics of Australia's interventionist record (two world wars, Korea, Malaya, Vietnam) apply similarly utilitarian calculations in their more isolationist assessment of the national interest. Rather than alliance, they have generally sought protection in Australia's remoteness from the world's centers of power, making a virtue out of a condition otherwise regarded as a vulnerability.

V

The dominance of Benthamite utilitarianism has not gone uncontested in Australia, even if it has not always been adequately understood. From both Right and Left, it has been challenged or rejected by those who do not share its assumptions. These critiques deserve notice.

The critique from the Right has been fitful as well as derivative. Australia is a large grievance to latter-day disciples of laissez-faire economics and inhospitable to radical conservatives. For so long has its economy been a mixed system, so intricately interdependent are state socialism and private capitalism in its affairs, that the free-marketeers have to take their stand outside the nation's historical experience and on the margin of its political decision.[22] If their rhetoric is useful to a defensive liberalism, their prescriptions are implausible for any party in office.[23] Theirs are the certainties and disappointments of scriptwriters for a production they will never direct.

The critique from the Left has been more sustained, and has largely defined the present understanding of ideology in Australia. The Left's tasks have included the construction and subsequent dismantling of a particular legend of national character-fraternity or "mateship"; the inclusion of culture, popular as well as elite, within the analysis of politics; and the incorporation of race and gender as dimensions of a historical sociology of class relations.[24] Yet, to adopt its language, the Left's paradigm has perhaps obscured its problematic. It has not sufficiently observed the extent to which capital, like labor, has been affected by the dominant ideology. The solitary individualist is as reluctant to be prised free from the weathered granite of Australian experience as the solidary class; the economic and political history that so offends the neoconservative proves scarcely more tractable for the neomarxist.

Once Australia is regarded as a society in which Chartism has succeeded, both Right and Left will face fresh problems in theory as well as in practice. Libertarian assumptions will clearly be in direct conflict with a successfully implanted Benthamism that rests its defense of individualism upon an explicit endorsement of state activity and regulation. A class analysis ultimately derived from Marxist theory will be unlikely to elucidate the puzzle of a labor movement that in its formative stages assumed a common interest between middle and lower orders. The conservatism of labor in Australia of which the Left despairs, like the timidity of capital to which the Right objects, reflects a utilitarian mental universe that classical theories of both Right and Left would regard as false consciousness.

A remaining response to the Benthamite ideology is rejection rather than critique. Manning Clark's five-volume *History of Australia* can be read as a sustained attempt to tell his country's story outside the constraints of triumphant utilitarianism.[25] "Cold, mechanical and ungenial" were John Stuart Mill's words for the popular notion of a Benthamite;[26] Clark's prophetic judgment upon those tendencies in the nation's experience seeks to redeem from it the heroic witnesses to a larger spirit. Addressing the past not with the moralist's narrow squint but from under the broader brim of what Mill called the aesthetic and sympathetic judgments, his concerns move beyond the distinctiveness of this society to the dilemmas of humanity. Clark's rejection can be total because his categories are no longer the individual and the state, but the individual and eternity.

VI

The distinctiveness of Australia's Benthamite ideology has been argued. Can it be put to the test? Some confirmation may be found in a comparison with another liberal society—the United States—on a specific issue, conscription during the Vietnam war. Both countries faced this issue, which exposes fundamental assumptions about the relationship between the state and the individual.

As the political career of W.A. Holman demonstrated, for Labor especially, conscription has been a traumatic issue in Australian politics.[27] The Menzies government's introduction of selective conscription in 1964 and, from 1966, the commitment of conscripts to the forces contributed as an ally of the United States in the defense of the Republic of Vietnam revived all the stresses of the past. The decisions of the sixties also presented new issues: this was the first occasion Australian conscripts had been sent beyond a limited zone of territorial defense and without a formal declaration of war. The conscription scheme, which was based upon a lottery of birthdates, was certainly inequitable; it was probably militarily inefficient as well.[28] Conscientious objectors were exempt from military service. However, although the test of conscience was not confined to religious beliefs, the objection to military service had to be absolute: no provision existed for selective conscientious objection.

The government defended conscription on two grounds: military necessity and legal duty.[29] No member of the governing coalition publicly questioned either the policy for which conscripts were used or the authority of the state to enforce their sacrifice.[30] Tortured by past rifts and torn by present rivalries, the parliamentary opposition was not united on this question.[31] Broadly, however, the response was to focus upon the particular war, rather than upon the general legitimacy of conscription. The government's fundamental claims concerning authority to conscript were not disturbed because they were in principle largely shared. The parliamentary debate, although impassioned, was about defense policy rather than about rights.

To those Australians who felt that their rights were being denied by these policies, there appears to have been neither a public language nor a central arena in which to articulate that sense. No Bill of Rights provided constitutional shelter for the anti-conscriptionists' position. These dissenters lacked any stilts upon which to elevate their claims. Even history was ambiguous: alongside the defeat of conscription in the referenda of 1916 and 1917, and a compromise limit upon the territorial sphere of compulsory service in 1942–43, stood the tradition of voluntary sacrifice immortalized at Gallipoli and Tobruk.

This record may be compared with that of the United States over exactly the same issue. While the draft and the war policy were entangled in public debate, it was nevertheless possible to distinguish these issues. The campaign against conscription could draw upon the language of civil rights protest and a tradition, enshrined in the Bill of Rights, that individual rights—certainly, that to life—were prior to citizenship and the state. Perhaps the most compelling evidence for the vibrancy of these assumptions and the tradition supporting them is the post–Vietnam War debate among American political philosophers and legal theorists about issues such as selective conscientious objection.[32] By contrast with Australia, the American tradition—with its distinctive assumptions based upon natural rights—provided firmer ground for individual challenges to authority as well as a more fertile soil for moral reflection upon that experience.

The case of conscription in the 1960s suggests why two issues concerning rights prove so difficult for Australia in the 1980s: women's rights—the equal opportunity debate—and Aboriginal rights, particularly land rights. These two issues doubly offend the utilitarian tradition. First, each couches present claims in the language of rights. While that basis for a claim may be resisted, a bargain can still be struck as an adjustment of interests. Second, and more radically, each is demanding compensation for past injustice. To add a retrospective dimension to a rights claim presents a utilitarian system with a demand it can scarcely recognize, let alone make allowance for. On this score, therefore, little headway has been achieved.

It is interesting that in both the equal opportunity and land rights arenas, the dominant ideology has to contend not only with the limits of its internal capacities, but also with the full force of an external challenge. For, those who are demanding these rights in Australia can call upon a global constituency that is not inhibited by the inherited constraints of utilitarian liberalism. Proponents of each of these causes have appealed to international conventions that rest upon natural rights doctrines.[33] Already, these external influences have begun to alter the constitutional balance and political debate as the High Court connects its judgments about the domestic division of powers to developments in international law.[34]

VII

The substance and transnational scope of these recent challenges to the dominant ideology point to the domestic changes and international transformations against which contemporary Australia must be assessed.

Domestically, the population itself has undergone rapid change. As the land rights protest indicates, Australia's indigenous inhabitants, dispossessed by European settlement, are now asserting the integrity of their participation in the politics of the present as well as in the consciousness of the past. The British boat people and their descendants have been joined by landings of northern, central, and southern Europeans, by communities from the eastern Mediterranean, and by a diversity of immigrants from Asia. The homogeneity that earlier made a rough-and-ready egalitarianism simple has been replaced by a heterogeneous society in which inequalities have to be justified between cultures rather than within a single set of social assumptions.

Internationally, Australia's setting has also been transformed. For most of its history, Australia's moorings were with Britain. The essential strategic, economic, and cultural ties were with London; the different strands were braided together, reinforcing the relationship. Those strands have now separated. The strategic thread became a line thrown to the United States in 1941 and secured a decade later; the main hawser of international trade was increasingly tied to Japan; the cultural link became an electronic wire to be plugged in wherever a connection was desired.

This global pattern reveals the uniqueness of Australia's international situation: its interests and identity cannot be enclosed within a consistent set of boundaries. Australia is a country without a region. Its future and its fate lie on the complex networks of global interdependence. The conditions of world order are the immediate conditions of Australian security and prosperity. This gives the country a high stake in defining these international conditions, but also means that changes in international norms and transnational regimes will have direct impact upon domestic politics.

* * *

What has been the impact of these manifold changes upon the dominant ideology? Is Australia still a Benthamite society?

Australia is indeed still a Benthamite society. The institutions created within the utilitarian mold persist and are notoriously difficult to change. The style and habits of Australian politics remain broadly consistent with the patterns of the past. The weight of this inheritance will not be shrugged off lightly; the Benthamite ideology's dominance persists if only by inertia.

Yet, despite its tenacity, I would argue that Australia's dominant ideology has exhausted its capacity to cope with Australia's most serious political predicaments. First, the ideology's inadequacy for defining policies consistent with Australia's place in the world may be seen in current debates about protection and immigration. Second, its inability to sustain democracy fully is evident in the damage caused by a convulsive legalism.

In his definitive analysis of Australia published in 1930, Sir Keith Hancock identified protection and restrictive immigration as Australia's "basic policies": these were the two "ring-fences" behind which economic and social life were pursued.[35] Each of these "basic policies" is now a matter of domestic controversy, yet in neither case does the debate appear to capture the full significance of these questions.

Protectionist policies must now face not only the internal conflicts of interest produced by a mixed economy, but also the demands of distributive justice within the global economy. The Third World will no longer accept its relative deprivation as the price of equality achieved among Australians. Established interests in Australian tariff politics do not provide breakthroughs because they do not represent the full dimension of the problem.[36] Determining the appropriate gates in the protectionist fence is neither simple analytically nor painless politically. (Is it an iron law of industrial democracies that over-protected industries are invariably located within electorally decisive marginal constituencies?) The debate over protection in Australia has been too narrow: it needs a new conceptual scheme.

The other "ring-fence"—the "great white wall" of the White Australia policy[37]—has been replaced by a discreet hedge of official and ostensibly non-discriminatory criteria. Nevertheless, old attitudes inevitably made Asian immigration a focus of concern as the non-discriminatory policy took effect, and as Australia applied to the refugee question of the 1970s and 1980s the humane response shown in the 1940s and 1950s. As the wisest and most informative contribution to this issue observes, "Opinions on Asian migration and settlement are one part of general Australian views about the way the economy and migration should be managed and about the place of equity in Australian society."[38]

Rather than generating a debate about equity, however, and regardless of the intentions of the protagonists, the current controversy over immigration has reinforced old rigidities. The challenge has been hyperbolic in its claims (even 7 percent of the total population by the year 2000 would not constitute the "Asianisation of Australia") and hypostatic in converting the data of attitude surveys into the actualities of social existence and public policy.[39] To have the wrong debate at the right time is one sign of the dominant ideology's inability to grasp the essential problems.

The content as well as the context of Australian democracy has undergone profound change. In the multiple crisis of 1975, which culminated in the dismissal of the Whitlam government by the governor-general and his installation of the parliamentary opposition as a caretaker administration, the damaging consequences of legalism upon elective democracy are forcibly displayed.[40] Scarcely a single element of the political system was left undisturbed by the events of that year, yet a decade later few of the structural weaknesses exposed or created by those upheavals have been repaired. A constitutionalism more confident in its fundamental principles would surely be less complacent, but the "constitutional crisis" itself demonstrates how far Australian democracy has been vitiated by legalism.

Doubtless, the principal actors in the central drama of 1975 differed in their individual philosophies of law. Sir John Kerr's legal positivism is revealed in his assertion that "the Constitution must prevail over any convention . . . the Constitution itself must in the end control the situation." By contrast, Gough Whitlam's legal realism is evident in his insistence upon convention: there was, he held, no convention sanctioning the power of the Senate to force the House of Representatives alone to the people. Yet, as the titles of their apologies reveal, each employs a juristic mode of analysis.[41] Each account sets out the cognitive closure to alternative strategies, the rejection of diplomatic—or classically political—maneuvers on the brink of catastrophe.

The grip of legalism is as evident in the subsequent interpretation of the crisis as in the behavior of the political actors. The definitive scholarly work on these events remains the province of lawyers.[42] For all that knowledge of the relevant constitutional law has been increased by these endeavors, inevitably they stop short of those questions of party, perceptions, and power that the politically systemic nature of the crisis provokes, and that need to be confronted if change is to occur. The rules of law are understood better than the rules of the game: 1975 has several Diceys; it awaits its Bagehot.

A paradox emerges, dramatized by the events of 1975 but more generally discernible. What was at first the most prominent element in the Benthamite ideology—the emphasis upon representative democracy—is now the weakest element of the political system.[43] The constitutional balance is altered more frequently and more significantly by the judiciary than by vote either of the legislature or of the people. The bureaucracy, cultivating a proprietary interest in "rational" decision, offers the surest route to policy. Consequently, it becomes the chief target of attention for those with specialist advice to offer "government." More than intellectual fashion has transformed "public administration" into "public policy." A reassertion of representative democracy would require a moral vocabulary capable of connecting social realities with political institutions.[44] Is utilitarianism any longer able to do this?

Its dominance makes the apparent exhaustion of the Benthamite ideology in the face of major challenges a problem for the political system as a whole. Yet why should a particular set of assumptions have achieved that hegemony? Why have not other ideologies contested equally for the Australian political mind?

A useful explanatory framework for answering that question is offered by Louis Hartz.[45] For Hartz, Australia's individuality, like that of other settler societies such as Canada, the United States, South Africa, and Latin America, is best understood as a historical fragment of European culture that has been transplanted into an alien environment. There, the founding characteristics are free to develop unchecked by the constraints, past and future, of the civilization in which they originated. Hence the dominance in each of these societies of a particular set of assumptions that undergoes its own metamorphoses unhindered by rival ideologies.

Hartz's description of Australia within this framework is of a "radical" fragment in which a radical democracy overthrows an early Whiggery and proceeds to define the national spirit in a mild but triumphant socialism. This is a caricature that the Left itself dismisses. My own account of the Benthamite ideology is intended to replace the specific treatment Australia receives at Hartz's hand, but I regard the explanatory dynamics he offers as an important insight into the development and limitations of these societies.

Like the other fragment societies, Australia is now confronting ideologies that its earlier course of development had enabled it to escape. If the confrontation with Marxist revolution in Asia—the ideological substance of the defense debate of the 1960s—was Australia's "delayed rendezvous with Babeuf,"[46] the appeals to international human rights covenants in the 1980s represent a late encounter with Locke. The mental universe of Australian politics is becoming more diverse, and future foreign observers may recognize more familiar elements than hitherto. Yet the mix will still be different. Even if Australia's fragmentary understanding matures into a more universal comprehension, its continuing distinctiveness will be explicable by its Benthamite origins.

ENDNOTES

The author is indebted to J.D.B. Miller and Judith Shklar for their comments on an earlier draft of this article.

[1]L.J. Hume, *Bentham and Bureaucracy* (Cambridge: Cambridge University Press, 1981), chap. 7.

[2]Elie Halévy, *The Growth of Philosophic Radicalism* (London: Faber and Faber, rep. 1972), p. 138.

[3]Nancy L. Rosenblum, *Bentham's Theory of the Modern State* (Cambridge, Massachusetts: Harvard University Press, 1978) emphasizes Bentham's modernity.

[4]J.S. Mill, "Bentham," in *Dissertations and Discussions* (London: John W. Parker & Son, 1859), p. 368; T.B. Macaulay, "Bentham's Defence of Mill: Utilitarian System of Philosophy," *Edinburgh Review,* No. xcviii (June 1829), Article i reprinted in Jack Lively and John Rees, eds., *Utilitarian Logic and Politics* (Oxford: Clarendon Press, 1978), pp. 151–178.

[5]Mill, *Dissertations and Discussions,* p. 336.

[6]A.W. Martin, *Henry Parkes: A Biography* (Carlton, Victoria: Melbourne University Press, 1980), pp. 48ff.; and see chap. 1 for the details of Parkes's Chartist associations. Parkes can be considered to have kept his Birmingham Political Union vow: no stranger to peril and privation, he devoted himself, three wives, and twelve children to his country's cause.

[7]Mill, *Dissertations and Discussions,* p. 333.

[8]W.K. Hancock, *Australia* (London: Ernest Benn Ltd., 1930), p. 71.

[9]John Tregenza, *Professor of Democracy: The Life of Charles Henry Pearson, 1830–1894, Oxford Don and Australian Radical* (Carlton, Victoria: Melbourne University Press, 1968), p. 41.

[10]Tregenza, *Professor of Democracy,* p. 42, citing Pearson's chapter "On the Working of Australian Institutions," in the influential Radical collection *Essays on Reform* (London: 1867). Pearson also commented on Australian affairs in Godkin's *Nation* and corresponded with Charles Eliot Norton.

[11]Tregenza, *Professor of Democracy,* p. 93 (citing Pearson's words in *Fortnightly Review,* May 1879, p. 688). Pearson's language here conceals a commitment to women's rights in education and politics.

[12]J.A. La Nauze, *Alfred Deakin: A Biography* (Carlton, Victoria: Melbourne University Press, 2 vols., 1965), vol. 1, p. 107. Deakin was a student of Pearson's. He too had an interesting American connection; he befriended and corresponded with Josiah Royce. L.F. Crisp, *Charles Cameron Kingston: Radical Federationist* (Canberra: Australian National University, 1984) describes Kingston and his father as Benthamites; see pp. 3, 11.

[13]See, for example, R.S. Parker's contribution (chap. 22) to R.F.I. Smith and Patrick Weller, eds., *Public Service Inquiries in Australia* (St. Lucia, Queensland: University of Queensland Press, 1978) and Parker's article "Responsible Government in Australia," in *Politics,* 15:2, 1980, pp. 11–22. See also David Butler, *The Canberra Model* (Melbourne: Macmillan, 1973).

[14]H.V. Evatt, *Australian Labour Leader: The Story of W.A. Holman and the Labour Movement* (Sydney: Angus and Robertson Ltd., 1940).

[15]Don Aitkin, *Stability and Change in Australian Politics* (Canberra: Australian National University Press, 1977), p. 270.

[16]Peter Loveday, "Corporatist Trends in Australia," *Politics,* 19:1, 1984, pp. 46–51.

[17]James Bryce, *Modern Democracies* (London: Macmillan, 1921), vol. II, p. 275.

[18]A.F. Davies, *Australian Democracy* (Melbourne: Longmans, Green & Co., 1958), p. 1.

[19]Until the publication of Hugh Stretton, *The Political Sciences: General principles of selection in social science and history* (London: Routledge and Kegan Paul, 1969).

[20]Vincent Buckley, *Cutting Green Hay: Friendships, Movements and Cultural Conflicts in Australia's Great Decades* (Ringwood, Victoria: Penguin Books, 1983).

[21]A problem dissected by Stanley Hoffmann in "Liberalism and International Affairs," Lionel Trilling Memorial Seminar, Columbia University, November 8, 1984.

[22]W. Kasper et al., *Australia at the Crossroads: Our Choices to the Year 2000* (Sydney: Harcourt Brace Jovanovich, 1980). See also Marian Sawer, ed., *Australia and the New Right* (Sydney: George Allen and Unwin Australia Pty Ltd, 1982) and Robert Manne, ed., *The New Conservatism in Australia* (Melbourne: Oxford University Press, 1982).

[23]Witness John Stone, "1929 and All That," (Shann Memorial Lecture, 1984), *Quadrant,* October 1984, pp. 9–20.

[24]See, as a sample: R.W. Connell, *Ruling Class, Ruling Culture: Studies of conflict, power and hegemony in Australian life* (Cambridge: Cambridge University Press, 1977); R.W. Connell and T.H. Irving, *Class Structure in Australian History* (Melbourne: Longman Cheshire, 1980); Humphrey McQueen, *A New Britannia* (Ringwood: Penguin Books, 1970); Humphrey McQueen, *Gallipoli to Petrov: Arguing with Australian History* (Sydney: George Allen and Unwin, 1984); Tim Rowse, *Australian Liberalism and National Character* (Melbourne: Kibble

Books, 1978); Ian Turner, *Room to Manoeuvre: Writings on History, Politics, Ideas and Play* (Richmond, Victoria: Drummond, 1982).

[25]C.M.H. Clark, *A History of Australia*, 5 vols., (Carlton, Victoria: Melbourne University Press, 1962–1981).

[26]Mill, *Dissertations and Discussions,* p. 386.

[27]K.S. Inglis, "Conscription in Peace and War, 1911–1945," in Roy Forward and Bob Reece, eds., *Conscription in Australia* (St. Lucia, Queensland: University of Queensland Press, 1968), pp. 22–65.

[28]Roy Forward, "Conscription, 1964–1968" in Forward and Reece, eds., *Conscription in Australia,* pp. 79–142. Jane Ross, "Australian Soldiers in Vietnam: product and performance" in Peter King, ed., *Australia's Vietnam* (Sydney: George Allen and Unwin, 1933), pp. 72–99.

[29]L.J. Hume, "Attitudes of Political Parties" in Forward and Reece, eds., *Conscription in Australia,* pp. 152–170.

[30]Although the Country party, which was vociferous in support of the military commitment and conscription, characteristically sought to obtain deferments for its sons to gather in the harvest to be sold to China. Hume, "Attitudes of Political Parties," p. 162.

[31]Hume, "Attitudes of Political Parties"; also Kim C. Beazley, "Federal Labor and the Vietnam Commitment" in King, ed., *Australia's Vietnam,* pp. 36–56.

[32]Michael Walzer, *Obligations: Essays on Disobedience, War and Citizenship* (Cambridge, Massachusetts: Harvard University Press, 1970); Michael Walzer, *Just and Unjust Wars* (New York: Basic Books, 1977); A. Gewirth, "Reason and Conscience: The Claims of the Selective Conscientious Objector" in V. Held et al., eds., *Philosophy, Morality, and International Affairs* (New York: Oxford University Press, 1974), pp. 89–117; Hugo Adam Bedau, "Military Service and Moral Obligation" in Virginia Held et al., eds., *Philosophy and Political Action* (New York: Oxford University Press, 1972), pp. 129–159; David Malament, "Selective Conscientious Objection and the *Gillette* Decision," *Philosophy and Public Affairs,* 1:4, Summer 1972, pp. 363–386; Donald A. Peppers, "War Crimes and Induction: A Case for Selective Nonconscientious Objection," *Philosophy and Public Affairs,* 3:2, Winter 1974, pp. 129–166.

[33]The same is true in a current education debate: see C.W. Collins, "Rights and Schooling," *Australian College of Education Occasional Paper* (Carlton, Victoria: Australian College of Education, forthcoming).

[34]As in Koowarta's case (*Koowarta* v. *Bjelke-Petersen* [1982] 39 *Australian Law Reports* 417). See Hugh Collins, "Aborigines and Australian Foreign Policy: Some Underlying Issues" in *Ethnic Minorities and Australian Foreign Policy* (Canberra Studies in World Affairs, no. 11, Department of International Relations, A.N.U., 1983), pp. 50–77.

[35]Hancock, *Australia,* p. 77.

[36]John Warhurst, *Jobs or Dogma: The Industries Assistance Commission and Australian Politics* (St. Lucia, Queensland: University of Queensland Press, 1982).

[37]Charles A. Price, *The Great White Walls are Built: Restrictive Immigration to North America and Australasia 1836–1888* (Canberra: Australian National University Press for the Australian Institute of International Affairs, 1982).

[38]Nancy Viviani, *The Long Journey: Vietnamese Migration and Settlement in Australia* (Carlton, Victoria: Melbourne University Press, 1984), p. 273.

[39]Geoffrey Blainey, "The Asianisation of Australia," *The Age,* March 20, 1984, p. 11.

[40]Judith N. Shklar, *Legalism* (Cambridge, Massachusetts: Harvard University Press, 1964).

[41]Garfield Barwick, *Sir John Did His Duty* (Wahroonga, New South Wales: Serendip, 1983); John Kerr, *Matters for Judgment* (South Melbourne, Victoria: Macmillan, 1978); Gough Whitlam, *The Truth of the Matter* (Ringwood, Victoria: Penguin, 1979).

[42]Geoffrey Sawer, *Federation Under Strain: Australia 1972–1975* (Carlton, Victoria: Melbourne University Press, 1977); L.J.M. Cooray, *Conventions, The Australian Constitution and the Future* (Sydney: Legal Books, 1974); George Winterton, *Parliament, The Executive and The Governor-General* (Carlton, Victoria: Melbourne University Press, 1983).

[43]Compare G.S. Reid, "The Changing Political Framework," *Quadrant*, January-February 1980, pp. 5–15.

[44]Of a kind similar to, though not necessarily identical with, Hugh Stretton, *Capitalism, Socialism and the Environment* (Cambridge: Cambridge University Press, 1976).

[45]Louis Hartz, *The Founding of New Societies* (New York: Harcourt Brace & World, Inc., 1964), part one.

[46]Hartz, *Founding of New Societies*, p. 45.

Donald Horne

Who Rules Australia?

IF YOU WERE ASKING YOURSELF "Who rules Australia?" and you imagined you could answer this by looking up the constitution of the Commonwealth of Australia, you would find you were in a world moving from the absolute monarchies of the seventeenth century but not yet reaching the constitutional monarchies of the nineteenth century: according to the constitution, the executive power is vested in the current English monarch, and the monarch's "representative," the governor-general, is governing Australia (appointing ministers at "his pleasure"), subject to certain checks provided by Parliament. There is also a somewhat more modern, or at least eighteenth century, check in the powers held by the states, but if you looked up the constitutions of the states you would again find it is the British monarch who, many and divisible, is also governing the states through the state governors as his representatives.

One cannot put any limits to the possible ignorance of voters but one can guess that it is not likely that many Australians actually believe that the British monarch or that monarch's "representatives" are engaged in ruling Australia—even if the representatives' powers to dismiss ministers and to dissolve parliaments have in fact twice been used to remove governments (in 1932 and in 1975) and even if, paradoxically, a great number of Australians see in these post-feudal powers the basic safeguard of Australian popular democracy. A former chief justice, Sir Garfield Barwick, has said: "The obligations of the governor-general are of the essence of our parliamentary democracy."[1]

It is more usually in the vague concept of "the Crown" that monarchically inclined Australians are likely to see the actual governing of Australia, and then (not that they would necessarily recognize this description) only as a legitimizing fiction. "The Crown" becomes a prestigious metonym for the whole apparatus of the state, lending it honor. It is "the Crown" that arrests citizens and puts them on trial before judges who are themselves also embodied with the spirit of "the Crown," and beneath one of whose icons they sit; the prison gates that clang behind those found guilty are also likely to carry royal insignia. Until recently, a crown was on the letterboxes. It is the Crown that military officers swear their allegiances to. For those who see it that way, the spirit of "the Crown" gives magic to various parts of the apparatus of the state, providing a sense of permanence and propriety found wanting in the sordidness of mere party politics, or in the untrustworthiness of the "transient majorities" of representative democracy. The imaginative power of the concept of "the Crown" was exemplified in Adelaide in January 1978, at a royal commission inquiring into the dismissal of a police commissioner who had been accused of misleading the premier in regard to the South Australian Police "Special" (i.e., secret) Branch. In justification of his actions, he gave a splendid expression of the useful mysticism of "the Crown" when he said: "I felt my loyalties were to the Crown and beyond the elected government."[2] By this language, he clothed in monarchic rhetoric his belief that the police were the true interpreters of the interests of the state.

Perhaps this seems a bizarre way in which to begin an essay on power in Australia. After all, feelings about the Britishness of Australia have been modified since the Second World War: British strategic power collapsed; British economic significance weakened; there was a dulling of London's cultural dazzle and an Australian cultural awakening; an active program began for immigrants not only from Britain but from "the continent" and even Asia; there are now declarations from the two main political parties that Australia is a "multicultural society." But one of the ways of beginning a discussion on power in a particular society is to look at some of that society's legitimating "myths"; those beliefs that have the magical quality of transforming complex events and actions into simple meanings that explain and justify action and that, whether altogether false or partly true, have the transforming effect of hiding the contradictions and inadequacies of reality. Myths make a good introduction to a society because the further they are from reality, the more they may tell us about a society's tensions. One can ask: if humans can delude themselves to this extent, what has gone wrong? What is (in effect, whatever the intention) being covered up?

In this case, what is being covered up includes all the usual things, all those realities of power that can disappoint the expectations people have about political action. But some things are covered up more than others. For example, a governor-general is not really a "representative" of the current British monarch: formally, he is appointed by the monarch for what is seen as a fixed term, but it is the prime minister who chooses him, and after his appointment the monarch does not in any way control a governor-general's actions. In this sense, Australia is not a monarchy, but what has been called a "governor-generalate"[3] or a "governor-generalship"[4]: the metonym of "the Crown" distracts attention from the realities of a conservative political institution of a perhaps unique kind. It might also be noted that the concept of "the Crown" is used with particular force within the armed services, the police, the prisons and, by extension, the intelligence services: in other words, it functions most strongly in regard to the coercive and surveillance apparatus of the state, where there is a less than public view of the "true" raisons d'état. In this use, it has the same legitimizing function as the phrase "the people" can have in those countries that employ it, but the magic of the phrase "the Crown" also summons up other meanings. Use of the phrase becomes a usefully polite encoding for British (or is it really English?) ethnocentrism, in that it can imply, without saying so, that it is the "anglos" rather than the "ethnics" who should still be engaged in most of the running of Australia. This perceived "Britishness" can also extend to being a legitimizer of political conservatism: Australia's most prominent ideologue of right-wing populism, Queensland premier Bjelke-Petersen, has attacked high taxation as "republican";[5] whenever the secret paramilitary organizations that formed in Australia during the Great Depression voiced their dreams of overthrowing "Bolshevik" (viz Labor) governments, it was always in the name of King George and Old England.[6] Perhaps most significant of all, is that by giving Australia a somewhat derived, dependent status, as if it were not yet a proper nation, the idea of "the Crown," by symbolic osmosis, can help make it seem natural that some of the most effective "ruling" of Australia can go on in centers of power outside the country. If the symbolic structure of the state celebrates the fact that Australians are not fit to choose their own head of state but must use the monarch from another country for that purpose, this helps reinforce a dependent mentality evident in "practical" fields such as military, economic, and diplomatic policy, in which it might be argued that Australia has become more "dependent" than, according to its economic size and strategic position, it need be. In the colonial style, Australians can fall in love with their own dependence: it can seem the most honorable thing about them.

These are arguments I shall return to later. They are worth raising at the beginning because, as a "traditional" rather than a "legal-rational" legitimation (in Weberian terms), the use of "the Crown" is a reminder of what should never be forgotten about power in Australia—that white Australia began as a colony and still maintains certain colonial habits. It was in the name of "the Crown" that the British occupied Aboriginal land; it seems fitting that where this concept may still have most retained its magic lies in distracting attention from the most secret powers of the state, the least democratic aspects of Australian conservatism, and the possibility that much effective power may lie outside Australia itself.

Premier Bjelke-Petersen and many others, including a Chichele Professor of International Law at Oxford,[7] have also attacked as "republican" any moves they see as weakening "federalism." So "federalism" becomes another legitimating myth worth investigating to see whose interests it serves. The Australian constitution is neither liberal (no Bill of Rights or any other formal statement on civil rights), nor democratic (no statement about a relation between voting and government), nor nationalist (it is, in fact, a declaration of national dependence) and it has been given effective meaning by a High Court that has always had a conservative majority. With this background, it is not surprising that the idea of "federalism" (although used by state Labor governments when it suits them) has, like the idea of "the Crown," mainly served conservative interests—in two particular ways. One of these serves the interests of "free enterprise"; after several decades of masterly legal legerdemain, a section of the constitution intended to prevent one state putting a duty on goods from another state became interpreted as meaning support for laissez-faire capitalism, so that "federalism" came to be seen as a protection against "socialism." The other serves to preempt use of the rhetorically valuable word "freedom" in its political sense, restricting it mainly to anti-centralism: this in turn can help maintain things as they are in two ways. First, it helps conceal the fact that the principal form of centralized government in Australia is in the bureaucracies of the state governments. Not only is the national government perhaps weaker in its powers than other national governments; local government in Australia is also weaker than local governments in most liberal-democratic societies, with many activities that are normally seen as matters for local government being absorbed into the bureaucracies of the states. Second, the accompanying paradox of this idea of "freedom" is that in time of peace it can be the state governments that have actually been the most suppressive: it is the state governments that hold most of the police powers and the state governments that have passed most of the discriminatory laws. It is not unexpected that a conservative constitution has been used by conservatives in such a way that "federalism" equals "freedom," which in turn equals laissez-faire capitalism (which is itself a highly significant myth, since Australian capitalism tends to be not laissez-faire, but oligopolistic and government-protected).[8]

THE MYTHS OF PARLIAMENTARIANISM

A right-wing official in a local branch of the Liberal party came briefly into the news a few years ago when he proclaimed that in Australia, loyalty was owed to the Throne, the Church, the Law, and the Army; he did not mention Parliament. Such a public confession would, however, be unusual. Parliament would probably be seen by most Australians as the prime symbol of legitimate power. This need not worry conservatives who still hold a belief in "the Crown": the constitution declares in its first section that the Commonwealth Parliament consists of the monarch as well as the Senate and the House of Representatives, and belief in Parliament is commensurate with general Britishry since, in all kinds of details (although not in essentials), the Australian system has many similarities with the British and its bards can delude themselves, in the British manner, that it was the British who invented what is in fact the distinctively *European* institution of the representative assembly[9]; but Parliament is also, of course, the prime symbol of the beliefs of representative democracy and, as such, can also appeal to liberal-conservatives, liberals, labor people, and radicals.

In fact, the institution of Parliament, whether state or federal, never lives up to expectations. For generations, people have been writing articles or making speeches about the decline of Parliament, but nothing is new about the moribund nature of Australian parliaments. They are, as it were, meant to be moribund: as with one of those insects that dies after performing its procreative function, a prime function of parliaments in Australia has always been to act as an electoral college, and then to become, in varying degrees, moribund. After a general election is held, the party or political grouping that has more votes than its opponents forms the government. When the determination has been made, the lower house has fulfilled its principal biological function. What is required of the majority grouping after that is to support the government. What is required of the minority grouping is to attack the government. In both cases, such meaningful debates as do occur are more likely to be conducted in the party rooms than in Parliament. Now and again, a leader is overthrown, or a government splits and loses its majority, but these are changes that come from fission in the party rooms, not because of a debate in Parliament. To the politicians themselves, parliamentary performance is assessed almost exclusively in terms of party, factional, and personal ambition.

If one believes in representative democracy (even if only in the Schumpeterian[10] sense that it is better to have the limited choice offered by the party system than to have no choice at all), the Australian parliaments, federal and state, could be most effectively criticized not because they lack the oratorical vigor of debates between Charles James Fox and Edmund Burke, but because they have three weaknesses as electoral colleges. The first is that, although they are not as bad as the Japanese, for example, or the British, the electoral systems for the lower houses do not always fairly represent voters' preferences.[11] The second is that the electoral college function is not defined in any of the constitutions: none of the constitutions says that a lower house chooses a government; they say instead that it is a governor or a governor-general who chooses a government. The third weakness is that in the Commonwealth and four of the state parliaments a government can be forced out of office if its money supply is blocked by an upper house—and an upper house elected on a different electoral system from that of the lower house. (One of these, the Western Australian upper house, is elected on what may be the most unfair electoral system in any democratic country.) It is one of the characteristics of political power in Australia that, of any of the parliamentary (as distinguished from presidential) democracies, Australia has the strongest upper-house system, and that this can threaten "responsible government," in the sense of the primacy of a lower house.

The second great function of Parliament lies in its ritualistic and mythic qualities: it lends legitimation to acts of government and the passing of laws, and it distracts attention from the realities of power (to which Parliament is certainly not central and to which even government may not necessarily be central.)[12] If anthropologists from a superior civilization in a distant galaxy came to Australia and investigated the ways of the natives, they would find no difficulty in writing learned papers on the difference between the manifest and latent functions of its parliamentary rituals. They would recognize that by voting for the restricted lists of candidates offered by the political system, Australians were acting out a myth that they were being "represented," and that by rituals in which pieces of paper called "bills" were transubstantiated into "acts" embodying the will of the people, Parliament was hallowing the making of laws. (Even if these laws had already been decided on within the prevailing political party of political coalition.)

MYTHS OF THE PARTY SYSTEM

So—the parties. What do they tell us about power in Australia?

By a variety of selection methods ranging from the decisions of local constituency branches to emergency head office interventions, it is the parties (made up of only 4 percent of the voters) that decide the names that go on the election menu. The candidates they choose are, overall, overwhelmingly unrepresentative. They are very much more male, very much less working class, and much more "anglo" than the population at large. In their own persons, the members of the Australian parliaments represent a male, middle-class, anglocentric Australia[13] and, on the whole, they act that way.

This stresses an overall similarity. But if one looks at the makeup of the party branches, their sources of financial support, their distinctive rhetoric and the patterns of voting support, one does find differences. In itself, the Liberal party is a hodgepodge. Its membership is mainly middle class and its voting support mainly white collar, but some of its voting support is blue collar and much of its financial support and its supportive social environment is that of big business. The Liberal party does, however, have a unifying language: its principal rhetorical device—the language of "free enterprise"—can seem the common language of Australians, and with a subtlety in which the same set of words can mean different things to different people. If you stand up on a platform and say "I believe in the free enterprise system," this can be decoded in a number of different ways that can provide simultaneous comfort to the managing directors of multinational companies *and* the owners of corner stores *and* working-class suburbanites paying off their mortgages: each group will think you are speaking to it. This common language can be so effective that, so long as it is presented with sufficiently heartwarming woolliness, it can obscure even the conflicts between the many types of business interest, so that most business people believe, most of the time, that the Liberal party is *their* party. In those regions where the National (formerly Country) party is strong, there can be a similar belief that this party gives special representation to farming interests; it can also seem to treat mining interests with special gentleness; and in Queensland, where it is the majority party, it can also seem worth contributions to party funds from big business. On the other hand, although the Labor party now chooses mainly middle-class people as its parliamentary candidates and its styles and policies are also middle class, blue-collar working people make up its largest group of voters: it has a special concern for welfare recipients; trade unions supply the bulk of its funds; and trade unions have direct representation at its state conferences (the proportion of trade-union delegates ranging from 60 percent to 75 percent). One way or another, just as the Liberal and National parties can seem to represent the special interests of business people, the Labor party can seem to represent the special interests of working-class people.

So, on the whole, most business people, from small farmers and corner-store owners to the managing directors of large foreign companies, can feel that, whatever its inadequacies, they have a political party of their own; on the other hand, many of those who define themselves as working class can also feel that, for better or worse, *they* have a party of their own.[14] These beliefs, along with those about the Crown, the constitution, and Parliament define reality in a satisfyingly mythic way, papering over some of the cracks.

As in the other cases, the reality that is papered over is complex. One part of this reality is that however much conservative governments may preach the virtues of free enterprise, what they actually practice is "managed capitalism," providing government bases of various kinds for the making of private profit; and however much they may speak of the virtues of individualism, what they practice is modified welfarism. In these cases, the differences between the conservatives and Labor might appear little more than rhetorical, and to those on either side with stronger tastes, the differences can seem, in effect, marginal. To say this is not to say, however, that the differences are unimportant. Politics in liberal-democratic countries must remain marginal: conflicts that go beyond marginality become more than the traffic can bear. The more important question is what *are* the margins between the parties?

The answer to that has varied. Up to about 1910, before the growing strength of the Labor party gave political theater the capital-versus-Labor look that has never quite departed from it, there was a generally "progressive" feel about Australian politics. The prevailing rhetoric was liberal, in the spirit of "Improvement" of nineteenth-century England; at times it was, by the standards of the age, radical. Australia was sometimes seen as a "social laboratory." Why Australia changed from a perceivedly progressive to a perceivedly conservative country is one of the great questions in Australian history (and, perhaps for that reason, not much discussed by Australian historians). I cannot compress my own answers sufficiently to include them here, but I can note that one result of this shift has been that since 1910, the width of the policy margins between the parties has usually (although not always) depended on the mood of the Labor parties. If they are in an active mood, the Labor people tend to be more concerned with welfare and equality and more open about the use of government intervention than their rivals; they are sometimes more inclined to be "modernizing" parties (in the sense of bringing in new ideas from overseas) and they sometimes give expression to the desirability of policies of greater national independence, occasionally even of isolationism.

It can become a conventional wisdom within the Labor party at times—especially if it has suffered electoral defeat—that "the Australian people" are conservative. But whether "the Australian people" are "conservative" cannot be judged simply from election results. There are biases in the electoral system, and according to one way of reckoning these things, the long period of Liberal rule, from 1949 to 1972, was artificial: the Labor party probably had majority support in three elections (1954, 1961, 1969) in that period. The much-analyzed defeat of the Whitlam government in 1975 is now produced as a prime example of Australian conservatism, and so, in one sense, it was. But it should also be remembered that Whitlam had won the 1972 election in a mood of reform, and when forced to an election in 1974 when his reform program was challenged, he won that election, too.

What matters most to the approach being taken in this article is that, despite the myths of a party system based on class division and however nastily conservative governments may shout abuse against the union movement, or legislate threateningly against the unions, in practice they deal with the unions in a much more circumspect manner. As governments, they know they depend on the unions (and union institutionalization of class conflict) to keep the work force working, and that if they risk a full union mobilization against them, they might lose. At the same time, the Labor party now so believes in its dependence on businesses to run a large part of the nation's economy that it has very largely given up even shouting; whether rightly or wrongly, Labor people have no doubt that if they acted in a way that mobilized business against them, they would lose.

Australia has not gone as far as the United States, where there is no labor party, or Canada where the labor party is a minor latecomer acting under an assumed name, but it may be that the single-member constituency system of voting for lower houses has given more of a class basis to Australian party-political divisions than they would have had under a proportional representation system. It was in the three upper houses where a proportional representation system operates, that there were small successes for the new party of the Australian Democrats that emerged in 1977 as a middle class "social issues" party. As such, this party reflects what is called in Australia "small-l liberalism" (viz, civil libertarianism), as distinct from the "big-L Liberalism" (viz, modified laissez-faire rhetoric) of the Liberal party: it also displays what is described pejoratively by its critics as "trendiness"—a concern with issues of environmentalism, feminism, multiculturalism, etc. If there had been a proportional representation system for lower houses, the Australian Democrats might have become part of the parliamentary "electoral colleges" that determine who will govern; they might, at times, have themselves participated in government, as part of coalitions. In either case, they would have strengthened a center bias in Australian party politics. (It is true that a proportionate representation system does operate in one state, Tasmania—but Tasmania is special.) There is a minority of small-l liberals and "trendies" in the Liberal party and a larger following in the Labor party (where they meet opposition from the traditional Catholic right-wing and from some working-class animosity to what can be seen as a middle-class lack of concern for pragmatic bread-and-butter issues.)[15] In fact, some of the most bitterly contested divisions in Australian politics, both between the parties and within them, are now over the "small-l liberal" and "trendy" social issues—which can be seen, especially by those who don't like them, as a symptom of a "new middle class" that has emerged in Australia from the (tardy) expansion of higher education that gathered some (limited) momentum in the 1960s. Abhorrence of this perceived "new class," which is seen by some as the dominant class in Australia, can unite the conservatives in all three of the traditional parties.[16] I shall return to the "new class."

To see as untrue the mythic interpretation of Australian politics as having a primary division related to class conflict is not to say that class conflict does not exist in Australian society—it does—but that it is not fundamental to Australian party politics. (Some would say that party politics "domesticates" class conflict.) What is more significant about this mythic view that there is such a conflict in Australian party politics is the theatrical sense of *priority* it gives to business, to the union movement, and therefore to "the economy." Government is seen as being primarily about economic management, and in this the business firms and the trade unions are seen as the principal actors. We are now approaching central questions of power in Australia, but I shall postpone them until I have dealt with a couple of other matters.

SETTING THE AGENDA

Another way of approaching the question of power is to pay some attention to the question of what politics in Australia can seem to be about, and why. I am assuming that society is a great arena of conflicts, but that only some of these conflicts become part of "politics"—or, as Schattschneider put it in his famous aphorism in *The Semi-Sovereign People:* "Some issues are organized into politics while others are organized out"[17]—so that an important element in the political struggle is to define what politics is about; one form of power can lie with those who have a voice in this matter.

What part do the parties play in organizing issues into, or out of, politics? Or as we might now put it: what part do the parties play in setting the political agenda? Whatever sense they might make in the United States with their independent legislatures, in Australia's case one can forget pluralist models of "interest articulation" in which the political parties are seen as acting as "brokers" between "interest groups." Perhaps the Liberal party does a bit of that in regard to conflicting business interests, but on the whole in Australia it is governments and bureaucracies, not political parties, that are lobbied, bullied, or bribed by those who want something out of them. An exception can be that rare occasion when there is a "conscience vote" in Parliament, or where there is a certain independence of action in an upper house through the existence of members of a minor party such as the Australian Democrats, or independent members, or, as sometimes happens, an independent-minded Liberal. There have been whole years of mindlessness when, apart from narrow economic programs, the parties have scarcely seemed to have any policies at all: there was a period when political leaders opened election campaigns merely by reading out shopping lists promising that they would spend money on this and that. It could be argued that, over the years, the media have been more significant than the politicians in setting the agenda. Parliament has certainly been of less significance than the media. The parliamentary meetings do allow, of course, for debate on public issues and for forcing disclosures about the administration, but they do neither very regularly or very well; since control by Australian political parties of what their members say and do in Parliament is even tighter than is usual in parliamentary systems, parliamentary debate is usually restricted to adversarial warfare of the crassest kind. In any case, the significance of parliamentary "debates" depends on how the media project them: one of the significant functions of the Parliament buildings is that they house the print and broadcasting journalists. The media proclaim what seems to matter in politics. In particular, between elections they proclaim what the "crises" are, and during elections what the "issues" are.[18]

It might be argued that in all the industrial societies, the media have very largely taken over what used to be the role of religion as a prime guardian of social reality.[19] For example, the various news services, whether print or broadcasting, throw up a regular "map" of reality that tells us what is, and what should be; it tells us what things are like, what is worth talking about, what is normal, and it suggests what is possible and what is not possible. Perhaps even more important are the media's entertainment services: these reinforce views of reality by the immemorial techniques of casting up typical images and telling us typical stories. Not all the people believe everything they see and hear in the media, nor do they all decode it in the same way, but what monopolizes the public culture can be effective even if its projections are not universally beloved: sheer monopoly can reinforce dominant views and inhibit the development of contrary views; above all, it can concentrate our attention on what it is that we are supposed to be disagreeing about. The media may not always be successful in telling people what to think, but they can be "stunningly successful" in telling people what to think about.[20] So one way of looking for a center of power in Australia is to peer past the myths of freedom for the media (which can mean freedom from government control but not equal rights to freedom of expression) and look for the professional projectors of social reality. One finds that most of the mass media are controlled by an oligopoly of four business firms and one government-supported institution, the Australian Broadcasting Commission. To those on the Left, this provides an easy answer—the media are owned by the capitalist class and reflect its values; on the Right, there is an equally easy answer—the media are dominated by "new class" "trendies." Although the second view is, in many instances, demonstrably untrue, there is enough in it for both views to be useful: it is true, overall, that the media accept as "common sense" the basic values of a capitalist society—the beliefs in individualism and private property and the dynamics of the market economy and the profit motive—but it is also true that they can offend the socially conservative by absorbing (but also, some would argue, "domesticating"[21]) social change. As with other liberal-democratic capitalist societies, it might be argued that Australia continues to change so that it can remain the same.

Theorizing about powers of agenda-setting must also take into account the fact that in the 1960s, a new element entered agenda-setting in Australia—the arrival of the protest movements. (It would be more exact to say that protest was an old form that revived and gained a new dimension from new media, especially television, definitions of "news.") At first, most of the media attacked the protests as threats to democracy, because they were happening in the streets and not in Parliament, and because they were directed against the policies of elected governments. But protests "made news," and however unfavorably most of the media represented them, the protest movements were "given a run." Although the peace movements had no success, in the fields of the women's movements, the civil liberties movements, the Aboriginal movements, and the various types of environmentalist movements, the protests had important effects on agenda-setting: the apocalyptic elements in the "It's Time" campaign that accompanied Gough Whitlam's elevation to the prime ministership in the 1972 election were largely a creation of the protest movements; people had turned Whitlam into a symbol of social regeneration. Now many of the first generation of protestors are themselves in the bureaucracies; the media now report the protests (or most of them) more sympathetically. Regarded by some as threat and by others as regeneration, they have become a recognized and influential part of political life in Australia. To social conservatives, this is further evidence of the growing strength of the "new class" in Australia.

THE CONCERNS OF THE STATE

It is significant that one of the ways of gauging the success of protest can be that some of the protestors now work in the government bureaucracies. Despite "Westminster system" myths of public service impartiality, bureaucracies are, of course, one of the principal agents of agenda-setting;[22] they have their traditions, very strongly held, of what governments should be concerned with, and their characteristic styles (usually of caution) of going about their business. To take an extreme example: in a state administration where one of the actual, if unintended, functions of the police is corruption (or, to put it another way, to assist in the organization of crime), part of the business of government becomes its own corruption and its style becomes one of continuing hypocrisy and cover-up. This is a view held of some state governments in Australia. To take a less extreme example: if a bureaucracy is enmeshed with business networks, as some of the Australian bureaucracies are, and sees its prime function as the encouragement of business enterprise, it will act as an extension of parts of the business community and, with or without corruption, the extension of favors will be one of its justifying tasks. All state governments in Australia act in this way. On the other hand, if a reform government takes over an administration, it is wise to move in new bureaucrats: all the new bureaus set up by new Labor governments and dealing with new agenda items (ethnic or gender discrimination, for example, or environmental protection) have been staffed partly with outsiders.

Almost right from the start of the penal settlement, two of the principal concerns of the civil officers of the colonies were the security of the state and a concern for the priority of its economic development. These remain the ingrained "common-sense," the unexamined (conventional) wisdoms, of most of the organs of the state in Australia and along with the endemic conservatism and self-definition of most bureaucracies, it is within the ambit of these wisdoms that government policy-making is usually deployed, or frustrated. They can be seen as the fundamentals of bureaucratic definitions of "the public interest."

For most of Australia's history, the concept of the security of the state was inextricably linked with the idea of loyalty to Great Britain—to such an extent that when an Australian secret service was formed during the First World War, it seemed quite natural that its head should be the official secretary of the governor-general.[23] It is now the United States that is honored with the principal expressions of Australia's loyalty. In overt declarations of these loyalties, there can be differences of view about the intensity with which they should be declared, but the covert loyalties of the various parts of the Australian intelligence community to the United States intelligence community is absolute. Australian self-interest is defined as naturally and always being the same as that of the United States to such an extent that towards the end of the Whitlam era, the CIA approached the Australian Security and Intelligence Organisation to see what they could do about the Australian prime minister.[24] In this context, the Australian intelligence community can be seen to have preserved a colonial mentality, and it is a mentality that suffuses other significant elements in the apparatus of the state in Australia.

It is to be found, in particular, in that loyalty to "great and powerful friends," of which the conservative R.G. Menzies, quintessentially colonial in mentality, boasted when he was prime minister and that comes to be seen as a matter not only of national interest but of national honor, and is still, so far as one can judge, also the prevailing wisdom among Australians generally. An example of this pride in dependence can be found in the contrasts between Australian memories of two incidents in the war against the Japanese—the Battle of the Coral Sea, in which a naval force led by the United States turned back a Japanese fleet whose mission was to invade Port Moresby, the principal town in Papua New Guinea; and the Battle of Milne Bay, in which an Australian force repelled an attempted Japanese landing east of Port Moresby and, in the course of doing so, inflicted on the Japanese military the first land defeat they had ever suffered. One would imagine that patriots, if they were looking for something to boast about, would have chosen the occasion of the first-ever defeat of the Japanese army for a demonstration of national honor; instead, the victory of Milne Bay is mostly forgotten and what is remembered and celebrated is the Battle of the Coral Sea. It is more honorable to be "saved" by an ally than to save oneself. There is a well-articulated "anti-Americanism" in Australia—"anti-American" in the sense of opposition to the United States bases in Australia that, by their signaling and surveillance facilities are part of the United States nuclear warfare program, and also in the sense of skepticism about, or opposition to, the ANZUS treaty—but opinion surveys suggest that, when it comes to diplomacy and military planning, most Australians do not question the old colonial commonsense of "loyalty." The only change is that the "loyalty" has shifted to the United States. When a few intellectuals suggest the possibility of a Swedish-style armed neutrality, this becomes such an affront to conventional wisdom that it seems beyond sensible, practical consideration, among the bureaucracies as among the people.

This belief in a dependent loyalty extends, among the bureaucracies of the state, to the economic sphere: in the days of empire, loyalty to the Bank of England was an important part of the imperial imagination; when the Great Depression hit Australia, a Labor government invited a governor of the Bank of England out to Australia to tell Australians what they should do, and, again, loyalty to the Bank of England was a matter not only of national interest but of national honor. There was much rhetoric of self-praise that Australia was almost alone among the nations in not asking for any moratorium on its debts. Such habits of belief live on in an attitude towards foreign capital that is far more deferential than mere considerations of prudence would dictate. It is as if foreign capital is good in itself and foreign money (at least from prestigious nations) is better than Australian money. As with "anti-Americanism," there is a minority opposition to what are seen as the evils of excessive foreign ownership and control of the economy, but within the apparatus of the state itself the belief in the absolute necessity for attracting foreign capital produces a wisdom of dependence even greater than in diplomacy (where at times there are minor acts of independence) and in military planning (where there is some talk of greater independence, but a failure of imagination and skill amongst politicians in doing anything about it). This belief in the need to attract foreign investment to Australia—at any cost, including the high costs of high deference—is one of those perceived facts of life with which politicians become acquainted when they take office. It can become so self-evident that in the International Bauxite Commission, Australia, although one of the world's main suppliers, almost always speaks up not for the suppliers but for the buyers. Insofar as one can speak of choice in human affairs, it was not by necessity but by "choice" that, after Canada, of the prosperous capitalist societies Australia is the world's most dependent and foreign-controlled economy.[25] And this "choice" is not related to economic pragmatism, taking one's economic good where one finds it, but to a whole inherited cast of mind that can see no alternatives.

In regard to habits of thought on economic policy, there are many general ways in which the growth of the state in Australia was much the same as that in other liberal-democratic societies: its growth came partly in response to the growth of capitalism. In one sense, in these societies the state *was* Marx's "executive committee of the bourgeoisie," concerned with reorganizing society to provide the conditions for the growth of business. But at the same time, the very conflicts between different forms of business produced a certain independent momentum, giving the state some mediating influence. The ugly face of capitalism, both threatening the social order and provoking conscience, produced many accommodating interventions on both the Right and the Left, providing, among other activities, welfare for the economically "useless." The state also developed in reaction to trade-union power, both restricting and protecting it. As in other liberal-democratic societies, it is seen as the duty of the government to maintain business confidence and, in general, to facilitate business activity, even if at an uneconomic price. Some of the traditions, as well as being capitalist, are, however, specifically "colonial." The European settlement of Australia got going at the dawn of the British "age of improvement," and the belief in national economic development has for long been one of the strongest Australian secular faiths. "National development," on the other hand, for Australians has tended almost exclusively to mean development of "natural resources" (at any cost), with a particular regard to farming and mining and the export (at any cost) of primary products.

In farming, there has been a strong and highly successful tradition of government intervention, supported by all the political parties. Australian farming and the processing of farm products is strongly research-based and the research is funded almost exclusively by governments (in fact, most of it is carried out by one government agency). The extension of this research is also funded by governments and the marketing of farm products is also controlled, or sponsored, by governments. Given the weaknesses of Australian capitalism (see later), only a similar type of government sustenance might have produced a lively and innovative manufacturing sector. There was no such intervention—except for lavish policies of protection, a policy that has the effect of operating for the benefit of foreign companies that set up plants in Australia. On the two occasions when government intervention might have most profitably occurred, the "colonial mentality" suggested otherwise. In the 1920s, when government sponsorship of Australian manufacturing might have succeeded, there was a declared policy of maintaining Australia simply as a supplier of raw materials; this was seen as Australia's appropriate contribution to the prosperity of empire trade. In the 1950s, there was another chance, when the government assistance to manufacturing that had been forced on governments during the Second World War might have been extended into peacetime. But the conventional wisdom was that the industrialization of Australia was better conducted by foreign companies. A Labor government, for example, when wishing to establish a motor vehicle industry, ignored Australian initiatives and called in General Motors. The result is, as I have put it in several books, that Australia is a "lucky country"; in its industrial imagination, it is almost entirely dependent and derivative. Practically none of the patents registered in Australia are for Australian innovations. The belief that active government intervention should be limited to farming and that, other than this, the main government initiative should be the encouragement of foreign investment, has also been part of the wisdom of the state.

The other appropriate question to ask about the Australian government bureaucracies concerns their rating in terms of class, gender, and ethnicity. The answer is that which any one aware of Australia's history would expect: in the upper reaches of the government bureaucracies, a disproportionate number of top people are male, Protestant, of British origin, and private-school educated.[26] The kinds of people who were dominant in the colonies at the beginning—privileged WASPS—are still there, and they are more likely than any others to get the best jobs (even if in some parts of the bureaucracies there can be competition from what is likely to be derided as a "Catholic mafia").

AN AUSTRALIAN ELITE?

Are these people part of a more general elite that runs most things in Australia? Increasingly, the answer would be "yes." But one must at once make a qualification: it involves the distinction Karl Kautsky made in 1902—that while the dominant interests in a society might be thought of as a "ruling" class, the administration might be carried out by a "governing" class working within the wider ambit of "ruling" class interests.[27] Leaving aside for a few more paragraphs the question of whether there *is* an Australian "ruling" class, one can at least now see that a new "governing" class has developed, people who sit at their desks and "make decisions." This is a product of the high bureaucratization of business corporations and perhaps, to a lesser extent, the bureaucratization of the union movement, along with an expansion in higher education. If there is a "new class," this would seem to be it—the class of the bureaucrats and technocrats (who also engender their own critics, the "trendies"). Its common basis is higher education—a novelty for Australia. The spread of higher education has meant that people with degrees or diplomas as well as controlling the professions are now also dominating the bureaucracies of both government and business, and also, to a lesser extent, even the union backrooms. It is as yet hard to know what this means: unlike higher education institutions in many modern industrial states, the Australian universities and colleges have not consciously set themselves the task of turning out a particular kind of governing elite. However, what one can now discern, within the bureaucratic institutions themselves, is an eagerness to abandon the old "give-it-a-go," "she'll-be-right" reliance on improvisation that used to be Australia's "lucky-country" style, and replace it with a "professionalism"—even if, as one might expect from a "lucky country," this "professionalism" is not only derived from overseas but also judged for its success by its degree of closeness to overseas models. This means there is a tendency for government, business, and union bureaucrats to speak in much the same language, or, if you prefer the expression, to use much the same "discourse." This can significantly modify the power of a "ruling" class (assuming, for the moment, that there is one), since a common discourse can mean a common way of structuring reality and this can have a special resilience of its own. To the extent that a "governing" class uses a style different from that of a "ruling" class, this is at least modifying the style of the "ruling" class (witness the continuing complaints about bureaucracies in both capitalist and communist countries, where they seem unnatural because they do not fit in with the prevailing legitimations of power); and if the contestants in social conflict use a common language, this will partly shape how the conflict will be defined. As it turns out, the language the Australian "new class" has learned appears, to a great extent, to be the postwar transnational boom language of high economic growth and a "fine tuning" in economic management (in which it was considered impossible that high inflation and high unemploymet could both occur at the same point on a graph). There may be a need for improvisation after all!

LOOKING FOR A RULING CLASS

It was this language that marked what became the famous National Economic Summit Conference, summoned by Prime Minister Robert Hawke in April 1983, in the afterglow of his election victory. Called to it were representatives of governments, business, and trade unions who, for the better part of a week, sat in the House of Representatives in the national Parliament in front of any citizens who cared to watch the live transmission on television, and enacted what Parliament would look like if Australia were, constitutionally, a corporate state. I will now examine this as a model of power in Australia.

As with the present Parliament, its very unrepresentativeness was significant. There was a disproportionate predominance of males of British origin, and a significant absence of the representatives of victims: the unemployed (more than one in ten of the work force at that stage, without counting hidden unemployment and under-employment); fatherless families (more than half of them below the poverty line); the single aged (half below the poverty line); the married aged (a third below the poverty line); the sick; the Aborigines. As a model of power, the absence of protest groups was a weakness, as was the absence of professional projectors of social reality. The symbolically significant place for the former, however, was *outside* Parliament house, protesting, and, for the latter up in the press gallery, projecting. In a society where priorities are overwhelmingly declared in terms of "the economic," what we had, in seeing representatives of government, business, and trade unions as the principal actors at "the summit," were the finalists in answering the question: "Who governs Australia?" The very fact that in their common rhetoric there was an almost complete absence of that basic rhetorical division over "free enterprise"—the convention in parliamentary debates—was an indication that we were now witnessing men of power speaking the private language of power, as distinguished from the public rhetoric of party politics: they were talking the bargaining realities of managed capitalism.

Let us now put on a playoff between the semifinalists to see if we can find a class of "rulers" in Australia. In using the word "rule," I am allowing for the distinction, already mentioned, between "ruling" and "governing," in which it is assumed that in a complex industrial state the "rulers" may not also be the executives: they can be thought of instead as those in whose interests the general structure of the society might seem to be primarily ordered and whose habits of thought and action dominate the public culture. There can be other beneficiaries from the prevailing habits of a society. Things are still ordered in Australia so that they best serve males or people of British origin or the employed, in general, and home-owners, in particular. In looking for a "ruling class," one is looking for a narrower group appropriating by what are seen as legitimate means a disproportionately large share of benefits and resources, and whose interests, in a showdown, are seen as decisive because they can be seen also as the public interest. "Prevailing" class rather than "ruling" class is perhaps a better usage: the former is composed of the kinds of groups who, when it matters, don't lose, and whose definitions of the situation make up the prevailing part of a society's common sense.

It seems to me there is little dispute about it: it is the business interests that prevail. It is business, not the government, that does most of the administering of Australian society. Governments are very largely dependent on businesses to keep things going; the state helps manage the economy so that businesses can make profits and continue to administer society. It is business, not the government, that makes the main decisions about the work force, about capital investment, and about what "choices" will be offered to consumers. Through the cumulative messages of advertising (greater than and different from the individual messages), they control the principal propaganda system. The production of most of the mass media is organized by business firms. It is mainly the decisions of businesses that decide the fate of both the physical and social environment. Business ways of thinking and acting tend to prevail in the public culture and throughout much of the society.

Despite their large memberships, unions have scarcely any fields of initiative, other than in reaction to business decisions. Unlike some liberal-democratic capitalist societies, "industrial democracy," allowing worker or at least union participation, does not exist, and moves towards it are very weak. Most economic decisions made by business firms are therefore not challenged by unions. Unions react not in fields of general economic policy but only in the narrow field of wages and working conditions (although the "Economic Accord" into which the unions entered with the Labor party and then the Hawke government showed a way for possible future developments of a more complex kind). That so many Australians should imagine that unions are the most powerful force in the country is itself a symptom of the weakness of the union movement, partly in the sense that the principal effects of strikes that most worry Australians (effects on consumers or the economy) are side-effects rather than declared primary objectives, and partly because while almost all types of business intervention are seen as normal, almost any type of union intervention is seen as deviant. Insofar as the unions have power, it is only in attempts to limit the actions of business managements and, sometimes, the state.

Both businesses and trade unions have what they can see as their "own" political parties, but in both cases this may be the lesser part of their influence on the state. This influence comes more directly, from the state's dependence on both of them, and businesses gain more from this dependence than unions. Since they are very largely "running the country," they can seem more essential to governments. Even with Labor governments, unions usually come into consultations only in the narrow range of industrial relations. The rest is settled before they are called in. Perhaps most significant of all, while business groups are usually in conflict with each other, if they see a threat to the institutions they consider most significant they can mobilize their resources against a government. So can trade unions if their existence seems threatened, but in some great political showdown, the powers of mobilization of business have, in the past, proved the more deployable, not least because the unions' ultimate weapon, a general strike, so unpredictably threatens the social order that most union leaders would not wish to risk using it. Business firms have powers of mobilization they can use; the unions have one great power of mobilization, but it is not one most of them would want to use.

From watching the conduct of Australians, one can put up a case for imagining the existence of a "ruling" (or, as I would prefer, "prevailing") class—a class of owners and of business controllers—whose habits of thought and action dominate the public culture and whose interests can seem to bear such a close relationship to a perceived public interest that it seems natural that the state should serve them and that in a crisis their interests should prevail. One can imagine such a class. Australians act as if there is one. There is only one difficulty: where is it?

The only people to look for it systematically are on the Left: some of them have found it, in a national bourgeoisie.[28] But is this a "ruling" class? On the whole, as I have already suggested, native Australian capitalism was feeble—and appropriately so. In the context of empire trade, that was what it was meant to be. Until the establishment of iron and steel making by the Broken Hill Proprietary (BHP) in 1916 (done partly with government assistance), the main areas of activity were in farming, mining, the retail and wholesale trades, and minor manufacturing (brewing, biscuit-making, etc): even the rich were not as rich as in most of the growing capitalist societies.[29] There was a ruling class, but it was the British ruling class. The native bourgeoisie were simply, in effect, their local agents (or, as the present pejorative phrase has it, their "compradors"). In both economic life and in their strategic imagination, Australian capitalists were part of the British Empire.[30] In the age of the "transnationals," they easily adjusted to defining their old modesty in a new way.

The weakness of Australian capitalism was illuminated by its failure to take command of the mining boom of the 1960s. The new potential for mining raised questions that went far beyond the intellectual capacity of a small-minded banking system and also went beyond the intellectual capacities of the few large Australian companies. As with manufacturing in the 1920s and 1950s, only government intervention might have saved the day. The conservative political parties were in power. One Country party leader and one Liberal party leader thought aloud for a while about more active Australian policies. Nothing happened. There was no political wisdom to draw on for this kind of intervention. The accepted wisdoms all seemed to point the other way. As a result, although in detail Australian economic life might seem more sophisticated, the economy is now even more dominated by overseas interests than it was with the British. Even native big businesses (the BHP and a few others) now work in partnership with foreign companies and become, in effect, their agents.

In answering the question "Who rules Australia?" it may be useful to imagine that, overall, despite a cultural awakening in intellectual life and the arts and despite the liberations of a declared policy of multiculturalism and despite a certain self-confidence in lifestyles and despite the development of new, if minority, approaches in strategic planning, Australia has remained colonial in its prevailing ideas about diplomacy, military planning, and, above all, economic policy. What can appear to be a "ruling class" is merely part of the "governing class." There is no Australian ruling class. There are ruling interests that seem naturally to prevail at some time of conflict. But these prevailing interests are not in Australia.

ENDNOTES

[1]Garfield Barwick, *Sir John Did His Duty* (Sydney: Serendip Publications, 1983), p. 115.

[2]Richard Hall, *The Secret State* (Sydney: Cassell, 1978), p. 123.

[3]Donald Horne, *Death of the Lucky Country* (Melbourne: Penguin, 1976).

[4]Colin Howard, *The Constitution, Power and Politics* (Melbourne: Fontana, 1980).

[5]See, for example, *The Weekend Australian Magazine,* December 24, 1983.

[6]See Keith Amos, *The New Guard Movement* (Melbourne: Melbourne University Press, 1976).

[7]Daniel O'Connell, "Monarchy or Republic," in Geoffrey Dutton, ed., *Republican Australia?* (London: Sun, 1977).

[8]For the difference between Liberal party rhetoric and practice, see Marian Simms, *A Liberal Nation* (Sydney: Hale & Iremonger, 1982).

[9]I have been influenced here by A.R. Myers, *Parliaments and Estates in Europe* (London: Thames and Hudson, 1975).

[10]Joseph A. Schumpeter, *Capitalism, Socialism and Democracy* (London: Allen and Unwin, 1950), pp. 250–273.

[11]John McMillan, Gareth Evans, and Haddon Storey, *Australia's Constitution: Time for Change?* (Sydney: Allen & Unwin, 1983), pp. 246–57.

[12]A subject not much discussed in Australian political science, although there is Brian Hocking, "Looking at Legislatures: Transformation or Decline?" *Politics* 13(2) (November 1978).

[13]James Jupp, *Party Politics: Australia, 1966–81* (Sydney: Allen & Unwin, 1982), pp. 161–64.

[14]For the relation betwen class awareness and party identification, see Don Aitkin, *Stability and Change in Australian Politics* (Canberra: Australian National University Press, 1982), pp. 118–142.

[15]Andrew Parkin and John Warhurst, *Machine Politics in the Australian Labor Party* (Sydney: Allen & Unwin, 1983).

[16]For example, Anthony McAdam, "Journalists and the New Class," *Quadrant* 26(11) (November, 1982).

[17]E.E. Schattschneider, *The Semisovereign People* (New York: Holt, Rinehart & Winston, 1960), p. 71.

[18]For an example, see Patricia Edgar, *The Politics of the Press* (Melbourne: Sun Books, 1979).

[19]The view of "reality" taken here is that of Peter L. Berger and Thomas Luckman, *The Social Construction of Reality* (New York: Doubleday, 1966).

[20]Bernard Cohen, cited in M.E. McCombs and D.L. Shaw, "The Agenda-Setting Function of Mass Media," *Public Opinion* 36(2) (Summer 1972).

[21]Along the lines discussed by T. Gitlin, "Prime Time Ideology: The Hegemonic Process in Television Entertainment," *Social Problems* 26(3) (1979).
[22]Elaine Thompson, "Democracy, Bureaucracy and Mythology," in Alexander Kouzmin, ed., *Public Sector Administration: New Perspectives* (Melbourne: Longmans Cheshire, 1983).
[23]Hall, *The Secret State*, pp. 13–14.
[24]Ibid., pp. 186–190.
[25]Greg Crough and Ted Wheelwright, *Australia: A Client State* (Melbourne: Penguin, 1982), p. 1.
[26]John Higley, Desley Deacon, and Don Smart, *Elites in Australia* (London: Routledge & Kegan Paul, 1979), pp. 74–104.
[27]Karl Kautsky, *The Social Revolution* (Chicago: Kerr, 1902), p. 13.
[28]Most notably, in R.W. Connell, *Ruling Class, Ruling Culture* (Cambridge: Cambridge University Press, 1977).
[29]W.D. Rubinstein, "Elites in Australian History," Robert Manne, ed., *The New Conservatism in Australia* (Melbourne: Oxford University Press, 1982).
[30]A view first expressed comprehensively in Brian Fitzpatrick, *The British Empire in Australia* (Melbourne: Melbourne University Press, 1941).

Hugh Stretton

The Quality of Leading Australians

MOST WRITING ABOUT ELITES or ruling or upper or managerial classes is about who their members are, how they get there or stay there, how much wealth or real power they have. This essay neglects those questions to ask only about the quality of performance. Whoever the leading Australians are, however they get there and whatever they do, how well or badly do they do it?

JUDGMENTS

If you ask how good leading Australians are at whatever they do, a common answer is this: Australia is an underpopulated, uncrowded country whose abundant natural resources make material living easy—perhaps too easy. There is a comparatively relaxed, friendly, uncompetitive culture. There nevertheless emerge respectable numbers of excellent painters, writers, musicians, scientists, scholars, doctors, lawyers, engineers, accountants and other professionals, and world champions at many sports and games. Only at two activities—business and government—do Australians seem to be incurably mediocre. Put simply, they do well wherever individual performance suffices. They do less well where, as in big business and government, the individual performances need complicated organization and direction. A national myth says that Australians are good at everything except leading and being led.

Right and left have variants of that theme. Some critics say that Australians have stupidly short-sighted, anti-intellectual, and self-destructive notions of equality. They idealize their uneducated, uninteresting selves as "the common man," they see little need for leadership, and they resist command or intelligent direction. They hate excellence and won't motivate or reward it. What they want is a leaderless one-class society, so boring conformity under third-rate leadership is what they get.

Others think that diagnosis mistakes the facts. Egalitarian Australians positively worship individual excellence. There is no shortage—indeed there is one of the world's better per-capita outputs—of Nobel prizes, Olympic golds, Covent Garden triumphs, best-selling books, brilliant political cartoons, pop-music fortunes. Ordinary Australians revere and richly reward them all. They spent more to build the spectacular Sydney Opera House than New York spent on Lincoln Center, and they pay La Stupenda more to sing in it than she earns at the Met. They pay their professors half as much again as the quality-loving British pay theirs. Millions of them have turned out to cheer the motorcades that carry the skipper and designer of *Australia II* through city after city. What, on the other hand, does not attract much respect or forelock pulling is eminence *without* excellence, i.e. ordinary personal wealth or high office. Leaders in business and government are not widely believed to have got there by merit. Inherited wealth, old-boy networks, bureaucratic time-serving, or political dexterity got them into position to exploit labor, order people about, or swan around the world at public expense. Cutting those mediocre careerists down to size (Australians think) has nothing whatever to do with undervaluing excellence.

Whatever the myths say, what do the scholars say?

First, it was not always so. Whatever the quality of business and government a hundred years ago, their achievements were not mediocre. Then, as far as economic historians led by Noel Butlin of the Australian National University can now tell, Australians ran level with Americans as the world's richest people. They did it by unusual means, helped by gold-mining, without much manufacturing, but with innovative, productive government. British and some local private investors developed a highly capitalized and profitable wool industry; that and some grain and mineral exports paid for the manufactured goods the colonies imported. Most of the colonists' own investment, public and private, did not go into business at all; it went to build their habitat. Public investment, much of it funded by borrowing in London, built roads, bridges, railways, water supplies, hospitals, schools and universities, some of the earliest secular welfare institutions, museums and libraries and art galleries, police stations and clock-towered post offices, domed and galleried law courts and elegant, extravagant town halls and Parliament houses. In 1872, Anthony Trollope found in Adelaide, only thirty-five years after its white settlement, "60,000 people in a new city with more than all the appliances of humanity belonging to four times the number in old cities." By 1890, Melbourne's taxable property values made it the third city (after London and Glasgow) under the British crown. Meanwhile, the people's private savings were organized by mushrooming credit institutions to finance capacious housing for them, more than half of it owner-occupied. In many of the years from 1860 to 1890 (Butlin discovered), new public investment exceeded new private investment. If houses built for owner-occupation are counted as non-profit investment, a surprising correlation appears: through the generation when Australians were comparatively richest, between two-thirds and three-quarters of all investment was non-capitalist, i.e., it was for use without profit.

During the century since, private capitalist investment has increased its share. With government aid and protection, it has made the country a substantial manufacturer. It has discovered oil and gas and rich mineral resources. It has at length achieved a normal mixed economy with the private capitalist sector as its biggest sector. And step by step through that "normalizing" process, the mediocrity has set in: the more capitalist Australia has become, the more manufacturing it has done, the more energy per head it has generated and the more copper and nickel and oil and gas and uranium its miners have discovered, the further Australia has slipped down the international league table of income per head, from equal, first a century ago, to a position below most of Western Europe and Japan now.

Hence the charge of mediocre leadership in business and government. The common grounds for it are these: for a developed, educated, and richly endowed country, Australia's economic growth has been slow. There have been too few home-grown entrepreneurs and too many of the few have been in property, corporate raiding, or other comparatively unproductive or antisocial trades. The tariff protection of industry has been done ineptly by government, often misused by business, and entrenched by organized labor. Between them, government and business have allowed unnecessary levels of foreign ownership, with various ill effects on national economic performance and potentiality. The following paragraphs spell out some of the charges of poor entrepreneurship, mismanaged protection, and undue foreign ownership.

In 1960, the proprietors of an old-established Adelaide optical firm used some of that firm's earnings to found a subsidiary called SOLA, a lens manufacturer. SOLA started with a thirty-two-year-old manager, nine employees, and the services of an ingenious engineer. It was soon one of the world's leaders in developing machinery for the mass production of fine lenses of plastic instead of glass. When they needed more land and factory space, state agencies financed and supplied them and were repaid from earnings. The technologists worked cleverly in Adelaide; the young manager traveled incessantly, first to develop his export markets and then to start manufacturing in many of them. The business came to employ 1,500 people with wholly owned subsidiaries manufacturing in the U.S., the U.K., Brazil, Singapore, Japan, Italy, and Ireland. Only two things distinguish the story from similar success stories in Sweden, Japan, and elsewhere. First, in Australia it is nearly unique—there are all too few technical or manufacturing successes to match it. Second, its owners came to fear their American competitors, especially for their greater financial strength: they could give SOLA a rough time through any long recession or price war. So instead of looking for better Australian backing, the owners sold SOLA to a British-based multinational. Neither business nor government would have let that happen in Sweden or Japan.

For their book *Elites in Australia* (Routledge & Kegan Paul, 1976), John Higley and his associates studied a sample of board chairmen and chief executives of the fifty-four largest corporations in Australia. Of their eighty-one business leaders, they classed only four as entrepreneurs. Six were foreigners managing foreign-owned corporations. Seven had moved to private enterprise after long careers in the Australian public service. Twenty-one had inherited family businesses. Forty-three had reached the top in a bureaucratic way after a long climb—average twenty-nine years—up the managerial ladder. Industrial managers had more education but earned less money than others. All the stockbrokers had degrees, none of the bankers did. Wider studies that included small as well as big firms have shown a higher proportion—about a third—of chiefs who got there by inheritance. At least they get there younger that way. The general impression of Higley's study was of an elderly, under-educated or narrowly educated business elite of a predominantly cautious, bureaucratic kind.

In November 1983, the magazine *Business Review Weekly* published a list of the hundred richest Australians with personal fortunes above $15 million. It shows what such lists tend to show in other English-speaking countries: luck, inheritance, and predatory activities figure largely, wholesome productivity rather less, in the making of multimillionaires. Nearly half those on the Australian list made their fortunes from property, some honestly and some corruptly, many by developing shopping centers of the modern, drive-in, lock-up, single-purpose kind that have wrecked the possibility of much lively and accessible town-center life in suburban Australia. Then there are two or three corporate raiders, and half a dozen each of share gamblers, and heirs or heiresses who let others look after their portfolios. Among the more productive people on the list are twenty clothiers and other retailers, fifteen manufacturers (not all of whom manage the firms they inherited), eight in building and construction, seven pastoralists and meat processors, and four or five each with fortunes from international trading, entertainment, and horseracing. Very few have invented anything or done much technical research and development; scarcely any have made any significant use of Australian science. The brainiest one who showed the greatest technical ingenuity got rich by inventing a computerized betting system.

Among the very richest, said to have more than $100 million each, are the three families who own most of Australia's daily and weekly papers and its highest-paying commercial TV broadcasters. Governments fear them and do them favors: TV licenses, a protected national airline, a state lottery monopoly. Many of the forty property fortunes should also count in greater or lesser degree as positive or negligent gifts from government—in Australia as elsewhere, millions have been made from the zoning and re-zoning and the escalating prices of urban land. The public has not got the share of those gains it could have got; alternatively (except in one or two small states) land and housing prices have not been restrained as they could have been. Similar failures of government have attended much of the nation's mineral exploration and development. The fast-growing postwar population of course needed minerals, radio and television stations, new shops and offices, and land development. But mediocre government has allowed a lot of private capital and tasteless talent to develop worse broadcasting, duller town life, and a poorer habitat at higher prices, than good public and private leadership might have achieved.

Why such poor performance?

Australian business men, supported by rising numbers of academic and public service economists, commonly blame the nation's indifferent economic performance on the behavior of Australian labor and its union leadership, especially on the wage levels that labor achieves, and its resistance to wage lowering. I believe the complaint is so absurd that it should count as further evidence of widespread stupidity among Australian owners and managers. There are enough individual examples of good management (including SOLA, and another noted below) to show that, given good management, the labor is as cooperative and productive as any in the world. Most of the overseas firms with whom Australian firms cannot compete (American, Dutch, German, Swedish, Japanese) pay their workers more and consult and listen to them more than do the Australian firms that blame their failures on "insubordinate" labor and "excessive" wages. All of the dozen or more countries that have overtaken Australian output per head through recent decades have done it (it goes without saying: perhaps that is why Australian leaders never say it!) with faster-rising real wages than Australians were paying. Many were also paying wage shares similar to those Australians were paying. More convincing explanations of the slower rate of Australian growth can be found in the record of unadventurous investment, indifferent management including a lot of quite bad "human management," and the misuses of protection and foreign ownership (to be discussed later). Meanwhile, two examples can illustrate the extremes of good, bad, and indifferent Australian management of labor: the great steel stoppage of 1945, and the productivity of labor at some Adelaide car plants before and after they passed from American to Japanese management in 1980.

The steel stoppage: Throughout much of this century, the symbolic target of anti-capitalist attack in Australia has been its biggest corporation and only steel-maker, the BHP Company. A few weeks after the Second World War ended, steel-making was stopped for fifteen weeks by what one side called a strike and the other side called a lockout. In that dispute, conservatives saw a communist plot to weaken Australian capitalism. Workers, on the other hand, believed, then and for a generation afterwards, that a Machiavellian management deliberately provoked a stoppage to reestablish its old pre-war whip hand over its labor, and probably also to save paying wages while it closed down and overhauled its furnaces. Thirty-five years later, the company, now managed in a different style, opened its archives to an economic historian who could not possibly be suspected of bias in its favor: Dr. Tom Sheridan was a working-class radical from industrial Lancashire who had already published a critical but sympathetic history of the militant Amalgamated Engineering Union. Sheridan entered the BHP archive with the "capitalist plot" as his working hypothesis. He emerged to conclude that

> the picture that BHP records reveal of the company's actions through the fifteen-week steel dispute in 1945 is not the popular one of calculated implementation of a strategy derived from careful weighing of all relevant factors in a cold, materialist balance. Instead the company is seen as much reacting to events as initiating them. Its managers did share certain attitudes and premises, but these proved something of a straitjacket which tended to constrain policy, often at considerable cost to the company, rather than to coordinate it. "Rational" maximization of profit, at least in the short run, hardly seemed to be the company's guiding light . . . Just as the records of the main steel union and its allies do not support the conservative accusation that the 1945 dispute was an infernal communist plot, so now the BHP records reveal no evidence of the premeditated, single-minded capitalist plot widely suspected by the contemporary left . . . Both sides had some coherent philosophy, but a good deal of incoherence and accident in action. (*Australian Economic History Review* XXII, 1, March 1982, p. 2)

Chrysler-Mitsubishi: The Adelaide plants where Chrysler did all its Australasian manufacturing began making a Japanese-designed car in the 1970s and were taken over by Mitsubishi in 1980. Mitsubishi has not been the most successful of Japanese car-makers. From time to time, they have misjudged their Australian models and markets and lost money on their Australian operation. But they have nevertheless revolutionized the productivity of their Australian workers. It has been done without much additional investment or automation, chiefly by reorganizing the existing resources, re-educating the Australian management and transforming its relations with the workforce. Within two years of the take over, the man-hours to build a car had been reduced from sixty to twenty, product quality was much better, absenteeism was down by a third, workers' compensation payments were halved, and there were no major strikes in what had previously been strike-ridden plants.

The achievement was an implicit reproach to the preceding American-Australian management. In May 1982, in a speech entitled "How management attitudes toward labor and technology differ between Australia and Japan and what we should learn from each other," Graham Spurling, the (Australian) chief executive of Mitsubishi Australia, made the reproach explicit:

I am firmly convinced that the Japanese worker is in himself no more subservient or dedicated than his Australian counterpart, but is better led, better managed. He has experienced better quality management, he expects it and he respects it. Better management gives him better motivation and better training from which comes better productivity and better product quality.

On the other hand the Australian manager, while professing loudly the egalitarian principles of Eureka, is not sufficiently confident in his own leadership ability to gain the respect of his employees without resorting to a dictatorial and adversative approach—a sign of lack of security.

The Japanese manager, however, who is quietly confident and well trained over a much longer period than we Aussie "hotshots," is willing to listen, to consult, to be patient, and to be firm when the time is right to be firm . . .

My philosopher friend Arai (director in charge of manufacturing for Mitsubishi in Japan) had a reputation in Japan for being tough on management and easy on the worker. Here in Australia generally we are the opposite. It's easy to blame the worker and it's uncomfortable to sit down and analyze the situation and accept that we, management, just might be wrong. We become so concerned with the need to motivate our managers, to keep them performing, to ensure they don't drop their bundle, that we let them cry on our shoulder and get away with saying "It's that production worker who screwed it up, or the union, or the vendor company . . . my design was alright, my tooling was OK . . . it's those idiots on the line." . . . Australians accept a one-line reason for lack of success and generally the dumb worker is part of that one line. The Japanese manager asks why, why, why, why . . . I will be accused of being scathing about Australian management—and I am, intentionally.

... I would like to say just a few words on the technology question.

I am not a great advocate of high technology investment as the path to productivity and profitability, and ... neither are the Japanese. Their philosophy is to get everyone—management and labour—working together to maximize utilisation of existing plant, and so conserving capital ... Only when every other avenue has been explored do they look to new capital facilities for the answer to greater productivity. This comes only when they have exhausted all other means of improvement—better organisation and planning, better use of people, all the time tempered with mutual respect and understanding between manager and worker.

We in Australia are all too ready to look to capital investment as the panacea to our problems. The Australian manager is too prone to saying that technology is the answer to higher productivity. He believes he should acquire a multi-spindle lathe when perhaps five single-spindle lathes will do a better job. He is inclined to believe in size for the sake of size. The defect in this line of thinking is that the result may just be to superimpose high investment on top of an inefficient structure, and when this happens the whole edifice may fall unless it is propped up with government protection, as the car industry has been for so many years.

Thus Spurling hammers his themes: left to itself, Australian management has often been expert in purely technical matters, but at management itself—at getting things done by other people—it has been lamentably uneducated, ill-trained, simple-minded, impatient, bullying, and unproductive. Especially, unproductive. The effects of its shortcomings are not minor or marginal. The magnitude of the Mitsubishi transformation suggests that the difference between normal Australian management and educated, intelligent management is more than enough to account for the whole difference between Australian and Japanese rates of economic growth, or Australian and Swedish income per head. (It should interest Japanese as well as Australians to see what Japanese management has achieved with Australian workers who have none of the oppressive conformist culture that critics see as a condition of Japanese performance at home.)

The passage from Spurling's speech concluded by drawing attention to the next general accusation against Australian business and government—that together they misconceive and misuse policies of economic protection.

Whatever economists say, protected industries are not usually slack or technically backward or uncompetitive. America's eighty or ninety years of outstanding industrial leadership were highly protected. Her farmers are still the most securely protected and the most efficient in the world. Germany, Scandinavia, Japan, and other late industrializers have protected very efficient and technically advanced manufacturing development. By contrast, Australia's mediocre industrial performance is unusual in conforming to the economists' expectations. Some of the reasons seem to lie in the choice and administration of the particular protective policies. Governments have often been uncertain about the effects of employment and productivity they wanted to foster, and have too readily seen the two as mutually exclusive.

A favorite target of criticism, as of Spurling's criticism quoted above, is the automobile industry. By one standard, that industry is a great Australian success: Australia makes a higher proportion of its cars than any other small country does. But the cars are dearer than imports would be. Too many manufacturers make too many models for such a small market—two American and three Japanese makers currently compete for less than half a million sales a year. Partly because of its uneconomic scale, the industry used to suffer from "protected under-investment"—by the 1970s, it was described as a museum of 1950s technology. Most of the makers are now modernizing and shedding labor as fast as they dare. As fast as they do, unemployment and the government's dole bill and budget deficit increase. That was predictable, but except for wringing their hands and slowing the process wherever they could, governments have thought of nothing effective to do about it, or about its social costs and consequences.

The last half century of protection gets more abuse than perhaps it deserves—I don't believe the country would have been better without it, free-trading in a protectionist world. But the protection could certainly have been better designed and managed. The countries that did it better—for example, France, Sweden, the Netherlands, and Japan, all of whose protected postwar industrialization has enabled them to overtake and surpass Australia's income per head—all arrived at protective policies that were elements of coherent long-term national strategies, and that did not discourage efficient performance. Australia has had no long-term national planning to speak of. Manufacturers, importers, farmers, miners, labor unions, and state governments with rival regional concerns all lobby a national government whose politicians—mostly reluctant, pragmatic, untheoretical protectionists—are advised by public-service departments and agencies with diverse and contradictory protectionist and free-trading beliefs. Tariffs and quotas and bounties issue from that melée as victories or defeats for this or that faction, not as the skillful implementation of a general plan for national economic structure. Least of all has there been any coherent strategy for the technical revolution that is now decimating employment in manufacturing and many services.

My own opinion—with which many Australian economists will disagree—is that industrial protection has been a good principle badly practiced. It was not wrong to diversify Australians' working skills and opportunities. It was not wrong in a materially comfortable society to put full employment ahead of faster growth. The way the world is going it may not be wrong to aim at more industrial diversity and self-reliance, rather than more specialization and import/export dependence. But indifferent public policy-making and private management have not served those good intentions as well as abler leaders might have. To attract five multinationals to a market uncomfortably small for one or two, then to vary their protective aids often and unnervingly, has not been a very intelligent way to stimulate car manufacturing in Australia. And other industries have similar histories of well-intended but imperfectly managed nurture.

Poor leadership is also blamed for the amount of Australian industry that is foreign owned. The economy has always depended on some capital inflow, but the relations between capital inflow and foreign ownership have varied. Back in the days when they were as rich as Americans, Australians used to borrow abroad to invest at home. The debts were eventually repaid, and the assets and any revenues were home-owned. One way to fall behind the Americans was to reverse that pattern, and throughout the twentieth century governments have encouraged the reversal. Increasingly, foreigners borrow in Australia the funds with which they acquire Australian assets and exportable revenues. The reasons for inviting foreign control have changed over the years. Between the wars, governments eager to encourage manufacturing did not try as hard as they might have done to encourage import substitution or export by native

Australian firms. Instead, measures were designed to induce the traditional British and American exporters to "come in under the tariff" and make or assemble their products in Australia. They came, and others like them have continued to come. They repatriate profits, in volumes that contribute increasingly to an adverse balance of payments, which it has become routine to offset by attracting more capital inflow, whose profit flows worsen the adverse balance, which has to be offset by heavier capital import, which can only be achieved by relaxing the rules about foreign ownership even further—and so on.

Moreover, that unintelligent policy has sometimes been incompetently applied. Its aim is to attract foreign capital, but its effect has sometimes been to trade ownership and control for little or no capital. Carpet-baggers with very little share capital (but all the shares) find that they can borrow most of their initial capital in Australia, hire Australian management and skills, get helpful tariffs or quotas or mineral rights from the national government, and factory sites and services and cheap power and transport and local tax exemptions from state governments, exploit the tariffs to price their products high enough to self-finance their further growth—and repatriate their profits freely. In the boom conditions of the early 1970s, the authoritative Fitzgerald report on Australian mining administration concluded—broadly speaking, with some hedges and exceptions—that Australian taxpayers were paying the mining companies about fifty dollars a ton to dig up and export the nation's treasure. Since General Motors was given some surplus government factories in 1944, they have repatriated more than a quarter of a billion dollars without investing one American dollar in Australia. If—so to speak—the GM directors had been in the business of governing Australia instead of making cars, they would have got the country a better deal than that. So would—and did—the French, Dutch, Swedish, Japanese, and other governments that have combined faster growth with tougher regulation of foreign enterprise.

Britain, Norway, and Australia discovered oil at about the same time. For transparent reasons the oil companies assured the three governments that the private multinationals alone had the expertise to prospect, extract, or market the stuff: public enterprises could not hope to acquire the skills or know-how. Only the Australian government fell for it. The Norwegian Oil Corporation now recovers most of the benefit, and the British National Oil Corporation much of it, for their citizens. Australians get sparse royalties and see substantial profits expatriated, and have developed no public capacity to prospect new fields. Through the British government's share of British Petroleum, British taxpayers own more Australian oil than Australians do.

A shorter, less anecdotal, more objective way to contrast Australians' excellence in arts and sciences with their mediocrity in business and government is this:

Australians make up 0.3 percent of the world's population
write 2.0 percent of the world's scientific papers
win 1.3 percent of the postwar Nobel prizes
make 0.7 percent of the world's patent applications
develop 0.2 percent of patents to production
produce 0.1 percent of the world's high-technology output

Australian science finds its practical application in Australian agriculture, but in British, American, or Japanese industry. The academic output is ahead of the OECD average, the Australian industrial uses of it are far behind. Two ironies attend that contrast.

First, many Australian business owners and managers are very ignorant and anti-intellectual, uneducated in anything except perhaps accounting. What stops them from understanding their scientific opportunities also stops them from knowing the above figures or understanding their implications. Many firmly believe and never tire of declaring that businessmen are Australia's dynamic and productive element while academics—at best cultural ornaments and at worst drones and parasites—are a luxury the country can ill afford. Accordingly, the conservative businessmen's government of 1975–83 began to reduce the universities' resources year by year, while in the name of supply-side economics increasing various business subsidies and tax exemptions. Australian business absorbed the aids and exemptions, and year by year continued to reduce its already small expenditure on research and development. Thus, the OECD country with the most extreme disparity between its academic and business performance is the least able to understand the facts or costs of that disparity, or to apply corrective policies.

To sum up, for and against: Australian business and government have not generally been corrupt, tyrannical, or seriously incompetent, but for most of this century they have been unenterprising, missing many opportunities. I risk two simplifications. First, the good qualities of Australian life have perhaps owed more to everyman and less to leaders than is common elsewhere. Second, a selective eye can see three phases in the history of broad class leadership, and they make a rake's progress from better to worse. Until 1914, the people were among the richest in the world while the leading class was less rich, less distant from the rest, and more progressive and innovative than most of its equivalents elsewhere. Then for sixty years it was more conservative, and its performance mediocre. Since 1975, there has been a third phase as some of the prevailing ideas and values of the leading class seem to have lurched to the Right to become actively reactionary, reversing long-standing trends towards greater humanity and equality.

When Australians stopped borrowing abroad to invest at home, it was not only money that they stopped borrowing. Through the nineteenth century, they had also been borrowing policies. English and American radical ideas, blocked by conservative resistance at home, used to get their first implementation in colonies that an English visitor likened to "Britain without the upper class." Australia and New Zealand were early with manhood suffrage and women's suffrage and first with old age pensions, fully lawful labor unions, industrial conciliation and arbitration, a legal minimum wage, and the range of state industries and services that a French visitor called "socialisme sans doctrines." The quick acceptance of Keynes's general theory was a late and by then unusual example. Already, in the 1920s—with some local state exceptions—more conservative styles of social and political leadership had set in.

Nevertheless, some reformist habits and values survived and kept the country roughly in step with the progress of welfare elsewhere, if not with economic growth elsewhere. The conservative governments of 1949–72 compromised willingly enough with a number of progressive forces and institutions. There was old-established machinery for industrial arbitration and wage-fixing. Governments of whatever color had to concede a good deal to a labor movement still strong in industry and in parliamentary opposition. The public services had some young, educated, and progressive leaders who had been appointed to the public service by wartime Labor governments and survived as useful servants and advisers of conservative governments keen to "hold the center" by a moderately progressive performance.

That combination of forces, though not very inventive, did achieve a good deal. They maintained industrial protection, very full employment, and very cheap money. They kept taxation comparatively low but they kept most of it direct and progressive, with capital taxes on gifts and bequests. They modernized Australian higher education and research. Their housing and financial policies extended home ownership dramatically from about 50 to above 70 percent of households—by 1970, 80 percent of Australian pensioners owned their houses. It was dull government, and many Australians stayed poor under it. But between them the labor movement, the welfare professions, the public service leaders, and the politicians did manage to deliver some substantial social goods, however poor the record of economic growth.

With the recession of the 1970s, many of those benign trends were stopped or reversed. Conservative government after 1975 became actively reactionary, and the reaction—Australia's "revolt of the rich"—has also characterized much of the leadership of business, the professions, and the public service. Since 1975, wealth and income have been redistributed upwards. Capital taxes have gone, other taxation is less progressive, more of the affluent avoid or evade it. Fewer Australians own their houses. Many more are unemployed.

The question for the rest of this paper is: why? Why did the old social laboratory stop importing and implementing radical ideas? What dulled and conservatized the country's leadership through the middle half of the twentieth century? Why has so much of its political, professional, and intellectual leadership lurched to the Right in the last decade?

EXPLANATIONS

It is of course absurd to characterize a century of complicated national history in a few pages, or to explain it as a product of half a dozen causes. With due apology for the absurdity, what follow are nevertheless half a dozen strands of explanation. First are two conventional ones. Next are three that I have distilled from the unguarded conversation or unpublished papers of some able historians, themes that they themselves have thought hazy or hard to prove, but which I here simplify and print as their more scrupulous authors might not. Last is a more general complaint about Australian leadership in the last ten years. In order, these themes ascribe some share in the dulling of Australian government to (1) conflict, (2) consensus, (3) women, (4) the native born, (5) war, and (6) the changing morality of the middle class.

Conflict

The federation that unified Australia in 1901 was achieved chiefly by progressives and was followed by some progressive policy-making in the creation of the new national institutions. But as the price of their consent to federation, conservatives had built some conservative devices into the new constitution. It created a time-lagged Senate, doubling the likelihood that innovative government would be frustrated by a hostile upper house. It divided powers between the Commonwealth and the states in ways that extinguished some powers and made others unusable for any radical purposes. It created a High Court that has often used its constitutional powers to frustrate elected governments. And it entrenched private property rights even more securely than before against democratic interference. Together, those measures changed the conditions of political conflict. Perennial conservative interests that had lost some battles throughout the decades of colonial radicalism have lost fewer battles since. Some of their legal and institutional defenses—for example, against the nationalization of existing industries—are so impregnable that radicals have given up trying.

Consensus

Perhaps conservatives and radicals have each got enough of what they wanted. Conservatives have a securely capitalist country in which the rich do very well. The intellectuals are doing well in the mushrooming academic and public services of the "information society." The workers have strong union organization, effective industrial arbitration and wage-fixing, a short work week, cars and homes and gardens and power mowers and barbecues, all the booze and gambling they can use, and a thousand miles of sunbaked beaches: bread and circuses. As with self-service, so with social conscience: as the welfare services have been extended and improved, there has been a corresponding increase in the proportion of the population—now, for the first time, a majority—who think the welfare provisions are at last sufficient, and need no further extension. So perhaps government has been dulled by success. The interesting, innovative work of developing the institutions of civilized society has given way, for the very best of reasons, to the boring care and maintenance of perfected machinery.

Women

We used to boast of the colonial radicals' achievements: manhood suffrage, religious equality, land reform, legalization of labor unions, industrial conciliation and arbitration, old age pensions, votes for women . . . until Dr. Barry Smith of the Australian National University uncovered a reason—perhaps—why the first and last items on that list did so decisively begin and end it. Smith searched the market research and opinion polls since they began in 1940 to find out how men and women voted. From the 1940s to the 1960s, the evidence is patchy and imperfect, but what there is of it suggests quite strongly that during those years the differences between men's and women's voting were greater in Australia than have ever been recorded elsewhere. Wherever political parties divide on Left/Right lines, it has been common to find two or three or five percent more men than women voting Left. Smith found indications that on some occasions as many as two-thirds of Australian men may have voted Labor and been outvoted by two-thirds of Australian women voting for the conservative coalition. There were still substantial differences when the differences began to be polled reliably in the 1960s. They soon afterwards diminished, some women becoming more radical and some men more conservative; the first symmetrical result was recorded in a state election in 1977.

The recent changes have come as more women got more education, more women entered the work force, the women's movement gained strength, and the Labor party tried hard for the first time to attract women's votes. But can those trends be run backwards to indicate how women voted earlier in the century? Some of the men who first gave women the vote expected them to be conservative, and enfranchised them for that reason. Women's leaders at the time, who tended to be less militant than their sisters in Britain and America, did often link the suffrage to the defense of moral and domestic values, especially against alcohol and "impurity." Writing about the state that enfranchised them first, a journalist reported eleven years later:

> the State has got into a condition in which it seems to think that nothing matters much so long as its Parliament is "respectable." Probably the arrival of the woman voter . . . has had most to do with this. The "nice man" who can cut a satisfactory figure at tea meetings and the like is swallowed wholesale, on the ground that "he wouldn't do anything wrong". Whether he will do anything right doesn't count. The consequence is a generation of political neuters . . . So we have the sorry spectacle of a State drifting along without ideals, and turning listlessly from the few men who are struggling to rouse it . . . (The Sydney *Bulletin*, May 4, 1905)

It seems likely—but still unprovable—that women's votes did help to conservatize Australian government for half a century or so.

Migrants and Native Sons

The early white settlers were all migrants governed by British governors. The change to a democratic, self-governing, predominantly native-born community came in the third quarter of the century: self-government in the 1850s, a majority of native-born about 1865. The following decades were the high time of inventive government and "socialisme sans doctrines." They also saw the growth of an assertive nationalism, radical and white-racist and anti-British, whose writers associated the radical achievements with the native-born majority. They depicted Britain as the source of conservatism, authoritarianism, imperial and class rule; colonial radicalism and democracy were home-grown Australian achievements. The native sons' successors have kept that spirit alive in nationalist and veterans' organizations, and done their best to block further immigration, or at least to keep it white, and keep immigrants from acquiring office or influence in politics, public service, or the professions.

Already in 1867, C.H. Pearson, an immigrant Oxford don who became a notable educational reformer, said those native sons were mistaken. Immigrants were the innovators. The native-born were already showing signs of "the conservative apathy of men partially shut out from the world, and coming to believe that the trodden way is the best." The trouble was, he said on another occasion, that "Liberalism has not been burned into them as it was into their fathers, by memories of class rule and of intolerable wrong in the old country." They are not reactionary, just satisfied and apathetic. "Democracy has given them what they want, and they feel grateful for it, and would resent any open attack upon it, but are not disposed to carry it out in new directions, to supplement a Land Act by a progressive land tax, or to add high schools to primary schools. The children of these men are, it is likely, even more apathetic." (*Fortnightly Review,* May 1879).

Those quotations are drawn from an unpublished paper that Pearson's biographer, Dr. John Tregenza of the University of Adelaide, read to the 1969 congress of the Australia and New Zealand Association for the Advancement of Science. His argument had three parts. First he analyzed the population records to show that for anyone interested in the provenance and quality of Australian leadership, the interesting date is not 1865 when the native born first outnumbered the immigrants; it is the date more than forty years later when the native born first outnumbered the immigrants among males aged forty to sixty-four, the group from which most leaders come. The first census to show that was 1911.

Second, Tregenza showed simply by listing them how many—how overwhelmingly many—of the colonial radical leaders, the founders of federation and the architects of the national institutions developed in the first decades of federation were immigrants. The Labor party, more successful than any party of its kind in the world at that time, governing or sharing power through thirteen of the first seventeen years of the Commonwealth (1901–1917), was led throughout by immigrants, including three prime ministers.

Third, Tregenza used a number of case studies to show what sort of things in their northern upbringing and experience had given those leaders such mixtures of broad vision and radical will. From the gold rushes on, from 1850 to 1890, Australia seems to have imported "on the hoof" plenty of youthful energy and talent, political discontent, egalitarian spirit, a surprising breadth and depth of education, and a wide acquaintance with British and American radical writing.

There was nothing surprising in the leadership the country got from such immigrants as long as they were there to lead it. What is puzzling is the blight that they allowed to descend on the upbringing of their native-born successors. Twenty-five years after immigrants had founded the University of Melbourne, it appointed its first homegrown professor in 1879. He had been a school inspector. He published nothing, and repeated the same lectures, for the next thirty-three years. He was the first of many: though there were individual exceptions, it was not until the 1950s that the Australian universities were reformed—chiefly by more immigrants or natives educated abroad—and again expected their professors to do original work. One exception during the lean years was the immigrant R.F. Irvine, an original and productive professor of economics. The University of Sydney sacked him, chiefly for beliefs that in many respects anticipated Keynes's. As at university, so at school: the well-built primary schools of the 1870s came into under-educated, unimaginative hands. As late as 1968, one state department of education responsible for primary and secondary schools and teacher-training for a population above three million had not one graduate in arts or science (and less than forty graduates in anything) among the seven hundred staff of its head office.

Tregenza's paper ended with the native sons' final inheritance of power after the First World War, as a lagged effect of the cessation of immigration in 1890. Having got power, they clung to it. All historians of the inter-war years agree that they were sterile years, miserably short of new ideas or initiatives. "How apt," Tregenza concluded, "that the [conservative] Prime Minister through most of the 1930s, Joe Lyons, was a native son of the most native state, Tasmania, which had taken in scarcely any immigrants since the convicts stopped coming in the 1850s."

Better things were in sight. A single shipload of European refugees who were allowed to land in 1940, against a good deal of anti-Semitic and anti-subversive opposition, have been like yeast to the native dough ever since. The oppressive sense of distance and isolation, and some of the philistine restriction of tastes, ended with the postwar revolutions in air transport and electronic communications, the modernization of the universities, the opening of the Commonwealth and then many state public services to graduate entry, and the new flood of British, European, and eventually Asian immigration. Since 1945, the life and culture have been transformed, almost all for the better.

But Tregenza did not spell out the deadliest implication of his paper. The time lags continued. Once in control of the political parties and government departments, the native-born kept hold of them: postwar immigrants got nothing like their pro-rata share of political or administrative power. Into the 1960s, the leaders of the national political parties were still trying to win votes by keeping the masses scared of the Chinese—the prime minister because the Chinese were now red, the Leader of the Opposition because they were still yellow. Until 1967, the Australian Labor party was led by a man born in the nineteenth century who remained to the end a racist "White Australian." The half-century of isolation from 1890 to 1940 cast a long shadow forward over the following decades.

Many of those born before the turn of the century were also, by the time they inherited power, products of Passchendaele and the Somme.

War

I owe what follows partly to my childhood memories but rather more to the published and unpublished work of Professor Kenneth Inglis of the Australian National University who as a young historian accompanied the Australian survivors of Gallipoli as they revisited their 1915 battlefields in 1965.

Australia had no military conscription for service abroad, and sent an army entirely of volunteers to fight in World War One. A high proportion of eligible men enlisted: nearly a tenth of the population, about half the men of military age, many more than half of those who were medically acceptable. Without much industry to equip them with heavy weapons or vehicles, most of them served as infantry or cavalry. They were effective soldiers and were given much fighting to do, in 1915 at the Dardanelles, then for two-and-a-half years in France. Only a third of them survived physically unscathed—of every hundred who reached the front, nineteen were killed and forty-six wounded. Australia had less than a twentieth of the United States population, but more Australians than Americans were killed in that war. The men who returned from it were half or more of their generation, and gave that generation its character.

They were celebrated at home as fine soldiers, tough and aggressive and independent—fair claims, though patriots often exaggerated their quantitative contribution to the Allied victory. They themselves more often told attractive tales of Australian soldiers behind the lines or off-duty, rioting around Egyptian and French towns, stealing ingeniously, upsetting stuffy British officers. But most of them said next to nothing about trench life and fighting. They had survived one of humanity's worst experiences of war—long, miserable, bloody, fear-gripping years of it. They were proud but even more, perhaps, desperately relieved to have borne it without visible cowardice or disgrace. Scarcely any of them ever talked about battle, about the fear and killing and dying, about handling the wounded and dying and the dead. They came home variously shocked, drained, exhausted, relieved, glad that it was over.

Some individuals were undiminished by the experience and went on to excel at other things. There was an urbane prime minister, a great headmaster, a good writer or two. A very few came home loving war and enlisted again eagerly in 1939. A few returned as rebels—there were returned soldiers in the Australian Communist party. But most of the survivors seem to have wanted safe and regular lives, among people as like as possible to themselves, rather than new challenges or any great enrichment of their culture or improvement of their institutions. They built many, many war memorials, all to the dead, some to the survivors, none (that I ever saw) to the victory. Twice a year on Anzac day and Armistice day, they held mournful, reverent memorial services at which they remembered the dead, then some of them would get drunk with old mates. If they remembered victories at all, I suspect it was private victories over fear rather than public victories over the Germans. As a child, I knew many returned soldiers, attended many services, heard many funny or boastful stories about life behind the lines or on leave—but never a hint of any "joy of battle," or anything at all that I could connect with the gung-ho derring-do described in all the books about Deeds that Won The Empire.

At home, some class war continued. Some returned soldiers hated the government or the unions, others looked to one or both to deliver the rights and preferential treatment they had been promised. But most conflict and consensus alike were concerned with veterans' rights or with class or individual shares of the cake, rather than with progress to any different or better society. Whichever political party they voted for, and however quietly generous and self-sacrificing and hard-working a great many of them were in their private lives, those survivors (always with a few blessed exceptions) conservatized Australia in profound, more-than-political ways. They emptied it of idealism and invention and, worse, of much regard for idealism or invention. They did not, of course, renounce idealism. As the prime minister's words quoted below will suggest, they gave it a new conservative meaning. Their ideal was now to preserve what they already were, and already had: the natives sons' ideal that C.H. Pearson had foretold, and feared, fifty years before.

Manning Clark, who writes elsewhere in this issue about heroes, wrote in his *Short History of Australia* (Mentor Books, 1963 and successive revisions since) about the nation's return to life after heroism:

> When Hughes [who had entered the war as a leading radical and changed sides to become conservative prime minister] spoke in the House of Representatives on 10 September, 1919, he told the members:
>
> We went into this conflict for our own national safety, in order to insure our national integrity, which was in dire peril, to safeguard our liberties, and those free institutions of government which, whatever may be our political opinions, are essential to our national life, and to maintain those ideals which we have nailed to the very topmost of our flagpoles—White Australia, and those other aspirations of this young democracy.
>
> He went on to pose the question, "Now, what have we got?" To which he supplied simply, national safety, White Australia, and freedom from communism. "Australia," said Hughes "is safe." The age of the survivors had begun.

One thing the survivors did was to bring up and educate, as far as they could in those values, the native sons who would inherit the national leadership through the third quarter of the century.

The New Greed

However dull the conservative leadership was, it did at least trundle the country along the middle of the ideological road. By 1970, Australia had reasonable welfare arrangements, high home ownership, very full employment and one of the flatter distributions of income in the Western world. What stopped that progress? Why have so many political, professional, and intellectual leaders turned on those standard achievements since 1975, spoken as if to dismantle many of them, and acted to stop or reverse the trend to greater equality? Does this recent "revolt of the rich" indicate a significant change in the quality of the society's leadership?

For a decade or so now, many of the rich of the Western world have been attacking its poor, increasing its inequalities, and denigrating its more compassionate ideas and institutions with renewed vigor and self-righteousness. In the lurch to the Right, the tax revolt, the use of deliberate unemployment as a macroeconomic device, the voguish cult of self and selfishness, and other manifestations of the New Greed, plenty of Australians have joined with a will. It was not surprising that the traditional "rapacious rich" should do so. What is frightening for the future is that they seem at times to be getting a popular majority for it.

In 1985, the Labor party is back in office and the lurch to the Right is supposed to be over. But the new government is not so far doing much to reduce inequalities, even to restore the levels of ten years ago; and many of its members avoid most of the rhetoric as well as most of the traditional policies of equality. They seem to have been scared into believing that to survive they must go to new and unusual lengths to propitiate the rich. The Labor leadership has always been predominantly moderate, middle-of-the-road, unsocialist, respectful of capitalist property, faithful to the American alliance of which it was the original negotiator. But it could once speak well of public enterprise, and harshly of "excessive wealth." It could and did collect gift and succession taxes and steeply progressive income taxes from the rich. What is new is what the rich can now get away with: the outrageous uses more and more of them are making of the outrageous exemptions from law and order and taxation that they now demand and get. A broad middle class of the professions, salary earners, self-employed, and skilled workers seems to have become greedier than it used to be, and is getting richer more artfully than it used to do, often by milking government and poorer taxpayers through their roles in, or their relations with, the public sector. What follow are notes on what seem to have encouraged these tendencies among leaders in business, the professions, the public service, the universities, and politics.

In business, there have been contrived booms in residential land prices and then in office and retailing property; share-gambling bubble-booms in mining and exploration stocks; new futures markets and currency gambling; bigger business than before in organized prostitution, drug-running, video pornography, and illegal gambling; and a burgeoning industry of offshore tax and law avoidance. These are mostly secondary or speculative or socially destructive markets that do nothing good for the allocation or efficiency of productive resources—but many of them pay better than (for example) traditional manufacturing and retailing do.

From about 1968, the rising rate of inflation began to have ill effects, two of which have not always attracted the attention they deserve. First, the housing finance institutions responded to the inflation in ways that redistributed access to housing credit upwards while at the same time lowering its real price. The national proportion of homeowners began to fall, while the financial resources went to fewer, richer people who used them to build richer houses than before. By that means, capital inequalities were increased. So also were income inequalities, as those excluded from home ownership paid rising rents to landlords mostly richer than themselves. Conservative government compounded the effect by simultaneously reducing allocations to public housing and increasing its rents.

Second, the inflation brought a sea change in mass attitudes to saved money. The country had run for a generation on cheap money with advantages to borrowers, producers, and marginal home-buyers rather than to lenders. A decade of inflation and conservative policies has reversed that bias. High rates of nominal and real interest now prevail. As noted, housing resources have shifted "upwards." Investment, especially by small business, dwindles. There has been a drastic shift of advantage from borrowers to lenders, from producers to rentiers. Governments of both parties have encouraged these trends by deregulating the financial system.

Among the rentiers are rising numbers of the middle class led by rising numbers of public servants. Their dear-money policies are increasingly self-interested, especially for tax and superannuation reasons. Australia has long had a dual system of superannuation. Wage earners retire on a non-contributory, means-tested, flat-rate state pension. Salaried and professional earners can belong instead to superannuation schemes. These schemes take employers' and employees' contributions into an investment fund and in due course pay pensions from the fund's earnings. Most of the employees' and all of the employers' contributions are exempt from income tax and so are the funds' investment earnings. The pensions paid are taxable if they are big enough to attract tax—but there has always been a capital alternative. Until 1983, a retiring member could take his whole benefit as a capital grant, paying income tax on only five per cent of it. (Benefits accruing after 1983 are to pay more tax, but not much more.)

These arrangements mean that most middle-class superannuants cost the taxpayers much more than most working-class state pensioners do. But the middle-class beneficiaries pretend the opposite: they say they are self-supported by their savings while the state pensioners are a welfare burden on the taxpayer. Not content with that well-concealed plunder, in 1974 the nation's federal and state public servants got themselves a spectacular extension of it. For public servants only, they arranged to combine the state pension principle with the private superannuation principle in a scheme that incorporates the old tax exemptions, higher employer contributions, high rates of interest, and no investment risks. Members retire with state pensions or capital grants guaranteed by government from tax revenue, but calculated on the basis of notional investment funds earning unrealistically high notional rates of interest, so that the pretense of "self-support" continues. The effect is that up to a fifth of a public servant's earnings, compounding at high interest, are tax exempt or nearly so, and entitle the servant to capital or indexed-pension benefits at retirement, benefits so high that very few of the taxpayers who must pay them can expect comparable benefits themselves.

The leading public servants who negotiated that scheme will retire with indexed pensions in the top one percent of the nation's incomes or with capital grants above half a million dollars. Some have since been leading advocates and designers of the conservative government's most reactionary economic policies: high interest rates, real wage cuts, high unemployment as a macroeconomic instrument, and severe restraint of welfare incomes and services and of public expenditure on education and housing. The Keynesian middle-of-the-roaders who used to lead the public services and head the economic ministries seem to have been replaced in the 1970s by simple predators.

The learned professions have gained less through superannuation but more in other ways. Doctors are widely believed to be greedier than they were, and bad government has certainly helped them to help themselves. Ill-designed and frequently changed arrangements for public and private health insurance, and for private medical practice in public hospitals, mean that institutions rather than patients pay most doctors' fees. Market disciplines do not apply, and governments have not managed to replace them with effective price and quality controls. Of course, many doctors continue to give excellent service and charge honestly for it. But others over-charge, over-service, or get unreasonably rich from using public equipment in public hospitals to supply private radiological, pathological, surgical, and other services. A few get rich by simple fraud, charging the government for services their patients do not get. The conscientious doctors suffer by association, and also from the rhetoric of their richer brethren and the spokesmen for their professional associations—rhetoric that has been provoked to self-righteous extremes by the suggestion that doctors might be included like ordinary mortals in the national incomes policy.

As with doctors, so with lawyers: most of them work for reasonable pay, including the many who provide low-paid legal-aid services. But some leaders of the profession have got rich and enabled other greedy Australians to get richer by inventing ingenious new methods of tax avoidance for capital owners, business executives, the self-employed, and many of the professions. Through the last decade or so, many of the rich have come to regard both avoidance and "safe evasion" as respectable, though they are outraged when the poor do such things—welfare cheats are hunted down relentlessly. One of the most ingenious inventors of some of the most unscrupulous tax-avoidance schemes was appointed to be a judge of the High Court where, together with a chief justice of like mind, he did his bit to keep such corruption lawful. Besides that legally protected avoidance industry, there has also been a multi-billion-dollar development of safe, unlawful tax evasion, also designed with the assistance of lawyers and accountants. Much of it is done by stripping tax-defaulting companies, then selling their shells to fictitious buyers, leaving trails too tortuous for investigators to follow or courts to prove. The names of thousands of beneficiaries have been listed and published, but they remain immune; in 1984, the conservative Senate is still blocking attempts to collect some of the lost revenue, estimated to be between two and three billion dollars. Thus, the leaders of the legal profession have contrived to put a lot of the nation's wealth beyond reach of the law. Consistently, they have joined the doctors in resisting any application of the national incomes policy to their own incomes. I write with feeling. As son, colleague, friend, and father of able and honorable lawyers I think the present leaders of the Australian profession are debauching it.

There is some, but not much, criticism of the new greed by intellectuals and academic social scientists. The critics tend to be uninfluential: women, social workers, Marxists, a few radical sociologists and political scientists. A social welfare research center at the University of New South Wales, an urban research unit at Macquarie University, a social justice project at the National University, some concerned economists at Queensland universities, a Catholic philosopher or two, and a sprinkling of individuals in other places are willing to argue about the good and bad purposes of public policy or professional behavior. The government has agreed to finance an academic study of the distribution of wealth and income. But such questions do not loom large in the journals or courses of study of most of the social sciences. Instead, "positivism" rules even from the grave: a generation of students has been taught that thought about social purpose or social justice or equity—moral thought—is childish; differences on such questions can only be resolved by violence or superstition (leading economics texts say) not by reason. (Academics need not and should not preach particular moralities at their students; but I think they should restore the discussion of social ethics and purposes to the central place it once occupied in the curriculum of the humanities and social sciences.)

With scarce exceptions, Australian departments of economics are strongly neoclassical, teaching the kinds of theory on which the cruel and ineffective economic policies of the last decade have been based. As happened elsewhere in the world, many moved to the Right in the 1970s. There is a sprinkling of dissenters—Marxists, institutionalists, "old" or "post" Keynesians—but they tend to be few and not in charge. When Labor returned to federal and state government in the 1980s and looked around the universities for experienced economic advisers with values and theoretical beliefs appropriate to the new governments' purposes, it found all too few, and most of the few were immigrants, British born, and British or American educated.

Political leaders of all parties shared responsibility for the shift to the Right. From 1976 to 1983, the conservative government led that shift, but the Labor opposition said and did very little against it and offered no radical alternative to it. Was the Labor party conservatized by its leaders or by its voters? Probably by some of both. Some Labor politicians were personally convinced by a good deal of the Right's economic reasoning. The party commissioned opinion polls of critical groups of swing voters and learned that they were an unfeeling lot, likely to vote for their immediate material interests rather than for any broader visions of good. So although some Left politicians and industrial labor leaders thought and spoke otherwise, the party's parliamentary leaders tended to accept and tacitly endorse a good deal of the conservative government's teaching. They outbid the government in offering to cut taxes. At various dates, often during election campaigns, they renounced their former commitments to direct rather than indirect taxation, to taxing rich gifts and successions, to taxing capital or capital gains. They abandoned as impractical their commitment to full employment. They offered an incomes policy that in practice would not restrain most property or professional or managerial incomes, so that its main promise was to restrain wage incomes more effectively than conservative governments were able to do. In those and other ways, they seemed to be acting much as their Marxist critics had always accused them of acting. Thus, thinking with some truth that they were adapting to the people's wishes, they were also at the same time teaching the people that those wishes were reasonable; that the shift to the Right, and the increasing inequalities of wealth and income, were right enough.

With the leaders of all parties leading and teaching and tempting the people in the same reactionary direction, and with doctors and lawyers and champion cricketers and media owners and professors of economics showing the way and endorsing the reasoning, it is not surprising that the people moved a bit—and politically, the "center" moved—in that direction.

GLOOMY CONCLUSIONS

Though they will be widely disputed, and deserve innumerable individual and institutional exceptions, I think these are fair judgments of the past:

- For seventy years past, Australian business and political leadership has been generally mediocre and uninventive, missing many good opportunities.

• For eight or ten years past, business and political and a good deal of professional leadership has been positively reactionary, and has encouraged popular values and beliefs that now make effective leadership in any productive, inventive, or compassionate direction more difficult and less likely than before.

Worse, some think that recent shift to the Right was not an oscillation, but a historical change of direction. Not only in the shift of opinion, but in the quietly selfish way in which so many educated people have been improving their incomes and evading their taxes and setting their sights on capital wealth as the reward of salaried service, alarmed observers all over the developed world have seen the rise of a new class interest, or, as some like to call it, a "New Class" interest. Where Marxists have traditionally defined the capitalist ruling class by its ownership of the means of production, "New Class" theorists see a broader governing class of owners, managers, politicians, administrators, intellectuals, and teachers—an information-rich class that uses its effective command of the complex business and administrative machinery of capitalist and communist societies alike to exploit the rest of the population for its own advantage. Is contemporary Australian leadership simply a case of such a trend? It is easy to see it so, in the intensified self-service and the diminished compassion of influential groups and individuals like those noted above, and in their success in persuading majorities to discard old commitments to equality and full employment and generous welfare, and vote further to the Right than they used to do.

And Yet . . . And Yet . . .

Must those trends continue, with leaders as stodgy as ever, but greedier?

For Australians who can't bear that prospect, the slender grounds for hope appear to be these:

First, there are the continuing virtues—the profound and lovable virtues and strengths—of a friendly, not-too-competitive society that is still the world's most egalitarian in style and spirit if not in all its tax and income arrangements.

Second, there are abundant natural and human resources that ought to make successful economic performance easy—though easy resources have rarely had that effect in the past.

Third, there have always been exceptions to the general mediocrity: able leaders doing inventive things in one field or another. For some years in the 1970s, Jack Mundey, a builder's laborer, turned the New South Wales branch of his union into an environmental crusader, and by militant industrial action stopped or shifted some hundreds of millions of dollars worth of socially or environmentally offensive building work. He now does more of the same by bureaucratic means, as a member of a state planning authority. A wide variety of leaders, including green activists, politicians of all parties and a majority of High Court judges lately combined to stop the hydroelectric development of Tasmania's wilderness. Throughout the shift to the Right, the rich proprietors of the Melbourne *Age* encouraged it to continue as an excellent Left-liberal paper. Through the same years, the program-makers of the Australian Broadcasting Commission made its radio services for many purposes a radical "university of the air." Other proprietors, whatever the tendency of their financial and leader pages, have not succeeded in conservatizing all their journalists. Nobody has succeeded in conservatizing all the schoolteachers. The universities have a sprinkling of progressive thinkers and courses. And, as will be noted presently, there is plenty of radical skill and will—however frustrated—in the labor unions and in the replenished Labor ranks in parliament.

Fourth, there is strong, all-class support for many radical environmental policies.

Fifth, the charismatic popularity of Prime Minister Bob Hawke, which is currently reconciling majorities to policies more conservative than many of them want, could as well be used with opposite intent, to lead people further in the progressive and inventive directions that many of his cabinet colleagues and a great many of his popular supporters would certainly prefer.

Sixth, the present Labor rule from Right of center cannot be expected to work very well for very long. Like other democracies with developed mixed economies, Australia faces novel structural, environmental, and technological problems for whose resolution past experience and present economic orthodoxy are unhelpful guides. Those problems may soon drive leaders of all persuasions to reach for more inventive policies.

And—finally—potential leaders do not appear to be lacking. The new leaders of the conservative political parties are offering to lead a more radical Right than Australia has ever dreamed of. Commanding the center is a Labor government with many members who would like to move it a good deal further Left than they have yet been allowed to do. Examples: Ralph Willis spent ten years as chief industrial advocate for the Australian trade unions; now as minister for employment he manages a national incomes policy that he would dearly like to extend to property and professional and managerial incomes. John Button, minister for industry and government leader in the Senate, is negotiating three-cornered agreements about industrial structure between government, business, and labor that may signify some intelligent long-term economic planning at last. Barry Jones, minister for science and technology, wrote the best-selling *Sleepers, Wake!—Technology and the Future of Work* (Oxford University Press 1982 and Harvester Press 1984), which is perhaps the best and certainly the most complicated and imaginative of contemporary studies of the potential economic and social effects of technical change. John Dawkins, the nation's youngest-ever minister for finance, made his first Australia Day in office the occasion for a radical manifesto. He spoke of the public sector as no minister had for seven years: "Great public commercial enterprises have in the last few years been vandalised as a side effect of the monetarist experiment. We intend to reverse that trend." He also intended to reverse trends in Aboriginal policy, education, the arts, energy policy, overseas aid, tax incidence, and youth employment, and income support; and he would invent "an effective and properly funded national superannuation scheme."

For anyone who still thought it was smart for the party of the Left to be commanding the center by preempting the economic policies of the Right, the clearest warning came from Neal Blewett, minister of health, who is also an eminent historian and analyst of the British constitutional crisis of 1910–11 and of British and Australian political history since. Soon after he took office, Blewett wrote and delivered the John Curtin Memorial Lecture which is a notable event in both the academic and the Labor party year in Australia. He chose to lecture about the choices that social-democratic parties face in times of economic difficulty. Though dressed in certain courtesies, his message was unmistakeable. Social-democratic parties that accept Right reasoning and economic policies in those critical conditions, as Labor parties did in Australia in 1914–18 and in Britain and

Australia in 1931, must expect double trouble: the conservative policies don't work as promised, and the parties' working-class supporters feel "sold-out" and rebel. Labor governments may safely stray to the Right in Australian states that have no real responsibility for economic policy or performance. But Labor parties that have tried that strategy in national government and economic management have split and gone out of office for long periods with their lost leaders remembered, if at all, for betrayal and failure.

Having learned that lesson, the British and Australian parties did better in government in the 1940s than they had in 1931. In the 1940s, neither achieved all they set out to do, but both managed to build solid elements of progressive reform into their compromise policies and left durable achievements behind them. Best of all—and in the worst of conditions in 1931—were the Scandinavians:

> Supping with the conservative devil . . . whether informally in accepting the existing consensus, or formally through coalition, seems hardly the response appropriate to democratic socialist parties in the midst of economic crisis. Such a conclusion is reinforced when we examine democratic socialist parties that took an alternative route.
>
> The Scandinavian social democrats responded very differently to the economic crisis. In Denmark the public sector was maintained and expanded during the depression and Steincke's social welfare reform, the basis of the Danish welfare state for over a generation, was a product of the depression. A fairly ambitious public works program was undertaken and an alliance forged with the peasant proprietors through novel subsidies to agriculture. In Sweden, where the Keynesian influence was perhaps most noticeable, the Social Democrats sponsored public works, expanded social welfare provisions, and a massive reflationary policy based on deficit financing. They too allied themselves with the peasant proprietors through protection for agriculture. Norway followed a little later drawing much on its neighbors' experience. The result was electoral hegemony for the Social Democrats in all three countries for the next generation.

Whatever American readers may think of such Left aspirations, it is evident that some of the new Australian leaders are not content just to be up there: they want to lead the country somewhere. Who knows! Historical turning points do occur, able leaders can sometimes take advantage of them, century-old trends are sometimes reversed. Certainly, something has changed. Dr. Tregenza noticed that Joe Lyons, the Labor leader who split his party and put it out of office for a decade when he turned Conservative in 1931, was a Tasmanian native son. Blewett is another Tasmanian native son. At very least, something has happened at last to the native sons.

Gordon Jackson

The Australian Economy

AFTER NEARLY TWO HUNDRED YEARS of European settlement, there may be some utility in reviewing the stewardship of this vast land. One hundred years ago, Australia enjoyed the highest per capita income in the world. This preeminence proved short-lived, however; early in the twentieth century the United States laid claim to the title, and Australia's ranking since has slipped steadily. The decline has been particularly marked in recent years; by 1982, Australia had fallen to sixteenth place, and currently her position is being further eroded as certain of the more vigorous Asian nations move steadily up the ladder.

Growth in gross domestic product is of course only a crude measure of change in national well-being: failing to take account of shifts in income distribution, it gives no weight whatever to improvements in the quality of life. Because Australians place a high value on leisure, they have to some extent chosen increased leisure in place of higher income. Owen Harries, former Australian Ambassador to UNESCO, described Australia as "simply a pagan country in which the only things to which the word 'worship' could be applied are the sun and the beaches."[1] While this may be true, there is today a growing concern that Australia may not be realizing its full economic potential.

This is not, however, the view of the world outside. Australia is today generally perceived as a rich nation; gold, the golden fleece, and, more latterly, black gold have all contributed to this opinion. In 1983, the French magazine *L'Express* voted Australia "country of the year." In explaining why it was braving custom and tradition in naming a country rather than a person, *L'Express* said that "no other country, no other eldorado in the world can express or incarnate to such a point the hopes, the aspirations of the old world . . . Australia is perhaps the last dream of the decade, the end of the voyage, certainly the last frontier."[2] How is it possible to reconcile such different perceptions? How much of the French weekly's assessment is grounded in reality? How much of it is based on a way of life that is long since gone?

In this essay I propose to explore the origins of each of these perceptions in order to establish the current balance between commonly accepted myth and Australian reality. Four decades ago, when newspaper editor Brian Penton asked, "Advance Australia—Where?"[3] he raised a question that has taken on greater urgency since. The early prosperity of the Australian colonies owed a great deal to a series of fortuitous gold discoveries. At the height of the gold boom of the 1850s, one-fifth of the total national income derived from gold mining; by 1920, however, income from gold had declined to less than 3 percent. The fading fortunes of gold brought home very clearly the interdependence of the various sectors of the Australian economy. Immigrants attracted to Australia by the gold rushes could be persuaded to settle and stay only by the promise of other employ; this was thought to require the protection of "infant industries," of Australian manufacturing.

Yet the mining sector was never abandoned; it rose to promise again in the 1960s when prices, output, investment, and exploration activity all showed astonishing increases. The nation was gripped by a fever not known since the gold-rush days. Prices on the stock market sky-rocketed; for a brief period, instant riches seemed wholly attainable. As world metal prices eased, however, the frenetic activity gradually slackened; share prices plummeted. When the dust had settled, it was obvious that the mining sector remained a more significant force in the economy of the country than it had been for more than half a century, but it had not attained the levels originally anticipated.

So, also, the worldwide oil price increases of 1973 and 1979 seemed to hold great promise for Australia's mining sector. The threat of new oil embargoes made many countries feel their economic and strategic vulnerability; it was reasonable that they should make strenuous efforts to become less dependent on oil. Australia was well placed to take advantage of these developments. Existing facilities were improved to make greater exports possible; major new projects were undertaken in the coal, oil, gas, and aluminum smelting areas. Most importantly, coal—black gold—once again came into its own.

The timing of this most recent resource boom had important macroeconomic ramifications. While the major world economies were gradually sliding into recession, domestic demand in Australia was still being fueled by a very rapid expansion in investment spending. Unrealistic expectations by both management and labor only exacerbated the inflationary pressures. The price of the Australian dollar rose in anticipation of increased export income; all the while, the competitiveness of Australian industry deteriorated sharply. By mid-1981, sagging oil prices and the prolonged world recession had taken the gloss off many resource projects; meanwhile, declining competitiveness was channeling an increasing proportion of Australia's domestic demand into foreign markets. A wage explosion in late 1981 only hastened the decline. Australia, before long, was in the midst of its own major recession.

Modern mining is a high risk enterprise by any measure: projects are typically very large and generally have long lead times; demand and prices are highly volatile. Unaided by government assistance, mining firms have had to adapt to this uncertain environment; they operate most effectively in a highly competitive world market. From its early history, mining has been an important part of the Australian economy. While the structure of the industry has changed dramatically, it remains a vital part of Australia's economy today, even though it is not without its problems.

While Australia is known internationally for its mineral exports, its exports of agricultural commodities have historically been even more important. A century ago, Australia's rural population accounted for 20 percent of gross domestic product (GDP): the mining sector, by comparison, produced only 5 percent. There has been a progressive decline in the importance of agricultural and pastoral production since; today, it accounts for only 5 to 6 percent of aggregate output—a far cry from the times when Australia was said to ride to riches on the sheep's back. Wool rose to prominence early in the nineteenth century. Apart from a brief period around the turn of the twentieth century, wool remained Australia's premier export commodity until displaced by rising mineral exports in the 1970s. In the hundred years before 1850 and 1950, wool's share of total export income remained remarkably stable at around 40 percent. It was the Korean War that sparked off an explosive rise in wool prices; at the height of the boom, wool sales accounted for as much as 65 percent of the total export income. The development of synthetics since has had a major impact on the market for wool, but it remains an important commodity, despite the fact that its share of export income has fallen to less than 10 percent. In 1983, wool's share of GDP was 1 percent; this needs to be compared with a peak of 18 percent in 1951.

Wheat has long been another major agricultural industry in Australia. By 1900, more than 2 million hectares of wheat were planted, and the area under cultivation expanded steadily, reaching some 12 million hectares today. Because the expansion has been into marginal lands, wheat production has become increasingly susceptible to adverse weather conditions. A severe drought in the eastern states, for example, had severe repercussions on grain production in fiscal year 1983.[4]

Australia's income from wheat and wool is today supplemented by the production of a wide range of other primary products. The advent of refrigerated shipping in the 1890s was an important stimulus to agricultural diversification. While meat accounted for 5 percent of export income at the turn of the century, it rose gradually to a peak of around 13 percent in 1979. Sugar production has also increased in importance over the last century. From a mere 0.5 percent of exports in the 1880s, sugar now provides between 3 and 5 percent of total export income. Long-term supply contracts with Britain played an important part in the postwar development of this industry. These contracts disappeared, however, when Britain entered the European Economic Community (EEC); the Australian sugar industry was compelled to diversify its markets, and succeeded in doing so.

Such changes, however, have not prevented the farm sector from becoming a much less important element in the Australian economy over the last century. The decline reflects many circumstances, not least of which were a deterioration in the rural sector's terms of trade and new restrictions on Australian access to foreign markets. The two factors are related: excess production induced by subsidies granted by governments of industrialized countries has contributed to keeping agricultural prices low; Britain's accession to the EEC proved highly disruptive to Australia's meat, butter, and sugar exports; protectionist policies, introduced particularly by the EEC and Japan, have greatly restricted Australia's export opportunities. Each of these developments has forced the pace of technological change and has contributed to structural adjustment in the farm sector. In the 1980s, Australia, one of the world's more efficient producers of wool, wheat, meat, and sugar, must face the fact that the market prospects for its farmers are very uncertain. The EEC in a few short years has shifted from being a large net importer of sugar to being one of the world's major exporters. This turnaround has been achieved largely by providing substantial subsidies to domestic European producers. In mid-1984, EEC sugar subsidies, for example, were equivalent to twice the world market price of sugar. The future of Australia's beef industry is also clouded by factors unrelated to its competitiveness. Japan and the United States are major markets for Australian beef. Access to these markets today is regulated by quotas. In the case of Japan, it is becoming increasingly apparent that political rather than market considerations govern the size of the imports that are permitted.

These trends, while disturbing from a world viewpoint, pose particularly serious obstacles to efforts by Australia to liberalize its trade regime. Richard Snape, the Australian economist, has argued that international trading rules such as those laid down in the General Agreement on Tariffs and Trade (GATT) "provide a framework in which economically or politically weak countries share more than otherwise in the benefits of trading when they engage in transactions with the strong and powerful; and they can reduce uncertainty in international trade and thus provide more confidence for planning international transactions."[5] For traders in farm products, however, GATT has so far proved disappointing, and there is no reason to believe that this will soon change.

One widely held misconception about Australia is that it has a large rural population. This view, doubtless related to the vast size of the continent and the sparseness of its population, conceals the fact that Australia is highly urbanized. Only about 6 percent of Australians live on farms; as many as 60 percent reside in the major metropolitan centers. Although nearly 90 percent of the farms are family owned, the urban/rural links are, in fact, weak. Steadily increasing productivity diminishes the need for people on the land;

there is a one way flow, with country children being forced to move to the towns to find employment.

"I love a sunburnt country"[6] is a familiar line from one of Australia's best known poems, but for many farmers sunburnt plains spell economic disaster. Despite technological advances, abundant seasonal rains are the lifeblood of the rural sector. Below-average rainfall for several years in succession culminated in 1983 in the worst drought in half a century. The drought, with its severe repercussions on rural towns, contributed to a steep rise in unemployment; the economy-wide recession only compounded Australia's problems. In a cruel twist of fate, when the drought finally broke, it did so with such vengeance that floods devastated the livestock and ruined the crops in many areas. The Australian bush is an exacting task master; those who choose to pit themselves against the land require all the fortitude and endurance of their pioneering forefathers.

These are not the experiences of other sectors of the economy. As has already been noted, from early in its history Australian manufacturing was nurtured by protection. Confronted with the prospect of large numbers of unemployed gold miners, several states—most particularly, Victoria—erected tariff barriers to encourage labor-intensive manufacturing. With the coming of federation in 1901, however, interstate tariffs were abolished, and external tariffs were eased. The next half century, punctuated by periods of war and recession, saw a progressive strengthening of tariff barriers, and the tide is only turning now, very slowly.

Australia emerged from both world wars with an overriding sense of vulnerability. The great open spaces were seen much more as a defense liability than as a source of pastoral and mineral wealth. "Populate or perish" became the national slogan. At the outbreak of World War II, Australia was heavily dependent on imported industrial goods. Although iron, steel, and non-ferrous metal industries have established a firm foothold in the country, and light industries such as textiles, clothing, and footwear flourished along with general engineering, the skill-intensive industries—motor vehicle, heavy chemical, and rubber—remained relatively small-scale. World War II pushed Australian industry into machine tools, construction equipment, heavy chemicals, and aircraft, and the momentum developed in the war years carried over into peacetime. Australia, like many other countries, was confronted with a serious shortage of foreign exchange just after the war and imposed import controls. This insured that local industries were the principal beneficiaries of rising domestic demand, and was an additional incentive to the development of a broadly based manufacturing sector.

There was a grand vision in 1945 that Australia would sustain full employment by building up its economy, especially in manufacturing, and by encouraging new immigration. The minister for postwar reconstruction, John Dedman, talking about the government's white paper on full employment in Australia, described the strategy as a "charter for a new social order."[7] *Argus*, in a characteristic newspaper comment, said that "the experiences of the war years have shown the Australian people that full employment can be obtained. They are not likely again to accept as inevitable the waste and soul-destroying bitterness of the depression years."[8] There was a strong Keynesian flavor to the strategy; an important role for government was envisaged in maintaining aggregate demand at full employment levels, with a fixed exchange rate instituted to insure a strong inflow of capital. It was assumed that as population expanded, industry would grow, become more efficient, be less in need of protection.

Throughout the 1950s and 1960s, Australia's manufacturing sector recorded continuous strong growth. Conditions deteriorated only in the 1970s when the overall rate of economic growth slowed and the growth in manufacturing slowed especially dramatically. From a peak of almost 30 percent of GDP in the late 1960s, manufacturing declined to just about 20 percent.

A number of reasons have been advanced to explain the poor performance of Australian manufacturing in recent years. The country's protection strategy ranks high on the list. The conventional argument is that protection tended to undermine industry's capacity to compete internationally and served to entrench implicit wage contracts often unrelated to the market situation. Also, it encouraged manufacturers and their employees to look to changes in tariffs as the appropriate response to market pressures, inhibiting their adaptation in more fundamental ways. In addressing the National Technology Conference in 1983, the chairman of a major electronics company stated that "it has been said that we in the private sector lack enterprise, play it safe and lack the entrepreneurial tradition which is a characteristic feature of American life."[9] While not disputing these propositions, he thought the government was to blame, arguing that the tax system discouraged risk taking. Given the high degree of risk taking characteristic of the mining and agricultural sectors, it is difficult to conceive why it should be so conspicuously absent in manufacturing.

Professor Ronald Johnston of the University of Wollongong participated in a survey of managers in Australian manufacturing, and suggested that "it is not risk aversion in general but a specific aversion to the risks associated with technology development which characterizes the attitudes of Australian management."[10] In Johnston's view, the increasing trend towards "a primacy of education over experience, of the short term over the long term, of the precise over the uncertain, and the calculation over intuition" has fundamentally altered incentive structures and has "led to a managerial ethos closer to that normally considered a feature of the Public Service where avoiding making mistakes . . . constitutes the first rule of action."[11] The research identified certain other shortcomings in Australian managers. According to Johnston, they regarded the introduction of technology "as being primarily for assisting in the defense of existing product ranges and markets through cost reduction, i.e., clinging grimly to existing but frequently declining products and markets."[12] This reluctance to press ahead with new products and new markets helped explain Australia's poor export performance in manufactured goods. The arguments were not wholly convincing. Others tried with other arguments.

A survey conducted by the University of Minnesota suggested that Australian managers had a high moralistic orientation, placed a low value on achievement, success, competition, and risk. In interpreting the results, George England suggested that the Australian managers were not very amenable to change.[13] Yet, in a comparative study, by Capon, Christodoulou, Farley, and Hulbert, of corporate planning practices of large American and Australian manufacturing companies, the most striking finding was the overall similarity that existed.[14] Indeed, these researchers suggested that there might be more professionalism in the planning of many Australian companies than among their American counterparts, with more substantial resources applied to corporate planning, and with tighter coordination of both long-range and short-term plans. It was true, however, that American plans were sometimes more driven by market considerations, and that this was a variable worth considering. Also, it ought to be acknowledged that to the extent that Australian manufacturing is foreign owned, or is otherwise linked with larger markets abroad, available choices or risk/reward tradeoff will generally tend against major research and development investment by the Australian operation. Australian society has evolved neither the group pressure for growth characteristic of Japan, nor the tolerance of successful individuals becoming very rich, as exists in the United States. In the absence of acute local turbulence, there has been no great motivation for change. Australia may indeed be the "last frontier," though the meaning of that phrase remains remarkably ambiguous.

With a growing sector of new Australia based on novel technology and showing an international outlook, the role of management has been placed high on the agenda of public discussion. The sharp rise in unemployment in 1983, particularly in the manufacturing sector, gave a new sense of urgency to the debate. It is now recognized that those made redundant by a contraction in manufacturing cannot be readily absorbed into the expanding sectors of the economy. As this realization has gradually taken hold, the foundations of Australia's ambivalent trade policies have come under increasing strain. Australian firms in the future will clearly need to view overseas markets as primary outlets for their goods rather than as outlets for residual production. How can they guarantee that such markets will exist for them?

While Australians see their country today as a great trading nation, as once indeed it was, the perception is largely founded in the past. Two-way trade flows amount to about 25 percent of GDP in Australia as compared with over 40 percent for Great Britain, Germany, and France. By OECD standards, Australia is a relatively "closed" economy. Australia's share of world trade has slipped to a low 1.3 percent from nearly twice that percentage only three decades ago.

Though Australia was one of the founding signatories of GATT in 1948, its early enthusiasm for the treaty soon waned. In successive GATT negotiations on eliminating barriers to trade, Australia consistently failed to find trading partners prepared to reciprocate for the tariff concessions that she was prepared to make. Agricultural products, still important among Australia's exports, have not had an easy time. With few exceptions, the EEC, Japan, and other major markets for Australian farm products have shown themselves unwilling to negotiate on their high, mostly non-tariff barriers to agricultural imports. Australia, as a result of standing firm on the principle of reciprocity, failed to participate in the mainstream of the post–World War II trade liberalization—a liberalization that contributed markedly to the growth of the major industrialized countries, opening up vast opportunities for the developing countries as well.

While Australia has in fact reduced its tariffs since the 1960s, it has done so more slowly than its trading partners. From around 24 percent in fiscal year 1969, the average tariff rate on manufactured goods was progressively reduced to 15 percent in fiscal year 1975, and then stabilized at this new lower level. When the Tokyo Round reductions have been fully implemented in 1988, tariffs of the major industrial countries will average around 5 percent. Australia's 15 percent may still be too high. Also, protection for the most highly protected Australian industries remains very elevated. In fiscal year 1982, the Industries Assistance Commission estimated that the tariff equivalent of the package of tariffs and quotas on automobiles was at least 70 percent; for clothing, textiles, and footwear, 60 percent. While Australia offers very liberal access to imports from the developing countries, these concessions do not affect its trade with others. The persistence of high levels of protection, however, does not necessarily presume a ready acceptance of the efficacy of protection. For a hundred years, Australians have argued with each other about external tariff policy. It was one of the major issues in the debates in the constitutional conventions that led to the federation of the states in 1901. While New South Wales argued for free trade, Victoria insisted on a protective tariff. The debate still rages today, but the premises have clearly changed.

The failure of infant industries to outgrow protection is now appreciated; in some circles, there is greater recognition of the long-term costs of protection. If the costs are widely spread across the whole community, the benefits accrue mostly to particular regions and groups who would certainly suffer if protection were reduced. Thus, for example, where employment in clothing, textiles, and footwear manufacture is dominated by migrant women who cannot move easily, and who in any case lack other skills, there are no easy solutions. Especially while unemployment is high, such short-term transition problems pose a major obstacle to reform.

In 1973, when the Whitlam Labor government unilaterally and without warning cut tariffs across the board by 25 percent, following soon after a cumulative 18 percent appreciation of the exchange rate, the manufacturing sector experienced a sharp decline in its competitiveness. The public came to view these tariff cuts as the principal contributor to the subsequent decline in output, a development that has seriously impeded the progress of tariff reform in Australia ever since.

Pre-war Australia saw itself as a far-flung outpost of Europe. Trade had been influential in shaping this perception; for over a century (from around 1830), the Australian economy fitted the classical colonial pattern—its role was to supply both food and raw materials to Britain and to buy British manufactured goods in return. These arrangements were formalized under a preferential trade treaty in 1932. They do not, however, describe the conditions that now obtain. From a mere 10 percent in the early 1950s, Japan and Southeast Asia now account for fully 40 percent of Australia's total trade. A number of factors have contributed to this massive reorientation: while Australia's agricultural exports faced increased barriers in their traditional markets, particularly after Britain joined the EEC, the products of its expanded mining sector found a ready market in Asia, particularly in Japan. At the same time, certain of the more efficient Asian producers made major inroads into Australia's market, frequently at the expense of British suppliers.

This rapid growth in trade with Asia has not been without its frictions. Australia maintains quantitative restrictions on imports of clothing, footwear, and textiles—commodities that are of particular interest to several of the less advanced countries of Southeast Asia. Australia was meanwhile the first country to introduce a generalized system of preferences for developing countries. The Australian Systems of Tariff Preferences, created in 1966, provided duty-free or preferential access to the Australian market for a range of goods from all developing countries, and the list of concessions included a number of items of special interest to the Asian region. This policy has not always seemed equitable to others.

It is an intriguing paradox that post–World War II Australia has sometimes seemed more open to the flow of people than to the flow of goods. A major element of Australia's postwar immigration program was its willingness to accept large numbers of refugees from war-torn Europe. As that war refugee flow subsided, migrants were accepted also from East European and Middle East countries, as well as from the traditional sources of Great Britain and Western Europe. In more recent years, Asians from a wide variety of countries and backgrounds have constituted about a third of Australia's migrant intake, with refugees from Indochina constituting the largest single element. Nearly one-quarter of Australia's present population was born abroad.

While the economic effects of this large-scale immigration have been immense—with recent migrants tending to find themselves at the bottom of the socioeconomic heap, particularly conspicuous in protected manufacturing—their drive to move upwards is strong and persistent. As with the United States in the last century, the multicultural society seems to generate diversity and vigor that appear only to increase from one generation to another. The infusion of new ideas is enriching the Australian lifestyle and culture in ways that few anticipated.

If protection, domestic and foreign, shaped the course of Australian history in the goods sector, in the primary industries it had an effect also in the tertiary sector of the economy, where regulation was common. Thus, for example, Australian banks, like their counterparts in Europe and the United States, have traditionally been subject to a wide range of controls. Prudential regulations date back to the bank crashes of the 1890s and the 1930s. Other incentives for bank regulation have included social ends, such as the provision of cheap loans to homeowners, farmers, and small businesses. A complex network of rules and regulations grew up covering interest rates on deposits and loans, portfolio composition, and maturity structures. Despite myriad controls, the banks appear to have been the net beneficiaries of all this regulation.

When interest rates rose strongly during the 1970s, deposit-rate ceilings prevented the banks from competing effectively for funds. The banks suffered a decline in their share of the market as the public shifted some of its funds out of the banking system. The process was accelerated by the development of a whole range of new products by innovative merchant banks. In particular, the emergence of cash management funds (equivalent to U.S. money market mutual funds) was instrumental in breaking down interest-rate controls in the retail banking sector. As the efficacy of the regulatory system came under increasing challenge, the government introduced minor changes; more important, it established a committee of inquiry charged with drawing up a blueprint for the reform of the financial system. The Campbell Committee contributed to a better understanding of the workings of the financial system, pointing the way also to major reforms. The committee, seeing lack of competition as a major source of inefficiency in domestic banking, recommended the issuing of additional banking licenses. Under the government of Prime Minister Hawke, interest-rate controls were substantially liberalized, the exchange rate was allowed to float, and foreign banks are to be authorized. There are many lessons to be learned from this deregulation of the finance sector, none more important than the central role that active public debate can play in creating a climate conducive to change. The question today is whether this deregulatory tide will now spill over into other areas of the Australian economy.

Regulation is pervasive in the tertiary sector, particularly in the area of transport. The ramifications of a high-cost, inefficient transport system are profound for a country as vast as Australia. As with the goods sector, pockets of efficient operation do exist. However, regulated enterprises predominate. The rail system, for example, has always operated as a set of state monopolies. Political considerations were significant in all decisions to expand the rail networks. As competition from road transport grew, taxes and license fees were introduced to control the increase of road haulage. Regulation of road transport permitted the railways to engage in subsidization, with rural communities being the principal beneficiaries. In recent years, some state governments have used their rail charges as a disguised form of tax on mining operations. In fiscal year 1984, the collective deficits of the state and federal rail system were expected to total around $1 billion—about 1.5 percent of total government outlays. As in the United States, these huge losses are attributable largely to low productivity and featherbedding. In contrast to the highly concentrated rail system, road haulage is characterized by a large number of owner/drivers. The industry is highly efficient; prices and output respond quickly to changing patterns of demand. Discriminatory taxes and charges on road haulage were abolished in 1979; a major confrontation with the New South Wales government, culminating in a blockade of highways, produced this happy result. Finally, there is the high cost of coastal shipping; closely regulated, this mode of transport has been prevented from providing effective competition for the railways.

This pattern of regulation and high costs has been repeated in the airline industry. After a number of mergers and substantial government interference, the number of interstate airline operators was finally reduced to two—one government and one private. In 1957, regulations were introduced that effectively abolished all competition between the two airlines: fares and equipment were to be identical; flights were strictly scheduled. "Rather than being a crucible in which to assay the comparative fineness of private and public enterprises, the two-airline policy became the alchemist's nightmare; it turned both enterprises to lead."[15] Despite a number of reviews, the deregulation of airlines on the United States model has yet to come to Australia.

Regulatory powers rest largely with the federal government, though the states exercise considerable control in certain areas. These arrangements owe something to the bitter and protracted wrangles that preceded the establishment of the Commonwealth in 1901. Alfred Deakin, who was to become the second prime minister of Australia, argued in the nineteenth century that "we should seek to erect a constitutional edifice which shall be a guarantee of liberty and union for all time to come, to the whole people of this continent and the adjacent islands to which they shall learn to look up with reverence and regard, which shall stand strong as a fortress and be held sacred as a shrine."[16] The founding fathers provided a constitution that could be altered only with a referendum. Sixty years later, Prime Minister Robert Menzies complained that "the truth of the matter is that to get an affirmative vote from the Australian people on a referendum proposal is one of the labors of Hercules . . . I don't think you will recall a single instance of the 'Yes' vote on constitutional change except a change designed to increase the amount of money being paid by the Commonwealth to someone else."[17] Similar views were voiced by the Commonwealth Parliamentary Committee of Constitutional Review in 1959: "Experience has shown that the Constitution is exceedingly difficult to amend."[18]

Frustrated by unsuccessful attempts at constitutional reform, the states and the Commonwealth have used the High Court to reinterpret the constitution. While some argue that this is a proper function for the High Court, others disagree. In the federation debates of 1900, John Cockburn, a former premier of South Australia, said that "the written words of the Commonwealth Bill are but the framework or skeleton to which the living form will be imparted by the interpretations placed upon it from time to time by the decisions of the High Court. That this will be the case may be inferred from the history of the American constitution, to which, as far as regards the balance between the central and State powers, the Commonwealth bears a close resemblance."[19]

The "fleshing out" of the constitution has not been painless. The process whereby the Commonwealth is pitted against the state has proved particularly divisive, as a recent dispute between the Commonwealth and the state of Tasmania suggests. The High Court, ruling in favor of the Commonwealth, prevented Tasmania from building a dam in an environmentally sensitive region. The decision marked a perceptible shift in the balance of power between the states and the Commonwealth, a balance that has been moving progressively in favor of the Commonwealth ever since federation.

Until the First World War, Commonwealth revenues were derived almost exclusively from indirect taxes. Federal income taxes, introduced to fund the war effort, persisted after the end of the hostilities. During the Second World War, the Commonwealth asserted the exclusive right to levy both individual and company income taxes. The states were to be compensated by unconditional grants. From 1976, they have been allowed to attach a surcharge or rebate on the national income-tax base, but so far no state has chosen to exercise this option. The evolution of revenue sharing has not been without its problems. During the depression of the 1930s, anti-Commonwealth feeling ran so high that Western Australia at one time voted to secede from the Commonwealth. The petition, turned down by the British Parliament, brought home unmistakably the need for major reforms.

One such reform was the establishment of the Commonwealth Grants Commission in 1933. This institution, guaranteeing that all Australians have equal access to public services irrespective of the income base of the state they reside in, has meant that income transfers are made from the high-income, highly populated states of Victoria and New South Wales to the lower income, sparsely populated states of the Commonwealth. The egalitarian principles that underlie the operations of the institution are deeply embedded in the national character, reflected both in wage-setting arrangements, and in a positive penchant for lopping off tall poppies. In reviewing the Australian system, Professor Edward Gramlich has said that "Australia has the most equalizing federalist system in the world."[20]

The growth in federal fiscal powers has been matched by a concomitant increase in its control over the states' borrowing programs. In the early part of the century, the states, in their own right, were large borrowers on the London market. From 1928, all public borrowing was assumed by the Commonwealth. In essence, the Commonwealth took on the credit risk of the states—not insignificant in the years of depression—in exchange for control of the size of the state capital expenditure programs. Over time, borrowing by semi-governmental authorities (such as the railways and electricity authorities) was also brought under the wing of the Loan Council. Increasingly, the Commonwealth came to use its power to influence the pattern of state expenditures. Specific-purpose grants were provided to encourage public housing, education, roads, and more recently, health. In the mid-1970s, under the banner of the "new federalism," the conservative government headed by Prime Minister Malcolm Fraser moved to ease somewhat the central government control of the distribution of state expenditures. This gesture, motivated in part by ideology, reflected also a pragmatic response to the mounting criticism of a steady erosion of state sovereignty. Concurrently, the Fraser government set about to reduce the Commonwealth budget deficit; in doing so, it squeezed federal transfers on to the states. Faced with burgeoning deficits, the states were in turn led to invent new ways of getting around federal controls on their borrowing.

Until recently, there has been little attention paid in Australia to the role of state governments as independent economic agents. Sharp rises in capital spending, escalating charges, and steep tax increases have, however, thrust the state governments into new prominence. There is today an increasing recognition of the role of the states, particularly in the growth and inflationary processes that now command such attention in the country.

Government outlays have increased progressively over the century. From around 15 percent of GDP at federation, expenditures by all levels of government had risen to over 40 percent of GDP by fiscal year 1983. The increases have not been continuous. The postwar period showed a high degree of stability, broken only in the early 1970s when expenditures rose sharply. This shift was associated principally with the introduction of a range of new social programs by Prime Minister Gough Whitlam. His Labor government's program of reform included the introduction of universal free health insurance, a major expansion of capital works programs, increases in pensions and social welfare payments, and the abolition of university fees.

Universal free health services proved to be an especially heavy drain on the public purse. By removing the price rationing mechanism, demand for such services rose sharply. A spin-off of free health care was the substantial enriching of those who provided these services; to defend their new financial status, they formed themselves into a rather powerful lobby. Yet standards of public health have not been markedly improved; life expectancy remains lower than that of Japan. Similarly, government-funded legal-aid services, while providing some assistance to litigants, has not appreciably altered Australian justice, while the legal profession has certainly benefited.

Social-welfare expenditures in Australia have nearly trebled in real terms since 1970. Particularly large increases have occurred in outlays for old-age pensions, family allowances, and unemployment benefits. Unemployment benefits have increased dramatically partly because of increases in benefit rates but principally because of the sharp rise in the number of the unemployed. From around 2 percent of the work force in 1970, the unemployment rate rose strongly in 1974 and remained at around 6 percent for several years. The most recent recession precipitated a major shake-out in the labor market; unemployment rose to a peak of 10.4 percent, or 730,000 people out of work.

Grants to the states rose sharply in the Whitlam years, facilitating a rapid expansion in capital expenditure on roads, educational institutions, public housing, and hospitals. Total Commonwealth outlays doubled between fiscal year 1972 and fiscal year 1976. A reluctance to fund these programs through tax increases resulted in a steep rise in the public sector deficit while also providing a major stimulus to inflation. Acquiring power after twenty-three years of consecutive conservative government, Whitlam's Labor government was driven by a compulsion to reform. There was no feeling that the pace of reform had to be moderated to accord with the availability of resources. The government believed that growth was assured; it saw its task as insuring equitable distribution. In this situation, real wages rose sharply. Profit share and investment, however, declined. The sweeping changes—many badly needed, a fair number surviving to this day—proved too much for the economy, the bureaucracy, and the naturally conservative Australian people. Unease over the balance of spending policies at home was matched by alarm in certain quarters abroad. Labor was maneuvered out of office after only three years and firmly kept out for another seven.

Although the programs introduced under Whitlam had a uniquely Australian flavor, the surge in government expenditure paralleled similar developments in other major Western countries. After two decades of uninterrupted prosperity, the Western world had begun to turn its attention to those who had failed to share in the postwar recovery. The United States put forth the Great Society programs of Lyndon Johnson; Australia greatly extended social welfare services. A general lack of fiscal discipline in most Western economies contributed to a great surge of inflation in the early 1970s.

Despite the large expansion undertaken in the 1970s, Australian government outlays are not an excessive proportion of GDP by OECD standards.[21] In 1982 (the latest year for which OECD comparative data are available), they were 34 percent—the same as for Japan and a little less than for the United States. This compares with 62 percent in the Netherlands, 59 percent in Denmark, and 65 percent in Sweden. While Australian government outlays have risen more rapidly than GDP in recent periods, partly due to automatic stabilizers but also a result of the pursuit of countercyclical policies, the Australian stock of public debt outstanding remains low by international standards, reflecting the somewhat modest public-sector deficits for most of the postwar period. The surge in the early part of the 1970s had been largely wound back by the close of the decade. While the deficit rose strongly in fiscal years 1983 and 1984 because of the combined effects of the recession and the government's fiscal policy, as the recovery gathers strength, the Australian government will have to choose between cutting taxes and reducing the deficit, thereby allowing room for an expansion of private demand for credit. Given that "consensus" seems to mark the style of Robert Hawke who first became prime minister in 1983, just as "crashing through" had seemed to define Whitlam's policies, and "imposing his will" seemed to be Fraser's aim, there is reason to expect compromise.

There is a striking difference today between the American and the Australian debates on the size of the deficit. By and large, there has been general approval in Australia of the government's plan to progressively rein in the deficit. In reviewing the Australian economy in 1983, Rudiger Dornbusch of M.I.T. referred to "the Treasury's deficit fixation";[22] he argued that "there is no case for believing that the 1983–84 projected 4.7 percent of GDP deficit is there for long: nor is there any case for believing that deficits of such magnitude do any serious harm at times of deep recession."[23] This view does not have universal approval in Australia. Hawke's government, for example, in involving the business sector in discussions leading up to the fiscal year 1985 budget, sought to dissipate some of the pressure that tends to find expression when such issues are aired. His open-government approach was intended to ease the making of difficult decisions on expenditure cuts. In addition to pruning back the deficit, a restructuring of expenditure patterns was high on his agenda. Australia had clearly drifted into the characteristic middle-class welfare quagmire: welfare payments had come to be viewed as a right rather than a support mechanism. The government was attempting to redress this imbalance by restricting access to broadly based welfare payments such as old-age pensions.

Control of inflation is also well up on the national agenda. Inflation is not a new phenomenon in Australia. The gold rushes of the nineteenth century generated substantial inflation, as did both world wars and the Korean War commodity boom. What distinguished these earlier episodes from the inflationary experiences of the 1970s was simply the speed with which the earlier inflationary pressures were dissipated. Inflation was running at around 22 percent per annum in fiscal year 1952; a year later it had fallen to 9 percent; by fiscal year 1954 it was less than 2 percent. By contrast, Australian inflation remained high throughout the 1970s and was still high in the early 1980s.

The precise causes of inflation are hard to determine, though it is clear that monetary and fiscal policies exert a strong influence. In macroeconomic management, as in so many other areas, Australia has always drawn heavily on the experience of other countries. Faced with rising outlays and declining revenues, Australia cut its capital spending during the Depression; Great Britain pursued similar policies, with equally disastrous results. The postwar period, however, saw a shift to Keynesian policies. The budget of fiscal year 1952 was the first serious attempt by Australia to use fiscal policy to counteract inflationary pressures. Over subsequent periods, the government tried its hand at "fine tuning," but only with mixed success.

From the mid-1970s, Australia's policies were directed primarily towards controlling inflation. Australia was again looking for ideas from other countries, and monetarism had come into vogue. Australia established monetary targets in 1976; they were seldom reached. Inappropriate exchange-rate policies and an unwillingness to accept the interest-rate consequences of a tight monetary policy lay at the heart of Australia's problem. Malcolm Fraser, the conservative prime minister after Gough Whitlam, placed a higher priority on macroeconomic management than did his predecessor. The rhetoric he used emphasized deregulation and the containing of wages and inflation; he failed to achieve much about either. Born into a farming family, his ability to act was influenced by deeply held rural prejudices about banks and interest rates. His rhetoric alienated many; the results were disappointing.

The election of a Labor government in 1983 raised the specter of increased government spending, high monetary growth rates, exaggerated wage claims, and high inflation. The experience, to date, has been quite the opposite. Hawke's government, taking pains to distance itself from the memories of the Whitlam years, directed its policies principally towards containing the growth in government outlays, while reducing the rate of growth of the money supply.

Wages policy still remains a major testing ground. For much of Australia's history, industrial relations and wage-setting arrangements have been central in all policy debates. Union aims and interests have traditionally been advanced at three levels: through the labor movement at large, including the Labor party; in the statutory state and federal tribunals that conciliate and arbitrate on wages and working conditions; in the work place, through collective bargaining and industrial action. In 1943, Brian Penton remarked that Australians "have an enormous faith in parliament's power to legislate happiness."[24] Nowhere is this more evident than in the labor market, where as early as 1892, legislation was enacted to provide for the compulsory arbitration of wages. Industrial courts were set up in

New South Wales and Western Australia; the other states, taking a less judicial approach, established wages boards. In 1904 the federal arbitration court was established. While this system has been modified repeatedly over the years, the broad framework has been little changed.

The institutional framework and highly centralized nature of the wage-fixing arrangements disguise the complex and cumbersome workings of this Australian arbitration system. As Justice Ludeke noted, "In the name of public interest, the Conciliation and Arbitration Act of 1904 has become a multi-armed miscellany which reaches into nearly every nook and cranny of industrial relations."[25] In addition to wage rates, separate state and federal tribunals regulate such disparate matters as hours of work, annual leave, sick leave, long service leave, penalty rates for overtime and shift work, recognition of union rights, and resignation and dismissal. The tradition of settling all such matters in an adversary situation before an impartial arbitrator, with parties represented at arms length, minimizes the opportunities for any local resolution of issues and may go some way towards explaining Australia's high strike rate. Still, strikes tend to be short in duration; the arbitration system seems to encourage strikes over quite trivial issues but tends to curb prolonged and bruising strikes.

The intrinsic complexity of the system is only compounded by the inappropriate structure of the institutions and organizations that work within it. Australia, with its 320 autonomous unions largely organized on craft lines, seems ill-suited to the industrial-relations needs of a postwar industrialized economy. The structures of the employer groups, similarly based on the accidents of Australian history, are no better suited to their tasks. Unions are so organized that even a medium-sized firm is required to deal with many unions. A union officer, inevitably, is obliged to deal with a very large number of firms. The philosophies of those involved and the mechanisms through which they operate tend almost always to inhibit communication. The results are generally both inefficient and divisive.

The arbitration system, while seeking to strike a balance between the competing claims of the "needs" of the individual and industry's "capacity to pay," is constantly challenged. From 1920 to 1953, award wages were automatically adjusted to provide for changes in the purchasing power of money. Wage-setting arrangements were further modified in the 1950s and 1960s. During this period, there was a constant presumption in favor of full adjustment to take account of movements in the general price level. Wage indexing, formally reintroduced in 1975 after a period of extreme turbulence in the labor market, was thought to be an arrangement guaranteeing equity. The notion of "comparative wage justice" is deeply entrenched in the Australian system. The usual practice has been for pacesetting unions to secure a wage increase that would then flow on to the rest of the work force. In the early seventies, the public service unions were among the principal pacesetters. Unconstrained by considerations of profitability, supported by a government committed to redistributing income in favor of labor, real wages rose strongly. The subsequent introduction of automatic wage indexing served to fix real wages at this new, higher, level, contributing inevitably to a steep rise in unemployment.

The arbitration system has led also to a compression of wage differentials, having deleterious effects on company incentives to invest in human capital. Faced with a conflict between "needs" and "capacity to pay," there has been a tendency to squeeze the more highly paid workers. While the resulting compression has been partially offset by a system of over-award payments, this compensation does not appear ever to have been complete. To the extent that the arbitration system has inhibited changes in relative wage rates, it has worked to impede the process of structural adjustment. By isolating the wage structure from the discipline of the market place, the arbitration system has worked against those forces that have supported a more open economy.

Australia's postwar development strategy was predicated on the expectation of strong growth in private capital investment. The results, at least in the 1950s and 1960s, were impressive: real fixed private investment increased by around 6 percent per annum. Following the surge in wages in the early 1970s, however, the profit share fell sharply, and remained low for the rest of the decade. These years, associated with sluggish growth and weak investment, were partially redeemed by the second oil shock, which boosted the outlook for profitability in the mining sector, leading to a very steep increase in investment in energy-related projects.

Foreign capital has always played an important role in the development of the Australian economy. In the early 1950s, about 12 percent of investment outlays were financed by funds from abroad; the percentage rose steadily to around 25 percent in fiscal year 1971. Rising nationalist sentiments and proposals to "buy back the farm" alarmed certain foreign investors, and for most of the Whitlam years foreign funds financed a mere 6 to 8 percent of total fixed business investment. The resources boom, however, returned foreign capital to its previous prominence, and in fiscal year 1982 overseas investment financed around 24 percent of private capital expenditure. Australian attitudes to foreign investment and views on the preferred forms of such investment tend to change in accord with fluctuations in the business cycle. While there has been a growing bipartisan approach to foreign investment over the years, an attitude that recognizes the important contribution foreign funds and know-how can make, there has also been a desire to insure that reasonable benefits accrue to Australia from the operation of foreign companies.

Just as a collection of pistons, rings, carburetors, and the like can only hint at the capabilities of a motor vehicle, so a broad overview of the main components of the Australian economy must necessarily leave a great deal unsaid. The performance of an automobile is crucially dependent on tuning and timing; similarly, the functioning of an economy is materially affected by the blend of policies adopted, with the timing of the changes being absolutely crucial. While all countries and regions confront the same international environment, countries grow at very different rates. This suggests that the domestic environment, even more than the international economy, may be the critical factor in determining growth. Japan, a closely regulated economy that operates in a highly restrictive trade environment, has registered exceptionally strong growth in the postwar years. New Zealand, on the other hand, has done poorly although it is a faithful model of a country that operates within a highly protectionist trade regime. Protection appears to be rather like a dangerous drug: applied judiciously, it can prove beneficial; administered in excess, it can prove lethal. The withdrawal process can be very painful.

While it is very much in the Australian tradition to consider the country markedly egalitarian—in the weakness of its class structure, in its openness to opportunity and upward mobility, and in its distribution of income—there are reasons to believe that the trend is otherwise, particularly as regards income. There are several explanations for this. At the bottom end of the income scale, the proportion of the work force that is unemployed or on welfare began to increase dramatically; at the same time, the payment of taxes became almost discretionary for many in the upper income brackets. Doctors, lawyers, and other privileged groups were able with ease to divest themselves of their tax burdens. This offended the community's sense of fair play, and tax reform is now on the agenda. Also, over the last two decades, while the share of federal government revenue from wage and salary taxes increased from around 20 percent to over 40 percent, these disparities have done nothing to moderate the pressure for higher wages. The trade-off between equality and growth remains a vexed question. While Herman Kahn and Thomas Pepper concluded that "mateship and egalitarianism make a business-as-usual alternative [for Australia] more likely than an intensely dynamic economy,"[26] the business community has argued that the highly equalizing tax system only stifles initiative, undermining the possibilities of rapid growth.

In the three decades after World War II, while the average unemployment rate in the United States was around 5–6 percent, the Australian rate was only 1–2 percent. Australia enjoyed virtually full employment. Given that situation, today's present unemployment is almost certainly bound to increase the sense of alienation, inadequacy, and bewilderment in those faced with long periods of being out of work. While there is ample public support for social service benefits being extended to the unemployed, the employed majority does not seem overly concerned to extend its natural compassion and generosity to assist in new ways this unfamiliar category of disadvantaged individuals. There is no public outcry demanding practical new policies to guarantee full employment. While this may reflect an increased sense of impotence rather than a lack of genuine concern for the unemployed, the community at large appears to have lost faith in the government's ability to bring about fundamental reform. The grand vision of 1945 has not just faded; it has been virtually obliterated.

Australians have tended to look abroad for inspiration, seeking in foreign example a confirmation of their own judgment. An increased acceptance by major Western economies of the inevitability of high levels of structural unemployment has certainly influenced Australia's reaction to this problem. So, also, with the acceptance of the fact that a disproportionate amount of this unemployment will fall on ethnic minorities. This has not prevented Australia from spending a generous half-percent of its GDP (U.S.$170 per household) to aid developing countries. The aid program appears to enjoy broad community support and does not today face the "donor fatigue" that is thought to be characteristic of America.

Why, then, does Australia, once at the top in living standards, now rank only sixteenth? The poor growth rate cannot be attributed to a lack of resources; it is impossible to argue that the nation lacks people or skills. Except for an occasional aberration, the management of fiscal and monetary policy has been adequate, if not uniformly impressive. Can it be that perceptions of the correct policies for growth have been unrealistic, out of tune with the nation's aspirations for higher current income? Australia, in many ways a derivative society, has tended to borrow ideas in good currency in Europe and the United States, and then to cling to these ideas long after the rest of the world has moved on. Thus, for example, there was little understanding of the argument that protection and restricted trade would over the long run provide less employment and less growth than an open economy and extensive trade. When the validity of these propositions was incontestably demonstrated by the experience of one country after another, Australia was either not looking or chose not to see. The idea of becoming internationally competitive was never very strong. Instead, there has been a penchant for regulation—of wages, fees, interest rates, exchange rates, prices. Institutions and organizations, accustomed to certain ways of handling their affairs, have tended to be rigid rather than adaptive. Repeated attempts to modernize the 1900 constitution have failed. The country has had more than its share of Olson's "distributional coalitions" seeking to maintain or expand their own share of the social pie, but in the end contributing only to new inequality.[27]

The question today is whether Hawke, recently reelected by a reduced majority, is the leader who will be able to persuade Australians to adopt more realistic policies for growth, adapting themselves to the world around them. Hawke's first major move on assuming office in March 1983 was to convene a national economic summit where business, trade unions, and the government could hammer out an agreement on a strategy for economic recovery. The results, though significant for reducing inflation, may have been less notable than the process, which possibly owed something to an idea espoused by Hawke and others in 1975, that those whose cooperation was necessary for the implementation of a decision ought to be involved in making it.[28]

In 1985, the Hawke government is to bring the summit technique to bear on issues as disparate and difficult as narcotics addiction and tax reform. Although uneasy about their lack of economic progress, Australians are yet slow to make needed changes in attitudes and institutions that are familiar and therefore comfortable. Faced with misgivings about a more international future, Australians tend towards inaction, and this is reinforced by distributional coalitions that see themselves as disadvantaged by particular reforms. In this setting, the Hawke idea of working towards a consensus on the directions and management of change stands a fair chance of success.

ENDNOTES

[1] Quoted in *The Australian,* May 14, 1984, p. 1.
[2]Quoted in *The Australian,* December 31, 1983, p. 2.
[3]Brian Penton, *Advance Australia—Where?* (London: Cassell and Company Ltd., 1943).
[4]The Australian fiscal year ends in June.
[5]Richard H. Snape, "Australia's Relations with GATT," *Economic Record,* March 1984, p. 21.
[6]Dorothea Mackellar, *The Witch-Maid & Other Verses* (New York: J.M. Dent & Sons Ltd., 1914).
[7]Quoted in Selwyn Cornish, "Full Employment in Australia: The Genesis of a White Paper," Research Paper in Economic History, no. 1, 1981, Australian National University, pp. 183–184.
[8]Ibid, p. 187.
[9]John Hooke, "Will New Technology Help to Solve Industry's Problems?," paper presented at the National Technology Conference, September 1983, Canberra, p. 5.
[10]Ronald Johnston, "Do Australian Managers Have the Right Attitude?," paper presented at the National Technology Conference, September 1983, Canberra, p. 4.
[11]Ibid, p. 5.
[12]Ibid.
[13]George W. England, "Managers and Their Value Systems," *Economic Impact,* no. 27, 1979, pp. 23–27.
[14]Noel Capon, Chris Christodoulou, John U. Farley, and James M. Hulbert, "Corporate Planning Practice in Major American and Australian Manufacturing Companies," Monash University, 1984, p. 18.
[15]Noel G. Butlin, Alan Barnard, and J.J. Pincus, *Government and Capitalism* (Sydney: George Allen & Unwin, 1982), p. 289.

[16]Quoted in Leslie F. Crisp, *Australian National Government* (Victoria: Longman, 1973), p. 1.
[17]Ibid, p. 40.
[18]Ibid.
[19]Ibid, p. 59.
[20]Edward M. Grambich, "A Fair Go: Fiscal Federalism in Australia," paper presented at the Brookings Survey of the Australian Economy Conference, January 9–11, 1984, Canberra, p. 66.
[21]*OECD Economic Outlook,* December 1983, no. 34, p. 159.
[22]Rudiger Dornbusch, and Stanley Fischer, "The Australian Macro Economy," paper presented at the Brookings Survey of the Australian Economy Conference, January 9–11, 1984, Canberra, p. 66.
[23]Ibid, p. 70.
[24]Penton, *Advance Australia—Where?,* p. 204.
[25]J. Terence Ludeke, paper presented at the Seminar on Changing Industrial Law, Australian National University, September 6, 1983, p. 7.
[26]Herman Kahn and Thomas Pepper, *Will She Be Right?* (Queensland: University of Queensland Press, 1980), p. 6.
[27]Mancur Olson, *The Rise and Decline of Nations: Economic Growth, Stagflation, and Social Rigidities* (New Haven: Yale University Press, 1983).
[28]R. Gordon Jackson and others, green paper "Policies for Development of Manufacturing Industry," Australian Government Publishing Service, 1975, p. 16.

T.B. Millar

The Defense of Australia

THE PRECAUTIONS TAKEN by any householder to preserve life and limb or to prevent theft or damage to his property or livelihood reflect the measure of his accumulated or unresolved apprehensions more than the accuracy of his judgments. So it is with nations, with the added complication that decisions are taken by groups of individuals, none of whom feels totally responsible for the decision nor totally concerned with its outcome, and all of whom are subjected to competing pressures, priorities, and incentives.

Since soon after the First Fleet set its cargo ashore at Port Jackson in 1788, the attitudes of the Australian settlers to the world outside have been characterized with remarkable consistency by a sense of remoteness from the sources of authority, power and protection, vulnerability to hostile forces deployed in the region, dependence accordingly on what Sir Robert Menzies came to call "great and powerful friends," and—especially since the gold discoveries of the 1850s—fear that the hostile forces will descend and take away the settlers' hard-won physical or social gains.

Those gains represented the notion of a separate Australian identity that developed alongside the sense of being an appendage of the British Empire (up to World War II), of the American alliance (since then), and of European culture (continuously). Australian nationalism did not come, as in the non-white British colonies, from a psychological and physical struggle against the visible constraints of imperial rule. Some of the settlers and their dependents resented the authority of Westminster and Whitehall, kicking against the bureaucratic pricks of the Colonial Office, yet at the same time the forces making for self-government resented equally London's relative lack of interest in colonial affairs, its reluctance to continue defending them, and the withdrawal of the imperial garrisons. The door they pushed at opened without difficulty. Nationalism grew more from identifying with "Australia," with their own land and people, the togetherness of a pioneer society, and shared (often harsh) experiences. Nationalist sentiment flourished alongside imperial sentiment, and although notions of imperial federation in the late nineteenth century struck little response, the need to defend the empire sent men flocking to the recruiting booths. Australians went to New Zealand to fight alongside British troops in the Maori wars of 1863–64. They went to the Sudan in 1885, to South Africa at the turn of the century to help defeat the Boers, and to China against the Boxers. Some 330,000 volunteers went overseas in World War I, and nearly 60,000 did not come back. In 1939, Australia was at war with Germany for reasons that constitutionally, politically, and electorally identified Australia with the British Commonwealth and Empire, Australian national interests with British national interests, Australian security with British security.

For most of the nineteenth century, Australians looked out on the world with the eyes and the perspectives of Europeans. Rivalry between the great metropolitan powers—Britain, France, Germany, Russia—was translated physically to the Far East but was also taken on board as their own by the Australian colonists. Thus, one of the main reasons for settling Western Australia was fear that the French might get there first. During the Crimean War (1854–56), Australian colonial governments built forts and raised volunteer forces out of fear of Russia and its Pacific fleet. German colonial aspirations prompted the Queensland government in 1883 to try to annex part of New Guinea. What caused a sea change in Australian apprehensions was the Japanese defeat of Russia in the war of 1904–05. For the next forty years and more, despite involvement in the two European civil wars, Australian political leaders saw Japan as the most dangerous threat to the Australian continent and people. For this reason, Prime Minister Alfred Deakin engineered a visit to Australia by the American Great White Fleet in 1908, and tried (though failed) to see a U.S.-British "Monroe Doctrine for the Pacific" enunciated. Successive Australian governments encouraged the continued renewal of the 1902 Anglo-Japanese alliance. At the Versailles peace conference, Prime Minister W.M. Hughes blocked Japan's bid for racial equality and the implication of unrestricted access to Eastern New Guinea and Australia. The "White Australia" immigration policy written into law by the nation's first parliament had been directed first against the industrious, formidable Japanese.

In the early 1930s, the Australian prime minister, Joseph Lyons, saw advantages in Japan invading Manchuria, in that this meant its energies were directed westwards rather than southwards; but within two or three years, Australian defense analysts concluded (as they had in the early 1920s) that Japan was Australia's most likely enemy. This led Lyons to propose a non-aggression pact for the Pacific that would include Japan, the Soviet Union, Britain, France, and the United States. Only the Russians expressed any sympathy; the others were too preoccupied by the gathering storm in Europe. The Japanese attack on Pearl Harbor, the thrust down through the Netherlands East Indies to the gates of Australia, and the bombing and shelling of Australian cities—all proved the point that Australia was under threat from Asia and that Japan was the enemy. World War II also proved that in the event of a major threat to Australian security, only the United States could provide the necessary protection. During the war, Australia sent some 550,000 servicemen and women overseas and lost over 34,000 of them. Of these, 8,031 died in inhumane conditions in Japanese prisoner-of-war camps.

Fear of Japan survived the war. Even with Japan defeated, exhausted, substantially destroyed, and occupied by allied armies, Australian governments and people believed that what Japan had once done it could do again. The soft peace treaty with Japan in 1951, acknowledging Japan's "inherent right of self-defense," was one of the major elements in Australia's successful bid for a security treaty by which the United States reassured Australia (and New Zealand). While of course offering Australia no guarantee of protection under any stated circumstances, the ANZUS treaty, or Pacific Pact, calmed Australian fears and appeared to interpose American power between Australia and any new "threat from the north." This treaty was negotiated under the shadow of a lightly rearming Japan, but by the time the treaty was signed (September 1951) it was seen by the new Liberal (conservative) government of Robert Menzies as relating primarily to the force that now seemed to threaten Australia: aggressive communism based in Asia.

Both the wartime-postwar Labor government (1941–49) and (still more) its Liberal-Country parties successor (1949–72) were troubled by the success of the Soviet Union in taking over half of Europe after the war and in supporting militant left-wing political parties and trade-union activities in many countries. The Chifley Labor government used troops to keep mines and wharves operating in the face of communist-led stoppages, and sent Australian aircraft to help beat the Soviet land blockade of Berlin. Communist insurgencies in South and Southeast Asia in 1948, allied to or competing with other nationalist movements directed against friendly (to Australia) European imperial powers, the communist takeover of China, and communist North Korea's attack on South Korea, coincident with communist-led industrial strife within Australia, convinced the Liberal government that the monolithic world communist movement was bent on taking over the world and imposing on it an alien and unacceptable ideology. Hence Australia's (unsuccessful) attempt to ban the Australian Communist Party, its contribution to the UN forces in Korea, and its involvement in the Vietnam War (1962–72).

During the 1950s, while "communism" remained the perceived threat, it was upon China that Australian apprehensions came primarily to be focused. After November 1950, China had become the enemy in Korea, where Chinese and Australian troops fought and killed each other. Like the United States, whose intelligence reports it regularly received, the Australian government saw a Chinese hand and Chinese support behind communist military activities in Southeast Asia. Some members of the government would have liked to enter normal diplomatic relations with the People's Republic but deference to the American alliance prevented this from occurring. When Prime Minister Menzies sent an Australian battalion to Vietnam in mid-1965, he justified this in terms of meeting a threat by China down between the Indian and Pacific Oceans, and the Australian public nodded its agreement. Elements within the Labor party, on grounds of ideology rather than of strategic assessment, resisted this concept but were barely heard. Chinese support of Vietnam reinforced the Australian sense of hostility, and those like this writer who urged on pragmatic grounds the recognition of China and its seating at the United Nations were considered at best ill-judged and ill-informed. A maverick Liberal minister for external affairs in an election address in 1969 (Gordon Freeth) declared that Australia should not be frightened at the sight of Russians in the Indian Ocean because they could act as a restraint upon the Chinese. (He lost his seat—partly because his electorate was in Western Australia, which fronts the Indian Ocean and feels more isolated, vulnerable, and thus defense-conscious than other states.)

Had Labor come to office earlier than 1972, it would almost certainly have recognized Peking, and, in the event, did so within days of assuming power that December. This, however, followed the American and Australian force withdrawals from Vietnam and the Kissinger-Nixon visits to China. By this time, China was ceasing to be seen as a threat, or as a real or potential enemy, and quickly assumed in Australian eyes the status of a major and important regional power with whose government one had to deal and whose political system was perhaps less evil than one had thought. China became "all right." It was even a useful counterweight to growing Soviet power in the region.

The decline of China in Australian perceptions of a threat to their country roughly coincided with the elevation of the USSR. During the long period of conservative rule, the Australian government had only slowly come to terms with the reality of Soviet power and influence. The first Australian minister for external affairs to visit Moscow did so only in 1964, and it was the Whitlam Labor government (1972–75) that recognized Poland and East Germany, and acknowledged de jure Soviet control of the Baltic states, as well as arranging formal relations with North Korea and North Vietnam. In the late 1960s, when a Soviet fleet entered and established a permanent presence in the Indian Ocean, with access subsequently to a modest base in Somalia and later Ethiopia, Australian apprehensions of the USSR as a potential direct threat to Australia rose, and were further "justified" by the Soviet treaty with Vietnam (1978) and its arrangements to use former American bases at Da Nang and Cam Ranh Bay and to erect a sophisticated communications and intelligence facility there. The Soviet invasion of Afghanistan in late 1979 raised further fears based on the alleged historical Russian desire for access to warm-water ports in the Indian Ocean. As part of the Western alliance system for more than thirty years, and a relatively close ally of the United States whose defense preoccupations since 1949 have been with the Soviet Union, Australia has seen the USSR as a continuing danger to its allies and to its own interests. Although the distances were still considerable, the Russians were coming steadily closer.

Since about 1960, one other country—Indonesia—has prompted a sense of insecurity in Australia. Australia had played a sympathetic, if somewhat ambivalent, role in the movement that led to Indonesian independence in late 1949, for which the new nationalist leadership was appreciative; but conflict of interest soon developed over Indonesia's claim to West New Guinea (West Irian, or Irian Jaya), which was the one part of the former Netherlands East Indies not transferred to Indonesian rule. West Irian lay only a line's thickness from the Australian-administered Territory of Papua and New Guinea, and Indonesia eventually obtained control only by the threat of force and the device (under the auspices of the UN and with the complicity of the United States) of a spurious act of free choice. Soon thereafter, Australia and Indonesia clashed physically in Borneo over President Sukarno's imperialist venture of "confrontation" of the new amalgamated state of Malaysia, comprising Malaya, Singapore, North Borneo, and Sarawak. During these few years (especially 1963–65), Australian fears of an Indonesia armed with some of the latest Soviet weapons reached their high point, and a new long-range bomber (the F-111) was ordered from the United States to be able to strike, if necessary, at Indonesian targets. While relations soon returned to normal after the fall of Sukarno, latent Australian concerns remain, especially over East Timor (where Australians fought Japanese during World War II) and over Papua New Guinea (in case of Indonesian intervention). Timor is only 250 miles from the Australian mainland, and there are some 25,000 Australian expatriates in Papua New Guinea, and strong historical links.

At the time, and in retrospect, were fears for their security on the part of the Australian government or public justified? And did governments of the day take appropriate action to meet the perceived threat? Deakin, early in the century, was undoubtedly not just a good guesser but extremely prescient, and his response—attempting to interest the United States in the security of the region including Australia, as well as building up Australia's own naval capacities—was entirely appropriate. Lyons was foolish to look sympathetically on Japan's conquest of Manchuria, the prelude to its great drive southwards. Subsequent apprehensions about Japan were entirely justified, but the proposal for a non-aggression pact was a poor substitute for the defense preparations that Japan's military adventures and the worsening situation in Europe demanded. Post–World War II fears of Japan were understandable, as a hangover from a brutal war, but unfounded. Fears of "communism" were simplistic, and the declared belief (of the Menzies government) that communist activities could rapidly lead to World War III—if genuinely believed in, and there is no reason to think they were not—were not translated into any serious military measures. Similarly, Australia's commitment to the 1954 South East Asia Collective Defence Treaty (usually known by the now-defunct organization it established, SEATO) was essentially rhetorical. Menzies promised to make two divisions available if necessary for the defense of Thailand, Laos, Cambodia, South Vietnam, and the Philippines, but Australia would have been hard put to find two battalions and could not have provided their logistical support. Similarly, when Menzies in August 1963 publicly ranged Australia alongside the new state of Malaysia, he delayed a further nineteen months before sending troops to Borneo where the action was. Fear of Indonesian attacks upon Australia was, as we now see, totally unjustified.

Again, as Senator Fulbright was unkind enough to point out, if the Australian military contribution had matched the Australian political rhetoric over Vietnam, several times the number of troops would have been sent. In other words, since World War I and apart from World War II, in the various apparent crises threatening her security, Australian apprehensions have not produced what might be deemed appropriate actions. This comes close to tokenism, and is certainly "defense on the cheap." Except in the two world wars, Australia has tended to want a front seat in negotiations but, like W.S. Gilbert's Duke of Plaza Toro, to lead the regiment from behind. Thus, the continuing sense of remoteness, vulnerability, and dependence has brought a major response only in a crisis extending far wider than Australia, and the sense of dependence was almost always stronger than any notions of self-reliance. Since World War II, only the United States has been capable of launching a major attack upon Australia, and—except perhaps for the purpose of recapturing the America's Cup—it has had no conceivable reason for doing so.

II

What then are Australia's residual commitments and current strategies? The strategy (if it can be so dignified) of what came to be called "forward defense" was the perfectly sensible if not especially bold one of encouraging powerful friends (Britain, the U.S.) to interpose themselves between Australia and its potentially hostile and sometimes communist near-neighbors. It suited the powerful friends because they had their own reasons for being there, and they welcomed the modest Australian military presence in its own right but even more as a political gesture. Forward defense began with the dispatch of the 8th Division to Malaya in mid-1941 and substantially ended with the final withdrawal of combat forces from Vietnam in early 1972. There is a residual presence in the region and forms of obligation, but "forward defense" in the old sense became unworkable when the British and Americans withdrew from mainland Southeast Asia. Australia gives significant defense aid, without commitment, to Papua New Guinea. At the time of writing, it has a squadron of Mirage III fighter-bombers, approaching the end of their operational life, located at Butterworth in Malaysia, and is part of the integrated Air Defence System (IADS) for Malaysia and Singapore. The Hawke Labor government has said it will withdraw this squadron when the F18 replaces the Mirage during the next two years. Unless Australia simultaneously withdraws from IADS and from the Five Power Defence Arrangements (involving also Britain and New Zealand), there will be continuing defense contacts and joint exercises which, while not constituting formal commitments to the defense of Malaysia and Singapore, imply a degree of defense cooperation. But to defend Malaysia from Darwin is a less credible enterprise than to defend it from Penang, and both Malaysia and Singapore would prefer a permanent presence.

The one residual obligation of the South East Asia Collective Defence Treaty is a commitment to the defense of Thailand. The treaty does not spell this out, merely affirming agreement to consult in the event of subversion, and in the event of "aggression by means of armed attack" to "act to meet the common danger in accordance with its constitutional principles." This obligation was reaffirmed in 1962 and again more recently by the government of Mr. Malcolm Fraser (prime minister from 1975 to 1983). The present Hawke government has neither confirmed nor denied the obligation that by its very vagueness leaves every option open. The most that Thailand could probably expect from Australia in the circumstances (say) of a major assault from Vietnam, would be the supply of arms and equipment and increased civil economic aid. Australia is even less likely than the U.S. to contribute armed forces. (Note that technically Australia is also committed under SEATO to the defense of the Philippines, but there appears to be no substance to the commitment.)

With five of the ASEAN states (Malaysia, Singapore, Thailand, the Philippines, and Indonesia) and with several of the small independent states of the Southwest Pacific, Australia has mutual cooperation agreements in defense matters, which in some cases are essentially camouflaged military aid agreements. They involve providing access to training facilities, transfers of arms and equipment, exchange of information, joint exercises, contributions to defense infrastructure, but in no case is there a formally declared obligation on any party to come to the aid of another. The ASEAN states also have their own growing web of cooperative defense measures without formal commitments. The fact is that no two of these states have identical national interests, and within ASEAN there are latent tensions that are sublimated by the common determination to gain added prestige and influence by presenting a common front to the world. This is one international institution where to sweep bilateral problems under the carpet, while it may leave some of the bumps visible, is of advantage to all; where the combined total of their objectives is based satisfactorily, though perhaps temporarily, on the lowest common factor of their interests.

Australia has never been seriously considered for membership in ASEAN, and ASEAN states have combined to belabor Australia over its tariff and civil aviation policies; but in the event of any foreseeable regional security crisis in which they stood together, they would expect Australia to be sympathetic and supportive. Australia would face a difficult dilemma if ASEAN were divided against itself; or if—in the most quoted scenario—some future Indonesian government were to trouble the waters of Papua New Guinea and then fish in them for political or territorial profit; or, worst of all, if the U.S. found itself torn between helping Australia and helping Indonesia. As the largest metropolitan power in the Southwest Pacific, Australia could be called upon (as it was in the insurgency on Espiritu Santo following the independence of Vanuatu, and responded by providing logistical help to a Papua New Guinea military force) to help preserve the integrity of one of the small island states.

Australia's main international security obligation, however, is not local or regional but global: its part in the defense of Western interests and the Western economic and strategic system, including Japan. Little of this relates any more to Britain: the empire is dissolved and the Commonwealth is not a political entity with mutual loyalties and commitments; only a handful of fragments remains. Australia's concern with global issues is as a partner of the United States. The ANZUS treaty is the legal framework and underpinning of that partnership, within a Western alliance system and historically developed arrangements that include Britain and Canada.

Cooperation takes many forms. There is a continuous interchange of intelligence information. Much of the Australian defense capital equipment is American. There are many technical cooperation agreements. There is a score or more of American defense-related facilities in Australia, the three main ones being the North West Cape Communications Station, used mainly for communicating with submerged nuclear-powered nuclear-missile firing submarines; the intelligence-gathering satellite ground station at Pine Gap in Central Australia, and the early warning satellite ground station at Nurrungar in South Australia. Joint naval exercises take place regularly, some involving other powers (Canada, New Zealand, Britain, Japan, Indonesia). American ships, including nuclear-powered and nuclear-armed vessels, have access to Australian ports for replenishment and minor repairs, and rest and recreation of crews. American B-52 bombers train over North Queensland, or stage at Darwin prior to onward flight to Diego Garcia or surveillance flights over the Indian Ocean. While the U.S. can drive a hard financial bargain and obviously regards Australia very much as a junior partner, the partnership is about as close as any in the Western world. Australia is not vital to American security, in the way that Canada or West Germany is, but it is very important, especially until defense technology will no longer require the Australian facilities. In the case of Pine Gap, this would almost certainly be well into the twenty-first century. Alternatives to Nurrungar are already being developed. The North West Cape station could be shifted at any time, although it serves the

Australian Navy. It is politically vulnerable to the left wing of the Labor party.

When those facilities were negotiated and installed, beginning in the early 1960s, they raised the possibility, virtually ignored at the time but now a matter of public concern and even alarm, that because of the relevance of the facilities to the American strategic deterrent, information gathering, and warning systems, they—and thus Australia—would be Soviet targets in any East-West nuclear war. While this cannot be confirmed short of a war, it would seem to be very likely, and Soviet representatives in an attempt to support the peace movement in Australia have confirmed the probability. Successive governments, including the present Labor government led by Mr. Hawke, have taken the position—or have acted as though they have taken the position—that the existence of the facilities is a net gain to Australian security in that, while they offer potential targets in a nuclear war, their contribution to the Western deterrent makes any such war less likely. Their importance cements the alliance and the alliance applies to other kinds of contingency. There is also the suggestion made by Desmond Ball[1] that the direction of prevailing winds, and the remote localities where the facilities are, mean that even in the event of a nuclear attack Australian casualties should be few. This does not reassure anyone who is opposed to the American alliance (a vocal minority) or who is emotionally committed to the proposition that nuclear war is imminent and that a situation that leads to any nuclear casualties anywhere is totally unacceptable, or anyone who is intellectually committed to the proposition that strategists are not necessarily infallible.

What, then, has happened to "remoteness, vulnerability and dependence"? They are still there in the Australian mentality, which is why the Hawke Labor government clings as firmly to ANZUS as its predecessors did, and appears to have accepted the Soviet Union as the main threat to the security of the West, including Australia.

On the other hand, it has reduced the defense perimeter by eliminating the navy's air-strike capacity, and there is no evidence that the government, its bureaucratic advisors, the media, or the body of academic and/or armchair strategists see any present or likely threat to the security of Australia. The Soviet Union is a potential threat because of its apparent global expansionist tendencies, its continuing increase in defense capacities, and the fact that it is locked into a cold war with the West. In the event that the cold war becomes a hot war, even a small hot war, Australia could become involved, especially if the United States wished to use its facilities in Australia. Should the U.S. become a direct party to war in the Middle East, for example, it might need Australia for staging transport and other aircraft on the Westabout route. Australian maritime reconnaissance aircraft based in Australia or at Singapore are part of the West's surveillance of the Indian Ocean.

Yet, the incalculable and potentially horrific consequences of an East-West war make a direct Soviet-American conflict far less likely than other kinds of conflict. In Australia, defense planners see a low-level threat to some mainland or off-shore facility or resource as the most probable threat to be faced in the next few years, as well as smuggling, illicit drug running, and illegal immigration into the northern half of Australia's long (12,200 miles) and largely open coastline. The Australian Defence Force, so long accustomed to the scenario of fighting a land war in Asia, is now slowly gearing to the notion of *first* defending the Australian mainland (three million square miles) and maritime environment (the EEZ has the same area). The problems here are complex and difficult enough. The distances are great (two thousand miles between Sydney and Darwin, for example), and the fact is that Australia is a land-connected archipelago of pockets of immense resource wealth, especially in minerals, particularly iron, bauxite, and uranium. A capacity to defend so large an area could, of course, be used for overseas deployments. While not rejecting the idea that Australian armed forces should serve overseas (there is a helicopter squadron right now in the Multinational Force in the Sinai), Australians are gradually gearing to the possibility that they may at some stage have to fight on their own soil. The scenario for this is difficult to create and even more difficult to publish, but with the end of European empires south of the equator, and with the British and Americans out of Southeast Asia, the largely European population of the world's largest island, rich and empty as it is, is coming uneasily to the realization that remoteness and vulnerability are even more difficult to bear when there is no great and powerful friend confidently at hand. Yet, once again, there is little evidence of any governmental, bureaucratic, or public intention to do much more than enjoy the sunshine while it lasts and hope for years of warning or for some god out of the machine.

III

It is possible to argue, with some cogency, that despite the assurance felt and benefits received, Australia has spent more than it has gained under the ANZUS treaty, or "produced" more security than it has "consumed." The treaty, after all, has never been invoked, i.e., Australia has never called on the United States to intervene physically in the defense of Australia. There has never been a situation where Australia *needed* to call for such help, although there have been several requests for reassurance, especially against Indonesia. On the other hand, one can say that Australia has made sacrifices. In diplomatic terms, it has not been able to pursue in the region a flexible foreign policy, geared directly to Australia's national interests and regional relationships, because of its obvious alignment with the U.S. and deference to American preoccupations. That attitude was excessively symbolized by Prime Minister Harold Holt's statement in Washington during the Vietnam War that Australia was (he quoted President Lyndon Johnson's campaign slogan) "all the way with LBJ." However much this may have pleased the president and his supporters, it offended Australian national sovereignty and independent image, and committed Australia to a military campaign whose prime purpose was not to save South Vietnam but to save Australia in some unknown future crisis—a crisis in which the U.S. would act not on the basis of past favors but of current interests. Participation in the Vietnam War (the Australian military presence totalled eight thousand men at the height of the commitment), had its costs in casualties and financial expenditure, but even more in the divisions it came to create within the society. The Australian commitments to Malaya and Malaysia, as well as to Vietnam, sprang from a dependence it did not need to feel (so the argument runs) because it was not in any danger, nor under any threat, and indeed was acting out a para-imperial role for which it was neither suited nor prepared.

Again, it has been contended that Australia's dependence on and emulation of the United States was the "easy way out" that deferred to the indefinite future any real attempt to determine a genuinely Australian foreign and defense policy, and pay for it, any attempt at "standing on its own feet." Some Australians saw little to choose between the imperialist attitudes of the United States and those of the

USSR, or between the brutality of their military forces, or the heavy handedness and unenlightened self-interest of their diplomacy.

None of the proponents of these views received significant support except for two or three years during the anti–Vietnam War movement late in the 1960s when the electorate had become confused about the war, its objectives and its relevance to Australia. In recent times, there has been a much more vocal movement opposed to the U.S. facilities (or "bases" as they are usually and incorrectly labeled) on the grounds that they make Australia gratuitously a target for nuclear attack. This movement has been allied to that opposed to all nuclear armaments, to Australian mining and export of uranium, to the dumping of Japanese nuclear waste in the Pacific, and to French nuclear tests. While this is a pluralistic operation with many facets, including support for "Peace," there is a thread of anti-Americanism running through most of them. Even so, the only activity to have real political influence has been the anti-uranium lobby, and it was out-gunned by Mr. Fraser and so far has been out-maneuvered by Mr. Hawke.

Within this varied assembly (whose total support would probably amount to less than 15 percent of the electorate), there has been very little attempt to find an alternative to the American alliance. Some people across the political spectrum would like to see greater "self-reliance," and a proportion of these would wish the taxpayer to finance the substantially higher level of defense expenditure that this would require. Others see little value—indeed, a definite evil—in defense preparations of any kind, and would like to rely on diplomacy, foreign-aid programs, or simple good will to ensure Australian security. Some differentiate between offensive defense and defensive defense, believing that any neighbor who saw that Australia was incapable of launching an offensive war would feel better disposed towards Australia and would never wish to attack or harm it. (How would they classify a submarine, one wonders?) On such innocent simplicities does much of the peace movement rest.

On selective issues, such as port calls by nuclear-armed ships, the anti-Americanism within these movements and within the Labor party could be politically embarrassing. It could force the dismantling of North West Cape, even though that would disadvantage Australia. It could lead to successful motions at some branch party meetings to get rid of the treaty, or to renegotiate it so that it would offer watertight "guarantees" to defend Australia (which is impossible) or enable Australia to evade any commitments under the treaty (which it already can do). But the Australian Labor party has come nowhere near the position of its New Zealand equivalent, whose party conference has voted that the country should leave the alliance. There is in New Zealand a restlessness with the treaty, and fear of a nuclear holocaust that has no numerical equivalent among the Australian electorate. Why is this? Why is there so much more apprehension, so much more anti-Americanism, in New Zealand than in Australia? I suspect that fear of being involved in regional conflict is much less in New Zealand, which is so much further from Southeast Asia than is Australia; hence there is less need of the alliance. Accordingly, the negative aspects of the treaty—especially the possibility of being dragged on the American coattails into a nuclear war—loom so much larger.

Then again, unlike Australia, the direct experience of New Zealand's armed forces in World War II was not in nearby Southeast Asia, nor in combat with the Japanese, but in fighting Germans and Italians in North Africa and Italy. Certainly New Zealanders operated in Vietnam and Malaysia, but there was and is very little sense of *threat* from Asia. New Zealand is a collection of islands in the South Seas, a South Pacific maritime state, remote from the superpowers. Why should it become involved in their arguments and confrontations at such enormous risk?

But Australia has been continuously involved since the Korean War (1950) with the support of the majority of the population. Today, no real alternative to ANZUS is being seriously considered in Australia at a political or significant public level. This may seem surprising in view of the growth in the volume and coverage of Australia's diplomatic voice around the world, the massive expansion of the economy, the steady erosion of formal links with Britain, and the consolidation of the Australian identity at home and overseas. Again, it may seem surprising in view of the greatly reduced sense of threat since the end of the Vietnam War. People troubled and vocal about the prospect of nuclear war are mostly on the left of politics and have little sympathy with the alliance.

Perhaps the reasons for dependence on ANZUS are more fundamental. The present generation of political leaders and newspaper editors experienced World War II and acknowledged the vital role of the United States in the defense of Australia. Within the generations of their children, fear of Asia was deeply engrained, even if it now exists alongside a desire to live on friendly terms with Asian neighbors. Australia is a nation of migrants and their descendants. Of the large proportion of the population (22 percent at the 1981 census) born outside the country, almost all will have considerably improved their standard of living and, like their native-born compatriots, want to preserve that standard at minimum cost. Many of the 3.7 million immigrants since World War II are refugees from communist regimes—in the USSR, Eastern Europe, Indochina—and for these the U.S. appears to represent resistance to their "oppressors," the ultimate defense, the only possible guarantor of stability or redress. Coral Bell writes of some of Australia's ethnic commitments:

> The Greek sense of nationhood centres around hostility to Turkey and has focused on the particular issue of Cyprus in recent years. Ukrainian, Polish, Estonian, Latvian, Lithuanian and Hungarian nationalism has been defined by hostility towards Russia and more recently towards Soviet Communism. Arab nationalism, originally directed against Turkey, now focuses against Israel, while the Australian Jewish community has adopted Zionism with as much enthusiasm as such communities elsewhere.[2]

Of these, probably only Arabs would not see value in American protection, although Egypt currently has a close relationship with the United States.

Yet, whereas there is this widespread-felt need to have American military power available for the ultimate defense of Australia, it is seen as ultimate and not proximate. Like the people of other democracies, Australians (and, even more, Australian governments) are reluctant to prepare for the unknown or invisible threat, to spend money on defense when it is not demonstrably needed at the time. Membership in ANZUS is an insurance policy. The fees (to most people) are low. Why terminate the policy when there is no alternative insurer, and considering that the policy might not subsequently be capable of renegotiation?

IV

The extent to which Australia will be or will feel itself to be dependent on others for its basic defense during the remainder of this century will relate above all to what happens in the world outside Australia. During its brief national history, Australia's foreign and defense policies have almost invariably been reactions to events elsewhere. No one knows with any certainty what will happen during the last seventeen years of the twentieth century, so it will be necessary to speculate on that and then speculate again on the likely Australian reaction.

If a global nuclear war were to occur, this discussion would be academic. Much more probable is a continuation of the nuclear cold war, with a steady improvement by both sides of their nuclear weapons, space technology, detection of tests and launches, etc., and a degree of commitment to managing the arms race. Whatever else happens will happen in the shadow of this Damoclean contingency. While it is always tempting to assume that events will go on much the same as they now are, the history of the world in this century suggests that change, including dramatic and revolutionary change, is almost certain to occur somewhere every year or two, and significant evolutionary change is going on in most places most of the time.

Let us consider first the state of the two alliance systems and relations between them. The Western alliance has been through many crises during the past thirty-five years, and emerged each time a little bloodied but largely unbowed. The dispute this past five years over U.S. leadership, economic aid to the USSR, and the theater nuclear defense of Western Europe, has coincided with a nearly successful attempt by the USSR to gain superiority in theater-based nuclear weapons through its deployment of the SS-20s and SS-22s. So long as the USSR dominates Eastern Europe and occupies the German Democratic Republic, there is no alternative to NATO. Members may demand a greater say in East-West negotiations and in Western decisions, especially any decision to launch nuclear weapons from their soil, but they dare not forsake the treaty and its organization.

Is the Warsaw Pact and organization similarly placed? A recent novel, *The Fall of the Russian Empire* by Donald James (London: Granada, 1982), is based on the proposition that nationalist sentiment in that empire, in the USSR itself, will break it up from within. This is plausible, if unlikely in the short term. In Eastern Europe there are periodic attempts to overthrow the dominance of the USSR and its satraps, as in East Germany, Hungary, Czechoslovakia, and Poland. The Soviet Union has shown that it is not omnipotent, and cannot perpetuate its influence against resisting national sentiment, as in Indonesia, Egypt, Somalia, the Sudan, and Afghanistan. Sooner or later it will go home from Eastern Europe: the only question is *when*. In the event of a serious disintegration of the Soviet empire, despite all the temptations, the danger of world war would in all probability force the Western powers to stay clear of the process except perhaps for some West German involvement in East Germany.

For the more predictable future, the Soviet Union may seek to expand its influence and stake in the Africa-Asia-Pacific region, but nowhere does it have obviously fertile soil in which to implant its authority. Even Vietnam, from whose defense facilities Soviet ships and aircraft can now deploy to the disadvantage of the West, has little evident desire for a more prominent Soviet presence. The mini-states of the Pacific Ocean are most vulnerable, economically and strategically, but a Soviet attempt to take any of them over would bring a great deal of international opprobrium, and probably a prompt U.S. response. And it is hard to see what objective it would serve.

Within the area from Vietnam to Papua New Guinea, there are internal and international tensions that could erupt into conflict during this period. Yet China, the USSR, and the U.S. combine as balancers to this system. The only situation that would seem likely to involve Australia more than marginally would be if there were a breakdown of law and order in Papua New Guinea, or if Indonesia were to engage in conflict with that state. In the event of major oil discoveries in the Timor Sea, a jurisdictional dispute between Indonesia and Australia is conceivable. Australia could also be confronted with dilemmas over sea-based resources in the South Pacific, with major friendly states (Japan, the United States) seeking to browbeat small Pacific states who then appeal to Canberra for political and military help. Competition for the resources of Antarctica could produce even less clear-cut and more dangerous problems, especially for resources located in territory claimed by Australia.

It is sometimes suggested that in the face of growing Soviet naval and air power throughout the western Pacific, the non-communist nations of the region should band together in some Pacific version of NATO. This looks simple enough, but the political basis is missing. Japan already has a treaty with the U.S. that commits the latter to the defense of Japan but commits Japan only to its own security. It does not want to extend its obligations to the security of other states, or to a general anti-Soviet strategy. Despite its general anti-communist leaning, ASEAN is in principle non-aligned and its members wish to remain that way, so long as the U.S. Navy is on call over the horizon. Australia already has ANZUS.

Paul Dibb, a former Australian defense intelligence analyst, has suggested the following additional unlikely but conceivable events during the next twenty years: a Sino-Soviet alliance, a Sino-Soviet war, a militarily expansionist Japan, an unstable and territorially ambitious China, a Vietnamese invasion of Thailand, a technological breakthrough giving one superpower decisive military superiority over the other.[3] Each of these would have an incalculable effect on the global strategic situation.

This leaves three areas of potential conflict: Central and South America, where Australia has little basis of involvement; the Indian subcontinent, where our historic concerns are greater but not so great as to require the deployment of armed forces; and the Middle East, including the Gulf, whose supplies of oil will continue to be vital to the Western world. Australia would inevitably be involved in any Western or American attempt to insure, against local or Soviet resistance, the continued flow of Middle East oil. In these circumstances, to paraphrase President Kennedy, it would not be a question of what the alliance could do for Australia but what Australia could do for the alliance.

Yet as Australia nears the end of the second century of its founding (1988) and the first century of its existence as a single, federal state (2001), there are few indications that it wants to make more than marginal contributions to the overall Western security system of which it is a part and on which it so heavily depends. Equally, there are few signs, in defense matters, of that rugged individualism and staunch self-reliance that form so large a part of the myth, the self-image—perhaps indeed the fact—of the Australian at war. Governments cling tightly to ANZUS, while denying more than a nudge and wink of comfort to the former colonial dependency of Papua New Guinea. Despite some modest and tentative moves towards Pacific cooperation, both Labor and Liberal administrations have retreated into an Australian-centered regionalism, a preoccupation with the immediate environment at the expense of wider involvements. The armed forces and the defense bureaucracy are only now beginning to realize that if Australia has to defend itself *at home,* this will entail a knowledge of the terrain, the development of communications, a comprehensive defense civil infrastructure, increased combat and logistical capacity, and forms of cooperation between federal and state instrumentalities never hitherto envisaged. The Citizen Forces, or Reserves, are slowly moving towards a continental defense role, having never fulfilled (because of inept planning and inadequate legislation) the expeditionary support functions required in overseas wars during the past century. On the whole, the government and the population are psychologically unprepared for the defense of the homeland. Apart from a brief period in 1942, war has always been something that happened somewhere else, a temporary if traumatic aberration from the norm of a peaceful and largely isolated existence. From the earliest colonial days, many Australians have been suspicious of the military, resisting the compulsive element behind civil authority, feeling that while all decent men flock to the colors in war, it is unnecessary and even a little disreputable to do so in peace. Perhaps only a physical threat to the continent would change such attitudes.

What are the defense policy options before Australian governments during the rest of this century as well as in the subsequent years that will ignore the shift of the calendar? Will they see themselves as *having* options to exercise? Most governments feel hedged about by circumstances, constrained by the logic of events. There have been very few Australian initiatives in foreign affairs this past eighty-three years. Foreign and defense policies have been largely, though not wholly, reactive. They have responded to an increasingly complex, somewhat frostier, international environment by a more vigorous and more flexible diplomacy, by espousing Third World issues and dosing them with aid and rhetoric, and by inoculating the white Australian populace with Asian migrants. These programs have had their own intrinsic value. They complement but do not replace defense measures that are high on quality if not on quantity. They add up to an ad hoc, self-propelling corpus of policies rather than a calculated external strategy.

In the millennia since land subsidence in the north made Australia into an island, the moat around it constituted the continent's primary defense. Despite the growth of technology and the multiplication of populations in Asia, this remains the case. Assault over water is a most difficult military operation. Yet in the long run, Australia must make its own terms with its alien and populous neighbors, and successive governments have probably been right to give diplomacy a priority over defense. The real question, however, may be whether inertia and hedonism will take priority over both diplomacy and defense.

ENDNOTES

[1]Desmond Ball and R.H. Mathams, "The Nuclear Threat to Australia," in Michael Denborough, ed., *Australia and Nuclear War* (Fyshwick, A.C.T.: Croom Helm Australia, 1983) pp. 38–54.

[2]Coral Bell, ed., *Ethnic Minorities and Australian Foreign Policy* (Canberra: Australian National University Department of International Relations, 1983), p. 24.

[3]Paul Dibb, *World Political and Strategic Trends over the Next Twenty Years—Their Relevance to Australia* (Canberra: Australian National University, Strategic and Defence Studies Centre Working Paper No. 65, 1983), p. 184.

Bruce Williams

Wealth, Invention, and Education

IN 1870, THE SIX BRITISH COLONIES that thirty years later became the Commonwealth of Australia had a product per head that was more than one-third greater than in the next wealthiest countries of Britain, Belgium, the Netherlands, and the United States. In the next century, Australia's product per head grew substantially, but the growth rate was so much less in Europe and North America that its product per head is now more than 20 percent less than in Switzerland, Norway, and the United States.

How did that small group of colonies with a population of less than two million achieve such a degree of affluence by 1870, and why in the next hundred years did Australian growth rates decline, while rates in Europe and North America increased? Were natural resources over-exploited? Was the small population an advantage at first but then increasingly a disadvantage? Were there more general changes in the conditions of economic progress that Australia could not create or simply failed to create? Are world conditions and Australian policies and attitudes now such that growth rates are likely to be high in the future?

Early inventiveness

Australia, it has often been written, rode to wealth on the sheep's back. The extensive cultivation of wheat also provided profitable exports, as did the large deposits of easily mined gold, silver, and copper. But unlike the gold and silver, Australian sheep and cattle were not "gifts of nature": sheep and cattle had to be imported and adapted to Australian soil and climates.

It was intelligent breeding programs that focused on fleece rather than carcass, the abandonment of British shepherding practices, the fencing of sheep runs, the development of the Australian sheep dog, and the invention of shearing machines that made it possible for Australia to become rich from the export of wool.

It was some time before Australia became an important producer of wheat. In the first area of settlement, European wheats did not prosper—they were prone to blight and rust. It was not until the 1830s, after the settlement of South Australia, that the production of European wheats flourished on Australian soil. But these two successes depended on inventiveness, and in particular on the invention of labor-saving machinery such as the stripper, harvester, and new plows that provided the means for very extensive methods of farming.

The very profitable trade in minerals that followed the discovery of rich deposits of easily mined gold in New South Wales and Victoria in the 1850s encouraged a great inflow of capital and the development of transport. It also changed the character of the population. In the decade after the gold rushes, the Australian population almost trebled, and coming just after the "hungry forties" in Britain, the potato famine and rebellion in Ireland, and the wreck of Chartism, this migration increased the population of self-reliant and enterprising people who wished to escape from the restraints of British life and were eager to make a more interesting and prosperous life in Australia.

Slower growth

But the remarkably high degree of affluence and growth based on the effective use of primary resources did not last.

The very rich alluvial deposits of gold in New South Wales and Victoria were almost worked out by the end of the 1850s, and although new deposits were discovered in Queensland in the 1870s and in Western Australia in the 1890s, in the forty years after 1860 the production of gold was little more than double the output of the 1850s.

The fertility of the soil was also reduced in many areas by poor farming, soil erosion caused by overgrazing, the excessive clearing of trees, and the spread of imported pests such as rabbits and prickly pears. Many Australian soils are deficient in phosphorus, and beginning in the 1870s wheat yields per acre declined, until farmers started to use superphosphate in the 1890s.

The climate was favorable in the years between 1850 and 1890, and sheep flocks grew from 18 million to over 100 million. That exceeded the carrying capacity of the pastoral regions at that time, and in the very dry years that followed the sheep population was halved and did not reach the 1890 level again until 1929.

The cultivation of wool and wheat in Australia was not labor intensive, and by 1870 only 30 percent of the Australian work force was in agriculture, compared to 50 percent in the United States, Germany, and France. In growth in output per head, Australia had become more dependent on productivity increases in secondary industry, and for that Australia's small and widely dispersed centers of population were a handicap. It was not until federation in 1901 that tariff barriers within Australia were abolished.

Inventive activities did not come to a stop. The stump-jump plow and grubber, which extended considerably the areas of economic cultivation, were invented in the 1870s and were followed in the next decade by the combine harvester. After twenty years of experimental work, W.J. Farrer produced strains of wheat that were less susceptible to drought and rust and so added still further to yields per acre and the areas of economic cultivation. In the extraction and processing of minerals, for which overseas capital was available and the size of the local market was relatively unimportant, there were also inventions of significance. In 1901, a Melbourne brewer and chemist patented the flotation process for the separation of metals and a selective flotation process soon followed. These inventions were soon adopted throughout the world mining industry.

However, these and many other inventions were not sufficient to maintain high growth rates. The new wave of growth in Europe and North America from the 1880s on was no longer based on inventions in mechanical engineering but on the application of discoveries in the fields of physics and chemistry. Those countries that exploited the opportunities for growth in the electrical and chemical industries had two things Australia lacked—substantial activities in higher education and research, and large markets.

A DEPENDENT COUNTRY

From the start, Australia depended on capital provided by the British government and the free settlers. Shrewd management of investment in primary production and the development of an export economy generated surpluses that financed further investment and growth. Discoveries of gold encouraged still more British investment and made it easy for the colonial governments to raise loans in London for the development of railways, roads, and other public services. The affluence of the average Australian in the 1870s and 1880s depended in large measure on capital inflow that was financing almost half the total capital expenditure in Australia.

In 1871, British investment in Australia was about £37 million per head. By 1891, the figure had reached £90 million. That was more than could be justified by prospective rates of growth. A considerable part of the public loans raised in London were squandered on unproductive investments. The price of pastoral exports fell by a quarter between 1873 and 1886 and left banks with many bad debts. An abrupt fall-off in capital inflow from the second half of the 1880s led to a major economic crisis in the 1890s.

An increasing proportion of employment was in high-cost manufacturing industries for which the separate state governments provided protection. As happened a hundred years later in Western Europe and North America, the long period of rapid growth induced a desire for greater leisure in the cities, and workers in both rural and urban areas pressed for wage increases that might have been justified by past rates of growth, but not by current economic conditions. The growth in real product per head fell from 2.5 percent a year in the 1870s to less than 1 percent in the 1880s. Growth then ceased, and product per head fell by between 5 and 10 percent in the 1890s. There was a recovery of annual growth to about 2 percent between 1905 and 1914 due to the recovery of export prices and volumes and the discovery of gold to Western Australia, but that was the end of substantial growth until after the Second World War.

Apart from its dependence on capital inflow and world export markets, Australia was becoming increasingly dependent on other countries for the knowledge and the mental and manual skills required for further economic growth. There was little understanding of the growing importance of chemistry and physics, of electrical and chemical engineering, for innovation and economic growth. Migrants have always played an important part in Australian inventions and innovations, but between the two world wars there was little support for substantial migration programs. Such programs might indeed have added to employment problems in the 1920s and 1930s, for the foundations for further industrial development were not very strong. It was the strengthening of these foundations by the necessities of the Second World War and the Japanese occupation of New Guinea that provided the conditions for a popular and major migration program after the Second World War.

Education for some

As late as the 1950s, fewer than 25 percent of all Australian pupils stayed at school beyond the age of fifteen. The next twenty years saw a substantial increase to 60 percent, but even today only one-third of Australian schoolchildren complete secondary education. This is less than half the figure for the United States, Canada, and Japan. There are continuing complaints about the low levels of literacy and numeracy among those who fail to complete school, and the unemployment rate for this group is disproportionately high.

Primary education became compulsory in the main Australian states in 1870, but not until the 1890s was the possibility of free secondary education seriously discussed. In 1900, there were only three state secondary schools in Australia. The main opportunities for secondary education resided with the church schools. Although the Roman Catholic schools made an attempt to adjust to the incomes of parents and to provide some scholarship, the dominance of fee-paying schools continued to ensure a strong social bias in education. To this day, private schools play an important role in secondary education, with the less affluent (mostly Catholic) schools receiving substantial grants from the Australian government. The influence of regions and parental incomes on secondary education is still very strong. In Canberra, for example, more than two-thirds of the students complete secondary school; in Tasmania, the figure is only one-fifth. Retention rates vary widely depending on the type of school: less than 50 percent in Roman Catholic schools; almost 90 percent in other private schools; and less than 30 percent in government schools.

The picture is little better for higher education. Universities were established in Sydney and Melbourne in 1850 and 1853, and in other state capitals between 1874 and 1911. But not until after the Second World War, when the number of universities had increased from six to nineteen and enrollments were boosted by scholarships and grants, did the proportion of the 17–21 age group receiving higher education exceed 3 percent.

The extension of education

When in 1901 the former colonies became states of the Commonwealth of Australia, the responsibility for education remained with the states. Unlike the situation with primary and secondary education, the universities, teachers colleges, and technical colleges were created by state legislation and tuition fees seldom provided for as much as 25 percent of even their recurrent expenditure. During and after the Second World War, the Commonwealth government assumed an increasingly active role in the planning and finance of educational facilities. During the war, it planned and financed an increase in scientific and technical manpower. After the war, it provided an increase in facilities and student grants for the higher education of veterans. In 1956, it appointed a high-powered committee to inquire into the problems of Australian universities, and this committee recommended continuing Commonwealth activity to ensure a great increase in university education of all kinds, to provide the manpower needed for a high rate of economic growth and the efficient conduct of public and social administration.

In 1959, the Commonwealth established a Universities Commission to provide advice on the finance needed for a balanced program of university development "for the greatest possible advantage of Australia," and a few years later, it set up another commission to perform a similar function for the teachers colleges and technical colleges engaged in post-secondary education. At first, these "colleges of advanced education" provided only non-degree vocational courses, but now about one-half of their students are enrolled in degree courses.

By 1975, the proportion of the 17–21 age group receiving higher education had grown to 10.2 percent studying full-time and 1.5 percent studying part-time. In the last decade, there has been a slight fall in that percentage, but that fall has been more than made up by an increase in the enrollment of students over the age of twenty-five who now constitute 40 percent of the student population.

Non-advanced post-school education—known as technical and further education, or TAFE—had remained a purely state activity. Following complaints from employers about the inadequate quality and quantity of technical education, in 1975 the Commonwealth created a TAFE commission to recommend grants for building and equipment and new activities. With this aid, the TAFE sector, which has much higher enrollments than the universities and colleges of advanced education (though most are evening and part-time students), has grown considerably in quality and range.

As part of a campaign to increase numbers in higher education and to reduce social and geographical barriers to access, in 1974 the Commonwealth government, by agreement with the states, assumed full responsibility for all capital and recurrent grants to universities and colleges of advanced education on condition that tuition fees be abolished. Then in 1977, the year in which expenditure on education as a percentage of GDP peaked at 6.3 percent, the Commonwealth created a Tertiary Education Commission, with subordinate councils for universities, colleges, and TAFE, in an effort to check the growth of expenditure by better coordinating programs and facilities in the three sectors. So in the space of a few years, the Commonwealth had abolished tuition fees, assumed full responsibility for the finance of higher education, undertaken major new responsibilities to aid the finance of secondary schools as well as TAFE, and made education a major item in the government's budget.

This rapid growth of expenditure that occurred during the economic recession and increased Australia's budgetary problems, led to modifications of plans for the extension of numbers and to a significant reduction in "resources per student." Taken together with a decline in the business sector's finance of research, these developments did not provide a good basis for a resumption of higher rates of economic growth.

Inducing research

Before the Second World War, the role of Australian universities in research was not at all distinguished, and the number of research students was very small. Financial support was inadequate, and the colonial habit of pursuing research or post-graduate work abroad was still strong. During the war, however, many university scientists and engineers were drawn into research, and plans were made for postwar reconstruction that included much greater provision for staff research and post-graduate studies in the universities. After the 1956 inquiry, the grants from the Commonwealth government greatly improved the financial state of universities. Staff research increased, and the number of advanced-degree students rose from less than 1 percent before the war to 12 percent of total enrollment. Today, about 40 percent of first-degree university students, 60 percent of graduate students, and 55 percent of academic staff are in the sciences and technologies. In 1976–77, expenditure on research and development in higher education was at 0.23 percent of GDP, 28 percent of the national effort. By 1981–82 it had risen to 0.30 percent of GDP and 30 percent of the total. About 75 percent of that expenditure was on the sciences and technologies.

Australia's overall expenditure on R&D is not very high. It was 1.3 percent of GDP in 1968–69, but thereafter increases in R&D failed to match increases in GDP. By 1981–82, research and development constituted only 1.03 percent of the national product, compared to 2.2 percent in Sweden and 1.5 percent in Canada (two countries with a distribution of employment similar to Australia). Although government-financed university R&D grew, industrial R&D contracted as profits in the manufacturing sector declined. The proportion of industry-financed research and development declined from 38 percent in 1968–69 to 21 percent in 1981–82. Government protection of fragmented Australian manufacturing industries had attracted overseas subsidiaries that rely in considerable measure on the research and development of their parent companies. These companies made major contributions to Australia's postwar growth, but did nothing to increase the indigenous capacity to generate industrial innovation from R&D, and they contributed to the very large imbalance in the technological balance of payments. In 1981–82, payments to other countries for "patent and licence fees and royalties and other technical know-how" were seven times greater than receipts from other countries.

One of the most difficult tasks in applied research and development is to address the right problems, and that difficulty is increased when R&D becomes separated from production and marketing activities. In Australia, a high proportion of R&D is performed in CSIRO (a Commonwealth government agency), state departments of agriculture, and the universities. In 1968–69, only 38 percent and in 1981–82 only 21 percent of R&D was performed by business enterprises. Although efforts have been made to make CSIRO and the universities more conscious of and responsive to market possibilities, it is only in agricultural and medical research, where experimental farms and teaching hospitals bridge the gaps between laboratories and production, that a reasonable solution has been found for the problems created by segregation. It is no accident that the outstanding fields of research in Australia in quality as well as quantity are agriculture (23 percent of the total), health (13 percent), and advancement of knowledge (27 percent).

Now no country, not even the United States, can afford to rely solely on the results of its own research and development in the fields of agriculture, industry, and services. Australia, with a population of only 15 million and a small proportion of highly trained manpower, must necessarily be dependent to a considerable degree on the results of research done in other countries. Even when Australia succeeds in assuming a larger role in applied research and development, her rate of economic growth will rest in considerable measure on the international diffusion of technological innovation. Australian firms still have much to learn about how to monitor overseas technical developments, and how to acquire and to adapt such developments to specifically Australian conditions. Japan has set an impressive example in this regard, balancing the two activities of generating innovations internally and adopting or adapting external innovations without depending on subsidiaries of overseas companies for technological knowledge.

Prospects for the future

Scientists, engineers, and financiers in Australia, as elsewhere, have been invigorated by the prospect of economic growth from the applications of information technology and, especially, biotechnology; Australia has a very powerful research capacity in the rural and medical faculties of her universities and medical-research institutes, and she could well make distinctive contributions in these fields. But it would be good neither for growth in output nor employment if excitement over sunrise industries diverted attention and talent away from the more traditional fields of production that will remain critical to the country's growth. Whether such contributions will be made depends, in large part, on whether the country's educational system continues to be improved and extended. The recent proposals from the Department of Science and Technology to raise school retention rates through year twelve from 36 percent in 1982 to 50 percent in 1995, and to increase higher-education enrollment from 10.5 to 20 percent, are based on a realistic appraisal of needs, though the financial authorities may regard them as too expensive. However, as shown by a 1979 report of the Committee of Inquiry into Education and Training, demographic conditions in Australia are such that even modest rates of growth in output per head would make it possible to spend substantially more on education without raising expenditure relative to the gross domestic product.[1]

The Department of Science and Technology also proposed an increase in research and development expenditure from 1 percent of gross domestic product in 1981–82 to 2 percent in 1995–96, and an increase in research and development conducted and financed by the business sector from one-fifth to one-half of the total. I do not think that such a plan for an increase in research financed by the business sector in little more than a decade is realistic. But it is important to reduce the proportion of segregated research and development in Australia and to encourage business sector activities. But business sector R&D is not likely to reach 1 percent of GDP by 1995–96 unless the state governments are prepared to place research and development contracts with the private sector. An OECD expert group recently recommended stronger government support for strategic research and exploratory development on "the enabling technologies" that could provide a range of possible applications over the several economic sectors.[2] There are lessons to be learned from abroad: Japan has a "next-generation base-technologies development program" that involves cooperation among universities, government laboratories, and the business sector. Great Britain has a government-sponsored program for advanced information technology that involves a similar type of cooperation.

Recently, there have been some very interesting proposals to create new institutions that would provide a mixture of financial and managerial support for small or new enterprises committed to developing new technologies. These should be encouraged, though the main case for the provision of government finance is for work on the enabling technologies. One government initiative that could have a major impact would be the reform of tariff policies. Support for particular industries could be made contingent on their successful use of modern technologies—whether homegrown, adapted, or directly imported—and an effort could be made to identify those areas in which Australia's natural disadvantages could be overcome by technological and institutional inventions.

Australia will have to struggle to recapture that degree of relative affluence that it enjoyed up to the final quarter of the nineteenth century. Its growth rate between 1950 and 1973 was more than three times the growth rate from 1870 to 1950, but even so it was only two-thirds of the average rate for the OECD countries.[3] With its rich reserves of coal and iron ore (which now provide one-quarter of export income), and its great productivity in the production of fine wool and wheat (that dominate the agricultural production that accounts for 40 percent of export income), there is a sound basis for higher growth rates—if the appropriate changes are made in education and in the scale and organization of research and development.

ENDNOTES

[1]Committee of Inquiry into Education and Training, *Education, Training and Employment* (Canberra: Government Printing Office, 1979).

[2]OECD, *Technical Change and Economic Policy,* (Paris, 1980).

[3]A. Maddison, *Phases of Capitalist Development,* (London: Oxford University Press, 1982).

[illegible] as a result of the provision of specific funds [illegible]

Leonie Kramer

The Media, Society, and Culture

An unusually perceptive observer might have been able to predict, soon after 1945, that in three areas Australia would be transformed. The First World War, which seemed to so many to symbolize the end of an era in Europe and to complete the destruction of traditional values and ways of life initiated by the industrial revolution, brought a sense of nationhood to Australia, and created the legend of ANZAC and Gallipoli. Yet old continuities were not ruptured, and from federation in 1901 until 1945, Australia was a much more homogeneous society than it has been since. In forty years, Australians have accepted and, on the whole, welcomed changes that could hardly have been imagined, even in the 1940s.

First, there was a fundamental change in the size and composition of the population. The pre-war influx of refugees from central Europe was succeeded after 1945 by waves of migrants from Britain and southern and eastern Europe, especially from Yugoslavia, Hungary, Italy, Greece, and Spain; and by displaced persons from iron-curtain countries; these in turn have been followed by large numbers of migrants from the Middle East, especially from Lebanon and Turkey, and most recently from South America and Southeast Asia. Second, the postwar influx of students, many of them ex-servicemen, marked the beginning of the rapid expansion of tertiary education. There were six state universities in 1945; now there are nineteen (including the Australian National University), and other tertiary institutions have proliferated throughout the country.[1] Third, communications have vastly improved, though there are still communities and remote country properties where communication is quite inadequate by modern standards. The introduction of television has changed the face of politics in Australia as it has elsewhere. In 1964, Henry Mayer wrote: "Federation reduced the political power of the Press."[2] Television, which both recognizes and overrides state boundaries, now exercises an influence potentially much greater than that of the press. In 1978, Mayer predicted, "We are moving towards a split between 'quality' and 'entertainment' press,"[3] a prophecy that reflects both the nature and power of television.

In a country that has as one of its most cherished concepts the independence, resourcefulness, non-conformism, and rugged individualism of its people, to talk of "the mass media" seems singularly inappropriate. It is nevertheless true that there are large-circulation popular newspapers, and that commercial television regularly attracts a substantial share of the total audience. The interpretation of these facts is by no means easy, and it should not be assumed that because large numbers of people read certain newspapers, and watch soap operas on television, one can draw firm conclusions about the tastes, preferences, and intellectual interests of Australians as a whole. The phrase "the mass media" might have more meaning for journalists and commentators than it can or should have for the general public. To the extent that it implies a common (and not too elevated) set of interests and capacities, it might well be at odds with the actual needs and potential interests of large sections of the community. In any case, the concept of "the mass media," while it might have some limited descriptive validity, is not a sound basis upon which to develop policy relating to newspapers or television and radio programs for a society that, while sharing some common experiences, is nevertheless scattered and diverse, and influenced by strong regional and local loyalties and affiliations.

Australia, which has to its credit some remarkable technical and scientific inventions and discoveries, continues to import ideas, even when their limitations have been clearly demonstrated in their country of origin. There is—it is acknowledged with disarming candor—a ten-year time lag between the acceptance of ideas abroad and their arrival in Australia. Thus, when progressive educational philosophies were displaying their theoretical flaws and practical inadequacies in the United States, they were running ahead like grass fire in Australia. Nor is it just that ideas and philosophies are imported; there is very little understanding as to whether or how they might be adapted to Australian conditions. The reason is that Australia still lacks a rigorous, constructive critical tradition. It is no accident that the word "knocking" has come to be recognized as an accurate term for a negative Australian habit of derogatory dismissal of an idea or achievement. There is a tendency to argue from extreme positions, and to question the status of objectivity. In Australia, Matthew Arnold would preach disinterestedness to a small (and possibly shrinking) audience. The general weakness in the practice of criticism is evidenced both in the ready acceptance of the latest doctrine, and in the tendency for criticism to be taken personally. This is so, for example, in criticism of the arts. In the nineteenth century, there were critics who tried to establish high standards of literary debate, and the relationship between Australian literary achievement and that of England and Europe was then, as it is now, a matter of contention. In spite of efforts to correct the so-called "cultural cringe," there is still an inclination to deal with local writers tenderly; and for some of them to respond to criticism with indignation or peevishness.

Political life provides an outstanding example of the lack of a critical tradition. Governments may now come and go with more assistance from the media than they had before the Second World War, but their philosophies suffer from a shortage of informed and purposeful critics. Labor governments have never decided whether they are socialist or not, and are therefore susceptible to internal dissension on that fundamental question. At the same time, when their Liberal/National coalition opponents (the National component of which has a substantially rural base) are in government, they show little inclination to limit the growth of the bureaucracy, or to put into practice their views about reducing government intervention in the lives of individuals and institutions. For example, the complexities of legislation relating to broadcasting are compounded by administrative regulations that no government seems anxious to rationalize. Labor governments tend to draw power and money to the federal sphere; Liberal/National governments profess to return it to the states. Both have uneasy relationships with the media, and have great difficulty in determining policy. Against this background, it is inevitable that discussions of such important topics as the nature and extent of Australian independence and the possibilities of republicanism should lack substance, and be shaped by emotion and personal responses to Australia's colonial past, rather than by rational analysis of the actualities of Australian contemporary life.

The structure of the broadcasting system reveals both the ad hoc nature of political decision-making, and the unexamined assumptions and confused philosophies that determine policy. There are three sectors in the broadcasting industry—national, commercial, and public. The two national broadcasting services, the Australian Broadcasting Corporation (ABC) and the Special Broadcasting Service (SBS, a multicultural service), are fully funded by the federal government on an annual allocation, and are governed by boards appointed by the governor-general, on the recommendation of the minister for communications. Certain anomalies are immediately apparent in the system. Though there are two national services free from commercial influence and motivation, there is an audience for public broadcasting (at present confined to radio) as well, though there is not so clearly understandable a rationale for it as there is in the United States. The ABC's charter requires the corporation to "take account of" the services "provided by the commercial and public sectors," and of "the multicultural character of the Australian community," leaving quite open the interpretation of "take account of."[4] Because it is a national service, the ABC has a responsibility for servicing the whole community, and thus those audiences sought and attracted by the SBS and other two sectors. The SBS's functions are "to provide multilingual broadcasting services, and, if authorized by the regulations, to provide multilingual television services," and "to provide broadcasting and television services for such special purposes as are prescribed."[5] No functions are prescribed in the act for the commercial or public sectors. The latter, however, defines itself against the other two sectors by claiming that "the ABC is resource-limited and commercial broadcasters must reach mass-audiences," and that diversity of programming and diversity of ownership "represents a counter-current to a disturbing trend towards aggregation in both ownership and programming. . . ." In practice, the public broadcasters represent an interesting assertion of a principle in that ". . . they are all non-profit, non-Government and—apart from ten licensed to universities or colleges—community owned and controlled."[6] This principle is enacted in the sector's policy of community access and target-audience programming. There is, however, overlap in principle and practice: in principle, with the SBS's responsibility for special groups; in practice, with, in particular, the ABC's classical music programming. There is evidence that the SBS's television service, especially its international news coverage and foreign films, appeals to an English-speaking audience as much as, or even more than, to its target audience. If this is so, it might be seen to be failing to fulfill its statutory function, by accident rather than design; and the ABC might be thought to be taking insufficient account of multiculturalism by not itself providing elements of the national service—especially in news and international affairs—supplied by the SBS.

One can speculate, but in the end infer very little about the social or cultural condition of Australia from the structure of its broadcasting system. One cannot even infer that the establishment of the SBS signified community recognition of the changed composition of Australian society, since, while there was pressure from some ethnic groups, its creation in fact implemented a political decision about multiculturalism, and expressed impatience with the ABC for not entering the field itself. The structure of the system does not in itself reflect "the will of the people," but rather a long history of inadequately considered decisions by governments. The public broadcasting sector displays an impulse towards community-based private enterprise, but still seeks government support. The commercial sector is disproportionately large in the Australian community, and in technical resources and its capacity to attract staff can easily outstrip the meagerly-funded ABC.

When it comes to programs, clear distinctions can be drawn between the commercial sector and the ABC. In television, the ABC's emphasis is on news and current affairs, drama and comedy (some of the best of which is British-made), music, documentaries, Australian drama series, and sports. (Fifty-seven percent of ABC TV is locally produced.) All commercial stations must comply with Australian Broadcasting Tribunal regulations concerning Australian content of drama on TV, and of music on radio. They run movies, quiz and variety shows, domestic soap operas, and adventure dramas of the cops and robbers kind. These are American-style programs. But they have also increased their news and current affairs output, and invested in Australian dramatic and historical series. Both in the provision of news services and in entertainment, there is a clear assumption that the audience prefers local (and often sensational) news items, and light entertainment. The SBS's television channel presents extensive international news coverage, foreign language movies, serials, and documentary programs. The diversity of radio makes generalization difficult, but the same broad distinctions may be drawn. The commercial stations provide a mix of light and popular music, and spoken word, with an emphasis on talk-back (call-in) programs. The ABC broadcasts much more "serious" music and talk, but it competes with the commercials on its "light" network. (Its sporting coverage is extensive.) The ABC's diversity reflects its obligation to provide for all Australians at some time, and it is largely successful in this. Certain of its program areas have no parallel in the other sectors. It makes high-quality children's television and radio, presents schools broadcasts in every state, contributes to general education through its rural broadcasts, science and public affairs programs, and, as one of its newest initiatives, broadcasts to Aboriginal people and Torres Strait Islanders in Central Australia and Northern Queensland. New proposals for a radical restructuring of ABC radio will, if implemented, greatly increase the range and diversity of its services.[7]

In its references to program policy, the ABC's charter is not without ambiguity, if placed in the context of broadcasting as a whole. It is required to produce programs of "wide appeal," which might be interpreted as inviting it to compete with the commercial stations in search of a mass audience; and it is also required (or is it merely permitted?) to make programs "for more specialized interests." This, in turn, might imply some encroachment on the responsibilities of the SBS, though in practice it is interpreted as a licence to produce high-quality programs, both on radio and television, which can be expected to attract a relatively small audience. This section of the charter gives some assurance that the ABC will not be persecuted for excellence, without implying that excellence is for the few, not the many. The charter is a serious attempt to describe the kind of community the ABC must serve, and goes some way towards identifying some of its characteristics. But the crucial debate about the relationship between normative and popular programming does not take place in public, though its terms are assumed every time some listeners complain about loss of quality in the ABC, and others about the taxpayers' dollars funding programs of minority interest.

The question of the adequacy of international news coverage in the media is a vexed one, complicated by statistical and geographical variations. In spite of its considerable news-gathering capacity, the ABC does not give significant *television* time either to international news, or more significantly, to background analysis of it. The SBS makes good this deficiency, at least so far as news itself is concerned, but neither in this area nor in others does it provide sustained critical analysis. A survey of three major newspapers from 1907 to 1967 examining the ratio of overseas to domestic news shows "that in the 'normal' course of events the demand for news about international affairs is not very different from what it was in the first decade of the century." Analysis of geographical sources, however, shows a considerable change in emphasis over the same period, the principal feature of which has been the "rise to prominence of Asia."[8] After some fluctuations (including a sharp decline in 1957), by 1967 "between a quarter and a third of all overseas news derived from Asia and that continent had come to be the main source of Australia's international news." In the same period, attention shifted away from the British Isles and Europe and towards North America. In the absence of later statistics, any assessment of the present nature of international coverage must be largely subjective. The prominence given to international news decreases outside the major city papers, and regional dailies, even in large country towns, give priority to local news. This is a reflection of the difference between the material available to the major urban centers of the eastern seaboard, and that supplied to the rest of the country.

In the provision of news services, the ABC has a special status because it is not dependent on the sources controlled by the commercial media monopolies. Restricted ownership of newspapers, and through them of the electronic media, has been widely criticized. In 1981, the *Report of the Inquiry Into the Ownership and Control of Newspapers in Victoria* summarized its views on the dangers of concentrated ownership and control as follows: "They are first, loss of diversity of expression of opinion and, second, the power of a very few men to influence the outlook and opinions of large numbers of people, (and consequently decisions made in society). While the first is not to be neglected, the second is the greatest danger."[9] A government view on this question was expressed in 1978 by the then minister for posts and telecommunications: ". . . government involvement in Australian broadcasting must be directed to ensure freedom of expression and enterprise in all forms of communication available to Australian society, particularly radio and television, and this freedom is best served by diversity of structures and outlets." He went on to say that it was the government's responsibility " . . . to make the necessary planning and administrative provisions, to obviate the risk of freedom of expression and enterprise for one sector, or group, being indulged at the expense of others, or of the system as a whole."[10]

Much of the criticism of ownership relates to the possibility of a monopoly of sources of news, and hence a deliberate bias, especially in news from abroad. (This is so even though ownership is Australian.)[11] The ABC act of 1983 empowers it to take syndicated wire services, but does not require it to do so, and so it is able to provide a service from sources other than those used by the rest of the media. It runs an independent news service staffed by journalists in thirty-eight centers, and twelve overseas bases, which provides the basis for its current-affairs programs.[12] Through its overseas news bulletins on Radio Australia, it is, especially in the Pacific region, an indispensable source of information to developing countries, and often their principal means of communicating with each other.

Public opinion of the performance of the electronic media is dominated by a system of ratings designed to provide the commercial sector with basic information about the effectiveness of advertising. It is perhaps inevitable that the ABC is caught up in the ratings game, since its programs appear on the list with those of commercial stations, almost invariably in last place. What could and should be a constructive discussion of normative and popular program policy becomes shallow sniping from sections of the press, public, and politicians about the ABC's failure to attract an audience it did not seek in the first place. Critics of the ABC frequently urge it to enter into more vigorous competition with the commercial sector, or merely to do something different, rarely specified. They claim that the ABC is essentially elitist in its programming, and that consequently it reaches a minority audience. This view persists despite the findings of a survey specially commissioned by the Committee of Review of the ABC (1980). The committee reported that:

> . . . a majority of Australians make use of ABC television and radio services, not a minority as is often believed. The real minority is the 7 percent of people who neither watch ABC television nor listen to ABC radio within any given week. Ninety-three percent turn to the ABC selectively for programs they particularly want to watch, or to listen to.
>
> Our ANOP study also showed that the idea that the ABC has an elitist or highbrow image is a misconception. True, the ABC does attract a high proportion of the better educated, but its audiences comprise an equally high proportion of the least well educated people in society.[13]

The list of the ten most popular commercial TV programs (in Sydney and Melbourne) contains a mix of movies, soap operas, news services, a quiz show, and a "profile" program. Differently based audience research surveys conducted by the ABC indicate, however, that if viewers are asked to assess their degree of familiarity with and appreciation of programs, ABC programs score top ranking.[14] The obsession with ratings and popularity exemplifies a general tendency to value quantity rather than quality of response.

Over the years, the ABC has demonstrated that there is a constant and significant audience for high-quality programs in music, drama, science, education, sports, general talks and documentaries, and news and current affairs, and that there is a demand for more specialized programs. There is no doubt that the ABC represents, even to those who are not its regular audience, professionalism and quality in programming. When it was suggested that the ABC FM network (largely devoted to classical music and high-quality spoken word) might be replaced by a radio network for the under-thirties, there was a public outcry supported by the press. A significant number of complaints from a wide cross-section of the public to the ABC concern the standard of programs. People express dissatisfaction if programs fail to provide mental stimulation as well as entertainment. It is clear that the ABC is expected, even by those who are not its constant disciples, to set higher standards than the commercial sector, not to follow fashions. This is but one example of a general tendency for leaders of opinion in Australia to be out of step with views in the community as a whole. It is a strange irony that some policy-makers seem resistant to excellence while many of the recipients of their policy are in favor of it.

What conclusions then can be drawn from the facts of the structure, programming, and reception of the three sectors? One conclusion might be that while commercial TV attracts a large proportion of the available audience, it does not necessarily satisfy it. If one assumes that large numbers of people will like certain kinds of programs, and one therefore provides them, one is restricting those people's choices and their ability to discover and enjoy new experiences. The choice between the three commercial TV networks is effectively a choice between variants of the same basic recipe. The structure of broadcasting reflects political decisions over time, the programming a contest between a concept of mass audience and a concept of an audience of individuals, and the reception by the public shows both a high regard for the national sector and a majority audience for commercial entertainment. There is no reason to suppose, however, that the total audience divides neatly into sectoral categories. Many people select across the sectors, and value variety of choice.

That variety of choice is, however, available only to audiences in the main capital cities. The rural population is, in general, poorly served by radio and television. There are regional radio and TV stations with some emphasis on local content, but there are many areas served only by the ABC through one outlet. Country people are culturally deprived. They have little or no access to concerts, opera, ballet, theater, and all the many forms of urban entertainment; so that while they need and appreciate local news and information, they also need to feel part of a larger community and to share its cultural life. When offered opera or ballet simulcasts, they respond with enormous enthusiasm. Their contribution to the economic well-being of the country is little understood or appreciated in the cities. Thus, the bombardment of the main population centers by the media results in a serious imbalance between urban and rural provision, and in an urban-monopoly programming policy that is, in the commercial sector, largely dictated by the size of the advertizing audience. Only in the 1983/4 federal budget has funding been made available for a second rural radio network, long sought by the ABC. In isolated areas, high hopes are held for the services the domestic satellite will make available. These scattered communities are small in numbers, but vitally interested in education and the arts. For the former, they make considerable sacrifices; the latter they experience only rarely.

There is a curious irony in the fact of urban domination, for Australians have an ambivalent attitude towards their cities, which, unlike European cities, are not lived in but are business and commercial centers. It is customary to speak of Australia as urbanized; it would be more accurate to describe it as the most suburbanized country in the world. Typically, the Australian family lives in a single-story house with a garden, as though trying to retain some elements of country life. The suburbs in Sydney and Melbourne stretch out thirty to forty kilometers from the city center and continue to expand. These outer suburbs have quite inadequate public transport, and many people who live in them rarely travel into the city. When newly established, they are more often than not entirely lacking in amenities. The new suburb is a cultural dead-heart. There is no inducement to community cultural activities. There are few, often no, suitable halls for concerts or exhibitions, and no place like the English pub or the continental cafe that can become a meeting place. The nearest equivalent is the club, which provides popular entertainment, and poker machines. Radio and TV are virtually the only means of entertainment. In the absence of cable television, video is capturing a large market; and when the domestic satellite is in operation, who can predict the impact on the established networks, especially in outer suburbs and rural areas? A receiving dish will cost less than the present price of a VCR, and the deregulation resisted by governments might be effected by technology. There are already expressions of anxiety from regional radio and TV stations that if the large commercial operators are allowed to network on the satellite, they will be extinguished. There are ways of protecting the small operators, but possibly only in the short term, and there is widespread anxiety in rural areas that regional news and interests might be submerged by networked programs from the Eastern seaboard.

In spite of the growth of the cities, the country (whether "the bush" or "the Outback") continues to exercise a powerful influence on the Australian imagination. The colloquial phrase "Sydney or the bush," meaning "all or nothing" (i.e., to make one's fortune, and live in the capital, or lose it all, and seek a livelihood in the bush),[15] is not just a metaphor for a distinction between the material benefits of city as against country life (Australia's version of the town-mouse and country-mouse fable), but for the implicit differences in values between town and country. The cultural nationalism so earnestly defended by Vance Palmer in the thirties and forties was largely based on the assumption (well-founded in the classical tradition) that country life forms certain qualities of character not likely to be developed in the artificial environment of the city. This attitude has not by any means been displaced. It influences political life, and it is therefore surprising that it has not been fully realized in either educational or media policy. It might even partly explain the rather grudging attitude that Australians seem to take towards the city; as might the fact that Australian cities are still in the process of being built, and some have only just outgrown their country-town habit. Whatever the explanation, a deep affection for a "bush" that might not even have been very fully explored, and for the life its image evokes, is an essential part of the Australian experience.

If satellite technology, as it promises to do, transforms the whole system of electronic media in Australia, it will bring greatly enlarged choices to the whole audience at a time when the cultural status of Australia is still surprisingly obscure. Even allowing for the fact that there are fluctuations in a country's artistic fortunes, and that a flowering in one area or period may be balanced by infertility in another, there is an air of fragility about the creative arts in Australia, evidenced partly by a certain defensiveness in artists, and partly by reluctance on the part of critics to subject local works to rigorous scrutiny. This latter tendency has been reinforced by a fashion for protective neutrality, and the practice of explanation and appreciation, in place of analysis and discriminating judgment. The notion of Australian creative life as a tender plant that needs special nurturing persists, though not necessarily explicitly. A cultural climate in which even minor talents are encouraged by government subsidy, might, however, prove discouraging to major artists, especially in the absence of challenging qualitative discriminations. In this context, the Australian Broadcasting Tribunal's role in ensuring that Australian content is at a prescribed level in the commercial and public sectors might be interpreted both as recognition that Australian material deserves and needs promotion, and as anxiety that imported material might otherwise be preferred. The tribunal's approach to its supervisory function is quantitative, not qualitative—perhaps another example of the tendency to treat problems administratively rather than philosophically.

Indeed, further evidence of the absence of a critical tradition is the poverty of criticism of the media. There are repeated complaints from the public about the inaccuracy of reporting and political bias to the left or right, but reviews of TV and radio programs are, on the whole, sketchy, and considered arguments about programming policy or broadcasting standards rare. There is great variation in quality across the main sections of broadcasting, ranging from the most superficial entertainment and sensationalism to excellent drama and documentary material, much of which is British-made. Good local comedy is scarce. In Australian-made programs scripting is often mediocre, and technical experimentation uncommon. Character is superficially treated, and there is a good deal of superfluous scenic camera work that creates its own imagistic cliches. By contrast, radio, and particularly ABC radio, has some outstanding achievements to its credit in many fields—science, music, literature, public and international affairs, and education. Yet neither the successes and failures of individual programs nor general critical questions receive significant attention in the press or in the electronic media, and there is therefore little incentive for program-makers to develop their ideas and improve their techniques.

With rare exceptions, the Australian media (while devoting a great deal of time and space to sports) deal with the arts and cultural questions in a somewhat perfunctory way. Weekend magazine sections in some newspapers are an exception to a general rule, but even in these, reviewing can be descriptive rather than analytical, and limited in scope. Extended discussion of ideas, either in newspaper columns, or on radio or television, is a rare phenomenon. TV programmers in particular are nervous about "talking heads," so their audience looks in vain for thorough and sustained examination of the background to news and public affairs. The fact that the medium of TV encourages a synoptic and simplified view of complex issues does not fully explain the dearth of informed, articulate discussion. Australians are prepared to take great pride in the achievements of their sporting heroes (as the time and space given to them in the media testify), but seem to have bad consciences about excellence in other areas. The cry of elitism is not heard in reference to sports training; it *is* heard in relation to university education, ABC programs, and the arts. A thoughtless preoccupation with egalitarianism, nervousness about intellectual accomplishment, and a simple-minded conviction that equal opportunity will produce equal results, combine to inhibit vigorous, learned, and fearless discussion of ideas. This is a serious cultural deficiency that affects Australian literary works, is detectable in the media and some of the most successful films, and prevents the development of a substantial critical exchange and commentary outside the learned journals and the little magazines.

It is difficult to account for the persistent anti-intellectualism in Australian life, especially since educational opportunity has expanded so much in the last forty years. Certainly, the influence of progressive educational philosophies has been pervasive. Their effect is to soften the rigor of learning, to encourage opinion rather than knowledge, and to arrest (especially in the humanities) the development of powers of reasoning and analysis. These tendencies make a marriage of convenience with egalitarianism. The idea of learning for its own sake is hard put to compete with strong indigenous traditions of pragmatism and utilitarianism. In his novel *Such is Life,* Joseph Furphy's narrator offers a satirical comment on an educated Englishman by means of a list of contrasting accomplishments:

> Without doubt, it is easier to acquire gentlemanly deportment than axeman's muscle; easier to criticise an opera than to identify a beast seen casually twelve months before; easier to dress becomingly than to make a bee-line, straight as the sighting of a theodolite, across strange country in foggy weather; easier to recognise the various costly vintages than to live contentedly on the smell of an oil rag.[16]

Even allowing for conscious irony, there is something typically Australian in the formulation of these contrasts.

Ideas about what is typical and traditional are the most confused of all. At the best of times, discussions of national identity are characterized by unprovable assertions. In Australia, they are complicated by ambivalent attitudes towards the colonial past, and misunderstanding of the ways in which artistic traditions are shaped. When John Perceval calls a painting "Homage to Buvelot," or James McAuley takes a phrase, "Surprises of the Sun," from Henry Kendall as the title for a group of poems, or Murray Bail writes *his* "The Drover's Wife,"[17] a tradition is being acknowledged; and through that acknowledgement its existence is verified. That this tradition has its roots in late eighteenth- and nineteenth-century British literature does not call in question its Australian character. Its genetic inheritance has determined its essential forms, but experience and conditioning have given it a life of its own. It constitutes a national tradition so long as one does not want to preserve "national" to describe that impossible utopian dream—a world that has no foreign antecedent. This restricted notion of nationalism is relevant only to a certain stage in a country's cultural development, and Australia has changed so rapidly in the last fifty years that such a notion is now anachronistic. In any case, concern about the sensitivity of Australian culture, arts, or institutions to foreign influence is justified only if one believes in the possibility and desirability of a "pure" descent. The ABC itself is an excellent example of an institution that is derivative, based on the Reith ideals of public-service broadcasting, but is nevertheless a distinctive Australian broadcasting organization.

The important consideration is not whether there is an indigenous culture, but what transformations the materials of culture have undergone in Australian conditions. To this question, there are some tentative answers. A distinctive tonal and idiomatic speech has evolved that must in some ways influence the written language. Even early writers claimed to be able to describe a physical type. No doubt, the dominance of sports in Australian cultural life reflects not just the climatic conditions, but also the respect for physical prowess that in the nineteenth century and later was necessary to survival. Resourcefulness and a talent for improvisation were also means of surviving the hardships of pioneering life. Since it is unlikely that these complex issues have been thoroughly considered by the formulators of media policy, the legislative requirement that ABC programs contribute to a "sense of national identity" is left to the broadcasters to interpret. Rejection of either traditional models or outside influences is a symptom of provincialism, though even the acceptance of the foreign and anterior is no absolute guarantee against it. Provincialism has always been a potential danger, though possibly Australia has exhibited insularity rather than provincialism, and anxiety at being out of the mainstream rather than smug satisfaction with the billabong.

But regionalism is another matter. The existence of a large number of regional newspapers, radio, and television stations, and the importance of the ABC's regional offices, is evidence of the strong sense of place and community felt by people outside the main cities.

The source of community spirit is identification with local interests and shared experience, but that spirit needs sustenance from outside, through the provision of news and information, discussion of public affairs, and access to a variety of entertainment. If the history of other countries is any guide, the regions, given the proper stimulus, might well have a significant contribution to make to the creative arts. Many artists have found their inspiration in the known and felt life of a small community more readily than in the impersonal anonymity of the large city. While the electronic media might well act as a stimulus to regional activity, they have as yet shown little inclination to do so. The effort is most likely to be made by the ABC, whose objective since its establishment in 1932 has been to enrich the lives of its audience. Its proposed second rural radio network should bring greatly enlarged choice and variety to the regions, and encourage a flow of ideas back into the cities. Such a movement would help to give substance to the concept of the "real Australia."

In his poem "Terra Australis," Douglas Stewart arranges a meeting in mid-Pacific between the sixteenth-century Portugese explorer de Quiros, sailing west in search of the Great South Land, and William Lane, the nineteenth-century Australian socialist, sailing in the opposite direction to found a utopian settlement in Paraguay. Perhaps it was inevitable that the last great continent to be discovered should have seemed to promise (as it did to de Quiros) a new start, a place to build a future free from the wars and inherited divisions of the Old World. But why should William Lane in 1893, less than ten years before federation and at the time when Australia was sensing the approach of nationhood, have sought his utopia in South America? The "burden of the past,"[18] as W.J. Bate has argued in another context, cannot be laid down, and it is tempting to speculate that the great expectations directed towards de Quiros's hoped-for Australia del Espiritu Santo long before its discovery and settlement, still haunt it, and that the impossibility of satisfying them is likely to sharpen, not blunt, a sense of failure to make the most of the "vision splendid."[19] Douglas Stewart's fanciful perception is a witty parable of that variable amalgam of fact and fiction that constitutes Australian cultural history. These imaginative and speculative matters are occasionally reflected in the mass media, but rarely inquired into.

If the power of the media—and especially television—is as great as some suppose, one would like to see it examine the character and style of the ambivalent attitudes that find expression in Australian life and that inspire Stewart's poem. Utopian idealism confronts pessimistic prophecy; ideology vies with pragmatism; preservation and restoration of the colonial past seem oddly compatible with anti-British sentiments, as does anti-Americanism with American-style consumerism; sentiment about bush values does not prevent neglect of rural needs; recognition of the importance of science and technology to Australia's future does not silence those critics of educational excellence who sneeringly call it elitism. If, as these and other ambivalences suggest, there *is* reluctance to scrutinize assumptions, examine arguments, and come to terms with the facts, then the problems facing the media might well prove intractable. They are certainly not likely to yield to the endemic Australian philosophy "She'll be right."

ENDNOTES

[1]The effect of the increase in the level of education between 1966 and 1979 is discussed in J.S. Western and Colin A. Hughes, *The Mass Media in Australia,* 2nd edition (St. Lucia: University of Queensland Press, 1983), part I, chap. I.

[2]Henry Mayer, *The Press in Australia* (Melbourne: Lansdowne Press Pty. Ltd., 1964, reprint 1968), p. 27.

[3]Henry Mayer, "Dilemmas in Mass Media Policies," (Canberra: The Academy of the Social Sciences in Australia, 1979), p. 5.

[4]Australian Broadcasting Corporation Act 1983, part 2, section 6, pp. 4–6.

[5]Broadcasting and Television Act 1942 (as amended to December 31, 1979), part IIIA, 79D.

[6]Michael Law, "Public Broadcasting in Australia," unpublished paper, p. 1.

[7]Peter Lucas, "ABC Radio—change is in the air," *Scan,* (Sydney: Australian Broadcasting Corporation, 1984), vol. 8, no. 1, pp. 1, 3, 4.

[8]Western and Hughes, *The Mass Media in Australia,* p. 118.

[9]J.G. Norris, *Report of the Inquiry into the Ownership and Control of Newspapers in Victoria,* report to the premier of Victoria, September 15, 1981, p. 98.

[10]Australian Broadcasting Tribunal, *Cable and subscription television services for Australia:* August 1982: vol. II: Report (Part B), page 12.2.

[11]For information concerning media ownership, see Australian Broadcasting Tribunal, *Cable and subscription television services for Australia:* vol. II, Report (Part B), (Canberra: Australian Government Publishing Service, 1982), table 12-3; and for views see Humphrey McQueen, *Australia's Media Monopolies* (Camberwell, Victoria: Widescope International Publishers Pty. Ltd., 1977), pp. 144, 198; Les Carlyon, *Paperchase: The Press Under Examination* (Melbourne: The Herald and Weekly Times Limited, 1982), p. 217; Lance Peters, ed., *Report of Proceed-*

ings, Mass Communications Conference, Sydney, 1969 (Sydney: Metro Press Pty. Ltd., 1969), p. 49. For a detailed and balanced discussion of ownership see Henry Mayer, *The Press in Australia* (Melbourne: Lansdowne Press, Pty. Ltd., 1964), chap. 10, pp. 152–172.

[12]ABC Annual Report, July 1, 1982–June 30, 1983 (Sydney: Australian Broadcasting Corporation, 1983), p. 2.

[13]A.T. Dix, *The ABC in Review: National Broadcasting in the 1980s*, review of the Australian Broadcasting Commission (Canberra: Australian Government Publishing Service, 1981), vol. I, part I, paras. 12, 13.

[14]*Television Program Appreciation Monthly Report*, November/December 1983 (Sydney: ABC Audience Research, 1983).

[15]G.A. Wilkes, *A Dictionary of Australian Colloquialisms* (Sydney: Sydney University Press, 1978), p. 331.

[16]Joseph Furphy, *Such is Life* (Sydney: Angus and Robertson/Sirius Books, 1962), p. 39.

[17]A reference to the story "The Drover's Wife" by Henry Lawson.

[18]W. Jackson Bate, *The Burden of the Past and the English Poet* (New York: W.W. Norton & Company Inc., 1970).

[19]From A.B. ("Banjo") Paterson's poem, "Clancy of the Overflow," in *The Man from Snowy River*, (Sydney: Angus and Robertson, 1895).

Nicholas Jose

Cultural Identity: "I Think I'm Something Else"

AMONG THE SUBTLEST OBSERVERS of contemporary Australian life is fiction writer Frank Moorhouse. He has written perceptively about the multiple choices offered by the present phase of Australian culture, and is particularly interested in the problem of self-definition that confronts artists and intellectuals. In his *Tales of Mystery and Romance* (1977) a brief encounter occurs between Moorhouse's narrator and his ex-wife:

> "Do you consider yourself an intellectual then—yes, I suppose you," she said, "I suppose you always have."
>
> "The new Australian style is not to be frightened of calling yourself an intellectual or an artist. Australians weren't allowed to once."
>
> "It still sounds arrogant to me."
>
> "I think I'm something else."[1]

Like Australian culture itself, the narrator aspires to recognition, or even self-recognition, in the face of egalitarian-utilitarian suspicions that it is all a bit of a joke. No sooner does the intellectual or artist find it possible to claim for himself a privileged, public role than he resists the title, sensing that it doesn't quite fit with what he thinks he is. He is unable to be seen, by himself or by others, to take himself seriously, especially not in the imported mold of an intellectual whose native ground is Paris, Frankfurt, or New York. Underlying the narrator's reluctance to define himself is uneasiness about Australia's authenticity as local habitation for cultural activity. What passes for culture may be simply "the new Australian style" with all the ephemerality that implies. Yet—and here is the distinctive puzzle—

the individual's refusal to claim an identity for himself is not seen as failure. For Moorhouse's narrator, it is a saving evasion.

Such complexes of feeling are a remote legacy of Australia's colonial past. From the first stirrings of national sentiment in the late nineteenth century to the tentative emergence of nationhood at Gallipoli, according to some historians, or after the Second World War, according to others, Australia developed in a provincial relationship with the mother country. Fledgling nationhood did not mean automatic cultural independence, despite the fervent hopes of nationalists. It merely institutionalized the cultural dominance of distant Britain, against which Australians had to define themselves and struggle for existence. Even when her power declined, Britain continued to be the center of the cultural and political empire that gave Australia a place in the world. As the imperial capital, London was the source of the ideals to which most Australians aspired, the apparent wellspring of intellectual achievement and the measure by which Australians would be judged. For Australians, London had taken over the position previously occupied by Greece and Rome, and writers and artists in the antipodean former colony faced the classic dilemma of the provincial. Their allegiances were divided between the stimulating peculiarities of their local world and the unassailably indifferent metropolis. They were spurred on, and daunted, by conflicting challenges: to find a voice for their new land, and to attain to the highest standards of the old. Some stayed at home to forge a defiant vernacular. Others heard the siren call of a more refined civilization and remade themselves as Europeans. But most, and perhaps the best, made art out of their dilemma, and scrutinized the conditions of life in Australia with a double awareness. From the encounter between the European heritage and the strange shaping circumstances of the new land have come the most influential visions of Australia.

What John Clive and Bernard Bailyn observed in two earlier provincial societies was also true of Australia for two-thirds of the twentieth century. As in eighteenth-century Scotland and colonial America, "the complexity of the provincial's image of the world and himself made demands upon him unlike those felt by the equivalent Englishman. It tended to shake the mind from the rock of habit and tradition. It led men to the interstices of common thought where were found new views and new approaches to the old. . . ."[2] In Australia's case, those "interstices" were not always comfortable, yet from the provincial anguish at being divided between two different kinds of home, fine fruits of the imagination have come. The immediate war and postwar years in particular witnessed an efflorescence of Australian culture, stimulated perhaps by the catastrophe and chaos that the old civilization in Europe was experiencing. The mythopoeic work of painters such as Sidney Nolan, Arthur Boyd, and Albert Tucker; novelists such as Martin Boyd, Patrick White, and Christina Stead; and poets such as Kenneth Slessor, A.D. Hope, Judith Wright, and David Campbell revealed new, grand, and sometimes tragic potentialities within the isolated and apparently ungiving circumstances of Australian life. Their perceptions were the culmination of Australia's growth towards nationhood. In their work, the deprived, challenging conditions of Australia were turned into national myth. The implacable alien majesty of the bush, the lack of European delicacy, the dry, empty center: such liabilities found symbolic and spiritual meaning, and vitalized art. A new way of seeing was achieved. It depended on all the straining energy between provincial adolescent and metropolitan parent, but it depended equally on a clear century-old certainty about which place played which role. Now all that has changed.

In the later postwar years, Australia's simple provincial relationship with Britain began to alter beyond recognition. The main reason was Australia's new military alliance with the United States: economic and cultural influence soon followed. But there had always been those Australians whose affinity with the Irish, by birth or maltreatment, made them resist English supremacy. As Australia grew more affluent and more confident and formed new relationships through immigration and trade with other European countries, with the Middle East, and eventually with Asia, there were fewer incentives to make Britain the primary reference point. In any case, technology, communications, and Western capitalism were rapidly making Australia as unprovincially, homogeneously "international" as anywhere else in the developed world. By the time of its disengagement from the Vietnam War, Australia was not, strictly speaking, a province of anywhere. Although the United States was visible as the new center, not all Australians reoriented themselves accordingly. Many preferred to stay marginal. In the words that conclude the history of Australia to the 1960s: "the Antipodes were drifting, though where they were drifting no one knew."[3]

If the complex provincial phase was past, what came after looked so confusing it was better not to think about it. With old bearings gone, the nationhood that had been glimpsed in the postwar decades was obscured once again. The traditions and values that had sustained Australians became the fading stuff of legend. The question of national identity, which had preoccupied Australians since the beginning, became more perplexed than ever. The growing stridency of Australian chauvinism since the early 1970s has concealed many uncertainties. As Patrick White remarked recently, "We have been served up a lot of claptrap about the need for a national identity. We have been urged to sing imbecile jingles, flex our muscles like the sportmen from telly commercials, and display a hearty optimism totally unconvincing because so superficial and unnatural." The imposition of a false, and falsely confident, image of being Australian has only disguised the fact that "Australia" is not just there to be proclaimed: it is still there to be formed. For that reason, every kind of cultural and intellectual life in Australia sooner or later gets tangled up with the vexed question of national identity. It will not go away, yet the desired object remains spectral.

In Australia, there is not the continuity and congruency of land, population, history, tradition, and language that knit together a people's soul. The search for that elusive center is the great Australian dream, as much today as when the early explorers perished in their quest for a life-giving source, where there was only the dead heart of the continent. Recurrent metaphors of heart, soul, and center reflect the geographical peculiarity of a country that is most knowable at its peripheries. Much Australian writing reveals a deep yearning for unity, perhaps as recompense for the breaking of bonds in the original severance from the old home, and the disruptive, violent arrival in the new. Center-seeking is a leitmotiv in Australian culture, whether it is the impulse to align the experience of the new society with the central traditions and values of the old world, or the search for a new center in the new land. The singleness of the island-continent makes the longing for a center look so feasible. Yet it is an aspiration of the most difficult metaphysical kind. It is the vision of a transcendent harmony between nature and nurture, between the "untouched" land and what "civilization" brings to it, between present selves and an enormous pluralistic cultural past. It is a grandiose dream on the scale of the land itself, an embryonic dream of *imperium* in which all are forerunners.

Yet here is the irony. If Australianness is elusive as a center, an essence, a destiny, it is everywhere to be found as a refracting perspective, a melange, a quirk. The baffling circumstances that defeat the search for a center may well prove to be the thing itself, and to think appreciatively in those terms may well be the first step away from mythology to the maturity that can rescue Australians from comic afflatus as well as tragic delusion. In the 1970s and 1980s, Australian writers have begun to explore the nature of their marginality. What they have discovered gives special brilliance to their work. As the high priest of marginal illumination put it, "A literature whose development is not . . . unusually broad in scope, but *seems* to be" can nonetheless contribute to "the stirring of minds, the coherence of national consciousness, the pride which a nation gains from a literature of its own . . . the spiritualization of the broad area of public life" and the other invigorating effects of cultural activity that does not deny its origins in a community.[4] Or was Franz Kafka thinking of somewhere else?

How Australia has been modernized is one of Frank Moorhouse's pet concerns. He is interested in what happens to the past as people try to change or abandon it. He is a chronicler of the "now," but his "now" prismatically reveals dimensions of history. His characters begin as children of conventional, rural, "old" Australia. They are brought up according to pragmatic country-town, small-business pieties, to be ingenious but straight. They are excited by a technological American future. They are otherwise untroubled by the relativities of world culture. But when these children grow up, they make the move to the cities, in a time of affluence, and do their exploring on quite different fronts from the early pioneers. They become students, academics, intellectuals, feminists, communists, homosexuals, artists, global travelers, drug addicts and/or transvestites. They adopt styles of life at odds with what they were brought up to expect. It is a quality of Moorhouse's art that he makes us see his characters' "alternative choices" in the context of continuous personal histories. The most explicit discovery his progressive sixties and seventies children make is the possibility of change itself: new ideas, and new ideologies. The trouble is, in Australia, that the pure form of the idea is always imported. How should Moorhouse's flexible Australians adapt their minds and lives to wave after wave of intellectual fashion? What to take and what to leave behind? In a story called "The Girl Who Met Simone de Beauvoir in Paris," a group of Sydney women take to feminism with comic gusto, while one of the husbands refuses it with pitiful self-isolating stubbornness. Moorhouse views the trends ironically, yet he is sympathetic to the evolutionary struggle towards the new, or against the falsely new, as central to human development. "The central dilemma is that of giving birth, of creating new life," he writes of his work.

His characters are marginal people. They are divided or thwarted in their hopes, perplexed and frustrated. They are relentlessly optimistic and experimental, yet doomed to the melancholy of failure or betrayal before they settle for a level irony. They are puzzled about their own natures, their politics, their spirituality, their sexuality, the orthodoxies of their society, old and new. They move ceaselessly into the future, yet they are dogged by a different past, part history and part nostalgia. They are on the move, yet drawn back to old fixities. In such ways, through his odd company of combatants in the field of modern life, Frank Moorhouse explores the bewildering choices of self and identity that face Australians at large.

Problems of identity are nothing new in twentieth-century literature, but Moorhouse's ear is especially attuned to the Australian particularities of his characters' difficulties. Their choices are not simply existential, but reflect political choices and social potentialities. Although he does not depict a range of representative Australian types, his fringe characters are significant because their peculiar circumstances point to the dilemmas of the country as a whole. They are adrift in a world of enormous diversity. Their dreams are not sustaining, because one dream challenges another. One imported artifact or concept vies with another for consumption. The talismans of old nationalism, such as the bush, childhood, and the past itself, are placed in disconcerting conjunction with the supermarket riches of the new cosmopolitanism. As a result, Moorhouse's characters end up rootless and unattached. At the end of each short, unconcluded stretch of story is a blank.

The major historical change in which Moorhouse's characters participate is the Americanization of Australia, after the postwar loosening of ties with Britain. Politically, economically, socially, and culturally, the range of American choices has been conferred on Australia, and Moorhouse's characters experience them in their personal lives. *The Americans, Baby* chronicles the impact of various transient Americans on the lives of susceptible Sydney-siders. The great American adventure is viewed quizzically, at once liberating and oppressive, frightening yet fascinating, funny and sad. It is not celebrated with the great intellectual energy of a Saul Bellow. Moorhouse considers America's abundant plurality a curious fact to be reckoned with, a strange new dimension in the life of Australia. T. George McDowell is an elderly soft-drink salesman from the South Coast of New South Wales, and a marvelous embodiment of a certain between-the-wars "ordinary" Australian. In one story, he recalls his visit to the St. Louis Rotary Convention of 1923, where girls from twenty-eight nations appeared with flag-waving Boy Scouts and an Italian choir to salute an innocent vision of international fellowship in the first flush of its American-style optimism. The recollection is poignant because it was the first, shining intimation of the brave new world to come—a world that turned out to be darker and more complicated than any Aussie Rotarian could have imagined. Between that first hope and the actuality that American-style progress has made of Australia, there is a considerable gap: McDowell is recounting his memory to a traveling American Coca-Cola salesman who has had a weird sexual fling with his mentally disturbed, city-gone, drug-addict daughter: "I have never seen anything like it in my life—it has never been equalled in my experience," says T. George, clinging to what the St. Louis Rotary Convention 1923 meant to him.

If Moorhouse is melancholy about change, its details afford him an increasingly rich and textured perception of the world. If the "Great Australian Emptiness" (Patrick White's desiccating phrase in 1958) has been overhastily filled, that is a condition that the writer cannot ignore. Indeed, it is a chance that the resources of his spirit, comic and humanizing in Moorhouse's case, may turn to something splendid. In one funny story, the narrator becomes uncomfortable when the visiting American poet Kenneth Rexroth remarks that even the behavior of Sydney's radical anarchists is derivative of the U.S..

"You should do something of your own," says Rexroth depressingly.

"Do your *own things* as the kids say in Haight-Ashbury," says his secretary.

We sit nonplussed and then I fall over backwards into silence like a skindiver. We have nothing of our own to do, I contemplate, nothing. We are culturally incapacitated and dependent. Everyone has known this in his heart now for some time. Actually we're Anglo-American. A composite mimic culture. Miserable shits.

Then I observe that, in a sense, all cultures are interdependent and derivative and that perhaps we are a remarkably rich synthesis. Perhaps we should go with the synthesis instead of painfully pursuing a unique nationalism. Exercising once again my capacity for finding countervailing partial truths for observation.

It is the characteristic Moorhouse sidestep, a melancholy marginal note that is also somehow cheering, hopeful because honest.

The truths of identity are complex and shifting. The world is fluid and so are Moorhouse's characters in it. Grand, simple meanings are elusive. "What is death? . . . What of the future of the world? . . . What is the purpose of life?" Another story takes its sly comedy from the fact that the narrator has one-line certainties to answer such questions, until the certainties themselves become meaningless: "Where do you get your new certainty, your new answers?" "I'm tired of people who pretend *not* to have all the answers." "Do the answers matter?" "No."

Curious things happen to the great issues of humanity as they are debated on Australian soil. Two paradoxes can be noted. The first is that the fundamental problems of mankind are rapidly transmuted to local questions. Who are we? What are we doing here? In Australia, such questions have a particular meaning and relevance apart from their wider metaphysical significance. They are inevitably tied up with questions about national identity, and the distinctiveness of existence in Australia, as if the larger questions cannot be answered without first answering the more socially specific questions: who are we Australians, and what are we doing *here*? Perennial philosophical questions raise particular anxieties in Australians, and Australians tend to respond to the general issues of the time in idiosyncratic and particularized ways. Worldwide discussion of nuclear disarmament, for example, is reflected in Australia chiefly through the dispute about whether Australia should export uranium mined from land to which Aborigines claim sacred rights. Australians characteristically have their own angle of viewing the universal concerns of our species and the larger movements of world history, and that angle has to do with being Australian. Australian skeptics suspect that universals, world trends, international crises, and the like are only so as seen from Europe or North America. That leads to the second paradox. From an Australian point of view, the great issues of humanity can easily look like someone else's problem. The point is not intended flippantly. Whatever else Australian thinkers and writers may do, whatever world problems they may engage with, their work also has a separate dimension of social purpose. They are writing and thinking Australia.

It might be observed that the doubts and relativities explored in current Australian writing can be paralleled in most other contemporary literatures. Australian writers and artists can be readily identified with trends, schools, and styles that have their origins abroad. In recent decades, the indigenous culture has been less separatist and less independent of foreign models than ever before, despite increased nationalist aspirations. The important point, however, is that the ideas and manners that are brought in quickly acquire a local color. They are subjected to local scrutiny. Crucially, they are put to different uses and have a different orientation with respect to the needs of the new society. Frank Moorhouse, for example, does not merely lodge his up-to-date intellectual concerns in a documentary Australian scene. More important, and to the contrary, his writing makes the intellectual uncertainties of the times symptomatic of the unfixed conditions of Australian society. It is the achievement of such a writer to understand the coincidence of Australia's development. Australia is aspiring to nationhood at a time when that is perhaps the least plausible, least possible thing to do. Australia is subject to every kind of international influence and pressure, and it is in those terms that Australians come to understand themselves, reluctantly and with a countermanding obsession with their own unique circumstances.

Moorhouse calls his Sydney bohemians an "urban tribe" because they live according to mysterious patterns and laws that often contradict the intellectual positions they consciously espouse. An unformulated, dimly perceived set of values persists, as both strength and liability. It is rooted in the past and in laconic rural pragmatism, transmitted through the vernacular and the strange decorums of

Australian social behavior, and includes at times a wild-man quality sanctioned and admired as "larrikinism." It is the loose gathering of attitudes, mores, and lore summed up for Australians as "the bush," a phrase that denotes uncleared native scrub and refers metaphorically to anywhere away from the urban and suburban centers. "Go bush" is Australia's version of "go West," but with an unoptimistic prospect. Frank Moorhouse's stories share the dry skeptical humor and melancholy of the early bush yarns, although the subject matter is vastly different. As his contemporary men and women find—or lose—themselves in the alien scrub of the cities, they bring to their encounter with the modern consumables of mind and matter the bush values they have inherited from an earlier way of life, from their scarcely articulated culture. Bush values are challenged and mutated in the process, but don't go away, any more than the bush itself has so far vanished. Although most Australians don't live there now, the bush still stands for a quality of innocent, doubting resistance to urbanity, internationalism, and the European mind. "Although he did not always feel easy in the bush—," Moorhouse's narrator says to himself on a camping trip, "in fact he sometimes felt discordant in it—he'd rather be out in it feeling discordant than not to be there." Meanwhile, his female companion is proving "her tenacity in the bush . . . not so much to win his approval as to demonstrate her Australian spirit."

Yet the intellectual world has largely drawn Moorhouse's attention. In a comic piece of social anthropology called *Conference-ville,* he charts the interactions of people at an academic conference. Australians love such meetings, less for the advancement of knowledge than for the opportunity to play games and to obstruct collectively. Typically, the intellectual proceedings are charged with extra-intellectual factors as the conference-going tribe groups and regroups: "like a huge, talk-inflated balloon the seminar bumps off the ground, bumps back again, and then rises, if things are right, and drifts in a wind of thinking, ridden by the participants all holding on, bumping, bumping across the terrain of the program, with the organisers working a useless rudder." Moorhouse appreciates the more energizing life of things outside the ordering, defining aspirations of civilization. He becomes more comfortably, evasively conscious of himself through a sidelong attachment to ordinary things than through the abstractions of theory alone:

> I ate in the park with the office workers and wouldn't have minded being back in their world of snatched physical touchings, kissings and resting hangovers.
>
> I was glad no one could see the inadequacy of my thinking.
>
> I was plagued by my inability to retrieve, there in the park, a nice summary, a decisive and confident summary of my "position."
>
> I'd been naive. That most dreadful political failing.
>
> Sometimes I had a position and sometimes I couldn't find it again. Oh well. I put it down as a personality deficiency, and went back to watching the office workers kissing.

Thus the narrator of *Conference-ville* snatches a moment's peace.

Moorhouse's perplexity springs from his efforts to measure new concepts and customs against "testable reality." He is no fantasist, but a sophisticated contemporary realist. In the context of Australian fiction, he is important because he refuses to mythologize the landscape, the pioneering tradition, or the country itself. He has not sought to write the Great Australian Novel. He has broken free of the archetypal exile-and-return of the major earlier works of fiction, the colonial journeying between the old world and the new that underlies Henry Handel Richardson's *Fortunes of Richard Mahony,* Christina Stead's *For Love Alone,* and the oeuvre of Martin Boyd and Patrick White. For Moorhouse, the dialogue is between a historical heritage and the rest of the world out there, the multiple options of the modern and future.

He labels each of his short-story collections a "discontinuous narrative." The discontinuities are essential as a means of catching the fragmented nature of contemporary Australian experience, of disclaiming ambition and the yearning for unity, and as a way of refusing to take oneself seriously. Yet taken together, all of Moorhouse's works constitute one big continuing "discontinuous narrative," with the wholeness that implies. It is the narrator's *éducation sentimentale,* a portrait of the artist as marginal man, the observer as hero. Here and there Moorhouse hints at his analogues. "The Jack Kerouac Wake—the true story" recounts the oblique "communal, subconscious respect" paid to Jack when no one turns up at his memorial gathering. Kerouac's raw, formless, all-inclusive autobiographical fiction is gigantic and artless, where Moorhouse's is lean and artful, but they share an impulse to redeem the complexities of the individual personality as it disappears in time. Kerouac found his own analogue in Proust, whereas Moorhouse is more circumspect. "I pulled out Anthony Powell's *Temporary Kings*. You always offend the sociability of the bar by reading. On our egalitarian scale though, I suppose, Powell was less unacceptable to read in a bar than say Proust." And Moorhouse's own books still less unacceptable, one might add. He has cultivated an un-highbrow image, but on turning forty, confessed that "at last Proust takes on his full meaning."

The allusion to French cerebration is not accidental. In habitual asides, Moorhouse worries away at the philosophical and psychological implications of things, as an argumentative, eclectic human scientist rather than a mythologizer. Christina Stead's observation that "critics . . . live in a world of fantasy," whereas "the writers . . . are the scientists" points to a traditional and reemergent quality of Australian literature. It is not characterized by its inventive capacity, its fiction-making, its pure and speculative thought. Rather, its strength lies in its origins, in the honest account of hitherto uncharted physical and spiritual territory exemplified in explorers' journals, natural scientists' records, colonial "lives" and, in due course, a flourishing historiography. In the same vein, Moorhouse's prose derives its spareness and concreteness from his commitment to argument and facts. As an intellectual, he is a figure of the rational enlightenment struggling with the romantic and post-romantic mysteries that haunt present-day (Australian) culture. In "The Airport, The Pizzeria, The Motel, The Rented Car, and the Mysteries of Life," the dispute between the narrator and his ex-wife becomes a dialogue between Rousseau and Saint-Simon. But the groping for lucidity is only intermittently successful against the chaos that Moorhouse also matter-of-factly embraces. If this is spiritual autobiography, it is as much *Tristram Shandy* as Proust.

The Australian colony was founded in the late eighteenth century. In many ways its literature devolves from, or keeps returning to, the thought and practice of that time. Moorhouse goes back, not to the classicism advocated by postwar poet-critics A.D. Hope and James McAuley, but to the quotidian shapeless picaresque, and behind that, to the seminal forms of the psychological novel, the diary-entry, the personal letter, the confession. It is a search that goes back to the beginning in order to scrutinize, not only the construction of fiction, but also the formation of the self, the construction of a nation, and the divergence of cultural identity. "All the time we drag the information and facts towards humbug and sensationalism," complains Moorhouse's narrator. The author's achievement is to work back behind that tendency in his analysis of Australian life.

In his funny, clever novel *Homesickness* (1980), Murray Bail describes a group of Australians on a package-tour of the world, or rather the world's museums. "The world itself is a museum; and within its circumference the many small museums . . . represent the whole."[5] Australians have become inveterate and capable travelers, and go everywhere. Perhaps it is a compulsion that arises from their fear of geographical isolation and cultural poverty, or perhaps it is merely a necessity if they are to know what is going on in the world. At any rate, traveling provides an appropriate contemporary metaphor for rootlessness, and a vantage point for looking back on Australia. Eagerly or wearily, as much turned in on themselves as outwards, Bail's tourists move through what the world offers, from Africa to Europe to Equador (where the bathwater goes down the plughole straight), from New York to Moscow, through museums of science, marriage, gravity, toilets, trains, corrugated iron, and more. As these motley Australians experience it, the world is a baffling, bizarre array of objects, labels, words—ordered and catalogued, but undifferentiated and devoid of other than curiosity meaning and value. An occasional illumination reaches through when the travelers see themselves through the eyes of an alien culture. In the English corrugated iron museum, they discover what appear to be "photographs of corrugated iron sheets," until the guide explains that they "are close-ups of Australian foreheads, taken at random. We believe it must be the loneliness and harsh seasons you have, the glare and the flies, the distance from help and the rest of the world that makes a man . . . perpetually frown. . . . By now it has probably established itself in the antipodean genes. Corrugated iron therefore matches the Australian psyche. So there you are."

Bail is reluctant to see himself as a national or realist writer, though he is skeptical of a spurious Esperanto internationalism, too. "That's what I like in other literatures, the Russians, for example. They don't really fool around with local problems at all. It seems to me that a lot of Australian literature—and painting too—is still primarily concerned with getting ourselves on our own two feet, of establishing our Australianness."[6] He is caught in something of a cleft stick here, because his preoccupation with the exoticism of the ordinary and the ordinariness of the exotic, as international travel brings it home, is the latest, most sophisticated stage of the attempt to gauge the special oddness of the Australian experience. Bail's subtlest perceptions are for local savoring. His tourists' fantastic encounters with the jumbled plurality of the world give an exaggerated, comic, apt expression of the cultural confusion Australians face daily. As Bail shows, the weird experiences of travel induce a kind of comparative anthropology. The Australian travelers refer back insistently to themselves and their pragmatic, vernacular home. Yet what *they* are is no more certain than the superficial conclusions they draw about others:

> "We don't speak very well. Have you noticed how the Americans are so descriptive and confident? Our sentences are shorter. Our thoughts break off. We don't seem comfortable talking, I don't know why. Have you noticed we make silly quips . . . ?"
>
> "You mean us, Australians?". . . .
>
> "We're embarrassed. We're not as confident as we look. We speak in jerks, or we're over-familiar. The quips you mention I think might be connected to our geographical location, and our land emptiness. . . . we seem to need encouragement. Quips help us along. . . . It's as if, in Australia, we're all in hospital. There's a lot of quipping in hospitals."

The uneasy speculation catches the awkward need of an identity that is threatened when Australians come into contact with the apparent superiority of other nations.

Elsewhere, Bail's jokey, cluttered, anti-rhetorical prose plays fantastically with the elusive mystery of what Australia might mean or be. The quest for a numinous Australian essence takes a parodic turn, a net that shows the shape of what falls through:

> "You mustn't be too harsh on your country," a voice called out. . . . "Other writers have been hypnotized by 'kangaroo.' 'Boomerang,' to a lesser extent. Those words represent the mystery of Australia—its distance and large shape."
>
> "You mean in particular D.H. Lawrence?". . . .
>
> "Not only him. It is a quite pronounced, if minor, trend in world literature."
>
> "Really? Go on?. . . ."
>
> "In particular, French novelists have long been attracted to kangaroos. The beast is biologically and visually surreal. The word itself is histrionic: a series of rhythmic loops. 'Implacable kangaroos of laughter,' wrote young

Lautréamont—a fine metaphor. Very fine. Young Alfred Jarry had his supermale box with not one but several kangaroos. You find the noun leaping like a verb from the hallowed pages of Louis Aragon, Malraux in China, and Goncourt's *Journal*—yes, he reported eating authentic kangaroo meat during the siege of Paris. Another naturalist is Gide. He described in his journal a monument in some little French village square, peopled with 'familiar kangaroos.' To Proust, an acquaintance ravaged by time looked unexpectedly strange, 'like a kangaroo.' There is Tiffauges, the ogre, astride his 'kangaroo-like horse.' (But then Michel Tournier can also throw a boomerang. It is said.) It appears in Boswell's *Life,* in *The Mill on the Floss* and 'Dear Kangaroo' is the nickname in Virginia Woolf's letters—ha ha. And who was that sad Irish clown who spent pages confusing the kangaroo with women and shirt-tails? The frequency of the word increases the farther north the writer is from Australia. Distance = novelty and a desire to conquer. Writing in Zurich, James Joyce recommended the Kangarooschwanzsuppe. 'Kangaroo-shaped' is a common metaphor. See Isak Dinesen's descriptions of hares, or the young philosopher in the Thomas Mann story, 'At the Prophet's.' Chekhov in his notebooks used it to describe a pregnant woman with a long neck; and in Ehrenburg's novel he has a vintage car hopping like one. The great Osip Mandlestam questioned the logic of kangaroos in Armenia. And when discussing the cosmos in his autobiography Vladimir Nabokov writes, 'a kangaroo's pouch wouldn't hold it.' Not bad? Very good. In a thunder-storm Henry Miller stripped naked and 'hopped around like a kangaroo,' the damn fool."

A more direct account of the mystery comes with the sudden eloquence of one woman in the group, at the end of the book:

"We come from a country . . . of nothing really, or at least nothing substantial yet. We can appear quite heartless at times. I don't know why. We sometimes don't know any better. . . . Even before we travel we're wandering in circles. There isn't much we understand. I should say, there isn't much we believe in. We have rather empty feelings. I think we even find love difficult. And when we travel we demand even the confusions to be simple. It is all confusing, isn't it . . .?"

Yet even that answer is subverted. The novel questions the relationship between the subjective self and the world, so that the woman's remarks are exposed as self-revelation as much as cultural analysis. Her remarks have a quality of literary gamesmanship, parodying, as much of *Homesickness* does, the bleakly oracular manner of Patrick White. More important, the novel itself stands as a substantial equivalent to that "nothing really." As an elaborate circumnavigation of a heart of Australia which is "nothing really," *Homesickness* makes that home into something. Bail's achievement is to remove that something away from a geographical description and to locate it instead as a quality of character and an angle of perception. Ultimately, the woman's *self*-revelation—the point from which she looks on—is as much or as little as the revelation of a culture can ever be. "We are an odd lot," says one of her traveling companions, and suddenly begins laughing. The land's original oddness has now been acquired as the defining characteristic of its people.

Another contemporary writer has been preoccupied with the richer understanding of the world afforded by an antipodean perspective. In the work of David Malouf, the dichotomy between Europe and Australia is brought into complex correspondence with the other polarities of his private mythology: light and dark, nature and nurture, wildness and civilization, words and silence, consciousness and unconsciousness. Those pairings do not line up neatly, however, as Malouf's mind moves variously among them. More thoroughly and austerely than other writers, he has found in his Australianness an unlocalized quality of the imagination. He has argued against the need for a writer to root himself in a particular world: the geography of one's place lives where it is internalized, as the geography of one's individuality that can go anywhere. Malouf's example shows the strength such a conviction can give. However disparately he roves, however extreme the oscillation between the northern and southern worlds of his imagination, the quality of his art is not discord and fragmentation, but their opposite. He finds continuity between the poles of experience, and harmony in the balance opposites achieve when they come together. His novel *An Imaginary Life* (1978) tells of the poet Ovid, exiled from Rome to a wasteland where a new sort of fellowship and community develops between himself and a wild boy, changing utterly the civilized poet's sense of his identity: "No more dreams. We have passed beyond them into the last reality. . . . I no longer ask myself where we are making for. The notion of a destination no longer seems necessary to me. It has been swallowed up in the immensity of this landscape, as the days have been swallowed up by the sense I now have of a life that stretches beyond the limits of measureable time. Is this what the shaman experiences. . .?"[7] The floating serenity of Malouf's prose reflects the harmony that the poet feels. Through relationship with his contrary, he moves into a new kind of imaginative completeness, "the last reality," a condition beyond the dreaming of culture, history, and identity. Unlike Moorhouse and Bail, who refer a complicated, relativistic sense of their world back to the individuals who live out those complications in a particular social reality, Malouf seeks resolution in an ever-encompassing breadth of perception, where the redeeming artistic imagination completes what is left partial in actuality. The pattern is repeated in poem after poem, and in all the novels.

In *Johnno* (1975), an exotic literary survivor retells the wasted life of his doomed friend. The book achieves what Johnno himself failed to achieve in life. Its inspiration is the vitality that the dead friend had communicated in youth years before, when the shy narrator stood "tongue-tied, ecstatic / . . . aglow only / in the darkness of myself," as a related poem puts it.[8] *Johnno* is a celebration of failure and an elegy for those sleepy, carefree, dreaming Australian values that could not survive. With the burden of doom characteristic of much Australian writing, its heart sides with what progress and prosperity annihilate. In the narrator's epigram, "Any story that matters here is a success story. The others are just literature."

In Malouf's novel *Child's Play* (1982), two people, a master of high art and a young terrorist who is the enemy of the master's culture, find their meaning and consummation through each other, in ways only the hidden novelist can grasp; and in *Fly Away Peter* (1982), a sensitive, silent, bird-watching young man is transported from a Queensland beach to die in the trenches in the First World War. In memory, and through the novel's art, that abbreviated life endures and is recorded as an absolute, if minimal, significance: "what life meant, a unique presence . . . and what was also, in the end, most moving."

Malouf has moved outward from Australia in his subject matter, and also in his approach to his readers, just as he has been consciously and gratefully receptive to outside influences in his writing: Mann, Stevens, Auden, Lowell, to mention a casual few. This is not out of any sort of cultural cringe, inverted or otherwise, but out of a simple belief that the experience of Australians and non-Australians is continuous and mutually enhancing. Malouf has said that Australian literature should not be presented "as a 'greenhide and stringybark' curiosity when . . . our real achievement, might be in pioneering the experience of suburban man and in presenting Europe with an image of itself that is both an imitation (which in its translation to a new place has become a new thing) and a critical revaluation."[9] But this remark, with the mirror held back to Europe, belies the extent to which the cultural dialectic in Malouf's work is freed from specific geography. Central to Malouf's imagination is the Conradian awareness that civilization is a fabrication that only conceals the things it most fears. His work is deeply informed by the experience of barbarism in this century, notably in the Holocaust. From that perspective, Europe and Australia are not so different. Both stretch a net of meaning over chaos. In "Notes on an Undiscovered Continent," he writes:

> centuries powder at a touch.
> The rest—since nothing happens—we must invent. . . .
> At the centre of our lives a big stone shines, we find a name
> for it, perhaps our own, settle the landslip with our bones.
> Such settlements are provisional. The nineteen tongues of Europe
> migrate to fill a silence. . . .

A darker poem begins: "We are all of us exiles of one place / or another—even those / who never leave home." The poet is "At Ravenna," remembering Dante, Conrad, and himself, and concludes:

> We all die
> under alien skies at a place called Ravenna. Whether the new atlas calls it
> that, or Sydney,
> or Katsangani formerly Stanleyville.

But Malouf also reverses the century's song of cultural disintegration. Beneath that plangency is the calm of perceived wholeness. Or perhaps it is the flattening caused by cultural overkill. As he jokes elsewhere, "Australia, like most other places these days, has more 'high culture' than even the hungriest of us can absorb."

Not just high culture, one might add, but more culture and more cultures of every kind. Frank Moorhouse's exploration of Sydney's tribal ways is paralleled in the work of Helen Garner, who takes for her material the countercultural world of Melbourne. The novel *Monkey Grip* (1977) is the story of a young woman's emotional addiction to a man who, in turn, is addicted to heroin. Its account of Melbourne bohemian life in the 1970s is lovingly accurate about everything from street names to turns of speech to ideological positions. The strength of the book is less how it treats the central relationship than its portrayal of a floating background of friends and lovers, their groupings, enmities, and alliances. In the concluding image, thirty or forty "people we knew" are gathered "at the kids' end" of an inner-city public swimming pool at the height of summer: a "gypsy encampment at the shallow end."[10] Thus, even at its most urbanized, Australian life offers an ancient picture of shore dwellers. In *Monkey Grip,* Garner respects a whole range of formless and drifting individualities. She exposes the laws by which the loose sub-community lives, and understands that its values are an attempt to socialize a deeper moral quest for personal integrity, freedom with responsibility, and selfhood within community. For Garner's venturing men and women, none of those things is chimerical.

Monkey Grip illustrates some of the paradoxes of Australianness. It is immensely and proudly local as it reveals how the lives of its people are shaped by the grid of streets and two sides of the river around which they act and move. But Garner's characters are also trapped by their locality. The reader, ultimately excluded by such intricate urban geography, peers in through prison bars at these young people as they move from Punt Road to Lygon Street. The novel is punctuated by scenes of arrival or departure at the international airport. Such occasions emphasize the obsessive nature of the Melbourne location. It is as addictive as drugs or passion, the novel's ostensible themes, and equally challenging to faith in the capacity of the individual spirit to transform an intractable world from within. It is a problem handed down from the first dwellers in the convict-settlement. Painfully, despite their rootedness in place, Garner's characters are culturally and morally rootless, impulsive or self-scrutinizing to a degree that makes it impossible for them to order or to control their lives. Their sense of identity, as individuals or as a group, is fluid and confused, while their sense of place is strong. It is the Australian dilemma again.

Helen Garner is a realist in her literary manner. She aims at a truthful description of her environment in order to highlight the points where it must be reformed. Her concentration on fractured relationships, especially the conflicting choices her women face, makes her an anatomist of emerging social forms. The inspiration of Virginia Woolf behind her writing is a means of bringing the accidentals of Melbourne lives into a traditional line of struggle. She is a radical in glimpsing, behind the mess her marginal characters make of their lives, the difficult, necessary impulse towards a different world in future: "We talked about things I had never talked about before: what it means to be alive in 1975, what change is and might be, how we see ourselves fitting in (or not) to this society, what the next step is or might be. We talked about these desolate things." The allusion to the crisis year 1975 suggests that it is Australia's potentiality for democracy and autonomy that is also at stake. Yet in that word "desolate," the dilemmas of identity resolve once again into melancholy.

A comparably complex analysis of a social group is to be found in *The Impersonators* (1980), a novel as rooted in Sydney as Helen Garner's is in Melbourne. Although its author, Jessica Anderson, is of an older generation, her best writing has appeared in the last decade. *The Impersonators* is crafted along Jamesian lines. An extended family, divided, yet bound by personal fortunes, rivalries, and social aspirations, is brought together greedily when the moneyed patriarch is about to die. Into this situation comes the woman most likely to inherit, who is returning to Australia in middle age after many expatriate years, chiefly in London and Italy. Through her once disaffected, now hopeful black sheep's eyes, we witness the ensnaring drama of Australian materialism, as it distorts and displaces other values. It is a rueful novel, the power of which comes from its recognition of the diverse possibilities of community that have been leveled by affluence. Money is the one unequivocal sign of "identity." As in *Monkey Grip*, the authorial consciousness is made desolate by the society's failure to form itself as something beyond the mere aggregation of its dispersed, flattening, competing interests. Yet, as in *Monkey Grip* and other Australian writing, the witnessing of failure, and the pity that brings, is also a sign of attachment and the determination to make it work after all, to pull the bits together and make a meaning of them—as Jessica Anderson's involuted novel in fact does:

> ... even as she looked incredulous, [she] began to see, in these perverse patriots, a reflection of herself. Her frequent sharp offendedness with the people of Sydney was the product of attachment, how ever much overlaid. It established her as a sort of patriot, just as her grief for her mother's dull and trivial fate established her as a sort of daughter. For when had she been so offended by, for example, fat and mendacious Romans, or grieved for the fate, when less than tragic, of anyone else's mother? She had exposed her wish, long hidden and denied, that the people of her country should excel, and that her mother should be wise and ripe.[11]

The novel's heroine wishes for wisdom and ripeness in herself, too, and her linking of those qualities with a concern for her country is indicative of the ways in which here and elsewhere in contemporary Australian writing, the complexities of personal and national being intertwine.

Jessica Anderson's other recent novel, *Tirra Lirra By the River* (1978), finely recounts one woman's sustained attempt to achieve such wisdom and ripeness, to apprehend the larger pattern, in respect of her own life. Again, there are the divisions: Australia versus Europe, home versus exile, cultural creativity versus passive mediocrity, selfhood versus dependence. In old age, a woman returns from England to her childhood home in Australia and reflects on the mixed waste and fulfillment of her life. The image she uses is a globe, only one side of which is in the light of consciousness at any given time, making it impossible ever to see it all: "There is always a nether side to my globe." It spins unpredictably, "Its surface inscribed with thousands, no, millions of images" from the different stages of the woman's past. The novel pieces together the images that come to light in an attempt to do what has never before been possible for the protagonist, to see her existence whole. This Nora's life has been divided, incomplete, inharmonious, yet from the perspective of old age a coherent pattern is revealed, as it is achieved in the novel's art. The globe in Nora's head that cannot be seen from all angles simultaneously is also, as the book's movement between northern and southern hemispheres suggests, the globe of our planet. Nora's—and Jessica Anderson's—impulse towards integration in the face of prismatic fragmentation reflects a broadly cultural (Australian) concern, as well as a personal one.

There is no happy ending here or in any other of the works I have mentioned. Nor is there a straightforward narrative line. The writers in question avoid such possibilities, as if they indicate too simple a conception of history and movement into the future. Jessica Anderson and David Malouf's more formally shaped works end just as inconclusively as Helen Garner's *Monkey Grip* or Murray Bail's *Homesickness* or Frank Moorhouse's continuing discontinuities. The completeness these writers move towards is different, a matter of working for a coherent, comprehensive understanding, scrupulously eschewing the simplicities of myth and, instead, reckoning with the resistance to coherence exerted by the stubborn, broken, actual world. It is a drama of hope that is enacted, but hope of a kind different from that which allows visionary futures and golden endings. The impulse towards pacific enlightenment and a changed world, in the work of these writers, is tempered at every turn by the recognition that such hopes are only realizable as they are grounded in a sharp accounting of actual circumstance. For a novelist, there is at once an artistic and a social challenge. To make hope substantial—not as a dream but as a potentiality for moral and cultural growth, already inherent yet requiring struggle for its realization—it is necessary for the writer to see without falsification what is, in order to reach minimally for what might be. Like Malouf's Ovid, Anderson's Nora finally moves outside the doll's house of her memory and imagination, determined to find what is there: "even if . . . only as small as a stone. . . . I believe I have found the river—the real river I disregarded on my first walks and failed to find on my last . . . ." From that glimpse of a real starting point, knowledge becomes possible, whence true hope.

No writer can be made to represent the generality of his society. Those whose works I have discussed have in common the fact that they are contemporaries and Australians. Their books have been published abroad (by no means the norm for Australian writers), but their audience is chiefly at home. They have won many Australian literary awards, and are reckoned among the most interesting current practitioners of the art of fiction. Their biographical circumstances are as widely different as their literary styles, and they certainly do not exhaust the varieties of Australian writing. Yet it is possible, for all their diversity, to identify affinities that suggest that their literary activity has special coherence and meaning, of the kind Kafka hoped for, in terms of their own community.

One way or another they share a consciousness of being Australian. As writers of the seventies and eighties with an eye on the international scene, they nevertheless share, by fate or choice, a concern with the peculiarities of Australia, and their writing places itself, at times elusively, in an Australian tradition. A corollary is that their international reputations are not, at the moment, on a par with those of their British and North American peers. This is a difficult fact of life. It is less a question of talent than a consequence of Australia's distance from the major literary marketplaces, and from the world's concerns. A few Australian writers have expatriated themselves successfully—Morris West, Thomas Keneally, and Colleen McCullough, for example—but the most exciting Australian writing continues to be that which is nurtured by the writer's originally challenging and inspiring social and psychological environment: the "flower" that may appear for a moment "at the sheer edge of a continent," as David Malouf puts it. That does not, of course, mean myopic nationalism. But it may mean sacrificing the larger readership for the sake of nuances and truths that only the smaller audience can judge.

"We are an odd lot," observes one of Murray Bail's characters. Australians have inherited an odd way of thinking about themselves. Towards the end of the eighteenth century, an ancient fantasy of the European mind was actualized in the Great South Land, which from the start acted out the ambivalent expectations of the antipodes. Its exotic fauna and flora were obligingly topsy-turvy by old-world lights. It was an uninhabitable waste yet the chance of a fresh start, a place of monstrous forms but strange virgin beauty, a last paradise yet also the antithesis of all that was civilized. It was the world upside down, a recognition that survives in its commonest nickname: Down Under. It has always laid claim to a particular feature of the antipodean myth, which has passed into its human forms too. Whatever else one may say about Australians, they take pride in being "an odd lot," set apart. If they do not claim superiority, they hold ironically or defensively tight to their uniqueness. It is not really an exportable commodity.

Good fiction is distinguished by its social particularity, and the flavor of the best Australian writing comes from its engagement with the specificities of place, time, and speech, and less literally, but fundamentally, with the society's particular deep questions, thought-patterns and perspectives. At the moment, there is a healthy relationship between writers and readers, to judge by the quality and popularity of the rather difficult, off-center books that have distinguished Australian fiction in recent years: a nexus between individual experience and social concern. Perhaps the integrative capacity of the novel is especially suited to the task of reckoning up the new, old, many-layered, divided, and contradictory elements that make up present-day Australia. A novel brings the parts together and adumbrates a whole. Narratives divided in time and space, interrelated gangs of conflicting individualities, selves divided by disparate perspectives: these are the characteristics of such various works as, among others, Shirley Hazzard's elaborate global dance, *The Transit of Venus* (1980); Patrick White's *The Twyborn Affair* (1979) with its tripartite transsexual protagonist; the ever more garrulous, ornate Hal Porter of *The Clairvoyant Goat* (1981); and Randolph Stow's wondrous *The Girl Green as Elderflower* (1980) in which the main character's life is haunted by a distant mystic past. Similar interests can be traced in playwrights and poets too, in Dorothy Hewett's multi-focused rural sagas for the stage, for instance, and Les Murray's encyclopedic poems for "the vernacular republic."

Through contemporary writing runs the awareness that older, simpler notions of what constitutes Australian society are no longer adequate. A rural Eden, a prisonhouse, a desert of spiritual mortification, an egalitarian utopia, a poor imitation of Europe, an Anglo-Saxon or white last stand, a place of unfettered exuberance and inventiveness, a place of surburban conformity: it was, and is, all these things and none of them. Important writers do not merely reflect their society but create it anew, discovering fresh images and conceptions of its meaning. Yet if earlier generations have labored to forge certain ideas of Australia, the current generation of writers seems impelled to displace itself once again, by looking on ironically at the mythic ways in which Australia has been imagined. Among critics, too, there is agitated debate about which of the contending schools is best able to draw out the true vitality of Australia's literature, and the literary life is characterized by a high degree of gang warfare. Nor is it merely academic. If Australia is to have a future history, there must be a careful estimation of the past and of the choices conferred on the present, without settling for myth. From all the possibilities, a concerted understanding of the place is needed, sufficient to guide it forwards. If older assumptions are unsettled in the process, so be it.

Three public debates are symptomatic of a reorientation in the Australian community's prime allegiances. The first of these concerns what as an official policy is known as multiculturalism, the incorporation of diverse cultural attitudes into the dominant Anglo-Saxon mode of the society. Through many small changes and decisions, an overall shift in the center of gravity has occurred. The status of England as "onlie begetter" has been challenged by Celtic and Gaelic claims, and the primacy of the British heritage itself has been placed in a different perspective by the influx of continental influences. Even Greece and Rome as the wellsprings of civilization are seen to be part of a larger, variegated, non-linear story. In consequence, the patterns to be adopted by future Australian societies become less predictable and more open to experiment. It is not a move towards cultural relativism, so much as a matter of making cultural values the result of wider discrimination and choice. From the side, marginal in numbers, the new arrivals embody a deep dimension of memory and wisdom. As the poet Les Murray sees, they possess the post-imperial knowledge that every new start is also a jettisoning:

> Bonegilla, Nelson Bay,
> the dry-land barbed wire ships
> from which some would never land.
>
> In these, as their parents
> learned the Fresh Start music:
> physicians nailing crates,
> attorneys cleaning trams,
> the children had one last
> ambiguous summer holiday.
>
> Ahead of them lay
> the Deep End of the schoolyard,
> tribal testing, tribal soft-drinks,
> and learning English fast,
> the Wang-Wang language.

Ahead of them, refinements:
thumbs hooked down hard under belts
to repress gesticulation;

ahead of them, epithets:
wog, reffo, Commo Nazi,
things which can be forgotten
but must first be told.

And farther ahead
in the years of the Coffee Revolution
the Smallgoods Renaissance,
the early funerals:

the misemployed, the unadaptable,
those marked by the Abyss,

friends who came on the *Goya*
in the mid-year of our century.

(Les Murray, "Immigrant voyage")[12]

Cultural diversity is not merely chaotic. It induces skepticism and judgment, and calls forth sensitivity to the balanced economy of gain and loss, material abundance against spiritual inturning.

The second related debate concerns not the newcomers but the oldest inhabitants, the Aborigines who make "New Australians" of the rest of the population. Whatever redress is made, it is unlikely that Aboriginal lands will ever be as they were when white men invaded. Yet the increased concern with the Aboriginal peoples' past and present denotes a sea change in white awareness. For many people, the intractability of the antipodean land, and the strangeness of Australia's form of civilization within it, has crystallized into a feeling that the land does not belong to Europeans in the way that it belongs to someone else: the Aborigines. Over and above the legal-political question of land rights for Aboriginals and other attempts to compensate the atrocities of the past, the issue has unsettled some of the basic claims of Australian society, such as every man's right to prosper freely on land he has won for himself. The world that has grown up through free enterprising exploitation is at the cost of other worlds. A groping awareness of the Aboriginal presence, as purposefully nomadic, acculturated husbanders of the land for centuries, leads indirectly to a questioning of the fitness and necessity of the kind of society Europeans have put in place of what was. The chastening realization that there existed a quite different way of living with the land also opens up the possibility of alternatives that present-day Australians may discover again.

The grim fate of the Aborigines warns that desolation may be visited upon contemporary Australians in their turn, too, especially if they do not learn to treat their land better. What was done to the Aborigines hangs like a shadow over the aspiration towards confident Australian self-consciousness. In *The Generations of Men* (1959), the poet Judith Wright treated the white man's intrusion on Aboriginal land largely from the white man's point of view, with his uneasy, bemused sense of himself as a hapless violator: "They were trespassing on country where they had no rights. This knowledge did not make for good relations. If they shot a turkey or kangaroo for food, it might prove to be a sacred animal to the people who were almost certainly watching unseen from the bush; or perhaps the lagoon beside which they camped held for the local tribes some incomprehensible significance, making their presence there sacrilege. Not that this would have troubled them." Twenty years later, in *The Cry for the Dead* (1981), she adopts an Aboriginal perspective, in a larger ecological context. The prose becomes harrowing in the power of its understatement. Wright's vision is tremendously strengthened and deepened by her determined capacity to see the legacy of her own civilization from the nether side:

> It was the loss of the land which was worst. As time went on, the Aborigines retreated or were driven out of whole territories into the inhospitable foothills which formed their boundaries. The land itself was now disfigured and desecrated, studded with huts, crossed by tracks and fences, eaten thin by strange animals, dirtied and spoiled, and guarded from its owners by irresistible and terrifying weapons. The all-embracing net of life and spirit which had held land, and people, and all things together was in tatters. The sustaining ceremonies could not be held, men and women could not visit their own birthplaces or carry out their duties to the spirits. The exiled camps were racked by new sicknesses; pale unfamiliar babes

were born to the women; deaths were now so frequent that proper burial became impossible and injustice had to be done to the rights of the dead.

The blighted camps dwindled, their food inaccessible or the hunters and gatherers too weak to find and bring it in. The elders and the children died. Some began to leave the camps and cling to the settlement where by clowning, begging and selling their women they could survive. Disease and listlessness increased. The rags they were given to wear became noisome, damp and filthy, for they had not been taught to wash them; slept in by night, they bred more disease and the survivors coughed their way to death.

It was a story which was to be told, with variations of misery, across the whole continent.[13]

For a long time, Judith Wright has fought to change Australians' relationship with their land. "Before one's country can become an accepted background against which the poet's and novelist's imagination can move unhindered," she wrote in 1965, "it must first be observed, understood, described, and as it were absorbed."[14] If that injunction goes for poets and novelists, it should also apply to planners, politicians, farmers, economists, and everybody else. The wording is vital: not mastered, tamed, settled, cleared, or utilized, but "absorbed." Throughout her writings, Wright argues for the need to live creatively with the land, to learn from it and care for it, not just as a question of good husbandry but as a matter of the cultural life of the community. Our relationship with nature is a dimension of our moral being and an expression of our social values. Wright is one of the leaders of the conservation movement in Australia, and her views are now widely shared. The argument between development and conservation makes up the third area of debate that is currently changing Australians' sense of their society. There has been a series of individual battles, with victories and defeats on each side. The most publicized was the successful campaign in 1982–83 to stop the damming of the wild rivers Franklin and Lower Gordon in southwest Tasmania. The decision to preserve a wilderness area "intact" is one extreme of solution. At the other end are mining enterprises that produce a total change in the landscape. Between those poles lie all the practices of Australian society in its dialogue with the environment, and any number of decisions about what the priorities are to be and where research efforts should go. Already, it is late in the day. In the case of the Murray-Darling river system, bad management now threatens serious damage to a major resource. Again, the effect of such problems is to stimulate questioning of whether the civilization set up in Australia, the kind of science and the concept of man's purpose, are appropriate or for the best.

These are large considerations. It is as if the trajectory into the future prescribed for Australia by its overseers has been disturbed, not by rebellion but by the realization that the older projection was too simple and too costly. There is not yet a concerted alternative proposal, however, only doubt, irony, and opportunism. Constrained by their dependent position in economic, political, and defense systems beyond their control, Australians fail to think much about their long-term best interests and are uncertain of what they should protect and nurture in their society. National identity is related to the question of national autonomy, which is largely an economic question in the current climate. As for the writers of the seventies and eighties, so for Australians generally, the hope of healthy future nationhood must be earned through a tough reckoning of the circumstances that presently underwrite the country's material well-being.

In its eagerness to participate on the world stage, Australia does not always act so as to prevent its capitulation to more powerful interests. As social analyst Humphrey McQueen writes, "While economic self-determination cannot be achieved without cultural, political and military independence, it is a material gain in its own right with its own set of benefits. . . . Once we are independent we will be able to enter into all manner of alliances and interchanges as equals and no longer as subordinates; internationalism begins with nationalism." That last phrase neatly sums up Australia's cultural dilemma, too, when one adds that internationalism is already rampant without a firm national base, whether one likes it or not. McQueen is quick to point out that the nationalism that can give meaning to Australia's international venturing is not one-dimensional, narrow-minded, or jingoistic. It is "that body of ideas and actions which helps us to make and then to keep our country independent."[15] It is a matter of identifying and uniting many diverse strands. On this issue, the social analyst and the creative writer occupy the same ground.

Australia may always be marginal to the rest of the world, but will seldom be content to seem so. It is a consequence of unignorable geography, and also the imperial legacy, a center-seeking vision of history in which the province rivals the capital and aspires in time to usurp its place, as England succeeded Rome and the United States succeeded Britain. Australia's advance and the comparative decline of the old center make mildly more plausible the notion that Australia might one day achieve a surpassing supremacy. The magnetic force of the myth has faded, however, to a niggling, unfocused discontent. Australian artists, writers, and intellectuals show the qualities of mind afforded by their position at the periphery—ambivalence, detachment, dreamy longing shot through with skepticism. Yet it is rare that those qualities have impelled the kind of radical self-scrutinizing found in other writers at the edge: Kafka in Prague, Svevo in Trieste, or Cavafy in Alexandria, for example. Creativity is abundant, but criticism in Australia has tended to be indulgent. When a cultural historian puts the hard question—is there really such a thing as Australian culture?—and suggests that the pursuit of Australian "so-called culture" has become a false substitute for the struggle towards "universal culture," the characteristic reply is a pragmatic plea for recognition of Australia's historical circumstances, the sociological context that is a form of mercy capable of transforming "even 'second-rate' writing" into something "instructive" and thus of worth.[16]

The crude quarrel between cultural cringe and cultural snarl has persisted partly because Australian cultural criticism has often been self-coddling. The editor of the *Oxford History of Australian Literature* (1981) has attacked the common assumption that "Australian writing is a delicate plant, which . . . cannot be expected to withstand the rough and unpredictable winds from the outside world." Good writing should not need special pleading. Consequently, the *Oxford History* makes a stab at the difficult task of establishing a *critical* history of Australian literature in which the vitality of the best writing generates criteria by which lesser writing can be judged. By implication at least, the best writing will be set against the best writing of the whole English tradition and beyond, just as it is entitled to its place in the wider tradition. At their most stringent, such comparisons may seem severe to the local product, but the reader who, for example, picks up the sustained allusion to *King Lear* in Patrick White's novel *The Eye of the Storm* can scarcely refrain from making the critical comparison such allusion invites. It is a question of proportion, and freedom of activity. "Protectionism can be prescriptive by laying down conditions in which literary values are less important than social attitudes." Although the gauging of such things will always be personal and provisional, it is important to recognize a distinction between substantial, vitalizing "values" and transient, conventional "attitudes."[17]

Yet the *Oxford History*'s approach has been accused of being "punitive."[18] The relationship of Australian writers and critics to broader cultural values has been made analogous to the predicament of the first convicts to their imperial overlords. Both yearn for release from penal judgments. Australians are traditionally tolerant, even affectionate, towards law-breakers and charlatans. They are reluctant to set up as judges except in groups, and are readily forgiving. In the cultural arena, mateship can outweigh discrimination. As the tax mess shows, Australians are good at finding ways to evade. They fumble when it comes to precise accountancy of their conditions, and may not express their pleasures and pains even as they feel them. Perhaps, like most people, they aspire to something else than the truth about themselves. Australians desire to turn their margin into another place, flourishing, manifold and central. Speaking of "our inherent mediocrity as a people," a character in Patrick White's *Voss* continues, "I am confident that the mediocrity ... is not a final and irrevocable state; rather is it a creative source of endless variety and subtlety. The blowfly on its bed of offal is but a variation of the rainbow."[19] *Voss* is sometimes credited with creating an Australian myth of triumph in ignominious defeat. White's uncomfortable formulation suggests how the defeating circumstances might be turned to splendid achievement. What is one to make of it? In the intellectual and artistic activities of many Australians today, that broad hope continues to be worked out, in a complex and sophisticated quest to harmonize the odd conditions of Australian life with the richest spectrum of cultural colors.

ENDNOTES

[1]Frank Moorhouse, *Tales of Mystery and Romance* (Sydney: Angus and Robertson, 1977). Moorhouse's other works include *Futility and Other Animals* (first published 1969; rev. ed., Sydney: Angus and Robertson, 1973), *The Americans, Baby* (Sydney: Angus and Robertson, 1972), *The Electrical Experience* (Sydney: Angus and Robertson, 1974), *Conference-ville* (Sydney: Angus and Robertson,

1976), *Days of Wine and Rage* (Ringwood, Victoria: Penguin, 1980) and, as editor, *The State of the Art: The Mood of Contemporary Australia in Short Stories* (Ringwood, Victoria: Penguin, 1983).

[2]John Clive and Bernard Bailyn, "England's Cultural Provinces: Scotland and America," *The William and Mary Quarterly*, April 1954, pp. 200–213.

[3]Geoffrey Blainey, *The Tyranny of Distance* (Melbourne: Sun Books, 1966), p. 339.

[4]Max Brod, ed., *The Diaries of Franz Kafka* (Harmondsworth, UK: Penguin, 1964), pp. 148–9.

[5]Murray Bail, *Homesickness* (Ringwood, Victoria: Penguin, 1980). Bail's other works include *Contemporary Portraits* (St. Lucia: University of Queensland Press, 1975) and *Ian Fairweather* (Rushcutters Bay: Bay Books, 1981).

[6]"Interview: Murray Bail," *Meanjin*, 41(2) (1982), pp. 264–276.

[7]David Malouf, *An Imaginary Life* (London: Chatto and Windus, 1978). Malouf's other prose works include *Johnno* (Harmondsworth, UK: Penguin, 1976), *Fly Away Peter* and *Child's Play* (both, London: Chatto and Windus, 1982), and *Harland's Half Acre* (London: Chatto and Windus, 1984).

[8]David Malouf, *The Year of the Foxes and Other Poems* (New York: George Braziller, 1979). Other collections include *Neighbours in a Thicket* and *First Things Last* (St. Lucia: University of Queensland Press, 1974 and 1980).

[9]"David Malouf Replies" (1979), reprinted in Moorhouse, *Days of Wine and Rage*, p. 187.

[10]Helen Garner, *Monkey Grip* (Ringwood, Victoria: Penguin, 1978). Garner's other work includes *Honour and Other People's Children* (Ringwood, Victoria: Penguin, 1982) and *The Children's Bach* (Melbourne: McPhee Gribble, 1984).

[11]Jessica Anderson, *The Impersonators* (Melbourne: Macmillan, 1980). Anderson's other recent novels include *Tirra Lirra by the River* (Melbourne: Macmillan, 1978) and *The Commandant* (London: Macmillan, 1975).

[12]Les A. Murray, *The Vernacular Republic: Poems 1961–1981* (enlarged and revised edition, Sydney: Angus and Robertson, 1982), pp. 184–5.

[13]Judith Wright, *The Generations of Men* (Melbourne: Oxford University Press, 1959), p. 14, and *The Cry for the Dead* (Melbourne: Oxford University Press, 1981), p. 27.

[14]Judith Wright, *Preoccupations in Australian Poetry* (Melbourne: Oxford University Press, 1965), p. xi.

[15]Humphrey McQueen, *Gone Tomorrow: Australia in the 80s* (Sydney: Angus and Robertson, 1982), p. 222.

[16]Eugene Kamenka, "Culture, and Australian Culture; the principles of Arnold in the ocker age," *Age Monthly Review*, October 1983, pp. 17–20; Jim Davidson, "So-Called Culture: A Reply to Eugene Kamenka," *Age Monthly Review*, November 1983, pp. 10–11; part of a debate on "tall poppies" (an allusion to the alleged Australian tendency to cut down to size those who excel), to be published in full in *Australian Cultural History*, 3 (1984).

[17]Leonie Kramer, ed., *The Oxford History of Australian Literature* (Melbourne: Oxford University Press, 1981), pp. 2, 23.

[18]John Docker, "Leonie Kramer in the Prison House of Criticism," *Overland* 85 (1981), p. 26.

[19]Patrick White, *Voss* (London: Eyre and Spottiswoode, 1957), p. 476.

Jill Conway

Gender in Australia

ANTHROPOLOGISTS, HISTORIANS, ECONOMISTS, and social psychologists have made the function of gender as a social category the subject of intensive study in recent years. In the West, patriarchal institutions have shaped the organization of the family, the workplace, and the state so as to sustain and strengthen male superiority. Their studies have shown the extent to which gender categories also shape the social process so that women and men live within an ideological framework that governs how they think, what they feel, and the identities accorded self and other. Gender, as a category for organizing the world around one, also serves along with class and ethnic difference to establish social boundaries. Since all social systems are in flux, subject to both internal and external forces driving change and adaptation, the boundaries may move around and the ideologies explaining them may develop new forms, but gender categories define boundaries in every social system we know anything about.[1]

The role played by gender boundaries and ideologies in the development of modern industrial societies is roughly similar. As the pace of technological development quickened, household and workplace separated. For the middle class, the household assumed many pseudo-sacramental functions as the guarantor of the one segment of society where men were free of challenges to status. It was the place of refreshment and renewal of male energies for the competitive world of commerce, and the sheltered setting for the education of the young in codes of moral behavior that could not be acted upon in the competitive economic order. At the level of the working class, female labor functioned as the labor reserve on which marginal economic activities could draw. Schools prepared the young for the hierarchy and routine of the work place and taught appropriate gender behavior. Church and chapel siphoned off the moral energy of the middle-class female and set her about the remedial philanthropy that attempted to rescue the victims of technological change and business cycles and thereby helped to avert social revolution. Gender conventions clearly shaped what could be thought and felt, and what could be talked about by nineteenth-century men and women, and those same conventions decreed what social territory fell within the sphere of competence of each sex.[2]

Rural societies had a different, but equally clearly discernable pattern. Where settled peasant societies were transformed by commercial agriculture, women became part of the displaced reserve labor force and migrated to industrial cities or to the societies of settlement made accessible by the transportation revolution of steam and rail. In the new world, the frontiers of rural settlement might open upon land suited for the family farm or the commercial plantation, and very often the sheer labor required to bring new land into production required some form of forced labor, a system at odds with the family as the agent of land settlement. Where the family was the unit of settlement, women's labor was of high economic significance, but the impact of this economic fact upon women's consciousness depended on the scale of settlement and the availability of institutions that could offer female sociability. The frontier could elevate a woman's status, or its isolation could leave her no psychic resources but the family. Tocqueville thought the loneliness of women on the American frontier profoundly alienating and in marked contrast to the position of influence occupied by women within the sphere of domestic life in settled American society. The difference in influence was related to women's opportunities for sociability and voluntary association. These opportunities changed the social process by which gender was experienced and the change had corresponding effects in consciousness and self-awareness.

In the political sphere, we know that the nineteenth century saw gender rise in importance as a category shaping the definition of liberal democracies. Grey's Third Reform Bill of 1832 introduced the idea that gender was important in the new polity by using the language "every male person" wherever the qualifications for voters were mentioned.[3] In some ways, the separate sphere of the household took on some of the characteristics of the old aristocracy as being "above" or "outside" politics, and women reformers were able to use the fact of their exclusion from the political system to influence the process of reform in industrial societies. The extension of the franchise to males was thus balanced by the formal articulation of a polity based on the total exclusion of women from participation in the formal political institutions of society except through the survival of hereditary monarchy in Great Britain.

The advent of industrial society and the rise of universal male suffrage produced these general patterns in gender relationships in Western Europe and its offshoots. Within these general similarities, however, there were distinctive cultural variations: variations in sensibility, styles of action, expressions of sexuality, structuring of family relationships, assumptions about work and leisure. These differences were the principal materials that excited the imagination of Henry James and inspired generations of nineteenth-century travelers' narratives about the differences between the United States and Europe. Less has been written about the characteristic Australian cultural patterns either as they emerged in the nineteenth century or were modified in the twentieth century. Australia was the earliest society to develop a set of institutions establishing political democracy which claimed to make the interests of the "common man" the central concern of the polity. Long before the age of mass communication, Australia's literary and artistic expressions exalted the experience of the working man. What did such a culture have to say about gender relationships? Did the celebration of the dignity of the working man change the traditional patterns of gender subordination on which Western culture was built? Or did it simply give that subordination a new and distinctive cultural expression?

Australian historians and social scientists have been so preoccupied with the study of class and class conflict in Australia that attention has been given only very recently to the history of women's experience. The context for the discussion of the subject since it claimed attention in the early 1970s has been shaped by the position held by the individual writer on the question of the uniqueness of Australian society and its culture. Those shaped by the left tradition in Australian historical writing tend to see Australian history as merely one chapter in the international class struggle and to deride a concern with national identity as bourgeois. For the left historian, the liberation of women must be subsumed within the class struggle, and exponents of feminism have been greeted with the male chauvinism of the traditional left. Conversely, those who wish to document Australia's development as a society with a highly sophisticated urban culture, in which the arts and the world of letters find a level of expression equal to that of the metropolitan societies of Europe or America, have been obliged to narrate Australian cultural history as though its nineteenth-century cities had a life not unlike provincial England. Landscape aside, Australians are assumed to have an inner life not unlike that of others of their class and education in modern Western societies. This point of view represents a reaction to the earlier tendency of Australian intellectuals outside the left to bewail the lack of cultivation in Australian life, the ugliness of Australian cities, the peculiarities of Australian language and diction, and so on.

This essay is written unabashedly from the point of view that there is indeed a unique character to Australian culture, that one aspect of that uniqueness is the extent to which the inner life (the landscape of the mind) of Australians is different from their equivalents in Europe or North America, and that one reason for the distinctive flavor of Australian culture and its expressions is the pattern assumed by gender relationships in nineteenth-century Australia. While this pattern has seen many twentieth-century modifications, a late twentieth-century Henry James could still delight in exploring the nuances of difference between the relationships of men and women in Australia compared, say, with England or the United States, and the differences could be made to sustain some of the larger significance James assigned to the same subject in the late nineteenth century. Such a view may be stated without assuming a negative position on the question of the level of cultural sophistication of Australia today. The artistic and literary achievement of contemporary Australia and the level of its learning clearly compare favorably with world standards. One reason for the level of that literary and artistic achievement, an extraordinary one for so small a population, comes from the powerful involvement of the Australian imagination with a social and natural landscape that is different from that of other countries, even though Australians may now drive Japanese cars and shop in American-style supermarkets. My perspective is that of an expatriate who has not lived for extended periods in Australia in the last quarter-century, a period when many claim that the pace of economic change and the revolution in modern communications has made Australia assume many of the characteristics of affluent North America, while immigration has brought a level of cultural mosaic to the society that defies generalization. Maybe. But the Canadian children of the Hungarians exiled after the revolution have developed a typically Canadian capacity for moderation, and the daughter of Italian immigrants who was recently a candidate for the vice-presidency of the United States has an authentically American voice. So when I visit Australia, I am struck by the continuities more than by the changes that are so visible to those who have experienced the last twenty-five years in Australia.

There is little dispute about the nature of convict society during the founding years of Australia. Its demography, the nature of its convict population, and the harshness of the discipline imposed by the convicts' jailers are clear matters of record. Among the population of minor offenders against the laws of property and the more alienated members of the lumpen proletariat who arrived in the early convict fleets, the women convicts, who had come from the culture of the pickpocket, prostitute, and petty thief of England's cities had the lowest status. Most social boundaries could not survive the voyage in the convict transport and the shock of settlement in an alien climate and terrain. Gender, however, could not be obliterated by these circumstances, and it became one of the certainties on which social boundaries could rest. It was a form of establishing social distance that worked very systematically while males far outnumbered women, as they did in the convict colonies until the closing down of transportation in the mid-nineteenth century, and as they did in the extended pastoral settlements of the inland, whether the original settlement was a penal colony or a free settlement such as South Australia.

The nature of the demographic imbalance between the sexes at the beginning of Australian society was striking. Between 1787 and 1800, some 5,195 male convicts, but only 1,440 women were disembarked at Botany Bay. In the First Fleet, the ratio was such that no possibility of stable family life existed. It carried 600 men and 180 women. In the eastern colonies of Australia, the entire episode of transportation had brought, at its conclusion in 1844, 130,000 convicts, of whom only 16 percent were women.[4]

This gender ratio combined with the unfree status of female convicts to produce a society of striking sexual exploitation of women. Contemporary commentators did not mince words: "It will perhaps scarcely be believed that, on the arrival of a female convict ship, the custom has been to suffer the inhabitants of the colony each to select one at his pleasure, not only as servants, but as avowed objects of intercourse, which is even without plea of the slightest previous attachment as an excuse, rendering the whole colony little more than an extensive brothel."[5] Such views might be attributed to simple opposition to transportation. But the evidence from all points in the society converges on this point. Historians have differed, however, about its significance. Radical feminist historians have argued that the mores of the convict colony were transferred to free society, and form the basis for a particularly strong form of male chauvinism in contemporary Australian society. Proponents of the view that Australia quickly approximated provincial England once free settlement set in, argue that this period was a brief episode quickly replaced by conventional evangelical sexual morality as the colonial cities grew and stable family life developed.

A further problem in interpreting the significance of this history lies in whether or not one sees urban culture and mores as the shaping force in the development of Australian society, or whether one sees the ethos and values of bush life as the dominant force in cultural development. If one sees the bush experience as the counterpart to the American frontier as a cultural force, then the persistence of demographic imbalance in the Outback until well into the closing decades of the nineteenth century assumes great significance, and the importance of male bonding in Australian life is emphasized by contrast with, for example, the American experience of family units engaged in homesteading across the continent. If one sees the city and urban life as the more important cultural influence, then one sees the nineteenth-century Australian experience as more comparable to the rise of Manchester or Birmingham, in which commerce, industry, and class conflict are the dynamics that shape culture. Thus, historians of the Australian city have seen the rise of a suburban culture characterized by a high degree of home ownership as an early development in Australian urban life in the decades between 1860 and 1890, when the profits of the gold-rush boom were invested in urban commerce and rates of marriage by native-born Australians were on the rise.[6] However, it is clear that the recession of the 1890s produced a reaction against urban values in favor of the independence of life in the bush, and that a cultural movement favoring an Australian version of urban domesticity and perfect womanhood was defeated by a return to the idealization of the independent male wanderer living off the land.

Certainly, in the Australian bush the scale of settlement and the fact of distance meant that no separate sphere could develop for bush women. Their economic contribution to the family might be enormous, but the absence of female sociability and the absence of the circuit rider, the camp meeting, and the regular social interchange that the American Methodist "women's classes" provided meant that the opportunities for raised consciousness were few, and the chances for collective action—as occurred in the American abolition movement—were slight. Gender could thus serve as an important social boundary in the bush culture, but not one for a division of power and influence that made the female area of domestic life of great political and social importance. If one remembers that the pattern of rivers and the development of the transportation system kept Australian inland settlement more isolated than was the experience in the United States and Canada, the absence of the sociability of the town also becomes important. American readers will grasp the significance of the Australian environment if they imagine a landmass the size of the United States without Alaska, which lacks the Mississippi and Missouri river systems. Europeans might try to imagine a similar sized landmass without a Rhine or a Danube. Such highways for settlement and for the dispersion of urban culture were simply not present in Australia. When these constraints on mobility were combined with a climate offering insufficient rainfall for small-scale agriculture, the result was a pattern of settlement where the family unit was marginal and the place of women one of isolation within a work force of single males.

This shortage of women is often thought of as conferring improved status on them, although the historical record for nineteenth-century England and the North American continent indicates that the major gains in status for women were made wherever women were an excess in the population of marriageable age and society was forced to consider some role for them outside the family. Hence, the upsurge of feminism in the northeast United States in the 1840s or in England in the 1850s, where the question of the "condition of women" was prompted by surplus numbers of females left in the population through the outmigration of males of marriageable age to the West or to the colonies. We should contrast the Australian bush woman's isolation with this description written at mid-century of the emerging culture of the back-country male world. At the time the description was written, there were some six thousand stockmen at work on the mainland and some fifteen thousand shepherds whose way of life was later to be idealized in the first outburst of patriotic writing about Australia. "A strange wild looking sunburnt race, strong, rough and taciturn, they appear as though they have never lived in crowds and have lost the desire to converse. So deeply embrowned were the faces, naked breasts and arms of these men, and so shaggy the crops of hair and beard that a stranger had to look twice to be certain they were not Aborigines."[7]

This type of worker combined with his urban counterparts by far predominated in the population. Indeed, by 1850 it is estimated that only 10 percent of the population of the rapidly growing cities was middle class. Thus, alongside the picture of the stockmen and shepherds should be placed the image of the urban male, recognized by visitors as a distinct type because of his typical patterns of social behavior. Visitors noticed the tendency of urban males to band together for leisure activities, whether in the gangs of "larrikins" whose mores involved rowdy questioning of authority, or the quieter concerns of the men whose leisure involved love of sport, gambling, and horseracing. Male bonding was a necessity in convict society. Men convicts needed a powerful sense of solidarity to sustain the pressures of forced labor in an environment where the predominant form of discipline was the lash liberally applied. The bonding remained after the jailers departed, and one of the most highly urbanized societies of the modern world kept the image of the solitary rural worker or the itinerant swagman as a powerful image of national identity, even though settled family life and the industrial city with its factories and suburbs became a shaping force in the economic growth of the colonies after the gold rushes and the influx of free migration.

The family that inhabited the suburbs had many of the recognizable suburban ideals—ownership of one's dwelling, the care and education of children—but leisure life was different. The pub, the game, and the races stood in constant tension with the family, and the emerging rituals of the culture gave a man a social territory away from women and children which was an important part of his identity. The elaboration of this important myth can be seen in the earliest Australian fiction, such as the authentic narratives of convict experience. It is given full expression in the poetry and prose of the 1880s and 1890s, which celebrate male friendship and loyalty and treat women as merely incidental to the important emotional experiences of life. The riding exploits of the Man from Snowy River and the unfettered freedom of the western drover are recounted by admiring male friends, who are nostalgic for the itinerant way of life, "for the drover's life has pleasures that the townsfolk never know."[8] The passing of this identification with the bush brought the anarchic hero into uneasy accommodation with the city and settled life, but such heros as C.J. Dennis's Sentimental Bloke cloak the conflicts that exist between male friendship and marriage with sickly sentimentality!

> I tells meself some day I'll take a pull
> An' look eround fer some good, stiddy job,
> An' cut the push fer good an, all; I'm full
> Of that crook mob![9]

The saga of the Sentimental Bloke and his Doreen shows us that this cheerful larrikin with the heart of gold will always want to go off with the boys and will always live in fear that his emotional ties to women and settled life may become too strong. In this literature, freedom is seen as the capacity to set limits to the claims of public authority and the family. Thus, by the Second World War, Chester Manifold's heroic Australian infantry officer dies in Crete defying fate and is seen as outside politics. We are never told whether he has a wife and family. Such ties are irrelevant in a poem that derives its power from its ability to persuade us that the fullest expression of heroism comes from an existential act of defiance.

> I could as hardly make a moral fit
> Around it as around a lightning flash.
> There is no moral, that the point of it,
> No moral. But I'm glad of this panache
> That sparkles, as from flint, from us and steel,

True to no crown nor presidential sash
Nor flag nor fame. Let others mourn and feel
He died for nothing: Nothings have their place.[10]

No matter whether we study high culture as in Manifold's poem or the popular culture exemplified by the Sentimental Bloke, we may see in the working of the Australian imagination the formulation of some basic life plots or mythic narratives that ignore or adapt the basic motif of bourgeois culture in the West—the quest for marriage, mate, and personal property—and gives the central development of the hero a quest to which an awaiting Penelope is more or less irrelevant.

The bush woman has her heroic dimensions also. She is always depicted in the fiction and poetry of the 1880s and 1890s as a solitary figure, alone with the children, living in hardship, capable of withstanding all the hazards of fire, drought, and flood. But she is older than her years, resigned and stoic. It was in rebellion against this stoic view that Miles Franklin wrote her satirical autobiography, *My Brilliant Career* (1901),[11] in which the heroine describes the truth about the cost of such stoicism and refuses romantic love. What inspired the young writer was a utopian socialist view of the future of Australia in which a more just set of human relationships would flourish in her beloved bush.

I am proud that I am an Australian, a daughter of the Southern Cross, a child of the mighty bush. I am thankful that I am a peasant, a part of the bone and muscle of my native land and earn my bread by the sweat of my brow, as man was meant to do. I rejoice I was not born a parasite, one of the blood suckers who loll on velvet and satin, crushed from the proceeds of human sweat and blood and souls. Ah my sunburnt brothers! sons of toil and of Australia! I love and respect you well, for you are brave and good and true. I have seen not only those of you with youth and hope strong in your veins, but those with pathetic streaks of grey in your hair, large families to support, and with half-a century sitting on your work laden shoulders. I have seen you struggle uncomplainingly against flood, fire, disease in stock, pests, drought, trade depression and sickness and yet have time to extend your hands and hearts in true sympathy to a brother in misfortune, and spirits to laugh and joke and be cheerful. And for you my sisters a great love and pity fills my heart. Daughters of toil, who scrub and wash and mend and cook, who are dressmakers, paperhangers, milkmaids, gardeners and candlemakers all in one, and yet have time to be cheerful and tasteful in your homes, and make the best of the few oases to be found along the narrow dusty track of your existence. Would that I were more worthy to be one of you—a more typical Australian peasant—cheerful, honest, brave. . . My ineffective life will be trod out in the same round of toil—, I am only one of yourselves, I am only an unnecessary, little, bush commoner, I am only a—woman![12]

Most non-Australian readers do not know that Franklin's next work was an equally satirical account of the heroine's disillusionment with Australian intellectual and literary circles, entitled *My Career Goes Bung.*[13] It was written in the years immediately following the publication of *My Brilliant Career* but not published until 1946. In it, Franklin justifies her decision to leave Australia and to look for a world more responsive to the woman of talent who wants to lead an independent life. By the time she was writing this second volume, Franklin had met the small group of women working for votes for women in Australia. She admired them, but sought a more congenial world where she could keep her freedom and escape the pressure of a society that relentlessly assigned women to marriage and motherhood. As with her heroines, her life was to be shaped by a quest for independence rather than for a mate and family.[14]

She was followed in this decision by a remarkable number of Australian women of talent in the 1920s and 1930s.[15] Intellectual circles in Australia were then dominated either by the goals and concerns of the radical left or by the refusal to consider women seriously which characterized the writers and artists influenced by Nietzschean aesthetics and the attitudes of D.H. Lawrence toward sex. There was thus no sustaining community to which women could make an internal migration to escape the pressures of family and social attitudes, and the consequence was departure overseas. Christina Stead is cited by Drusilla Modjeska in her study of Australian women writers of the 1930s as presenting the psychological motivations for this departure in her most autobiographical novel, *For Love Alone* (1944):

In a few months she would leave them forever, this herd teaming shoulder to shoulder in its home march. They married, settled down in the Bay or in the suburbs along bus routes to the city, in order to reach their work in the shortest time, and that was the end, then came the marriage-sleep that lasted to the grave. She would sail the seas, leave her invisible track on countries, learn in great universities, know what was said by foreign tongues, starve in cities, tramp, perhaps shoeless along side roads, perhaps suffer every misery, but she would know life.[16]

Stead's novel, as Modjeska points out, uses the heroine's quest for the ideal lover as a thinly veiled rationale for a quest for self-discovery and the encounter with personal fulfillment.

Women writers who did not leave had only one escape route which was to enter the culture of the radical left, and if this carried them as far as the Communist party, to accept the party dictates on what might be written. Thus, Drusilla Modjeska points out the great talent of Katherine Susannah Pritchard was directed toward party hack writing, although her earlier years of creative work had produced some of the first and finest fiction in Australia to examine the sexual exploitation of black women, and several powerful fictional explorations of the inequities of the marriage relationship in Australian culture. The world of the CP was totally male dominated and there seem to have been no counterparts of the female-led centers of intellectual and sexual rebellion such as the salons of Mabel Dodge in New York and Taos, or the feminist male circles such as Margaret Sanger met in her expatriate years in London.

The absence of the female rich from the centers of social and intellectual rebellion has not yet been the subject of serious historical inquiry, but the explanation seems likely to reside in the character of the educational and philanthropic organizations that developed in urban Australia after the closing years of gold-rush prosperity. The abolition movement in the United States and England linked concerns with women's education and their right to pursue their moral concerns through political action with evangelical culture. Thus, a Rockford Female Seminary in Illinois, founded out of the determination of Methodist and Presbyterian leaders to raise up a group of Christian women to civilize the West, had links to the abolition movement, and its students saw themselves as obligated to follow in the footsteps of the great Emancipator. As a result, its graduates contained an extraordinary number of women reformers. A recent study of the early graduates of the Advanced School for Girls established in Adelaide in 1879 concludes that its graduates were reinforced in their acceptance of the prevailing ideology that women's place was in the home. Those who entered the professions saw their responsibility as educated women to concern themselves with the care of babies and the instruction of mothers in child health, but these concerns did not link them with questions relating to Aboriginal rights, nor were they interests that prompted concern with the right to vote.[17] Philanthropic organizations also seem to have recruited and utilized female talent in ways that did not call in question the need to preserve social elites against the challenges from impoverished, smallscale agricultural settlers, or the urban working class.[18] In this context, the condition of women and children did not become a question that subsumed class interests as it did in the United States and Canada in the 1890s.

The private school for women, an important focus for female sociability and the development of intellectual ability, led, as in North America and England, to the admission of women to Australian universities. Beginning with women's admission to the University of Adelaide in 1874, the opportunity grew in each state to attend lectures, to matriculate, and eventually to study in residence at colleges founded for women. But popular opinion was united on the reason for creating such opportunities. The New South Wales Minister for Public Education justified the founding of the Women's College at the University of Sydney in 1889 by the following statement:

> We must recognize the fact that the women are the mothers of the nation . . . it behoves us to see that we strengthen their judgment; that we so improve their mental faculties and so raise their intelligence that they will be better able to perform their duties in training the rising generation. If we wish to have better men we can only hope to have them by giving our children better proclivities, and giving their mothers increased power to promote their intelligence.[19]

The Bulletin, the purveyor of all unquestioned Australian assumptions, agreed. "Women cannot be too learned," the editors wrote, "provided the learning she has helps her to fulfill her varied functions of mother, nurse, educator and trainer of children."[20] Anything that detracted from her performance in these important roles was "most emphatically a curse." These attitudes have been enduring. Even though women have been approximately 20 percent of graduates in Australian higher educational institutions since the beginning of the twentieth century, they have earned only about 17 percent of masters degrees and 5.9 percent of doctorates. The climate with respect to gender within the academic environment may be bluntly stated by quoting a simple statistic: of the 950 full professors in Australian Universities in the mid-1970s, only 2 percent were women. Women make up just over 4 percent of the lower ranks and their numbers rise in part-time employment.[21]

Another fruitful avenue of employment for graduates might well have been the Australian public service, which has always been one of the largest employers of university graduates in the country. Limitations on women's employment were, however, severe within the Federal Public Service until 1966, when a total ban on the employment of married women was abandoned by the Public Service Board. Nonetheless, women employees remained clustered in the lower grades and within the part-time staff. We may see the impact on the lives of Australian professional women of the recently altered Australian rule about giving up employment on marriage in *The Half Open Door: Sixteen Modern Australian Women Look At Professional Life and Achievement*, published in 1982.[22] In her autobiographical essay in this collection, Kathleen Fitzpatrick describes the loss of her first regular academic job in 1932, upon her marriage. She did not resume her career as a historian until 1939 when she was in her thirty-fifth year. She noted the frequency of discrimination against women in Australian academic life, but astonishingly reported that her evidence on this point was "heresay . . . I never experienced sexual discrimination myself." When the opportunity to apply for a chair came her way, she did not apply because she felt that she did not meet the standard for the highest academic rank:

> I have always believed that no one should be appointed to the highest academic rank unless he or she is either a profound or original thinker or a truly erudite person. There have been appointments which do not meet this standard but they are not, in my opinion, good appointments. I felt quite equal to the rank I held as an associate professor, but I had not spent my life in universities without learning that I did not meet my own criteria for a Chair.[23]

The possibility that Fitzpatrick may have met her standard without the lost years and the struggle to establish herself in junior positions does not seem to occur to her. The later generation of women whose lives are recorded in the collection have a different consciousness. It was this generational development that gave rise to the new wave of feminism supported by middle-class, educated women in the late 1960s and early 1970s. This new wave of feminism has carried with it many of the characteristic institutions and concerns of the North American feminist movement of the 1970s. Consciousness-raising groups, agitation for the right to abortion and for equal pay, and radical lesbian organizations advocating women's rights all developed in urban centers in the 1970s. What did not accompany these developments was the parallel concern for access to higher education, the professions, and the management levels of business, all of which developed in North America. The national data do not indicate a noticeable broadening of educational aspiration for women. More males than females complete high school, and in the late seventies, 8 percent of males over fifteen years of age compared with 3 percent of females over fifteen years of age, were engaged in post-secondary education. During the decade of the 1970s, the number of women entering professional fields based on the hard sciences and mathematics actually declined, and the percentage of women engineers stayed level at 1.1 to 1.2 percent.[24] The arrival of the professional classes thus introduced the helping professions for women—nursing, librarianship, social work—but the rates of the entry of educated women into non-traditional fields, and their rates of persistence in higher education do not indicate major social change. The fact is the more striking to an observer familiar with North American trends. In the United States, for example, the statistics for graduate degrees conferred in 1982 were as follows:

Field of Study	Males	Females	% Females
M.D. in Medicine	11,867	3,947	25
J.D. degree (Law)	23,965	12,026	33
Master's degrees			
Biological Sciences	3,426	2,448	42
Business and Management	44,359	17,069	28
Computer and Informational Systems	3,625	1,310	27
Engineering	16,311	1,628	9
Law	1,510	383	20
Mathematics	1,821	906	33
Physical Sciences	4,318	1,196	22

While these figures show the strength of women's entry into fields such as engineering and medicine, the more striking fact is the strength of women's recruitment into the world of business and management. The most recent statistics indicate that 20 percent of all managers are women. While it may be argued that the private sector is less important in Australian recruitment terms than it is in the American context, too exclusive a focus on the role of government in changing employment patterns can easily mislead as to the long-term direction of change.

Indeed, until the recent past, the major work-related consequences of feminism in Australia may, in contrast to the United States and Great Britain, show more noticeable results among working-class women. Between 1870 and 1900, the colonies developed the characteristic forms of female labor associated with industrialization. Women worked in textile, boot and shoe, and cigar-making factories, and as sales clerks and waitresses. These early industries were regulated as to conditions of work and rates of pay by the various colonial governments in the 1890s and by the federal government after 1904. Australia's unique pattern of arbitration and conciliation by means of government intervention in setting wage rates and mediating wage disputes has been much vaunted as a sign of the extent to which government concerned itself with the creation of a stable working environment and with a reasonable distribution of the profits of labor to the working class. It has not been so frequently reported that the system gave the sanction, first of colonial governments and then of the Commonwealth, to differential rates of pay for women and men doing the same work. Australia's much vaunted egalitarianism vanished where questions of gender and work were concerned. The early leadership of the Labor party operated to exclude women from apprenticeship in skilled trades, and to foster the idea that women should be paid at well below male rates for the same work. As the government regulation of the wage system developed, many award agreements were negotiated with pay scales that specified that women could only be employed in the work assigned the lowest grade by the arbitration court. The courts operated through establishing what should be understood as a "living wage" for each of the gender groups. For males, this wage was defined as the rate of pay which would enable a man to support a wife and two or three children through full-time work. For women, the rate was defined as that rate which would reimburse her family for the expenses of her upkeep but not return them a profit.

A boy knows from birth he will be a breadwinner: that is his lot in life. A girl learns that in all probability she will marry. Her work will only be an episode in her life. . . The great majority will live with their parents, and these should receive a wage which will relieve their parents of the whole expense of their upkeep but not necessarily one which will give their parents a profit.[25]

Women labor leaders fought against these views by asserting the importance of work outside the home for women and by drawing attention to the necessity for minimum wage standards that would enable a woman to support herself living alone.

Only the demands of the 1914–18 and 1939–45 wars brought such a recognition to women workers. These years saw wage rates for skilled women rise to 100 percent of the male rate, although the return of peace brought a quick reversion to the established pattern of wage inequality. These inequities endured until the 1970s, despite isolated protests. Typical of the incidents of protest were the strenuous efforts of such groups as the middle-class United Associations of Women and the Council of Action for Equal Pay to fight the policy of the New South Wales state government limiting employment opportunities for married women teachers, and the campaigns of the Victorian Teachers Union to secure equal pay for equal work for women teachers.[26] These efforts were largely unsuccessful until the election of the Whitlam Labor government in 1972. At the time of the election, a complaint had been brought before the Federal Arbitration Commission involving the principle of equal pay for equal work, and the newly elected Labor government chose not to oppose the application brought to the commission by women's groups and union representatives seeking a decision in favor of equal pay for work of equal value. The commission's judgment outlawing discrimination in pay on the basis of gender was followed by a ruling from the Australian Conciliation and Arbitration Court, which established an "adult" minimum wage rather than a "male" minimum. These combined efforts of the federal government and women's groups changed the legal basis on which wage awards were made but did not reverse the historic pattern of differential earnings for men and women. This pattern was the result of a secondary market in women's labor in which levels of skill for women did not produce the same entry-level opportunities as they did for men. New systems of job classification and promotion quickly followed the rulings of the Whitlam years, and these combined with interruptions in work-force participation and reduced educational aspiration to keep women's aggregate earnings at about 75 percent of male earnings. Nonetheless, the changed legal basis for wage rulings changed a tradition relating to gender in the workplace and did so very rapidly.

Given that nineteenth-century Australia developed a style of political life in which the interests of the common man were pitted against those of pastoral and commercial property, it is not surprising that women's political action emerged focused around the interests of working women in securing better conditions of work and wages and the concerns of elite women with the family and health care. Concern with the family and its supports fits closely with the national concern for the preservation of a white Australia so evident by the opening of the twentieth century. Thus, women who worked for the suffrage in Australia expected that there would be a base of support for them in elective politics which did not in fact materialize. The weakness of local government in Australia meant that there was no municipal experience available to a woman who wanted to build a political network. The traditional stress on mateship and male bonding meant that working women could not break into labor politics via the factory and the trade-union movement. Thus, although Australia was the earliest society to extend the suffrage to women, it was not until 1940 that the first women members took their seats in the national Parliament in Canberra. Women who worked within the traditional structure of the labor movement faced genuine hostility from union leadership. Muriel Heagney, one of the pioneer workers for equal pay for women, despaired of building support for her cause because of the strength of Australian male attitudes: "Frankly I have given up hope of achieving anything worth while immediately because here in Australia the Labour Movement and the ACTU executive officers are so terribly reactionary in their views on women workers. One commences about half a mile behind the starting post in a mile race here when women are involved in any issue, and the trade union officials and Labor Ministers as a rule are more difficult to deal with than many big employers of labour."[27] Under these circumstances, it was not surprising that early research on rates of political participation in Australia showed a significantly lower level of participation and interest in politics on the part of women compared to men. By way of contrast, it should be noted that the first efforts to delineate the contours of postwar Australian society documented high rates of participation in cultural organizations on the part of Australian women whose support of the fine and performing arts was to bring them into direct relationship with state and federal government as cultural nationalism and pride in the achievement of Australian artists and performers became more important in the 1960s and 1970s.[28]

The impact of the most recent wave of feminism experienced in Australia in the 1970s is evident in changed rates of political participation and in the ability of organized feminist groups to bring political pressure to bear on national party structures. The importance of this changed level of participation has been emphasized in Australian politics because of the operation of its electoral system through preferential voting, and the resulting ability of small groups to disturb the balance of power in the national Parliament where political forces have been very evenly balanced. By the 1970s, the leadership of the Australian Labor Party had become convinced that its path to political office depended on reversing the historic preference of female voters for non-labor parties. Both the Whitlam and Hawke campaigns were marked by pledges to introduce legislation implementing important objectives of the feminist movement. The result has been a flurry of legislative and executive actions that have outlawed discrimination on the basis of sex in employment, education, and the provision of goods and services by government; have changed the status of women with respect to pensions, reinforced the definitions of rape and of sexual harassment, and introduced important new initiatives with respect to the appointment of women to governmental bodies. The Hawke government also made the Office of the Status of Women part of the Department of the Prime Minister and Cabinet to move the effort to improve women's position high in the national priorities.[29] The results of this activity and the demonstrated willingness of the government to appoint women to key positions have made those Australians concerned with women's issues highly optimistic about the rate of change, the possibility of achieving and consolidating the drive to equal opportunity, and the likely enduring consequences of the government actions and shifts of attitude of the last ten years.

One's judgment of the future depends on how typical one thinks the Australian experience is in the context of other modern societies. Will the decade of the 1980s evoke the response in the Australian psyche that the 1970s did in the United States? Is there an Australian Mrs. Thatcher in the wings? It is too soon to say, but the possibility is real. No one predicted the reassertion of conventional values about women and the family that has accompanied Ronald Reagan's leadership of a return to the values of an older America. Indeed, in the heady years of the major United States civil rights legislation of the sixties and seventies, the rejection of ideals motivating the drive for the rights of women and minorities seemed unthinkable. Even if the thrust of current civil rights concerns is blunted by a future swing in public opinion and political fortune, will we see women among the highest earners in fields such as brokerage or investment banking, occupations which persist in a mixed economy whatever the thrust of state economic policy? At present, we can only guess, but it is clear that such developments could not occur without a major alteration in levels of educational and occupational aspiration.

For this reason, it is important to look at the archetypal Australian values expressed in the works of the creative artist whose vision and recurring images may tell us about the inner life of the emotions censored in most public utterances. These patterns, like the American western, endure through what may appear to be monumental shifts in the direction of technological change or in the nature of economic and political organizations. The France of Louis XIV, Napoleon, and de Gaulle was different in political tone and social ideology, but all three had the *mission civilisatrice* in common. So it seems to me with Australia today. Much has changed. Yet when I visit, I see the same embattled heads of women's colleges work to overcome the same crude hazing of women students in the universities. And they are met by the same bland university authorities who believe "boys will be boys," and fail to notice the deep hostility to women expressed in rituals of intimidation which are not just "fun," and which have clear symbolic meaning. There are many such rituals alive and thriving despite the changed legislative climate. On the female side, the current cult of Princess Di does not exactly symbolize the world of achievement Miles Franklin had in mind for women, nor do the statistics about women's completion of high school. It is admirable that the current government is taking steps to improve the benefits of part-time workers, but instructive that more than 70 percent of women workers occupy so marginal a position. There is as much debate about what these archetypal patterns are as about any other aspect of Australian history. For the left historian, they are part of the acquisitive dreams of capitalists to usurp native peoples and to destroy the balance of nature that accompanied the expansion of the west. For the Australian environmentalist, they have to do with an attitude to nature that has much inspiration yet to be derived from the attitudes of Australia's Aboriginals. For the Australian nationalist, inspiration comes from a powerful identification with Australian landscape and the heroic virtues that are indisputably part of Australia's history of settlement and of its military history. All are valid points of view, and all convey important dimensions of the Australian contemporary consciousness.

If one's concern is with the cultural construction of gender, these views are not particularly helpful unless linked to an examination of underlying Australian attitudes about nature. Western concepts of gender have been derived from biblical texts, theology, the romantic view of nature, and finally from the molecular biology that has given us a new understanding of the biological basis of sexuality. Historically, what one sees in the natural world and the way one responds to it provide the imagery through which we understand the forces of generation, birth, fruition, and death. For the historian of culture, it matters what the landscape of the mind looks like and whether nature and natural forces stand for growth or sterility. For a people settling a new continent, this constellation of emotional forces is of primary importance as Perry Miller demonstrated in writing about the cosmology of Puritan New England,[30] and as Northrop Frye has shown in writing about the history of Canadian literature.[31] The reasons why the vision of nature mattered for the settler were existential. For the New England Puritan, the wilderness was a backdrop for a world-historical drama in which the Puritans were principle actors. For the Canadian looking "home," the northern woods were a menacing threat that home and all it stood for would be engulfed. If we ask what the bush has meant for Australians, it has stood for anti-romantic attitudes towards an unfruitful nature. The continent and the landscape have for historical reasons not permitted the development of the pastoral ideal or the bourgeois romance. They have been the setting in which a man or woman shows that they are not "soft" Europeans, that they do not give in to nature or to corrupt authority. Their errand, to borrow Perry Miller and the Puritan divine whose words he quoted, has been to learn to do without Europe, and to see life without the "illusions" of European culture. Australians in their wilderness live without the romantic agony, for it is an attitude the bush cannot evoke. As A.D. Hope writes in the poem "Australia," the land is "a nation of trees, drab green and desolate gray." Its natural world wears "the field uniform of modern wars."

> They call her a young country, but they lie:
> She is the last of lands, the emptiest,
> A woman beyond her change of life, a breast
> Still tender but within the womb is dry.[32]

Nature and nature's forces stand for menace and power, as for instance in W.S. Fairbridge's verses about the arrival of evening.

> Over the open belly of the earth
> Lingeringly the sun has pressed
> Its scorching iron. Muscled
> like wrestlers, the banking clouds
> Hold in ambush their thunder,
> A menace from over the scarp,
> So longed for and aloof. . . .
> And now arising in the air we feel
> The dews, and over all the housetops now
> the heat's steel cramp
> Most carefully
> Unscrews.[33]

In Judith Wright's poem "The Cicadas," the image of birth and fertility is given a new twist. It is bought at too great a price and too short-lived. "On yellow days in summer when the early heat presses like hands hardening the sown earth," the cicada stirs in its womb that is also a grave and begins the struggle toward light, birth, mating, and death.

But now in terror overhead their day of dying breaks
The trumpet of the rising sun bursts into sound
and the implacable unborn stir and reply.
In the hard shell an unmade body wakes
and fights to break from its motherly-enclosing ground.
These dead must dig their upward grave in fear
to cast the living into naked air.[34]

This searing vision of the forces of nature deliberately reverses the categories of romantic poetry and focuses on death rather than fruitfulness. For such a consciousness, few romantic stereotypes have meaning, and the physical expressions of sexual attraction occupy the same emotional climate. Much Australian fiction explores the relationship to nature and the inevitability of disillusionment. Patrick White's *Voss* (1957),[35] a fictional account of the explorer Ludwig Leichardt's death on an expedition to cross the continent, depicts a hero who is consumed by the natural forces of the land that has become his obsession. It is a universal statement about the Australian "errand," which is a journey to destruction with no shadow of redemption at the end. In such a situation, it is safer to deny or to deflate the emotions and settle for sexuality as a source of physical comfort but otherwise not to be at risk. So it is also with relations between the generations. When Hal Porter recounts his mother's death in *The Watcher on the Cast-Iron Balcony*, his grief is real but instantly deflated. As she draws her last breaths the watching hero says "I begin to make sounds I did not think I could, hard and harsh, bestial and elemental sounds."[36] This autobiography of the youth of a product of small-town Australia comes to an end with a powerful evocation of the hero's sudden coming of age on the event of his mother's death. But we are left feeling that the emotions accompanying so basic a life transition have diminished him, and have been wrung from a reluctant heart.

Thus, although a substantial portion of the Australian population lives in the relative calm and affluence of Australia's five major cities and their suburbs, it may be argued that Australians' inner life, like the landscape, is different, and this difference matters where we seek to understand what gender means in Australian culture. Australian suburbs, like their counterparts in North America or England, are hives of middle-class family life lived with all the ubiquitous accompaniments of modern comfort and international tastes in food, drink, and the pleasures of senses. Today, the middle class has grown from the early colonial 10 percent to 46 percent of the population. But we have the evidence of a great literature and a great tradition in painting to suggest that they live in a bleaker emotional environment than history has given other bourgeois societies, and this affects the relationships of love and work that make up adult life in our times. Many Australian historians will disagree with such a view, but the history of the affective life of Australians is still to be written. We cannot yet know whether the current climate of political change will be an enduring one, one of those marking points at which a people sets out in search of new meanings. To those who have lived these recent decades in Australia, the change seems momentous. To the occasional visitor, the continuities seem more profoundly striking. Thus, it seems no accident that Australia's recent great outpouring of achievement in film has reworked the theme of the isolated male hero, and the woman who must reject her sexuality for achievement. They seem larger-than-life figures whether in Technicolor or in the pages of *The Bulletin* where they first appeared.

ENDNOTES

[1]The best general discussion of social theory relating to gender is in Susan C. Bourque and Kay B. Warren, *Women of the Andes: Patriarchy and Change in Two Peruvian Towns* (Ann Arbor: University of Michigan Press, 1981), chaps. 2 and 3, pp. 41–86.

[2]See Bourque and Warren, *Women of the Andes,* p. 80.

[3]*Representation of the People in England and Wales Act,* June 7, 1832, chap. XLV, 2 and 3 W.4. C.45.

[4]For the clearest exposition of the composition of the early convict population see A.G.L. Shaw, *Convicts and Colonies* (London: Faber, 1966).

[5]T.W. Plummer to Colonel Macquarie, Park St., Westminster, May 4, 1809, *Historical Records of New South Wales* (Sydney: Bligh and Macquarie, 1809), vol. 7, p. 120.

[6]See Graeme Davison, *The Rise and Fall of Marvelous Melbourne* (Melbourne: Melbourne University Press, 1978).

[7]G.C. Mundy, *Our Antipodes* (London: R. Bentley, 1855).

[8]Banjo (A.B.) Paterson's "Clancy of the Overflow" first appeared in *The Bulletin* in 1899 and is reprinted in the centennial edition of the magazine for January 29, 1980, along with a fine selection of 1890s Australian verse and fiction.

[9]Clarence James Dennis, *The Songs of the Sentimental Bloke* (Sydney: Angus and Robertson, 1916), p. 16.

[10]J. S. Manifold, "The Tomb of Lieut. John Learmonth, A.I.F.," *Penguin Book of Australian Verse,* selected and ed. John Thompson, Kenneth Slessor, and R.G. Howarth (London: Penguin Books, 1958).
[11]Miles (Stella) Franklin, *My Brilliant Career* (Edinburgh: W. Blackwood, 1901).
[12]Miles (Stella) Franklin, *My Brilliant Career* (Sydney: Angus and Robertson, 1966), pp. 231–232.
[13]Miles Franklin, *My Career Goes Bung* (Melbourne: Georgian House, 1946).
[14]See the very insightful discussion of Franklin's life by Drusilla Modjeska in her *Exiles at Home: Australian Women Writers, 1925–45* (Sydney: Angus and Robertson, 1981).
[15]See Modjeska, *Exiles at Home,* chap. 2, pp. 16–42.
[16]Modjeska cites this passage from Stead's *For Love Alone* (1944) as a clear indication of her state of mind when preparing to depart from Australia. See Modjeska, *Exiles at Home,* p. 29.
[17]See Alison Mackinnon "Educating the Mothers of the Nation: The Advanced School for Girls, Adelaide," in Margaret Bevege, Margaret James and Carmel Shute, *Worth Her Salt: Women at Work in Australia* (Sydney: Hale and Iremonger, 1982), pp. 62–71.
[18]See Judith Godden's essay on a typical figure in New South Wales philanthropy "Portrait of a Lady: A Decade in the Life of Helen Fell, 1849–1935," in Bevege, James, and Shute, *Worth Her Salt,* pp. 33–48.
[19]W. Vere Hole and Anne H. Treweeke, *History of the Women's College within the University of Sydney* (Sydney: Angus and Robertson, 1953), p. 32.
[20]*The Bulletin,* May 10, 1890.
[21]See Sol Encel, Norman MacKenzie, and Margaret Tebbut, *Women and Society: An Australian Study* (Melbourne: Cheshire, 1974). More recent trends are reported in John S. Western, *Social Inequality in Australia* (Melbourne: Macmillan of Australia, 1983) and Bettina Cass, Madge Dawson, Diana Temple, Sue Wills, and Ann Winkler, *Why So Few: Women Academics in Australian Universities* (Sydney: Sydney University Press, 1983).
[22]Patricia Grimshaw and Lyn Strahan, eds., *The Half-Open Door: Sixteen Modern Australian Women Look at Professional Life and Achievement* (Sydney: Hale and Iremonger, 1982).
[23]Kathleen Fitzpatrick, "A Cloistered Life," chap. 6, pp. 120–33 in Grimshaw and Strahan, eds., *The Half-Open Door.*
[24]See the discussion of recent data on education and occupations for women in Australia in Western, *Social Inequality in Australia,* pp. 137–155.
[25]*Bulletin of the New South Wales Board of Trade: Living Wage, Adult Females 1918 Declaration* (Sydney: Government Printer, 1921). This subject is treated in detail in Edna Ryan and Ann Conlon, *Gentle Invaders: Australian Women at Work, 1788–1974* (Melbourne: Thomas Nelson, 1975).
[26]These are discussed in a series of essays collected under the title *Women, Class and History: Feminist Perspectives on Australia, 1788–1978,* ed. Elizabeth Windschuttle (Sydney: Fontana/Collins, 1980).
[27]This revealing comment is cited by Jennie Bremmer in "In the Cause of Equality: Muriel Heagney and the Position of Women in the Depression," in Bevege, James, and Shute, *Worth Her Salt,* p. 292.
[28]See Encel, MacKenzie, and Tebbutt, *Women and Society,* pp. 274–5.
[29]I am indebted to Dr. Cherry Collins for making available to me a copy of Anne Summers "The Power of the Vote: Women and Parliamentary Politics," a paper

delivered at the Women's Caucus of the ANZAAS Conference, May 15, 1984, which provides a useful summary of recent political events touching on women's concerns.

[30]See Perry G.E. Miller, *Errand into the Wilderness* (New York: Harper and Row, 1956).

[31]See Northrop Fry's introductory essay in Karl F. Klinck, ed., *A Literary History of Canada* (Toronto: University of Toronto Press, 1976).

[32]A.D. Hope, "Australia," *Penguin Book of Australian Verse* (London: Penguin, 1958), p. 119.

[33]W.S. Fairbridge, "Evening," *Penguin Book of Australian Verse,* p. 240.

[34]Judith Wright, "The Cicadas," *Penguin Book of Australian Verse,* p. 205.

[35]Patrick White, *Voss* (New York: Viking Press, 1957).

[36]Hal Porter, *The Watcher on the Cast-Iron Balcony: An Australian Autobiography* (London: Faber and Faber, 1963).

Michael Davie

The Fraying of the Rope

PROFESSOR GEOFFREY BLAINEY HAS COMPARED the fluctuating relations between Australia and England to "a long rope that safeguards and strangles." He was referring to the Australian end of the rope. The British take the relationship for granted. The subject rarely, if ever, features on the agenda of the Cabinet. Inside the Foreign and Commonwealth Office, the official in charge of Anglo-Australian affairs day-to-day is to be found obscurely sited at the South Pacific desk. No discussion of British relations with Australia surfaces among the continuous argumentative chatter that is characteristic of British metropolitan life. Newspaper coverage of Australia is scanty. Australian books are virtually unobtainable. Twelve thousand miles away, however, things are different. Insofar as Australians are at all inclined to reflect on the problems that confront them, or the nature of the society they have constructed or wish to construct, they soon find that they are involved in discussion of the British link. British influences are pervasive, peculiar, and tenacious. Non-Australians, particularly those who know the United States, are often surprised that Australia has not thrown aside these influences more than it has. Great changes have taken place in relations between the two countries in recent decades, and the rope is fraying. But it is still in place.

The point may be illustrated by a simple image. Soon after Melbourne was settled by an expedition from Tasmania in 1835, the bones of the future city were laid out on a straightforward grid system, of the kind employed in many American cities. The city was sited, which was the reason for its beginnings, on the northern bank of a river that flows into one of the few good harbors on the continent's southern coastline and thence into a capacious strait. The southern bank rises from the sluggish Yarra in a gentle slope, and it was on the crest of this slope that Government House was eventually built—the seat of the governor of Victoria, the representative of Her Imperial Majesty Queen Victoria, after whom the new colony was named. And there, on its crest, the governor's mansion still stands: brilliantly white, implacably Victorian, the whole edifice a copy of Queen Victoria's residence at Osborne, in the Isle of Wight. Remarkably little has changed at Victoria's Government House over the years. The herbaceous borders are immaculately maintained. The ample hallway is adorned by portraits, ancient and modern, some of them signed, of the royal family. Formal receptions are held, at which traditionally minded matrons of Melbourne wear hats and gloves; and a governor still resides there. He is an Australian citizen, nowadays, to be sure, and he is chosen by the state government. But technically he is still British-appointed, and he continues to possess and to exercise a constitutional role in the government of the state: a safeguard, as some believe, of the federal system. At the top of the gleaming white tower, visible from almost everywhere in central Melbourne, flies the Union Jack, modified by the addition at its center of a gubernatorial crest. The image of mansion and flag is imperial. And every Australian state capital, though none so prominently as Melbourne, has at its heart a similarly undigested symbol of Britain's former dominance and of the present British connection, raising questions as yet unresolved. It is possible to chronicle and even to date quite precisely the great changes that have taken place between Britain and Australia in politics, trade relations, defense, and population statistics. Culturally, though, the changes are much more elusive. Yet it is in cultural relations—using the word in its broadest meaning—that the deepest problem for Australians crops up, since it poses the question of what an "Australian," these days, really is.

The question—"What is an American?"—was asked two hundred years ago and the answer was, "The Americans are a new race." When the English novelist Evelyn Waugh was traveling by train across the United States in 1947, a railroad attendant, becoming philosophical about his fellow countrymen, remarked: "We are all foreigners here." The same is true of Australia. As in North America, so in Australia there exists, and has existed for at least forty thousand years, an indigenous population, the Aborigines. What are the Australians—relative newcomers—doing in the great brown southern continent? One early thought that must strike any visitor from continental Europe, still more from Britain, is that he has reached a land of which vast tracts are fundamentally unfriendly to those raised even in the bleakest stretch of Scotland. The European explorers who brought back the first publicized reports between 1606 and 1644, the Dutch, thought the barrenness of Australia showed no commercial promise and was not worth settling.[1]

Why, then, did the British settle it? It is only in the past twenty years that Australian historians have begun to investigate their own origins, an omission attributed, by Australian historians themselves, to a misguided absorption in European history, especially British history, at the expense of their own. An outsider may surmise, without evidence, that the omission may have been connected with a feeling that the first years of Australia were, until very recently, too painful to contemplate. A nation needs a myth about its origins. For Americans, a myth was readily at hand: the founders of their country, independent spirits, had sailed away from a harsh mother country to found a new kind of commonwealth, free from persecution and the corrupt ways of Europe. Australians had no such noble myth with which to justify or to explain their presence in so remote a part of the world. They could not claim to be "a new race." They did not, for the most part, choose to settle in Australia. Whether English, Scottish, Irish, or Welsh, they were dumped against their will by a British government. They were rejects. The best and the most famous of the convict novels is *For the Term of His Natural Life,* by Marcus Clarke. It has been justly said that "what seems most crushing" in this novel "is the aloneness of the abandoned outcasts, their condition as rejected 'things' rather than human beings."[2]

Once latter-day Australian historians began to investigate the origins of Australia, they questioned the old idea that the pathetic occupants of the prison hulks had been shipped off to the other side of the world merely to get them out of the way. The British government's motives were, as now seems established, largely imperial. It sought a naval base for exploits in the Indian Ocean and the Pacific, to counter other expansionist European powers. It is a very odd circumstance that a modern industrial country, two hundred years after its foundation, should only now be searching intensively for the reasons why it exists at all. But whatever London's motives, the fact remains that the new colony was born in great brutality. One can glimpse these conditions today among the preserved ruins of Port Arthur, a penal settlement in Tasmania. On sale at the tourist shop are T-shirts that show convicts in leg irons, with a caption underneath that says, in a witty extension of an axiom produced by Mr. Malcolm Fraser, "Life Wasn't Meant To Be Easy in Port Arthur." But despite the joke, it would be surprising if the average Australian tourist, gazing into the cells in this terrible place, did not feel a surge of resentment towards the British grandees who subjected the earliest settlers of his country to such harsh treatment so far from home. Comparing the gap between the crimes committed and the punishments administered, every thoughtful Australian of British and, still more, Irish descent must harbor profoundly ambivalent feelings about a "mother country" that used transportation of its offspring as an instrument of policy.

Australians were treated as an inferior breed by the London establishment, and they have not forgotten it. Some would say that they have not been allowed to forget it—by the British. In 1899, a new governor of New South Wales, the 7th Earl Beauchamp, arrived in Australia by the mail steamer "Himalaya" and was asked by a reporter from the *Sydney Morning Herald* if he had a message for the people of Sydney. Lord Beauchamp loftily declined to give an interview, but his private secretary a little while later presented the reporter with a verse written by his lordship on his own writing paper in his own hand:

> Greetings! Your birthstain have you turned to good
> Forcing strong wills perverse to steadfastness.
> The first flush of the tropics in your blood,
> And at your feet success.

Beauchamp had taken the lines from Kipling, but it was an unfortunate message, patronizingly reminding the citizens of New South Wales that, despite the convict origins of many of them, they had made good. Beauchamp never recovered from this "birthstain" message, and resigned his post well before his term expired.[3]

Such attitudes survived. Even Churchill, angered by the Australian government during World War Two, burst out with the comment that "the Australians came from bad stock." For their part, plenty of

Australians still instinctively think of the present-day British as descendants of the eighteenth-century landowners and magistrates who supplied the wretches who filled the holds of the First Fleet, and who marked the early pages of Australian history with blood, misery, and injustice. From the beginning, the new colony depended on the mother country. The surprise, looking back, is how long that dependence survived. Consider the most fundamental marks of national sovereignty: defense and the conduct of foreign relations. From 1788 until 1942, Australia relied on the protection of the Royal Navy. The country had been founded in order to provide a British naval presence in the region. Britain was still providing this presence when the Japanese, after Pearl Harbor, crushed southeast Asia. The sinking of two British battleships, the *Prince of Wales* and *Repulse,* in Malayan waters on December 10, 1941, and the subsequent surrender of Singapore itself, marked a fundamental change. In 1940, when R.G. Menzies went as prime minister to London to seek help for Australia's frail defenses, he received, in the words of a French historian, the "usual sort of lavish, patronising welcome that the British are so good at."[4] The writing was on the wall. On December 29, 1941, Menzies's successor, John Curtin, announced a revolution in Australian policy: "Without any inhibitions of any kind, I make it quite clear that Australia looks to America, free of any pangs as to our traditional links or kinship with the United Kingdom. We know the problems that the United Kingdom faces . . . But we know, too, that Australia can go and Britain can still hold on. We are, therefore, determined that Australia shall not go, and shall exert all our energies towards the shaping of a plan, with the United States as its keystone, which will give our country some confidence of being able to hold out until the tide of battle swings against the enemy."

In World War One, Australia had come to the aid of Britain. In proportion to her population, Australia made much heavier sacrifices of fighting men than did Britain, and most of her soldiers died in Europe. She achieved her nationhood, as the national myth has it, fighting a European battle at Gallipoli. World War Two was different. Australians fought at Tobruk and Crete, but Australia's main military effort was in her own region. This strategy did not always please London. Early in 1942, two Australian divisions that had been fighting in north Africa were withdrawn, and although Churchill wanted them to go to Rangoon to defend the frontiers of India, the

Australian government ordered them back to Australia. Their return coincided with the arrival in Australia of General MacArthur; henceforward Australia's principal role was to be the United States base in the South Pacific in the war against Japan. The emotional effect of these events would be hard to exaggerate. Churchill was "astounded" by the withdrawal. But rightly or wrongly the Australian public believed Japan was attempting to invade Australia. Suddenly the streets were full not of British but of American soldiers.

Here was the crossroads. Britain was seen to have turned its back on Australia. Since then, there has been a total change in the balance of defense as between Australia and the United Kingdom, and Australia and the United States. Britain's withdrawal from Aden showed that it had abandoned any pretence of being able to defend the traditional route to India and the East Indies. With the expiry of the lease in Hong Kong, British territorial interest in the Far East will be at an end, concluding the long story that began in the seventeenth century. Australia has never been able to defend itself, given its vast coastline and small population. Politicians and voters alike have been reluctant even to try, and the defense budget has been kept small. Australia is necessarily exposed, and everyone knows it. Britain still from time to time shows the flag in Australian waters, but under increasingly ambiguous circumstances. When HMS *Invincible* in December 1983 put in to Sydney Harbor, she was refused docking facilities on the grounds that her captain, in accordance with British government policy, declined to state whether or not she was carrying nuclear weapons. Both the Labor government in New South Wales, whose capital is Sydney, and the Labor federal government are, at least in theory, and in public, disinclined to welcome the presence of nuclear weapons on Australian soil. The U.S. government was more agitated about the ban of *Invincible* than the British. It was the U.S. secretary of state, not the British foreign secretary, who urgently asked the Australian federal government whether the ban represented a change of policy. Nobody admits it, but nobody denies it either, that Australia is visited from time to time by U.S. nuclear submarines, and in all probability also by U.S. aircraft armed with nuclear weapons. The Royal Navy, in this context, is irrelevant. The "keystone" of Australian defense, as it has been since Curtin's speech in 1941, is the United States. True, connections with the British armed forces survive, and a British serviceman can expect a warmer welcome in a Sydney bar than an American serviceman can; but as Australia increasingly buys ships and aircraft from elsewhere—from the United States and, very likely, in the future from Japan as it moves into defense technology—so these connections too will wither.

As in defense, so in external relations. Before World War Two, Australia thought itself lucky to be allowed to post an Australian diplomat inside the Foreign Office as a liaison officer. In 1939, Australia's entire diplomatic representation consisted of one high commissioner in London, a post established in 1910, one counselor attached to the British embassy in Washington, and a handful of trade commissioners. By the early 1970s, Australia was represented overseas by forty-five ambassadors, eighteen high commissioners, six heads of mission attached to the United Nations and the European Economic Commission, and forty-five trade commissioners. Between 1972 and 1975, when the new Labor prime minister, Gough Whitlam, in a frenzy of diplomatic activity, recognized China, brought home the last Australian troops from Vietnam, and withdrew recognition from Taiwan, it became plain that Australia was wishing to show itself determined to have a foreign policy of its own. Since then, Australia has scaled down its ambitions. Its sphere of interest lies in its own region, seeking good relations with non-communist powers and with China, and keeping a wary eye on Russian expansion in the Pacific and Indian oceans. In pursuit of these aims, Washington is a far more important ally than London, whatever stripe of government is in power in Canberra. When Hawke took office as Labor prime minister in 1983, his first concern was to reassure President Reagan—from whose general political stance Hawke could scarcely have been further removed—that Canberra's adherence to the U.S. alliance would not be affected by the change of government. An Australian prime minister's problem these days is to avoid being seen too much as a satellite of Washington, not of Downing street. Australia's main foreign policy business with Britain these days (though the intelligence services work closely together) arises from membership in the Commonwealth, rather than through independent dealings. It is only at Commonwealth heads-of-government meetings that an Australian prime minister, whose visits to Washington and London attract relatively little attention, can appear on a reasonably sized stage and make an impact. Australia has acquired much credit in black Commonwealth countries—

more than it has in Britain—through its consistent oppposition to apartheid in South Africa. In words, and sometimes in deeds, Australia under a Liberal (conservative) prime minister, Malcolm Fraser, showed itself much more sympathetic to the aspirations and needs of black Commonwealth countries than was always convenient for Mrs. Thatcher. Here again, Australia has moved a long way since Menzies regretted the departure of South Africa from the Commonwealth. He never concealed his belief that, to him, the Commonwealth really meant the white Commonwealth, joined by ties of blood, and grouped around Britain.

The United States has replaced Great Britain as Australia's principal defender and foreign-policy ally. Two great events have underlined the shift: Britain's entry into the European Economic Community, and the constitutional crisis, arising from the powers of the governor-general, of 1975. Britain's move into Europe confirmed, rather than caused, a radical shift of trade relations. Australia's exports to Europe were already declining while her exports to the Far East were growing rapidly. The blow to Australia, though long expected, was psychological rather than economic, particularly when new rules about immigration into Britain came into force, and Australians passing through British ports and airports found themselves queuing up with foreigners. With the new passport and immigration laws, imposed both by Britain and by Australia, another strand in the rope was broken, forcing Australians to recognize that henceforward the mother country would award them no special privileges.

The political crisis of 1975 was especially disturbing. A Labor prime minister was dismissed by a governor-general, the representative in Australia of the queen, on the grounds that the government was having such difficulties in securing the passage of financial legislation through the houses of Parliament that it was only by replacing the Labor by a Liberal prime minister that orderly administration of the country could be carried on. The governor-general was an Australian citizen, a lawyer, who had been appointed on the advice of the Labor prime minister himself. But it was thought that the power and trappings of the job had gone to his head. Constitutional lawyers argued, and still argue, about whether he had or had not properly exercised his reserve powers;[5] but most Labor supporters, outraged by the abrupt sacking of the government for which they had voted, saw the crisis in terms not of law but of the anachronistic continuing power of the queen's representative in Australian domestic affairs. Republicanism was given its biggest boost since the foundation of the colony.

Even without the 1975 crisis, though, the surviving legal links between Australia and London would probably have been severed. The High Court in Canberra, housed in an uncompromisingly modern concrete building on the edge of the lake in Canberra, and very different in looks from its American equivalent in Washington, is on the verge of becoming Australia's final court of appeal, replacing the privy council in London. The state of Victoria has been slowly weeding out the residual links of colonial legislation from the statute book.

So, judged by every formal indicator that distinguishes relations between states, Australia and Britain have slowly but surely moved apart: in defense, diplomacy, trade, the law. The Australian constitution is also under sharper criticism than it has been at any time since it was written. This weakening of the structure of Australian-British relations has undoubtedly been accompanied by a shift in attitude at the very head of the Australian state. Here again, a useful reference point is Robert Menzies, Australia's dominant postwar politician. Menzies did not come from a socially elevated background: he was born in a small town in Victoria, and his grandfather had been president of the Victorian miners' union. He attended the University of Melbourne. He did not fight in World War One. Yet he developed, and displayed, profound veneration for Britain and British institutions: the monarchy, the church, Parliament, the law. A fine orator and a considerable actor, he liked nothing better than making after-dinner speeches to appreciative British audiences in London, or dressing up in the antique costume of Lord Warden of the Cinque Ports, staying in one of the Lord Warden's sixteenth-century castles on the English Channel and performing ceremonial duties. Being British meant something very special to Menzies. The same cannot be said of Malcolm Fraser, although he, in many ways, was Menzies's political successor. Fraser is much more skeptical about Britain, despite—or perhaps because of—his Oxford education. These days, the Australians would never tolerate in a prime minister the deferential view of Britain adopted by Menzies (though they would tolerate a deferential view of China, Japan, and the United States). Fraser's accent, to a Briton, was Australian; but to many Australians it sounded suspiciously British. It was a political disadvantage. Hawke has two accents, one of them more Australian than the other, and it is noticeable that when he speaks in public he stresses his Australian vowel sounds, in the same way and for the same reason that Lyndon Johnson became much more Southern when he was on a platform in the South. Very few Australians wince when they hear Hawke's Australianisms. On the contrary, his use of the vernacular is one reason for his popularity, even among those who would regard themselves as his social superiors and whose own parents encouraged them to modify their strident native vowels. Nobody, these days, wants an Australian prime minister to sound as if he was educated at Oxford—even if, like Hawke, he was.

With increasing, if not necessarily sought-after Australian independence, the political ties between the two countries have become more distant. Only twice since the war has an Australian prime minister played any considerable part in British affairs. During the Suez crisis of 1956, Menzies, through his close association with the British and American leaders and through his position as the elder statesman of the Commonwealth, led an international but unsuccessful mission to Cairo in an attempt to mediate between Eden and Nasser. Malcolm Fraser played an important role at the Commonwealth Conference in Lusaka, in modifying—possibly in changing—the British government's attitude towards independence for Zimbabwe. (The British government was not pleased, however, when Mr. Fraser himself explained to journalists the importance of the role he had played.) Britain took no part in the most crucial Australian political decision of the postwar years, when Australia sent troops—as Britain did not—to support the United States in Vietnam.

Occasional links are formed between politicians of both countries. Mr. John Howard, the Australian federal treasurer in the Fraser government, had his first taste of a political campaign when he helped, in a very humble role, a British MP, Geoffrey Johnson Smith (now Sir Geoffrey), fight an election in the 1950s. In recent years, there has been one Australian-born and educated MP, Russell Kerr, in the House of Commons, and an Australian baroness, Lady Gardner, in the House of Lords. Politicians of both countries meet at Commonwealth parliamentary conferences.

Left-wing contacts go back a long way, but have not been conspicuously stimulating. Sidney and Beatrice Webb, the Fabian socialists who helped to found the London School of Economics and who started the *New Statesman*, visited Australia in 1898, seven years after the formation of the Australian Labor party. They were not impressed, however, either by the Labor leaders they met or by the working class. Beatrice Webb wrote in her diary of the tour: "The working men seem largely non-political." Professor Bolton finds underlying all Beatrice's comments "a note which can be detected time and time again in the comments of British visitors to Australia. It is a note of resentment that these descendants of British and Irish working-class migrants should be prospering so unabashedly and enjoying themselves so greatly. The Australians were those fortunate members of the lower orders who had broken loose from British hierarchy and were exercising their own choices about their style of life. It would be very difficult for members of Britain's ruling classes and still more for Britain's intellectuals to accept the legitimacy of those choices."[6]

The Webbs found nothing to learn from antipodean social experiments, even though Australian and New Zealand governments were then laying the foundations of the modern welfare state. The radicals were timid about factory legislation and the taxation of wealth, the Webbs concluded, and the labor politicans seemed happy under the capitalist system. The Webbs were collectivist; what they encountered was individualism. Australian radicals of the day, by the same token, found more to excite them in the ideas of Henry George than in the municipal socialism of the Webbs.

Nor have modern Labour party intellectuals in Britain found much to interest them about the Australian Labor party (ALP). The formation of the largely Catholic, anti-communist Democratic Labor party between 1955 and 1957, following a split in the Labor party, made the Australian movement's problems seem very different from those of the British. Similarly, the splits and arguments that have preoccupied the British Labour party—Britain's possession of the atomic bomb, nationalization, Britain's relations with the Common Market—have no parallels in Australia. Australia's present Labor prime minister, the apostle of "consensus," shares few political ideas with either the present British Labour leader, Neil Kinnock, or the last, Michael Foot—still less with the left-winger Tony Benn. It is a long time since Labor leaders in Australia became wary about describing themselves or their political aims as "socialist." In 1963, the ALP leader Arthur Calwell, fully aware of the electoral problems of being associated with socialism, specifically stated that, if elected, the party would not implement any socialist policies. In 1962, a prominent English Labour leader, Douglas Jay, published a book called *Socialism in the New Society,* in which he set out "to restate the case for democratic socialism in the 1960s." Jay became president of the Board of Trade in the Labour government of 1964. It is true that both labor parties, today, formally describe their links as extremely good. Labor politicians from Australia call at Labour party headquarters in London; both parties belong to the Socialist International. Mr. Hawke used to attend Socialist International meetings; Mr. Gough Whitlam attended a meeting in April 1984. But the ALP was not represented at the Socialist International meeting in Sheffield in June 1984; and neither Mr. Foot nor Mr. Kinnock has ever found time to visit Australia.[7]

The doctrines of Mrs. Thatcher, likewise, have had little impact on Australia. The Australian electorate gave the Liberal party three solid victories in 1975, 1977, and 1980. The results—particularly the rather unexpected result of 1977, which almost repeated the record majority of 1975—showed that the party had recaptured the center ground of Australian politics, winning back the urban voters who had deserted it for Whitlam in 1972 and 1974. To a degree, it faced some of the same problems as Mrs. Thatcher: inflation, unemployment, fractious unions. But Australian Liberal leaders did not believe, as Mrs. Thatcher believed, that radical surgery was needed to put the country on the road back to health. By 1980, the Australian government had brought inflation substantially under control, and, though Fraser huffed and puffed about the unions and had many disagreements with them (particularly over wage hearings before the Arbitration Commission), he was not elected, as was Mrs. Thatcher, with a mandate to reduce over-mighty union power, and the expected confrontation between the unions and the Liberal party did not occur. It was only when the Liberal party found itself doctrinally naked in the wilderness, following the electoral triumph of Mr. Hawke in 1983 and his massive 78 percent popular support in the early months of 1984, that it began to flirt with Thatcherite doctrines such as the distancing of the central government from wage-fixing, the sale of government assets ("privatization"), and the withdrawal of government backing for sectors of industry that, left to themselves, would collapse. These moves, however, were received coolly even by the Liberal voters to whom they were intended to appeal.

Among all the signs of changing relations between Great Britain and Australia, one measurable indicator is the makeup of the population. On the eve of World War Two, 98 percent of the white population of Australia was of British or Irish origin, though there was a small Chinatown in the heart of Melbourne, Chinese market gardens elsewhere, and pockets of Italians, Greeks, Germans, and Maltese. After World War Two, the supply of Anglo-Saxon migrants was not large enough to meet the ambitious targets Australia had set itself, and Australia was forced to turn elsewhere, particularly to Italy and Greece. The great period of postwar immigration occurred between 1947 and 1972. During this time, the Australian population rose from 7½ million to 13 million. Her net population gain through immigration was 2.4 million settlers. Preference was shown to immigrants from the British Isles, nine out of ten of them receiving assisted passages, compared with just over one in four of those from southern Europe. Even so, the non-British—Italians and Greeks especially, but also Dutch, Yugoslavs, Poles—made up 56 percent of the new arrivals.

This flood has greatly changed Australian social and cultural life, moving it away from its British roots. Five years ago, when the Australian artist and cartoonist Arthur Horner returned to Australia after a long spell in London, his work soon began to reflect his observation that the national physical stereotype was no longer the tall, rangy figure of legend but a short, black-haired overweight fellow wearing shorts and thongs, and carrying a transistor radio.[8] But if the migrants have had profound effects on all parts of the national life, it should not be forgotten that 40 percent of all postwar migrants have been British. One-sixth of the population may be non-British, but the rest is of British origin. Many Australians of British descent may not, these days, be especially proud of their ancestry; and the descendants of nineteenth-century migrants very rarely still have close kinsfolk in Britain. But twentieth-century family networks are considerable. During the devastating bush fires of 1983, the telephone lines from Britain to Australia were jammed by anxious Britons seeking information about their relatives. One reason why young Australians continue to travel to London as soon as they can rake the money together is not only that they speak the language, or that they have a sentimental interest in visiting what used to be known as "home," but because they have an aunt somewhere who will give them a bed.

Family and social ties are infinitely dense and varied, and are found at the most exalted as well as the most humble level. The queen's deputy private secretary, Sir William Heseltine, who was at the University of Western Australia with the Australian prime minister (a useful link from all points of view), has a brother who is a professor of English literature in Townsville, Queensland. The British prime minister's daughter, Carol Thatcher, has been a hard-working reporter on the *Sydney Morning Herald*. Besides the young Australians who visit Britain as tourists, or use the country as a springboard for a once-in-a-lifetime tour of Europe, others take jobs—the hard-pressed British national health service is always ready to employ an Australian-trained nurse. The Labour candidate at the disastrous (for Labour) by-election in Bermondsey in 1983 was a young left-wing Australian employed by the social services. There is rarely a day of the year when there is no British sporting team of one sort or another touring Australia, or an Australian team touring Britain. Australian jockeys have been markedly successful on the British turf. The Australian wife of the world's most prominent bloodstock owner, Robert Sangster, a Briton, was formerly married to the leader of the Australian Liberal party, Mr. Andrew Peacock. Thirty years ago, Sir Alexander Carr-Saunders, then director of the London School of Economics, used to maintain that in thirty years' time the most important bonds, perhaps the only important bonds, between Britain and her old colonies would be universities. Carr-Saunders had much to do with the setting up of new universities in the Commonwealth after World War Two. His prediction has come true. Not only are the last two Australian prime ministers, Fraser and Hawke, Oxford graduates; so is the head of the Australian treasury, who often wears the tie of an exclusive Oxford sporting club, Vincent's; so is Rupert Murdoch, the owner of the *New York Post* as well as the London *Times;* so is the chairman of his main company; so is the chairman of John Fairfax and Sons, one of the country's most powerful newspaper empires; so is the editor of *The Age* in Melbourne; and so is the prominent businessman Sir Roderick Carnegie. The last governor-general of Australia, Sir Zelman Cowen, had been an Oxford don at the same college as Cecil Rhodes, whose scholarships are still given to those who, in the opinion of those who award them, will one day be prominent in the affairs of their home country. Three decades ago, aspiring Australian parents with money still sent their boys to Oxford or Cambridge. They rarely do so today. But the Rhodes Scholars keep coming, even though for the sake of their careers in a world increasingly dominated by technology they might be better advised to try to get into the University of Tokyo or MIT.

Culturally, connections are equally intricate, though Australians are more aware of the connections than are the British. Many of the best-known Australian publishing houses are British offshoots, and the Australian market is still the second most important export market for British books. A steady procession of British writers visits Australia, usually at Australian expense, to lecture or to take temporary posts as writers-in-residence. The best of modern Australian landscape painters, Fred Williams, studied at the Chelsea Art School. A former professional racing cyclist who became one of the leading Australian painters of his generation now lives in England, laden with honors, as Sir Sidney Nolan, O.M.. The director of the Art Gallery of New South Wales is an Englishman. One of the dominant names in British ballet during the past decades has been Sir Robert Helpmann, originally from Adelaide. The opera houses of Britain, as of Europe, are rarely without an Australian voice. The master of the queen's music, Malcolm Williamson, is an Australian. Actors and actresses go back and forth between the two countries, though it is true that the more successful an actor or actress is in Britain, the less likely he or she is to sign a contract for an Australian tour. Academics are almost equally mobile. Most Australian universities have a Briton or two, or more, on the campus; the Regius Professor of Medicine at Oxford University is Australian. So is the Director of the highly regarded International Institute for Strategic Studies.[10]

On the British general public, Australian films have made more impression in the last few years than any other cultural product; all the more so since the BBC, looking for a source of moderately priced films suitable for "family viewing"—American films are more expensive and less likely to be family "material"—has acquired rights in most of the best Australian films. They have thus been seen by millions of viewers. Most of these films are set in the past; and most of these in the bush, taking advantage of the Australian landscape. To British audiences, they have something of the charm of the old American westerns: they present a simpler, somehow more honest and more virtuous way of life lived amid breathtaking scenery. It is doubtful whether these films, good though many of them are, have given the British much idea of modern Australian multicultural society and its problems; but they have at least, perhaps for the first time, made the British understand the vast scale of the continent, and the privations, triumphs, and myths of its inhabitants. Films are one recent Australian export that has made an impression in Britain. The other is Australian tabloid journalism, which, as practiced by Mr. Rupert Murdoch's papers the *Sun* and the *News of the World*, has transformed the British popular press—not, most critics would say, for the better.

Elsewhere, the promise of the early sixties, when it seemed that Britain was about to feel the force of an Australian cultural renaissance, whose forerunners were Ray Lawler, Patrick White, and Sidney Nolan, has not been fulfilled. This is partly because the announcement of a renaissance was premature, but also partly because the British have largely failed to take note of such excellence as has been achieved. A review of a new novel by the Australian writer David Malouf illustrates the point. Francis King wrote in The *Spectator:* "Recently the following item appeared in *The Times* Diary: 'I hear that the Australian Broadcasting Corporation and the *Australian Book Review* are to compile a list of the 10 greatest Australian works since the war. Nominations on a postage stamp please.' As an English judgment on any literature other than our own, nothing could be more typically provincial and patronizing. Graham Greene apart, what male postwar English novelist has the stature of Patrick White? Ivy Compton-Burnett apart, what female postwar English novelist has the stature of Christina Stead? How many postwar English novelists are the equals of Thomas Keneally, Randolph Stow, David Ireland and David Malouf?"

Despite the links that survive, Australians visiting or living in Britain often feel a lack of sympathy for Australia in certain quarters. Englishmen in Australia have been known to make the same complaint. Each group feels a victim of powerful stereotypes. The stereotypes go back a long way. In 1869, Marcus Clarke described the "preposterous follies" of the English in Melbourne; heads in air, superior, disdaining colonial society without condescending to investigate it.[9] He also described Australians in England making themselves equally ridiculous and disliked by "blowing" about their achievements, and by boasting about how easy it was to get rich in Australia. A shrewd contemporary Australian journalist has observed that Australians in Britain find it hard to be themselves. They tend either to wish to disguise their origins and turn into Englishmen, or they exaggerate their Australianism.[10] The British upper class and middle class still seem to feel the need, like the Webbs, to think of Australia as an uninteresting country inhabited by beer-swilling louts who talk in a comic accent. Their misconceptions are fed by some of the best-known, and highly talented, Australian expatriates. When Germaine Greer reported on a recent return visit to her home town, Melbourne, she deplored the lack of change there in twenty years. She made no mention of the impact on the city of the influx of hundreds of thousands of migrants from Greece and Italy since she left. The comedian Barry Humphries, a frequent performer on British TV who can also fill the Drury Lane Theatre for weeks with his one-man show, presents a savage picture of Australian suburbia and culture that brilliantly fuels the prejudices of his audience. Clive James wrote an account of his early years in Sydney that became a best-seller in Britain (though not in Australia) and must have given many British readers the impression that James's home country was so brash that the only course for a man of his talents was to emigrate to Cambridge. If more Australian voices and opinions were heard in Britain, the picture of Australia presented by this nationally known trio would make less impression. But the media in general—even the four national newspapers owned by Mr. Murdoch—make no attempt to report Australia steadily and in the round. The notion lingers, possibly a survival from the earliest days when Terra Australis Incognita was first seen by Europeans as somewhere wholly remote and exotic, inhabited by kangaroos and incomprehensible naked savages, that the news the British will digest from Australia is limited to tales of bush fires, plagues of ants that halt trains, or—most recently—Aborigines physically damaged by British nuclear tests in the desert thirty years ago. Australian businesses go along with the tide. Qantas airline advertisements feature sheep, koalas, and men with corks suspended from their hats on strings to ward off the flies (both the koalas and the hats are rare sights in the country itself).

Australian winemakers have tried to ingratiate themselves with British drinkers by labeling one of their red wines "Kanga Rouge," which suggests that even the producers do not expect their product to be taken seriously. But the willful ignorance and snobbery about Australia, particularly as exhibited by the British middle class without Australian relations, are not shared by the poor of, say, Liverpool, who are aware that their opposite numbers in Perth or Brisbane are much better off than they are themselves.

The British image in Australia has changed more than the Australian image in Britain. Few Lord Beauchamps survive even in England, and still fewer visit Australia. The British in Australia, like the Americans in Britain, are less resented these days than they were twenty-five years ago, and for the same reasons: both Britain and the United States are inherently less to be envied. Australia knows that in some cases it has handled its affairs—for instance, immigration—better than Britain, if not as well as it might. What Australians resent about Britain these days is more likely to be its export of awkward shop stewards than its export of the head-in-the-air young men described by Marcus Clarke. As films are belatedly helping to educate the British about Australia, so television is helping to educate Australia about Britain. The Australian Broadcasting Commission, which was modelled on the BBC, preserves close connections with London and takes many BBC programs. True, the ABC's ratings are much lower than those of the commercial stations that are more American both in style and content; but one effect of the BBC programs is to help dissipate the notion that the British Isles are populated by an effete and idle people who talk with a plum in their mouths. British "working-class" comedies and soap operas are almost as much a staple diet of television viewers in Melbourne as they are in Manchester.

What will happen to the relationship in the years ahead? Its principal symbol is the monarchy. Many Australians (like many Britons) are bored by the monarchy, not caring whether it lives or dies. But there is a solid 28 percent of the country that seeks a republic. This block is unlikely, though, to achieve its aim in the foreseeable future, if only because of the extreme technical difficulties of amending the constitution, quite apart from the fact that any Labor government seeking to bring in a republic would find itself so bitterly opposed by a number of not uninfluential organizations—for instance, the Returned Services League, the local equivalent of the American Legion—that it would be utterly distracted from what it regards as much more urgent tasks. Mr. Hawke's predecessor as leader of the Australian Labor party, Mr. Bill Hayden, did not regard the question of a republic as a live issue; certainly he never mentioned it in the 1980 federal election. Mr. Hawke's position is that he is sure Australia will be a republic one day, but he declines to say when, or to indicate what he will do to bring that day closer. Serious republicans, such as Professor Manning Clark, the historian, or Patrick White, the novelist, argue that it is only by abolishing the monarchy that Australia will be able to look Britain in the eye, like a child that finally learns to say "No" calmly to its parents.

And it seems to be true that a certain lingering deference still survives.[11] For instance, Australian universities have continued to look to Britain not only for staff, which is perhaps natural, but, much more surprisingly, sometimes for vice-chancellors. Why should this be so? In recent years, Britons have also been imported as editors, scientists, cultural administrators, broadcasters, and headmasters, though the practice seems to be declining. Since in many of these instances, equally well-qualified Australians were available, it is hard to find any other explanation for these imports than a lingering Australian belief that the benefits of experience outside Australia outweigh knowledge of the country itself.

For Australia—and here we approach the heart of this ambiguous relationship—is still to some extent in the grip of what A.A. Phillips has called the "cultural cringes," defined as an Australian inclination to assume that anything British is better than anything Australian. Historically, Australians have often mocked and scorned the cultivated British, while at the same time paying exaggerated attention to their views, especially their views of Australians. Americans will find such attitudes familiar. The Jamesian expatriates pursued European culture, feeling that American culture was worthless unless somehow connected with and justified by the salons of London and Paris. Today, a painter in Kansas City, much though he or she may disapprove of New York, may well feel that regional success is not enough: what does Kansas City know? So the painter moves to New York, to compete in the highest league. Similar forces have been at work in Australia. Australian culture flowered in the late 1950s and early 1960s, with painters such as Nolan and Drysdale, writers such as Patrick White, and playwrights such as Ray Lawler. But it was only when Nolan was hailed as "a born painter" by Sir Kenneth (later Lord) Clark, Patrick White as a genius by the London *Observer,* and Lawler as the first truly antipodean dramatist by London theater critics that the Australians themselves began to sit up and take notice. Patrick White is one of the few Australian writers who, perhaps because he was educated at an English public school, Cheltenham, and an English university, Cambridge, and because his family had a long and secure social standing as landowners in New South Wales, never felt any undue respect either for English society or for English intellectual society. He returned from Europe to Australia, drawn especially by the landscape, in order to develop his talents. But these talents, he has always maintained, were rubbished by critics in his own country even after they were recognized abroad. It was only when he won the Nobel Prize for Literature, the ultimate accolade, that Australians accepted the fact that they had a great writer in their midst.

The shadow of Europe lay over Australian culture for a long time. Generations of Australian schoolchildren were taught history and poetry from English textbooks designed for English pupils. How far Australia has escaped this shadow, or how far it should try to escape it, is a question that preoccupies a certain type of Australian intellectual. Cultural nationalism is on the march. In the schools, there has been in the past decade a dramatic shift towards Australian studies. Murray Bail, the novelist, has complained that "anyone who desires a normal knowledge of the world . . . is a cultural cringer." Graham Rowlands, discussing the poetry of Bruce Dawe in the August 1983 issue of the literary magazine *Overland* (whose motto is "Temper democratic, bias Australian"), writes: "Dawe isn't a poet who happens to live in Australia. He's an *Australian* poet." Rowlands goes on to say that "many of Dawe's poetic predecessors and contemporaries have written in a language scarcely distinguishable from educated British English. The younger Canberra poets (excluding Les Murray) still seem to be as oriented to Europe as A.D. Hope ever was, while the Modernists, of course, imitate their American models. The old Cultural Cringe with a new vengeance. If, however, our film industry succeeds by consisting of Australians making films about Australian experience, why shouldn't the same argument apply to our poetry? Why would Australians want to read anything but Australian poems about Australian experience?" Nothing in these words, or in the rest of the essay, suggests that their author is being ironical. Nor does Rowlands go on to ask why the same argument shouldn't apply to "our" painting, novels, or music. The demand, which can be vociferous, for an "Australian Culture" is principally a demand for independence from British models.

But the cultural links will survive. So will economic links. Australia is very much a trading country,[12] and Britain in the past was the main market for its agricultural products: sheep, meat, butter. In recent years, the significance of the U.K. as an export market for Australia has dramatically declined. In the early 1950s, 33 percent of Australia's exports went to Britain. By 1975, the U.K. took a mere 4 percent, while the Japanese, who took 6.3 percent in the early 1950s, took 33 percent. But by contrast, the export of capital from Britain to Australia has grown. These trends are likely to continue, as Britain becomes more integrated with the EEC, and Australia continues to build up its strong ties with Japan and the other Pacific rim countries. China has itself suggested taking shares in Australian steel production, which is typical of the way the trade winds are blowing.

The main areas of financial activity are direct investment by British firms, the holding of Australian portfolios by U.K. institutions (pension funds and insurance companies), and the provision of debt finance. Since the Australian financial system is being rapidly deregulated by the Labor government, the capital flows from London are likely to increase substantially. Barriers to inward investment and the transfer of funds have been dismantled. British merchant banks—Hambros, Warburgs, Schroders—want to be part of the flow. The so-called "high street banks"—Natwest, Barclays, Lloyds—see Australia more and more as a rare overseas safe haven for their funds.

British banks have been lobbying Australian politicians for years, seeking deregulation so that they could establish their own presence in Australia and not merely service it from overseas. Only the present government has listened to them. With a population of only 15 million, the Australians realize they themselves cannot provide the finance the country needs, and must therefore tap overseas markets. More and more, financial advisory contracts are going to British banks. For instance, the State Energy Commission of Western Australia, needing to put in a natural-gas pipeline of some 1500 kilometers at a cost of A$800 million, did not possess the in-house experience to finance the scheme itself, and so put it out to tender. The contract went to the Orion Royal Bank of London Wall, a British merchant bank.

However, there is not, and probably will never be, an open-door policy about investment in Australia, whether from Britain or elsewhere. There are restrictions on real-estate ownership, ownership of the media, and mining—especially uranium mining. Australians are fully aware of the implications that a large foreign financial interest has for undue political and economic influence. Direct British ownership of companies in Australia will remain, accordingly, much as it is. Australians want to control their own destiny. If British companies take shares, they will want directorships, which will involve them in making decisions. The Australians want to make their own decisions, which they can continue to do if they are using British loans. But even with these qualifications and remaining restrictions, the capital market sector is expected to grow in order to satisfy what may become a very large Australian appetite.

Sophisticated people are not worried that this development will increase London's influence on Australian affairs. But not all Australians are sophisticated. There are certainly fears in some quarters that Australia will find itself in the grip of London bankers—fears that echo the cry of the late sixties and early seventies that Australia must "buy back the farm." Those with long memories recall the humiliating episode when the governor of the Bank of England visited Australia during the Depression to tell the Australian government how to conduct the economy. However, though left-wing members of the Labor party may rumble, they are not likely to shake the government, which knows that a Fortress Australia policy is impossible, and that its electoral fortunes will be much more helped by a flow of capital from London and by the good opinions of the business community than they will be damaged by criticisms from the left wing. So the financial links seem likely to strengthen even as Australia's trade with the Pacific rim countries increases—at least until Singapore mounts a challenge to the City of London.

Not all Australians are certain, in an uncertain world, what they want to happen to their country in the future. Japan may have demonstrated its determination to try to understand Australia by translating into Japanese Xavier Herbert's powerful novel, *Poor Fella*

My Country, a long saga of Aborigine life known to disrespectful Australians as "Poor Fella My Reader." But the Australians do not instinctively find the Japanese easy to understand, or a natural ally. They continue to want to be understood and appreciated by the English-speaking countries. Whitlam in 1976 supplied government money to set up a chair of Australian studies at Harvard "to promote awareness and understanding of Australia in the United States"; Fraser did the same in London on a more elaborate scale, establishing under the wing of the University of London an Australian Studies Centre opened in June 1983, with one of its aims the furthering of Australian studies at British educational institutions. It would probably not be an exaggeration to say that for every British academic professionally interested in Australia there are fifty British academics whose job is to study the United States. Mr. Hawke was present at the center's opening ceremony (and did not object to having his photograph taken, it was noted, with the Queen Mother), and said that his Labor government would continue the Liberal government's support.

Australia's view of itself has greatly altered in the past twenty years, and few Australians would contest the notion that it must in future regard itself as an Asian as well as a European nation. Australian prosperity depends on Asia. But the population is still overwhelmingly European. Increasing independence causes tremors as well as satisfactions. "And always keep a-hold of nurse for fear of finding something worse" is a sentiment that finds an echo throughout the continent. Australians are few, and Asians are many. The United States may be their protector, the Asian nations of the southern Pacific their neighbors, and Japan their new economic partner; but it will be a long time yet before Australians' feelings fully correspond to their geographical position.[13] The American colonists' loyalties were first tested by mismanagement in London, then dissolved by London's stupidity, and then irrevocably ended by war. But Australia never had a Lord North, and America was independent before Australia was settled. Given the nature of its roots, its small population, and the novelty of its independence, perhaps the persistence of British influence is not to be wondered at. Time alone will change matters. Even if Australia became a republic tomorrow, and all the governors' mansions were turned into casinos (a suggestion that has been put forward, at least half-seriously, in Melbourne), the threads would still survive.

It is to be hoped that this fact of life will not be too unpalatable in the growing mood of Australian nationalism. A wise Australian, Professor Sir Keith Hancock, has quoted with approval an Indian professor as telling Australians that they will be of no use to India if they repudiate their European inheritance. Meanwhile, the British could help Australians to treat their inheritance calmly and seriously by themselves taking Australia more seriously, and by asking whether British society is, as they often assume, so superior to Australian arrangements. The problem of the future is Australia's, not Britain's, however. Britain will accept any proposals that Australia makes about legal or constitutional links, without argument. It is hard to resist the conclusion that Australia will become more and more preoccupied by its relations with Asia and the United States and less and less concerned with its relations with Britain. The rope will thus continue to fray. But it will be a very long time indeed before it parts altogether.

ENDNOTES

[1]G.C. Bolton, "The Image of Australia in Europe," *Journal of the Royal Society of Arts* (London), February 1984, p. 172.

[2]L.T. Hergenhau, introduction to *A Colonial City, Selected Journalism of Marcus Clarke* (Queensland: University of Queensland Press, 1972), p. xvii.

[3]Harry Gordon, *An Eyewitness History of Australia* (Melbourne: Currey O'Neil, 1976), pp. 174–5. Beauchamp's contribution to Australia was not entirely negative. It was he who financed a visit to England by the writer Henry Lawson. Lawson, on his return to Australia, said that Beauchamp denied having sent a message to a reporter. But the reporter had kept Beauchamp's verse written in Beauchamp's handwriting. It is now in the Mitchell Library in Sydney. Few Australians who watched Laurence Olivier playing Lord Marchmain in the television series of "Brideshead Revisited" will have realized that a former governor of New South Wales was the model for Marchmain.

[4]Robert Lacour-Gayet, *A Concise History of Australia* (London: Penguin, 1976), p. 341.

[5]See letter from Senator Gareth Evans, former Australian attorney-general, in the *Times Literary Supplement*, June 22, 1984.

[6]Bolton, "The Image of Australia in Europe,", p. 176.

[7]Harold MacMillan was the first incumbent British prime minister to visit Australia, in 1958. The Japanese prime minister, Nobosuke Kishi, beat him to it by a year.

[8]The same physical change had been noted earlier by a historian at the Australian National University: "Australians appeared to have softened and developed

comfortable little paunches." John Ritchie, *Australia as Once We Were* (Melbourne: Heinemann, 1975), p. 256.

[9]L.T. Hergenhau, ed., *A Colonial City; Selected Journalism of Marcus Clarke* (Queensland: University of Queensland Press, 1972), pp. 40–62.

[10]Peter Smark, *The Age,* October 25, 1983.

[11]Bruce Grant, former Australian high commissioner in India, recently wrote that Australian style is "still hindered by reverence and timidity in the presence of Royalty." See *The Age,* August 30, 1983.

[12]Trade represents 14½ percent of Australia's GNP. The figure for the United States is 3½ percent.

[13]*Japan and Australia,* edited by Peter Drysdale and Hironobu Kitsoji (Canberra: Australian National University Press, 1981), p. 9, reports a poll of 1,145 Australians and 160 Japanese businessmen in Australia. When the Japanese respondents were asked "What do you think Australians think of the Japanese?" 27.5 percent replied that they thought they were regarded as "trustworthy." Only 3.8 percent of the Australian respondents in fact thought the Japanese trustworthy.

Henry S. Albinski

Australia and the United States

TWO AMERICAN-RELATED EVENTS have been among the most powerful agents in shaping Australia's development. The American War of Independence closed the colonies to Britain and caused it to turn to Australia as a convict settlement. Hence, the birth of the United States made Australia British: "George Washington may have been the father of the United States: he was assuredly the stepfather of New South Wales."[1] A century and a half later, the U.S. role in the prosecution of World War II in the Pacific ushered in a period during which Australia's society and its official and economic connections have become measurably more American.

By now, American intellectual as well as popular cultural trends are the dominant overseas influence in Australia. About seventy thousand Americans are domiciled in Australia on a permanent or long-term basis, and over a hundred thousand American tourists visit annually. There are extensive scientific and technical cooperation programs between the two nations. By the early 1980s, the U.S. had become Australia's principal source of imports and its second most important export outlet. The United States had also become the foremost overseas investor in Australia across a broad range of industrial, resource, agricultural, and service industries. Since 1952, Australia's security has been linked to the U.S. through the ANZUS alliance. Bilateral military exercises and planning and intelligence exchanges are widespread. Jointly with Australia, the U.S. maintains elaborate communications and surveillance facilities on Australian territory. American military aircraft deploy through Australia on reconnaissance and training flights, and U.S. naval vessels frequently call at Australian ports.

The present study examines Australian social features, outlooks, and practices in relation to the United States. It highlights national and community feeling, socioeconomic priorities, and responses to the external environment. Such an inquiry can provide insight into comparative trends in societal development, and into why Australia may or may not have borrowed or learned from American experience. As a secondary theme, this study attempts to suggest the extent to which the United States has become pervasive on the Australian scene, and the factors that may have predisposed Australia to such influences.

Australia acquired a sense of community *before* it became a nation; its sense of nationhood, and of nationalism, has been dominantly social, not nearly as explicitly political and state-related as in America. The U.S. had its origin in overtly political acts—a declaration of independence, war, and the crafting of a novel constitutional document as a guideline for a new order. American national mythology became heavily infused with constitutional reverence, the Constitution serving as a touchstone for both defining and shaping the country's purpose. Even the pre–Civil War debate was conducted largely within the framework of deciding among various interpretations of the Constitution. When the Civil War finally laid nullification to rest, the liberal-democratic assumptions of America's politics—themselves an outgrowth of the revolutionary tradition—were restored as the major principle of organized political life. Much later, during the McCarthy era, both those in favor and those opposed to the silencing of ostensibly subversive elements made elaborate reference to constitutional guarantees. Cross-national survey data have noted the continued American propensity to take pride in and to remain loyal to existing political institutions. A rising cynicism about individual political leaders does not jeopardize support for these institutions.[2]

Australian federation in 1901, by contrast, was a leisurely process, inspired mostly by considerations of efficiency. The new Australian constitution drew heavily on American federal experience, but was more of a synthetic than a bold and original document. Australia slipped into formal nationhood, almost unobtrusively; it had no specific legacy of emotive political symbols; it lacked heroic figures, and has not developed them since. The emergence of political nationalism was arrested in part by the fact that the country did not become a genuinely sovereign international actor until almost half a century after federation. The British imperial tie was sufficiently strong to create a sort of surrogate political nationalism, though not strong enough to evoke resentment or disaffection, from which Australian national feeling might have emerged. While Australians have distinguished themselves in numerous wars, their military exploits testify more to the nobility of individual character than to the power of national causes. The "spirit of ANZAC," derived from World War I, commemorates Australians more than Australia. In the United States, wars have generally been fought and recalled more as national events, glorifying such principles as national destiny or the bringing of democracy to other peoples. Such distinctions carry large implications for contemporary U.S.-Australian relations, as will be demonstrated.

American nationalism, politically laden and impassioned, has often linked national purpose to social ends. Historically, Americans have been almost superstitious in their dedication to popular sovereignty; American liberal and egalitarian values are politically based. Australia, becoming a nation after the age of liberalism and indeed, after the full force of the industrial revolution had spent itself, did not make the state a "final value." It is easy to agree with Richard Rosecrance that the Australian state was primarily instrumental: "It was not the embodiment of the nation; it was the nation's tool."[3] American experience in winning and settling the frontier celebrated a certain kind of opportunity. So, also, did the assimilation of great numbers of diverse immigrants and the regionalism of the country which reinforced a nationalism that, while shaped by distinctively American institutions and political temper, helped create a climate of energy and optimism, of individualism and competitiveness.

Australia, already homogenous, evolved into nationhood without comparable sharp differences. Many of its social priorities had already been formed: its egalitarian principles, for example, were paramount. Australia's brand of nationalism emerging in the decade before nationhood owed much to literary and folk publicists such as Henry Lawson, A.B. (Banjo) Paterson, and Joseph Furphy. These men vigorously extolled a proud, resourceful, indigenous Australian man; the state was not their hero. Then and later, Australian literature placed greater stress on equality than on freedom; American literature, "more equable and more positive,"[4] seemed to reflect the more self-assured, optimistic blend of social and political nationalism so characteristic of America. In Australia, the Labor party, which emerged as a political force even before federation, helped foster nationhood. Quickly becoming a prominent national actor, it manipulated the levers of power, without, however, having to fight for democratic institutions or for universal suffrage. Labor was and remains today a highly nationalistic party with its nationalism being informed by social purpose.

Australian nationalism has since changed; its more distinctive political forms are the product of the events of the late 1960s. Bruce Grant, writing of the period, suggested that "the 'withheld self' that D.H. Lawrence [had] glimpsed on his visit to Australia [in the early 1920s] was at last released; the search for identity had become a display of self-expression."[5] John Gorton's larrikinism and Gough Whitlam's "new nationalism" contributed to these changes. But so, also, did Australia's new position in the international community, and especially, its changing relationship to the U.S. and to all things American.

Despite its great land mass—roughly the size of the continental United States—Australia has not developed the regional and subcultural identities that are common in America. This has strengthened Australian homogeneity, making it easier to live with the sense of there being an all-Australian community. America's sectional and subcultural pluralism, by contrast, has etched its own, all-American, national/patriotic myth, emphasizing the success of its melting pot. The increased incorporation both of blacks and of Hispanics into American society has often been held up as an example of what a country with a diverse racial and ethnic population can achieve. In Australia, for political and constitutional reasons, the Australian states remain powerful; the recent transition of Queensland and Western Australia from mendicant to prosperous status has only accentuated the weakness of the federal government as national spokesman and image-builder. Also, the newness, smallness, isolation, occupational unrepresentativeness, and artificiality of Australia's capital, Canberra, has hindered the growth of nationalism. This is not a national society in the way that the United States is.

The strength of the Australian states has had its own effects on local government: "The idea that . . . local institutions formed part of a federal system and could play a part in political integration or national development was never considered."[6] For the most part, Australian local political institutions have had severely limited formal authority. In a nation where party is important, local elections are often not contested under party labels. In a nation where egalitarianism is sovereign, local suffrage often revolves on arrangements other than an unqualified one-person, one-vote, criterion. American local institutions, by comparison, appear viable, more attractive. Over half a century ago, the Australian historian W.K. Hancock noted that in America, a free habit of local association fostered a voluntaristic impulse, while in Australia that impulse was stifled. In Australia, moreover, the absence of viable, intervening local government bodies has meant the absence of effective barriers between the individual and central authority, whether that authority is national or exists in the form of powerful states.[7] The Australian, in short, has been consigned to reacting to larger, more impersonal, less accessible strata of official authority.

This is an important point because traditionally the two countries are thought to have radically different outlooks on authority. Australia, generally portrayed as an almost archetypical anti-authority society where there is little respect for government, in fact tolerated considerable governmental intervention, which does not detract from its skepticism of authority, its limited empathy for the state's institutional dignity. In America, the high regard placed on political institutions does not inhibit public discomfort with excessive or unnecessary governmental intervention. The American tradition of disdaining and deploring state intervention, of romanticizing the idea that the government that governs the least is the one that governs best, reaches back at least to the eighteenth century and to Tom Paine. In truth, during the American colonial period and for much of the nineteenth century, American government did not "govern" very much. The frontier, social variety, and atmosphere of movement and fluidity all contributed to an individualism that looked for little help from state or national organs of government; local grass-roots institutions supplied many of the basic services. The "state" could be held up and patriotism praised precisely because the state was not an intrusive mechanism.

The patterns of settlement and consolidation were very different in Australia. Convict origins, authoritarian strains in the early administration, experience with settlement and consolidation that was not nearly so freewheeling and opportunity-presenting as in America, the smallness of the population, the dearth of skills and capital to allow development under private auspices: all contributed to making government in Australia *the* prominent agent. Also, a social ethos that emphasized socioeconomic egalitarianism—in some respects, collectivist principles—made the state its natural instrument. The early record of Australian state-owned railways, together with the passing of legislation to guarantee and protect employment and social assistance, not to speak of the industrial arbitration and conciliation machinery, all guaranteed a key role for government.

The Australian party system necessarily reflected these conditions. As has been suggested, the Labor party achieved its political success very early, the party system having quickly embraced and proclaimed the special interests of the working-class, rural industry, and specific urban business constituencies. All, in their own fashion, have had a stake in some form of government intervention, ownership, and regulation; none have had an interest in laissez-faire doctrine. In the U.S., by comparison, A. Lawrence Lowell, late in the nineteenth century, said that the prime object of American government was, at bottom, negative. The majority's will over minorities and over individuals ought to be limited, except within very definite limits where the feelings of the popular majority are clear. Weak parties and conciliating politicians served this purpose well.[8] A more recent assessment complements this Lowell thesis: "The party system was never asked to *effect* sweeping social change," and has been well suited to a national political system "in which the principal impetus for modernization comes from outside government, in which conflict over social change is minimal."[9]

Twentieth-century American government interventionism has been incremental, for the most part reactive rather than socially blueprinted, and usually—as with the New Deal—couched in terms that defend private rather than state enterprise. Contemporary American debates over deregulation have carried noticeable overtones of principle as well as of cost-effectiveness. Both in the U.S. and in Australia, there has been a decline in the electorate's party system allegiance with issues and leadership-image emerging as more consequential. This is not necessarily an evidence of conventional myths about the proper functions and legitimacy of political authority being discarded. Though confidence in American institutions has not been compromised, culturally borne idealism and leeriness of government intervention have probably exacerbated the country's disappointment in the performance of government and the party system. Vietnam, Watergate, failed social programs, and other such developments have also contributed to the new misgivings. Yet, simple distrust of big government is being displaced by more subtle outlooks, with government and politicians being challenged for their mistakes as well as for their encroachments on individual rights. It is fair to say that Americans are still faithful to a system that has helped migrants and others, that once served a local social function of integration, and know the uses of an intervening power that does not depend on action in state capitals or in Washington.

Both Americans and Australians modeled their national political institutions to reflect the principle of countervailing authority. Australia did not move as far as the U.S., choosing instead to fuse its executive and legislative domains along British parliamentary lines. But as in the U.S., Australia carefully divided power between the central government and the states. Judicial review in both countries has de facto enhanced the central authority, though political expediency even more than constitutional constraints limits the range of its effective action. It is instructive that the author of a major treatise on American precedents in Australian federation commented on the indulgence the Australian founders showed in giving attention to American precedents of limitations on centralized power.[10] The Australian public's traditional resistance to all constitutional referenda designed to enlarge the authority of the national government, or appearing to do so, suggests the persistence of misgivings about all concentrated, offical authority. Complementary Australian practice reaching back to the turn of the century includes the formation of many rule-making, administrative, and quasi-judicial bodies whose accrued powers might otherwise have fallen to the open market or been assumed by legislative bodies. The fact that such bodies were created, that they came into existence very early, suggests that elaborate rule-making functions were acceptable to a society accustomed to—indeed, culturally disposed towards—authoritative socioeconomic resource allocation. As Robert Parker has suggested in his treatment of the subject, this reflects the institutionalization of conflict in Australia, where the burden of conflict resolution has been taken from the high table of political authority, and where the popular mistrust of concentrated authority is apparent.[11]

The conventional Australian attitude towards elitism—political elites in particular—further underscores the argument. The cultural traits of leveling, egalitarianism, and mateship are seen as evidence of the public's concern to "lop off the tall poppies," the symbols of the very authority on which Australians have become dependent. With some allowance for literary license, Henry Lawson, the great social commentator and nationalist, believed that at bottom Australians were antagonistic towards most laws and to law as a whole; towards magistrates, judges, and police; towards lawyers, spies, pimps, and informers of all descriptions.[12] Various consequences follow from such a cultural orientation. Russell Ward's often-cited conclusion is that "our profound suspicion of authority and pretentiousness provides some safeguard against the main danger of our time: dictatorship from either the right or the left . . . it is possibly harder to imagine a Hitler, a Stalin or even a Perón flourishing here than in any other country on earth, including England itself."[13]

But such suspicions of authority carry a reluctance also, more noticeable than any in the United States, to recognize and to reward superior ability. Recent Australian party leaders—Evatt, Menzies, and Whitlam, for example—faced problems because of these popular prejudices. Similarly, Australian political parties, for a very long time, chose to nominate members of their respective support constituencies for major elective office; Labor, for example, looked to trade-union officials; the Country party to farmers and graziers. Conspicuously missing were lawyers, a group that popular orthodoxy branded as somehow beyond the national Australian pale. The U.S., moving in almost exactly the opposite direction, has been partial to lawyers; there has been an early and continuing flow of lawyers to elective politics. American practice, in this regard, appears wholly consistent with its basic national traits. In the United States, where there is no tradition of denigration or fear of institutions of political authority, personal high-status achievement such as that demonstrated by a highly trained lawyer is admired. Law, an inherently conservative profession, tied as it is to rules, texts, precedents, and ordered procedures, is eminently suited to the relatively gentle and incrementally laid-on hand of government, as traditionally preferred in America. It is not surprising that litigation as a method of dispute settlement is considerably more widespread in the U.S. than it is in Australia.

Australia's ambivalence towards authority and authority's symbols has not, however, produced a markedly stronger tolerance of individual political rights than has been common in America. Still, the United States has at times exceeded Australia in the passion with which it has denounced and prosecuted alleged political subversion, especially in its Left-radical form. In 1951, for example, in the heyday of anti-communist feeling in the West and Australia, the Australian electorate rejected a government-sponsored referendum that would have outlawed the Communist party. One writer speculated that a similar referendum in the United States at that time would probably have carried. Why? The Australian frontier experience is more recent; the trend toward conformity has gone less far in Australia than it has in the United States.[14] Australian norms do not call for active hostility towards those who, flying unorthodox colors, challenge political authority. Nor have these values supported a notion of political nationalism that allows the state to anoint itself as judge, to act as warden of patriotic norms. Perhaps basic attitudes are much more complex than this simple formulation would indicate. Australia's relative political permissiveness is grounded *not* on a philosophical defense of individual rights. With an ethos more social and collectivist than individual, the emphasis in Australia has traditionally been on *group* privileges. As a result, even in the political arena the right of dissent has been championed more vigorously in America as a matter of birthright; especially in recent decades, this has been accomplished through the reaffirmation of a constitutionally entrenched Bill of Rights guaranteed by a system of law and courts on which Americans rely.

It is in the domain of opinion and behavior that the Australian community emerges as significantly less tolerant than the American. The dominant strain of the Australian social-nationalist myth favored egalitarianism, with stress given to likeness rather than to diversity. This nurtured an Australian parochialism that was powerfully reinforced by disdain for the Aboriginal population and by the perceived threat to Australia's racial and sociopolitical integrity created by the country's position as an outpost, on the edge of a densely populated, almost certainly covetous Asia. Until well after World War I, Australia pursued strongly assimilationist policies, as much out of conformist impulses as to avoid social unrest among its people. The U.S. has also had its fair share of nativist and xenophobic outcroppings, but has been too large, diverse, self-confident, and far removed from potentially hostile forces to cultivate habits that could overturn its individualistic ethic.

With consequences that will be discussed later, distinctions between these two national ethics have accounted also for quite different perspectives on both accomplishment and destiny. It has not been uncommon for Australians, whether or not they have visited or studied the U.S., to speculate whether Australia had the potential to become as great as America and would have done so had it been granted America's population and natural endowments. The widely circulated, late nineteenth-century interpretations of Australian nationalism conveyed a confident message, a belief in the scheme of evolving progress. But the sociological material out of which Australian society was fashioned could not sustain such hyperbole. We are again reminded that Americans mastered their environment; Australians were often compelled to retreat from their own. Jeanne MacKenzie dwells on the seemingly limitless possibilities for expansion that marked much of America's experience, encouraging "a boundless optimism, vitality, and drive and joy for living"; the Australians, however great their achievements, found the "going was always too tough to leave any energy for the sheer joy of the struggle." MacKenzie contrasts the optimism of America with the cynical pessimism of Australia.[15]

While American culture evolved a myth of equality, of the *process* of opportunity—from rags to riches, from log cabin to White House—equality's texture in Australia became one simply of *being*. In America, "life, liberty, and the pursuit of happiness," with happiness eventually growing into something well beyond Locke's original term, "property," became symbolically ritualized. A faith in human nature has continued to be revealed in all American survey data, and continues to foster interpersonal trust and the extension of voluntaristic, cooperative action. In Australia, a more egalitarian socioeconomic ethos has produced an essentially relaxed, detached, and not especially aspirational/optimistic attachment. It declared, in effect, live and let live and allow a fair go: far more prosaic impulses than life, liberty, and the pursuit of happiness. One consequence of these differences, in the mind of a British observer, has been that the dynamic of life itself, which contributes to national economic performance, has been affected: "the element of perfectionism, which is so marked in the American character, is conspicuously absent in the Australian."[16] Australian critics have not been averse to lamenting their society's lack of verve and optimism, exhibited in part in their self-depreciation, their preoccupation with cultural cringe. Hence, Robin Boyd's indictment in *The Australian Ugliness* is that while Americans and Australians are both aware of their respective nation's shortcomings, the typical American is self-critical, not self-destructive: "He recognizes faults and difficulties, but he sees them set against a sunny background . . . [and] an ever-broadening horizon."[17]

Much of our assessment so far, in dwelling on the predisposing influences on Australian and American national community feeling has neglected to emphasize change. Because neither society has remained static, it is important to note how susceptible Australia has been to influences from abroad, and how America and Americanization have figured in this regard. Popular American culture—films, plays, and second-rate printed materials—have been common in Australia since the First World War. These American exports have had a mixed reception. While American cultural products were widely consumed in educated and even in popular circles, they were often derided as expressing a cheap, flaunting, violent, and in some respects unreal America, not fit for Australia to consume. During World War II, nearly a million Americans were stationed in or passed through Australia. They were regarded with a combination of admiration and envy, with what has been referred to as the overpaid–oversexed– and over-here syndrome. Some fifteen thousand Australian women became U.S. war brides. Many were disillusioned; a number returned home, their expectations deceived, having shown little ability to adapt. Since the war, and especially since the arrival of television, rapid travel and communication, and a far greater economic and defense involvement with the U.S., the American influence in Australia has grown. Many in Australia were concerned that these relations would do little to create a more self-confident national feeling. Australia, because of its linguistic, political, cultural, and other affinities to the United States, was thought to be especially vulnerable to American influence. The country's declining affinity with countervailing British influences, together with the absence of other plausible sources of influence, made the country uneasy. Isolated Australia's deference to imported products and imported ideas seemed only to aggravate the situation.

But postwar Australia soon changed, and it did so rapidly. Its population doubled in less than forty years. Its ambitious migration program led eventually to the dismantling of the White Australia policy, and also to the acceptance of large numbers of non-Anglo-Celtic white migrants. Educational and cultural pursuits multiplied; the economy became more diversified. Assimilationist policies towards ethnics and Aborigines were replaced by pluralistic policies; money and effort were committed to anti-discrimination programs to assist minorities and women. Australia became more cosmopolitan, more lusty, more self-assured.

Some of these changes in policy and public acceptance were helped by the traditional Australian community and national values. For example, the postwar migration program was justified as an effort to achieve rapid population growth, both to enhance Australia's defense capabilities and to foster economic development. Other programs, such as the efforts to provide greater opportunities for depressed groups, were thought to be a partial fulfillment of egalitarian precepts; a satisfaction of *group* interest, concepts familiar to most Australians. Still others, such as the elimination of racial migration barriers, were undertaken gradually and unobtrusively. Australia's traditional aversion to doctrine and abstractions—its pragmatic face—made change acceptable; the more passive/apathetic features of Australian culture may have helped.

But the American factor was also important. One overall effect of the pervasive American influence was the transmission of ideas, methods, styles, and values that had little to do with the easily targeted Hollywood tinsel. While Australian critics of the U.S. and of American influence within Australia have not relented, they have generally acknowledged and borrowed from America's example, including the example of protest, pressure, and accomplishment. Hence, for example, the Freedom Rides in northern New South Wales on behalf of Aborigines, the anti-Vietnam marches, the teach-ins, the criticisms of environmental neglect, the raising of women's sociopolitical consciousness, all owe something to American models and ideas. The impact of the Australian Germaine Greer through her book *The Female Eunuch* on the feminist movement was first felt in the United States and elsewhere overseas; then, as a recirculated effect, within Australia itself. Australians increasingly came to admire much of what America produced, and not just by contrast with what was available in Australia. More important, Australians came to take a more balanced view of America because of America's capacity to review and to regenerate itself. Selma, Alabama; Vietnam; Watergate—these became symbolic evidences of vitality. As Grant avers, it helped Whitlam come to power as head of a reformist rather than a traditional Labor government. Whitlam, pointing to America's diversity, was able to explain how Labor could also identify with such tendencies.[18]

Australians have not become Americans; survey data as well as impressionistic evidence testify to this. While, to be sure, in a garish grotto setting Australian admirers erected a memorial to Elvis Presley in Melbourne's historic General Cemetery, and a 1984 survey showed young Australians relating closely to the U.S. and to things American, it also showed quite plainly their pride in being Australian.[19] The survey responses in their frequent references to the 1983 America's Cup race, suggested that the race was not a transient event, that it engendered a sense of national pride in an unprecedented defeat of the Americans. Australia had no need to be content with coming in second in its rivalry with America. While the resurgence of national feeling among Australians in the early 1980s could be viewed as a reaction to, but no longer a resentment of America, it also took place, in part, because of the cultural renaissance in the media and in the arts, especially in cinema, which since the 1970s had been accorded considerable official patronage precisely because the barrage of American materials had stifled the Australian film industry.[20]

The Australian sense of community and national feeling has been altered but not transformed. As the author of a wide-ranging assessment of America's effect on Australia concludes, America's most important contribution to Australia has not been to provide a glamorous pattern for successful nation-building, but "a measure against which whatever was distinctly Australian could come to be recognized and cherished."[21] The process of cultural change in Australia has been influenced by America, both in what has been borrowed and in what has been set aside. The change, is, of course, uneven, as our analysis of the country's economic priorities and practices must suggest.

At or near the top of Australia's inheritance has been its propensity for egalitarianism, which we will now consider in its socioeconomic rather than in its political context. Where Australian egalitarianism has stressed equality, its American counterpart—even allowing for populism, the New Deal, and the Great Society—has focused largely on individual rights of opportunity and achievement. Some critics have argued that Americans are, in effect, libertarians who tolerate and encourage inequalities of all kinds.[22] The distinction is often ascribed to the different societal origins of the two countries, to their distinctive class features. The free settlers in Australia, for example, were on the whole more uniformly working class than were the nineteenth-century migrants to America; there was little of a genuinely Australian middle class to create an individualistic ethic. As Seymour Martin Lipset argues, frontier and other such factors meant that by the end of the nineteenth century, when an Australian ethos had congealed, it was the "Left"—the bearer of socioeconomic egalitarian priorities—that had helped to define social institutions and thought.[23]

Class constructs, then, are helpful in appreciating Australian egalitarian notions. Australia's development generated something approaching not a *classless* but a *one-class* society, in which privilege, social gradations, and elitism were deprecated, where similarity of income and lifestyle were prized. Australia was and still is less extreme than is the U.S. in disparities across the income spectrum; the incomes of those in the middle- and upper-middle-class are more severely taxed and redistributed. The phenomenon is noticeable in a variety of situations, ranging from the resistance of organized labor to piecework or automation, to considering holiday and weekend work (and wages) as extensions of a normal work schedule, to practices of extended paid vacations and of long service leave, and to popular enthusiasm for ex–post-facto legislation aimed at recovering otherwise technically legal tax-shelter proceeds.

The evidence suggests that Australians subjectively associate themselves far more with middle-class status than Americans do, even though by objective measures Australia is a less middle-class society.[24] There is a dual point here; Australians regard themselves as members of a *common* class—and that class is *middle*. This perception is important for what it says about Australia being at neither end of the spectrum but in the egalitarian middle. Apart from what one might imagine the substance of middle-class values to be, it is, in other words, a self-perception of a reasonably level society, and perceived as desirably so. In the United States, socioeconomic egalitarianism has mostly meant opportunity to achieve status: position, power, and wealth. In America, distinctions in wealth and status are more conspicuous and seemingly more acceptable than in Australia. One must also say that, because of its wealth, it is possible for America to make fairly expensive investments in social-support programs without undermining opportunities for individual gain and success.

While traditional outlooks have certainly eroded over time, the Australians' ethos continues to affect practice, influencing the country's social and economic style and performance. Also, while Australian literature is much less personal, subjective, and individualistic than American literature, and while there has certainly been an anti-intellectual strain in America's history, it has usually been surmounted by countervailing achievement and an insistence on pluralist norms. These norms are not traditionally shared by Australians; intellectual creativity and recognition were long regarded with suspicion by a culture that had little patience with the esoteric, the abstract, and the ostensibly un-utilitarian. Australia introduced compulsory education early, but for a very long time emphasized only basic primary education. Few students went on to complete secondary school and even fewer attended university—far fewer, proportionately, than in the U.S.. Well into the postwar period, university education emphasized the acquiring of professional qualifications—in law, medicine, and engineering—with little attention paid to a broader curriculum. Despite reforms, Australian schools are still more likely to emphasize skills and specialization over cognitive training and social adaptation than are the American, with the American youths' "sheer articulateness and range of viewpoint (however shallow) . . . [setting] it apart from the vast majority of Australian adolescents and young adults."[26] The absence until recently of a leisure and/or educated class, combined with a narrowing of income ranges and a tradition of government action, dampened impulses for philanthropic venture, be it to ameliorate social conditions, to promote the arts, or to cultivate science and invention.

Whatever its positive effects on social justice and the civil order, the Australian egalitarian norm has probably been reflected most conspicuously in the nexus between work and efficiency/productivity. Values of security, comfortable living, and leisure are not entirely congruent with values of aspiration, exertion, and the search for new skills needed for social mobility. Less powerful than before but still present today is a general social ethos that tolerates a low-key work ethic and deems ordinary performance as good enough, even for the business and educated classes. The fault has been noted among both providers and consumers: "Australians are poor at providing personal service and are reluctant to demand it."[27]

Conceptions of egalitarianism are kin to conceptions of individualism and collectivism. There are, of course, individualistic and collectivist threads in both societies, but in Australia collectivism has left a stronger imprint. The interpretative literature often reduces individualist/collectivist (as well as egalitarian) distinctions to the major role that a conventionally understood middle class has, from the beginning, discharged in America, but not in Australia.[28] Then in addition, one must consider the implications of the notion that there was a "small man's frontier" in America, which stood in contrast with the "big man's frontier" in Australia.[29] Australians found the land locked up; though the grip of squatters was broken, land conditions remained such that a rural proletariat rather than small farmers became the norm. Unlike Americans, Australian settlers required intervention from state authority, and so did urban dwellers, both because of the stern conditions that prevailed and because private capital and social effort were so scarce. The Australian inclination towards a collectivist style expressed the society's version of an egalitarianism that preferred the norm of redistributive social justice to that of personal opportunity.

It is ironic that rural, bush circumstances helped to shape collectivist norms in a country that historically has been one of the world's most urbanized. The popularization of Australianism as a community phenomenon represented a blend of radical social commentary and nationalism. A rash of major strikes in the 1890s, both in rural and urban settings, failed, but they served to coalesce views on social justice and lay the ground for subsequent political action.

Urban concentration, expressed in few but relatively large and well-placed cities, a homogeneous population, labor shortages: all of these served to focus attention on unions as the spokesman of working people. Quite simply, "the trade unions were the effective organizers of a political party, the Australian Labor Party, which helped to make Australia a welfare state and more a collective economy than the U.S.A."[30] Australian workers, while not badly off by international standards, could not compare with their American counterparts, who in imbibing a strong individualist national settlement, found themselves in both real and subjective terms becoming better and better off with the advent of industrialization. Then and now, Australians admired many of America's accomplishments; they could not, however, relate easily to America's rugged individualism, to the distortions and injustices it appeared to spawn and countenance.

The United States did not develop a powerful labor movement or an electorally meaningful labor/socialist party. Whereas, in Rosecrance's generalization, capitalism captured the radical myth in America, the opposite happened in Australia; as labor became the gadfly of American politics, business was subordinated to become the gadfly of Australian politics.[31] This has not prevented American influence from contributing to Australia's collectivist consciousness, even to its left-of-center political thrust. The American populist theme was known, and American writers such as Henry George, Edward Bellamy, Laurence Gronlund, and Ignatius Donnelly were widely read and discussed in Australia in precisely the period when that community was ripe for their radical messages. These critiques were all the more influential because they were primarily written for popular rather than for academic audiences. William Lane, the foremost Australian radical publicist of the time, championed Bellamy's ideas advocating a cooperative society. There is a distinct link from Bellamy to Lane, to the strikes in the 1890s, to Lane's and Mary Gilmore's flight to Paraguay to launch the New Australia experiment. Like the strikes, that last endeavor failed, but from it all, as Robin Gollan has argued, came not so much an adoption of Bellamy's (or other radical Americans') explicit prescriptions, as a major contribution to the creation of a climate of opinion that gave birth to the Labor party.[32]

The Labor party has continued to be at the center of Australian politics. Mostly under Labor auspices, significant socioeconomic innovations in Australia were undertaken at both federal and state levels until the 1920s. The other parties, when in office, have not dismantled these collectivist/redistributive programs; and, since its own terms at office, beginning in the 1970s, Labor has instituted still more programs of social importance, some of them quite creative. For a host of electoral, institutional, and cultural reasons—particularly Australia's distaste for doctrine, formula, and overbearing authority—the party has continued to be moderately reformist, never aspiring to anything more. Barely two decades into the twentieth century, Bryce saw Labor's caution in perspective: theoretical doctrines had little charm, and the majority held to common-sense moderation: "There was no passion, because there were no hatreds, no wrongs to avenge, no abuses to destroy, like those which had often roused social ferocity among revolutionaries in countries that have never known, or had lost, constitutional government."[33] The Labor party became socialism without doctrine—not even socialism as such—but its policies suited a national collectivist frame of mind all the same. Americans also grew up without doctrine, but they chose to take their cue from individualism.

Lingering collectivist and socio-egalitarian cultural dispositions, combined with a certain blockage imposed by non-individualist norms against innovation, enterprise, entrepreneurship, and risk-taking continue to color behavior in ways that affect Australia's contemporary economic performance. No single explanation suffices, but cultural factors have contributed to a reluctance or an inability to perform and to excel. A mid-1980s international survey of chief executives disclosed that Australia's top executives were complacent, out of touch with technological needs, and un-innovative compared with other industrial countries.[34] In order to correct this state of affairs, an Australian School of Management has been founded at the University of New South Wales, modeled on Stanford and, to an extent, Chicago's business schools—essentially, to make Australians more competent to manage business. Australia has a historical fascination with gadgetry, and Australian science and technology can claim world-rank achievement in fields ranging from microsurgery to marine biology and military radars. Yet a survey published in 1984 found that Australia's research and development spending as a proportion of gross domestic product was the lowest among all OECD countries save Italy. Also, Australian R&D was disproportionately funded by government rather than by private industry, and, within the private sector, by foreign firms based in Australia rather than by domestic companies.[35]

The behavior of workers and their unions is thought to be another aspect of cultural trends that have tended to depress productivity and otherwise distort Australia's performance and international competitiveness. As the archives reveal, U.S. diplomats posted in Australia between 1935–1945—including the period when World War II was in progress—almost invariably began their assessments by referring "to the emphasis placed in the Australian ethos on not working too hard, on not striving for excellence, but happily accepting mediocrity with the cheerful cry of 'she'll be right,' and on class conflict rather than collaboration."[36] Recent reflections by many observers, foreign and Australian, suggest that not much has changed.

In *The Lucky Country,* published in the mid-1960s, Donald Horne suggested that, partly because of their concern with happiness for ordinary people, Australians believed they were already "ahead" of America.[37] According to certain social-justice values criteria, Horne's assessment is valid. But Australian cultural values, including aspects of the work ethic and general social expectations, have deep and troubling implications. Fifteen years after Horne wrote *The Lucky Country,* Herman Kahn and Thomas Pepper argued in their suggestively titled book, *Will She Be Right?,* that Australia may have acquired the values and styles of a post-industrial society without securing the undergirding foundations to sustain such an order.[38]

Reflecting on the symbolic figures in Sidney Nolan's art, the American historian Robin Winks wrote that Nolan captured the Australian frontier and its differences from the American: "alone, alienated, and yet fascinated with a mechanical civilization where, however far across the horizon train tracks might run, they inevitably ended at a port, beyond which stood the world upon which Australia depended."[39] Australian society evolved in, indeed, inhabits an island continent; Australia's international environment is composed of societies and political orders very different from its own; Australia's economic well-being is inordinately linked to overseas markets.

Insecurity has been the lietmotiv of Australia's external outlook. Its mainsprings, however, have been as much a product of Australian society as of the external environment, investing that insecurity with exceptional durability. Feelings of insecurity, bred in part by the uncomfortable presence of Asian and Pacific Islander workers, hardened the socially exclusive attitudes that became incorporated into the myths of Australian purpose and development. Australians felt that they had something very special to protect. One remedy was to entrench exclusionary migrant practices; "White Australia" became settled policy from the outset of the Commonwealth.

However Australians went about molding their own society, beyond Australia's shores there lay other, complex, far less tractable environments. Australia's small population, modest resources, and lack of full sovereign status only heightened its sense of vulnerability. Australians were prone to magnify the dangers to their safety from the spillover effects of regional colonial rivalries, not to speak of the major power advances both in Asia and the Pacific.

In sum, Australia's sense of insecurity impelled a close reliance on the military and diplomatic protection of a great and powerful friend. In the nineteenth century and until World War II, Britain served that function. Humphrey McQueen has summarized the result as "the peculiar nature of Australian anti-imperialism which accepted British domination of the world as a precondition for Australian independence."[40] From this perspective it is easier to appreciate Australia's willingness to contribute to remote British conflicts: to fight in the Sudan, the Boer War, World War I. It was a sort of premium, paid on insurance, in order to avoid humiliation and defeat for the principal protector. Well before full international sovereignty was assured and even before federation, Australia also attempted to secure its own, vitally defined interests: this explains, for example, Queensland's seizure of Papua in 1883; the later forcing of British acquiesence to bring Papua under Australian administration; pressures on Britain to establish an imperial presence in the Hebrides; Billy Hughes's successful campaign against the inclusion of a racial equality clause in the League of Nations Covenant; Australia's acquisition of New Guinea under a Class C Mandate.

While Britain was both mother country and principal security guarantor, Australians welcomed also what they regarded as an unfolding American interest in the Pacific, construed as an added counterweight against Japan. Hence, the outpouring of Australian enthusiasm for the 1908 visit of the Great White Fleet, and for the later major American naval visit in 1925. Many rank-and-file Australians could neither understand nor condone America's tardy entry into World War I, nor its apparent hesitation to offset the rise of Japanese militarism, let alone the commercially inhibiting measures that depression-time America was disposed to take.

Japanese entry into World War II traumatized Australia. Northern Australian cities were bombed and there was a chilling fear of invasion, at least until the Battle of the Coral Sea. Australia's insecurity, aggravated by its relative military unpreparedness, the deployment of most of its trained troops in North Africa, and the collapse of a protective British screen in the Pacific led Prime Minister John Curtin late in December 1941 to put the matter plainly and publicly: Australia's traditional kinship with Britain was not in doubt, but "without any inhibitions of any kind, I make it quite clear that [for its security] Australia looks to America."[41]

Since World War II, Australia has continued to be exercised by the volatile conditions that prevail in its Asian/Pacific neighborhood, created partially by decolonization and its aftermath, exacerbated by the rise of revolutionary regional powers. Postwar Australia has variously identified Japan, China, the Soviet Union, and Indonesia as likely threats to world or regional stability, threats also to itself. Feelings of insecurity have not been simply the expression of alarm by the publicists or politicians. Survey data have indicated strong, persistent currents of public unease about threats from overseas, and, in comparison with polls taken worldwide, there appears to be an inordinate Australian tendency to foresee regional or world war.

Australia's continuing desire to maintain the mantle of a great power's protection is easily comprehensible. The Australia of the last quarter of the twentieth century, certainly economically and socially more vigorous and indeed more nationally oriented than it was at federation, has more, not less, to lose if perceived security threats materialize. Its great and powerful security partner today is the United States, the nation predominantly responsible for the goods, services, capital, and techniques that have given Australia the kind of materially improved society that Australians wish to protect. The substantial increase in American intellectual, cultural, and artistic influence has inevitably affected Australia's security connections with the U.S.. The Australian public at large has, over the decades, supported these ties. In 1984, 73 percent of the public felt that, as a device for protecting Australia's security, the American alliance under ANZUS was either very important or fairly important; only 12 percent thought it was not very important, or not at all important.[42]

There has, of course, been criticism, often sharp and trenchant, of the value, propriety, and extent of the American presence in Australia. Our interest lies not so much in the criticisms themselves as in their significance in explaining new and old Australian norms, and how these norms relate to the United States and to American society. First, given the inherently asymmetrical relationship between a great and a middle power and all that this implies in various domains, even those Australians who strongly favor the American connection must at times be expected to feel uneasy, sometimes critical. America and American behavior, even on matters unrelated to Australia, are constantly communicated to Australians by the media, and by tourism and direct contact. The U.S. is, therefore, under close and continuing scrutiny. Also, while much that is American is admired and emulated, Australians retain an uneasy feeling about America's wealth and power, a discomfort linked "with a dislike of alleged brashness and arrogance, combined with a contempt for softness."[43]

Such reservations relate not only to America's great power status, but also to the cultural and historical dispositions that have symbolized America's reaction to international affairs. The United States in the present century has tended to swing from being inner-regarding and isolationist to being worldly and internationalist. When American idealism has been bruised, or when there have been reasons for a preoccupation with domestic concerns, Americans have tended to turn inward. This has been disconcerting for a country like Australia whose security appears predicated on an interested and active American role worldwide, especially in the Pacific. Inevitably, questions have been raised about long-term American reliability. It has also sharpened criticisms of so heavy a reliance on the U.S.. In dealing with America, recent Australian governments, like their predecessors, have found it prudent as a matter of policy to extend encouragement, lest the U.S. experience feelings of loneliness and discouragement and eventually use these as an argument for withdrawal. This helps explain Australia's extended involvement in Vietnam on America's side. Yet the involvement caused considerable divisions within Australia, created deep doubts whether the war itself was worth fighting, and whether the American effort was worth supporting. After

Vietnam, there was a widespread feeling in Australia that the U.S. should be sent strong signals of encouragement; otherwise, its post-Vietnam depression could lead to demoralization and to a diminished interest in the region's security.

The other side of the coin has been the problem of dealing with an enthusiastic and indeed overzealous America, which at times has led to a certain embarrassment. The American tendency for zealousness is often associated with moralizing. While the U.S. may be magnanimous in its gestures of enlightened self-interest, as it was with the Marshall Plan, it may also be sanctimonious, as it was, for example, in its crusade against international communism—many thought the policy unrealistic, dangerous both to friends and allies. Ernest Lee Tuveson's characterization of the United States as a "Redeemer Nation," animated by millennial conceptions that justify visions of destiny in dealing with the outside world,[44] needs to be set beside George Kennan's observation that Americans suffer from an "inveterate tendency to judge others by the extent to which they contrive to be like ourselves,"[45] and that this leads to constant proselytizing. Such American habits, traceable to the self-congratulating, optimistic, and idealistic thread in American culture and tied also to a sense of pietism and accomplishment that has facilitated the absorption of territories, the waging of war, and the overseeing of international order in the Western hemisphere and beyond is acknowledged. It is also a problem for others.

In a special but quite limited sense Australians also have a sense of mission, of destiny. More than occasionally they see themselves as models of the good, sensible society, having certain prescriptive rights to arrange conditions, at least in their immediate neighborhood. Some of this sentiment has pre-federation roots, but it has been manifested more recently by Hughes, Evatt, and Whitlam, all three leading figures in the Labor party—the party of traditional Australian nationalist expression.

Still, Australia's small capacity to influence external circumstances, combined with its cultural norms, so uncongenial to a sense of international vision, limits what it can do. Aside from trade, Asia has historically been a place to be wary of, to be defended against, rather than to be shaped. Contrary to American proclivities, Australia has not been given to norms of exuberant self-confidence, optimism, idealism, and high achievement. Whatever its feelings about the insecurity that lies beyond, Australia has been a relaxed society. For this and other reasons, Australia has not been inclined to accept unthinkingly America's own foreign policy impulses. On the contrary, criticisms of the U.S. connection have always emphasized the *costs* for Australia, including the hazards of being drawn into unwanted and unnecessary American adventures and of sustaining collateral risks.

As we have seen, American influences on Australia have been deep and varied, on balance welcomed, rarely actively resisted. Lloyd Churchward, concluding his historical account of the relationship, underscored the effects of the consensus, but the last sentence in his book is a lament: "It is clear that a practical re-assertion of Australian nationalism in present circumstances is impossible short of a socialist revolution,"[46] which is unlikely. Churchward's premise about nationalism may be mistaken. Australian society has become more open, more questioning, and more self-confident in the political as well as communal sense. American influence has led to a *selective* borrowing of foreign styles and preferences, and has served as a catalytic impulse for self-examination and self-renewal. The newer layers of Australian society will not necessarily wish to disengage from the United States, losing the advantage of certain security and economic ties. Alan Renouf, a former Australian ambassador to Washington, has found that as the Australian and American *people* have proceeded along their distinctive national cultural paths, the two *countries* have in fact moved closer together. Renouf, not at all displeased that quite different societies can be friends and allies, finds the relation all the more encouraging because it is no longer unexamined; it has matured.[47] America and Americanism may, on balance, have done more to foster Australian national definition than to submerge its identity.

ENDNOTES

[1]T. Dunbabin, address to the Australasian Association for the Advancement of Science in the *Report* of the nineteenth meeting (1928), p. 250. Cited in R. Else-Mitchell, "American Influences on Australian Nationhood," *Journal of the Royal Australian Historical Society*, vol. 62 (June 1976), p. 3.

[2]See the data and argument as presented by Alan I. Abramowitz, "The United States: Political Culture Under Stress," in Gabriel A. Almond and Sidney Verba,

eds., *The Civic Culture Revisited* (Boston: Little, Brown & Co., 1980), pp. 177–211.

[3]Richard Rosecrance, "The Radical Culture of Australia," in Louis Hartz, ed., *The Founding of New Societies: Studies in the History of the United States, Latin America, South Africa, Canada, and Australia* (New York: Harcourt, Brace and World, 1964), pp. 296–97.

[4]T. Inglis Moore, *Social Patterns in Australian Literature* (Sydney: Angus and Robertson, 1971), p. 242.

[5]Bruce Grant, *The Australian Dilemma. A New Kind of Western Society* (Sydney: Macdonald Futura Australia, 1983), p. 258.

[6]R.J.K. Chapman and Michael Wood, *Australian Local Government. The Federal Dimension* (Sydney: George Allen and Unwin, 1984), p. 11.

[7]W.K. Hancock, *Australia* (London: Ernest Benn, 1930), p. 273.

[8]A. Lawrence Lowell, *Essays in Government* (Boston: Houghton Mifflin, 1889), pp. 22, 106–108.

[9]Everett C. Ladd, Jr., *American Political Parties: Social Change and Political Response* (New York: Norton, 1970), p. 45.

[10]Erling M. Hunt, *American Precedents in Australian Federation* (New York: Columbia University Press, 1930), *passim.*

[11]See R.S. Parker, "Power in Australia," *Australian and New Zealand Journal of Sociology,* vol. 1 (October 1965), pp. 85–96.

[12]Henry Lawson, "Wanted by the Police," in *Prose Works of Henry Lawson* (Sydney: Angus and Robertson, 1940), p. 617.

[13]Russell Ward, *The Australian Legend* (Melbourne: Oxford University Press, 1958), p. 239.

[14]A.L. McLeod, *The Pattern of Australian Culture* (Ithaca, New York: Cornell University Press, 1963), p. 19.

[15]Jeanne MacKenzie, *Australian Paradox* (London: MacGibbon and Kee, 1962), p. 104.

[16]H.C. Allen, *Bush and Backwoods. A Comparison of the Frontier in Australia and the United States* (Sydney: Angus and Robertson, 1959), p. 107.

[17]Robin Boyd, *The Australian Ugliness* (Melbourne: Cheshire, 1960), p. 67.

[18]Grant, *The Australian Dilemma,* p. 65.

[19]Australian National Opinion Poll survey, cited in the *Sydney Morning Herald,* May 9, 1984.

[20]The point is made with special force by Gary Sturgess in his extensive analysis of "The Emerging New Nationalism," *Bulletin,* February 2, 1982.

[21]N.D. McLachlan, "The Future America: Some Bicentennial Reflections," *Historical Studies,* vol. 17 (April 1977), p. 383.

[22]As for instance in the exposition of H. Mark Roelofs, *Ideology and Myth in American Politics: A Critique of National Political Mind* (Boston: Little, Brown & Co., 1976), pp. 137–49.

[23]Seymour Martin Lipset, *The First New Nation. The United States in Historical and Comparative Perspective* (New York: Basic Books, 1963), especially pp. 248–68.

[24]See, for instance, David Kemp, *Society and Electoral Behaviour in Australia. A Study of Three Decades* (St. Lucia: University of Queensland Press, 1978), pp. 12–16; 51–52.

[25]Joan Kirby, ed., *The American Model: Influence and Independence in Australian Poetry* (Sydney: Hale and Iremonger, 1982), especially the editor's preface, pp. 6–8.

[26]Ronald Conway, *The Great Australian Stupor. An Interpretation of the Australian Way of Life* (Melbourne: Sun Books, 1971), p. 168.
[27]Ronald Taft and Kenneth F. Walker, "Australia," in Arnold Rose, ed., *The Institutions of Advanced Societies* (Minneapolis: University of Minnesota Press, 1958), p. 145.
[28]Perhaps in its best, terse form as expounded by Kurt B. Mayer, "Social Stratification in Two Equalitarian Societies: Australia and the United States," *Social Research*, vol. 31 (Winter 1964), pp. 435–65.
[29]Brian Fitzpatrick, *The British Empire in Australia. An Economic History, 1834–1939* (Melbourne: Melbourne University Press, 1941).
[30]Geoffrey Blainey, *The Tyranny of Distance: How Distance Shaped Australia's History* (Melbourne: Sun Books, 1966), p. 169.
[31]Rosecrance, in Hartz, *The Founding of New Societies*, pp. 304–06.
[32]Robin Gollan, "The Australian Impact," in Sylvia E. Bowman, ed., *Edward Bellamy Abroad: An American Prophet's Influence* (New York: Twayne, 1962), pp. 119–36.
[33]James Bryce, *Modern Democracies* (New York: Macmillan, 1924), vol. 2, p. 257.
[34]See Jane Ford, *Australian*, May 4, 1984.
[35]See Peter Roberts, *Age* (Melbourne), April 26, 1984.
[36]P.G. Edwards, ed., *Australia Through American Eyes 1935–1945* (St. Lucia: University of Queensland Press, 1979), p. 11.
[37]Donald Horne, *The Lucky Country: Australia Today* (Baltimore: Penguin, 1965), p. 95.
[38]Herman Kahn and Thomas Pepper, *Will She Be Right? The Future of Australia* (St. Lucia: University of Queensland Press, 1980).
[39]Robin W. Winks, *The Myth of the American Frontier: Its Relevance to America, Canada and Australia.* Sir George Watson Lecture, University of Leicester (Leicester: Leicester University Press, 1971), p. 35.
[40]Humphrey McQueen, *A New Britannia. An Argument Concerning the Social Origins of Australian Radicalism and Nationalism* (Melbourne: Penguin, 1970), p. 34.
[41]Curtin, article in Melbourne *Herald*, December 27, 1941.
[42]Morgan Gallup Poll, no. 1200, June 7, 1984.
[43]W.F. Mandle, *Going It Alone: Australia's National Identity in the Twentieth Century* (Melbourne: Allen Lane/Penguin, 1978), p. 37.
[44]Ernest Lee Tuveson, *Redeemer Nation: The Idea of America's Millennial Role* (Chicago: University of Chicago Press, 1968), especially pp. 208–14.
[45]George F. Kennan, *American Diplomacy 1900–1950* (New York: Mentor, 1951), p. 127.
[46]L.G. Churchward, *Australia and America 1788–1972: An Alternative History* (Sydney: Alternative Publishing Cooperative, 1979), p. 195.
[47]Alan Renouf, "Australia *v* the U.S.: The Foreigners Who Look Like Us," *Bulletin*, July 7, 1981.

Richard Walsh

Australia Observed

IMAGINE, IF YOU CAN, a country without any universally accepted national anthem[1]—but a pronounced devotion to a rousing ballad that sings the praises of penury, theft, the solitary life, and suicide. Its title ("Waltzing Matilda") is such an obscure piece of vernacular that few of its citizens understand its meaning;[2] fewer still know all its words by heart.

Imagine a nation that celebrates, apart from a smattering of hand-me-down Christian festivals and, rather half-heartedly, its founding by 736 petty criminals and their 227 armed guards,[3] only two events with marked enthusiasm—a horse race (the Melbourne Cup) and a notable military debacle (Anzac Day).[4] It is only the horse race that successfully brings all activity to a halt as the nation huddles around its television sets for the few minutes it takes to race 3200 metres at 2.40 in the afternoon of the first Tuesday of November.

This is a country that lacks a distinctive national flag,[5] that lacks the constitutional power to appoint is own head of state,[6] that has no strong sense of history or tradition (although this is changing), nor any perceptible desire to extend its sphere of influence. It is the only country in the world, outside the great neutralist tradition of Europe, where in its whole modern history less than one thousand men have lost their lives under enemy fire on native soil.[7]

It is, of course, the ultimate enlightened state, a true nation of the twenty-first century, one that spurns—or even transcends—those narrow notions of nationalism that have seduced lesser states in the past to the brink of disaster. Or else, depending on your viewpoint, it is a political neuter, a country so totally devoid of ideas and passions that it is an utter non-event. On this Australians themselves cannot decide.

If Australia is indeed a portent of the world to come, it is hardly surprising that it is one of the most urbanized countries in the world (three quarters of its people live in cities or towns of over one hundred thousand people). Six state capital cities and their urban satellites cling tenaciously to the outer rim of a mainland that offers some of the most inhospitable terrain on the planet. They live in sprawling suburbs (in area, Sydney is the second largest city in the world, behind Los Angeles) that are closer to the American than the European model.

Bruce and Kaylene are old friends of mine who live on Sydney's Upper North Shore (despite the name, it is not within view of Sydney Harbor); they are typical of the Australian upper-middle-class and are a local variant of similar people I have met from the Californian suburbs, Connecticut, and Surrey's stockbroker belt. They live in a single-story, sprawling double-brick home on a traditional quarter-acre block that faces north (to catch the sun). The front garden is sparse: a few native shrubs and two large eucalypts plus a gravel driveway. Their pride and joy is the backyard: a spacious sunroom gives out on to a wooden deck, where, except during winter, they sunbake, drink, and have frequent barbecues. Beyond is the swimming pool and the half–tennis court.

The name of their suburb (St. Ives) is borrowed, like many Australian suburban names, from an English place, though nearby there are some borrowings from the Aboriginals who inhabited these parts about two hundred years ago (Turramurra, Kuring-gai) and some commemoration of pioneering Australians. The people here are mainly professionals and senior management with a comfortable home costing $150,000 to $250,000. They are predominantly Anglo-Saxons who claim on their census form to be Protestants; they are notoriously materialistic, hedonistic, and philistine, supporting few good restaurants, art galleries, little theaters, etc.

Traditionally, most Australian suburbs have developed around a railway station, an above-ground island between two tracks, providing shelter and facilities on the British Railways provincial model. The nearby shopping center is strung out along the main thoroughfare and provides a choice of supermarkets plus specialty shops including the greengrocer, chemist, dry cleaner, butcher (selling relatively cheap, by world standards, lamb and beef), the grog shop (liquor outlet), news agency (who provides a morning delivery of newspapers and magazines to his suburb and sells over the counter a wide variety of books, stationery, toys, and lottery tickets), a TAB (betting shop), milk bars (purveying the traditional Australian milkshake, plus ice creams, soft drinks, and sweets), and takeaways (fast-food outlets). Often the milk bars are run by Greek families and the greengroceries by Italian or Chinese families; the fast-food can be everything from Colonel Sanders to Lebanese kebabs.

However, St. Ives's development as a fashionable suburb has happened post World War II by encroachment into formerly afforested parkland. During the bushfire season, some of its houses are usually threatened. This fact, together with the proximity of some small farming (the area even boasts an annual show), inculcates a sense of the traditional bush to this neighborhood that is less than ten kilometers from the central business district and yet five kilometers from the city's outskirts.

For the purposes of local government, Sydney's suburbs are organized into municipalities (each with its mayor and aldermen). Most municipalities would hope to boast an Olympic-size swimming pool, public tennis courts (and private tennis clubs), at least one public golf course, lawn-bowling clubs, a large number of parks in which children can play, public gardens, an oval or two that sporting groups can hire to play cricket or football, commercial squash courts (ten-pin bowling is rarer and indoor cricket is a growing pastime), and a municipal library. Places of worship are plentifully provided for those of the Anglican, Uniting (a coalition of the old Methodist, Congregational, and Presbyterian faiths), and Catholic persuasions; less plentiful are synagogues, mosques, and churches for the Eastern Orthodox congregations. Twenty-six percent of Australians claim to be Catholic and 50 percent Protestant.

Bruce and Kaylene's two boys go to a nearby Anglican private school. They themselves long ago gave religion away, but all, bar one, of the major private schools in Sydney are church-affiliated and, even if Bruce were less wealthy than he is, he would scrimp and save the $6000 (almost one-fifth of his take-home salary) needed to cover school fees each year for the boys rather than allow them to go to the local high school, which he regards as inferior. In actual fact, the private school system is educationally no better than the government school system but it certainly offers a much wider range of extra-curricular activities, is much better endowed with facilities, and can offer better individual assistance to the struggling young scholar. Despite the fact that 18 percent of Australian secondary students go to non-government schools, there is little evidence of the English old-school-tie syndrome, and former students from the government school system encounter few obstacles to success in professional, academic, and business life.

Bruce drives a company-owned Holden Commodore (General Motors' 3.3 litre car, which has recently been supplanted by Ford's Falcon in popularity) and his wife, a 1.5 litre Ford Laser (Ford, the outstanding motor manufacturer in Australia, has recently been successful in incorporating Japanese expertise into its small cars). He drives the boys to the railway station in the morning and Kaylene collects them in the afternoon. In between times, she does the housework (domestic assistance is rare and expensive but usually takes the form of an "ironing woman" and professional cleaners once a week) with half an ear on the talkback radio or half an eye on daytime soapies or chat shows on TV. She "goes up to the shops," takes her turn at the school tuckshop, plays mid-week tennis and solo whist or just cools off around the pool. Although there are many prominent successful women in Australian commercial, academic, and artistic life, most upper-middle-class women give up work when their children are young and rarely return to the full-time work force.

The Australian school (and university) year is broken into three terms with three major holiday breaks. The longest are the Christmas holidays, beginning in early December and ending in early February. In most parts of Australia this period is very hot, although with recent changes in weather pattern, December can be mild and January and February the most unbearable months. Temperatures can rise above 100° Fahrenheit and the humidity in Sydney and Brisbane is very high; in the south there are often disastrous bush fires while elsewhere there can be cyclones and floods.

December is traditionally a time of pre-Christmas carousing—office parties, picnics, barbecues, and cruises, usually accompanied by heavy drinking. Beer and wine are inexpensive; spirits much more expensive and American-type cocktails a rarity. Drunken driving is sufficiently a public health problem that major blitzes, involving random breath-testing conducted by squads of police in "booze buses," have been introduced in recent years to discourage loss of life. (A regular item in the daily newspapers is the "road toll," and the number of deaths sustained on the road in the current year as compared to last year and other memorable holocausts.)

On Boxing Day begins one of Australia's best-loved sports events, the Sydney-Hobart Yacht Race; at this time there is also often an international cricket match (preferably against either the English or the West Indians), and in the days of our tennis supremacy it was traditionally the first day of the Davis Cup (usually against the USA). Few people work between Christmas and New Year; January is the time when most people prefer to take a family holiday, often camping or renting a house near the coastal beaches or in some other way savoring Australia's great outdoors.

The other two school holiday breaks, of less than a month each, are around May and September. There is also usually a week's break at Easter, which in Sydney coincides with the Royal Easter Show. Each major city of Australia has something equivalent to The Show, which is not dissimilar to the traditional American country show with its proud displays of primary produce and rural skills (horse jumping, sheep and cattle drafting, tree felling, etc.) together with manufactured goods and carnival rides. The fact that Sydney, a highly urban and reasonably sophisticated city of 3.5 million people, still boasts a week-long country show is fitting testimony to Australia's persistent perception of itself as an agrarian nation.

In recent years, the school curriculum has slowly developed from a colonial to a nationalistic mode. Twenty years ago, Australian children knew more about the kings and queens of England and the twilight of the British Raj in India than the names of their own prime ministers and the history of Indonesia; they followed in the great English public school tradition that Latin and geometry developed one's reasoning powers and had little use for the Chinese, Japanese, and Malay languages. This has changed a lot, although English literature still dominates over Australian and there is rarely a nod in the direction of American writing.

In the middle of the morning, the young scholars have their morning break, "recess," which the very young call "play lunch," and about 1:00 p.m. there is lunch itself, during which informal sports games will be played—"tip cricket," "touch football," marbles, a pick-up game of soccer, or swimming if a pool is handy. At about three, they emerge in restless hordes, often to take up their sports in a more serious way. The girls will play netball, field hockey, softball, cricket, or turn their attention to dance or a musical instrument.

The kind of good life my friends Bruce and Kaylene live is not celebrated in Australian fiction. While the late Jacqueline Susann might have made a good fist of it, Australian novelists tend to concentrate on literary rather than commercial fiction and the life of the Australian bourgeoisie simply lacks the texture needed. Nonetheless, much of its broader outlines are celebrated in highly popular TV soap series (most notably one called *Sons and Daughters*), and such diverse geniuses as Patrick White and the theatrical satirist Barry Humphries know how to put their talented fingers on its most unsympathetic features. Our own version of Neil Simon, David Williamson, and also Alex Buzo have captured a slightly trendier version of these people in some of their plays.

But the real trendies live a long way from sprawling suburbia and congregate in the inner-city terrace houses in Sydney and Melbourne, where they share their space with the genuinely indigent (including large migrant populations) and the young and restless student/dropout populations. Real trendies are usually junior academics or those engaged in communications/cultural activities (advertising, journalism, arts administration); they are childless, affluent, and engaged in restoring nineteenth-century slums to high-gloss coziness by means of up-to-the-minute (or beyond) decorating ideas.

My friend Micky is definitely not an affluent trendy. She is a radical feminist who left her husband five years ago and migrated with her eight-year-old son from the suburbs to an old terrace house in Melbourne's Carlton, a traditional working-class suburb that abuts Melbourne University.

She shares with another single mum, a young (female) student, and a (male) gay actor. Formerly a clerk in the public service, she attempts to survive on the government's Supporting Parent's Benefit of $110.00 per week.

The house is part of an informal cooperative that buys fresh food in bulk at the nearby wholesale market once a week. Clothes are bought from the op. (opportunity) shop run by a religious group. Transportation is a bike. They grow their own herbs, lemongrass (for tea), and dope. There is communal ownership of a fridge, an old washing machine, a dryer, and a TV (their third—the other two were stolen from them). What they lack in worldly goods, they make up for in camaraderie. The other single mother in the house works and there is some pooling of income. There is much inter-house visiting, child-minding, hair-cutting, etc. There are interminable cups of tea, shared joints, and cheap flagons of wine. There are spontaneous celebrations on the flimsiest pretext.

Two doors away is an Italian couple, Gino and Nina. Externally, their house is identical but inside it is sparser, minus the posters and objets trouvés of Micky's but with some gaudy decorations and a pious portrait of the Virgin Mary. Gino and Nina both work (he is a daytime textile worker and she an office cleaner in the evenings) and their combined income is around $400 per week, but they have four children and mama (Gino's) living with them. They enjoy the camaraderie of the very large local Italian community and the consolation of their church.

Gino catches a tram to his nearby factory, working 8:00 to 4:00. To demonstrate his adoption of local mores, he stops off at the pub on his way home to have a drink with his polyglot mates. After dinner, Nina leaves for her 8:00 to 12:00 PM job. They save madly; since they regard Carlton as a poor place in which to raise children, they ultimately hope to buy their own free-standing home in the outer suburbs (from which, as it happens, their neighbor Micky feels she has "escaped").

Most of Australia's "mediterraneans" in fact arrived in the fifties and sixties, when they were called "reffoes" or "New Australians" or "Continentals," and suffered much hostility. In time, Melbourne became the fifth largest Greek city in the world (behind Athens, Salonika, Chicago, and New York) and developed an even larger Italian population. Finally, the mediterraneans became accepted as part of the landscape and contributed enormously to its way of life with their pastas, pizzas, and exotic sausages and coffee. In their turn, the Slavs, the Lebanese, and the Turks became the victims of those who wanted to keep Australia "pure," and now it is the turn of the Vietnamese.

In Australia, no one is expected to admit to liking work; workaholics are such a curiosity that serious articles intermittently appear offering miracle cures for this bizarre disease. You work from

Monday to Friday so that you can afford to indulge in expensive leisure activities on the weekend and holidays. The ordinary Australian male expects to own a car, a TV, a fridge, a washing machine and clothes dryer (or the Australian patent rotary outdoor clothes-hoist). His expectation is that he will be able to afford to spend most of his statutory four weeks' vacation away from his home with his family and he will own some of the essential impedimenta of the outdoor life, such as a portable barbecue, golf clubs, a small boat, a caravan or trailer. Basically, those who are able to do better than this are regarded as well-off—aspiring in their turn to two cars, expensive electrical equipment (hi-fi, video cassette, home computer, etc.), a weekender (second home), a large watercraft, a below-ground swimming pool, private education for their children, and regular travel abroad.

My friend Micky and her Italian neighbors do not aspire to such grand recreations, but nonetheless their leisure time is important to them. In summer on the weekends both will try to go for picnics; in winter the Italians will go to their social club (affiliated with the local soccer team) while Micky will take in a movie. For holidays, Micky leaves her son with a friend and heads north to Sydney or a rural commune in northern New South Wales. On one memorable occasion Gino and Nina went back to Italy, but camping is their usual style.

Less well off than working-class families and those like Micky, who are able to share a home, are the unemployed families, attempting to survive on the dole of $149.00 per week (for a couple without children; $89.00 for a single person). In the country, these may be Aboriginals, the dispossessed original people who, displaced from their traditional nomadic life, are forced to eke out an often squalid existence on the outskirts of country towns. Some drift to the city's slums but an active minority is not only beginning to assert its rights but gain the education and power positions necessary to do something about it. Pat O'Shane is the first black Australian to run the N.S.W. Aboriginal Affairs Department, and she and other Aboriginal leaders are fighting hard for governments to hand back land rights to their people.

The contemporary life of Aboriginals is captured in Richard Beilby's *The Brown Land Crying*, and the stories of Nene Gare and of Colin Johnson. The life of Melbourne's young dropouts is seen in the book (and film) *Monkey Grip*. The classic humorous account of newly arrived Italians attempting to adapt to Australia is *They're a Weird Mob* (also a film).

And yet, however statistically insignificant rural life is in modern Australia, it continues to grip the imagination at home and abroad and somehow pass itself off as both typical and characteristic. Even today, a surprisingly large number of our writers and artists were either born in the country or have lived there for a significant time and confront city life with a rural sensibility (our foremost poets like Judith Wright and Les Murray; our novelists like Patrick White, David Malouf, and Randolph Stow). To complicate matters further, many of our major cities (and most notably Brisbane and Adelaide) feel like large country towns, and the nation really only boasts five industrial cities (Sydney, Newcastle, and Wollongong, which form a kind of megalopolis, and the virtually twin cities of Melbourne and Geelong).

My cousin Bob is a mixed sheep and wheat farmer in the Riverina, an irrigation area in southwestern New South Wales. His house is a typical Outback dwelling, made of timber and with wide verandas to provide shade. The roof is galvanized iron; large peppercorn trees provide some shade and, across the home paddocks, willows bend low over the canal.

He works his property from sunrise to sunset with the assistance of another family, who are his tenants. He kills his own meat, runs his own laying hens, milks his own cow. He goes into the nearby town once a week, on Saturday mornings. As in the rest of Australia, this is a traditional shopping time because, until very recently, nowhere in Australia were major retailers open on Saturday afternoons or Sundays. He drives in his old ute (pick-up) and takes on board fresh fruit and vegetables plus assorted groceries and toiletries. At the pub, he irrigates his throat and picks up liquor supplies and local gossip (for detailed information on commodity prices and weather futures, he relies on the excellent ABC rural broadcasting programs).

Bob is forty-three and served in Vietnam, but, apart from that, has never been abroad and has no plans to travel. Whereas his city counterpart dreams of getting away to Asia and Europe, his idea of a holiday is a month beside the sea, swimming and fishing. He genuinely despises city life and urban do-gooders with their fanciful ideas about conservation (attempting to thwart his right to eradicate the accursed kangaroo, which tramples down his crops and destroys his fences) and their willingness to use good taxpayer's money to support "bludgers" (parasites) like the unemployed and the Aboriginals.

An authentic rural conservative, in fact Bob is unwittingly a closet socialist in so far as he expects government intervention to provide a variety of schemes that minimize his risks, soften his hardships, and protect the market price of his produce. He is a card-carrying member of the National party, a rural party that is currently in power in the Queensland state legislature.

In the country towns, there are few diversions. The metropolitan papers usually arrive by mid-morning; radio and TV have recently been supplemented by the VCR boom. But, as in the city, there are the pubs and the clubs which in the evening are alive with the sound of music, usually rock 'n' roll but occasionally jazz and country. New South Wales is the home of clubland—licensed clubs that offer drinking and eating facilities plus the opportunity to lose your surplus cash on the "pokies" (slot machines). The profits the clubs make from their poker machines enable them to provide live entertainment, often imported acts, on a lavish scale at attractive prices. These clubs are usually either RSL clubs (the Returned Services League is an association of war veterans) or Leagues Clubs (associated with the professional football code, Rugby League).

Australians like to think of themselves as a classless society and, although generations of social scientists have earned their keep systematically debunking such a simplistic myth, the truth is that most people see themselves unselfconsciously as middle-class, belonging to either an upper or lower division within that class. The pubs and the clubs are part of this great mythology—they are places where people with very different incomes and employment responsibilities congregate in their leisure time as equals. The racetrack and other sporting venues, the beaches and picnic grounds serve a similar function. No Australian likes to be thought of as a "snob," as "up himself," seeking insulation from his or her fellow citizens.

Each year in Sydney there is a free performance by the Australian Opera Company in an open grassland area known as The Domain (famous for its Sunday-afternoon soap-box orators). The star in recent years has inevitably been Dame Joan Sutherland. Some TV footage of the 1982 Opera in the Park performance still lingers in my memory, providing my fondest images of egalitarian Australian society at its best. There were brief TV glimpses of the Great Diva peeping out, like a naughty schoolchild, from her makeshift dressing-room caravan; Dame Joan herself is a good example of a certain kind of hearty "good sport" Australian woman. For all her international fame and travel, she retains many of the qualities Australians admire: a certain naturalism, a sense of humor, a lack of pretension. In the audience that evening the camera caught sight of Tom Keneally, whose novel *Schindler's Ark* (*Schindler's List* in America) won the prestigious British Booker Prize, sitting beside his Esky (a portable cooler carrying beer, etc.), beaming from under a toweling hat with a dab of white sun-cream on his nose. In another part of this vast milling throng sat former prime minister Gough Whitlam, the closest we have to an elder statesman, chatting amiably with well-wishers. Even current prime ministers attempt to survive without any obvious security guards, but retired leaders have little status and the country is the poorer for having evolved no formal way of turning their talents and experience to some formal purpose. The famous—the singers, the writers and former statesmen—cannot expect much in the way of special treatment.

There are, of course, some extraordinarily wealthy Australians, but they are mostly at pains not to set themselves too much apart from their fellow citizens. Traditionally, wealth arose from the ownership of vast land tracts handed out by the early colonial government. This often resulted in British-born absentee landlords. Australian-born pioneers built up their holdings by personal exploration and by other, more dubious, methods of land-grabbing. None of this has really allowed the development of an indigenous aristocratic gentry, and those families that have attempted to assume an air of inherent superiority are mocked as a "bunyip aristocracy" or "squattocracy" (the squatters occupied Crown Land and made it their own, sometimes legally but often not).

Today, the big rural landowner is expected to ride out with his station-hands and muck in with them. On more formal occasions, they will join him for dinner at the Big House, but during the day there is a rough kind of egalitarian camaraderie. In the city, the boss is often on first-name terms (in both directions) with his employees, rubbing shoulders with them and "being one of the boys" (a key phrase in the Australian lexicon). Young Australians in England, employed in casual work, are notorious for knocking on the front doors of the grandest houses rather than going to the "tradesmen's entrance" (a concept virtually unknown to them); most Australian men and some women, when traveling in a cab on their own, prefer to sit beside the driver (a habit they have to unlearn fast in New York!). Tipping (10 percent) is usual in good restaurants but elsewhere is nowhere near as common as in the U.S. and some Australians find American customs in this area offensively condescending.

Meritocracy is not merely a mighty theory but a pervasive practice. Australia is a land where schooling, kinship, and other ties seem even less important than in the U.S. The children of the rich (such as Rupert Murdoch) more often seek to outdo their ancestors than to indulge in the easy life. If he had been American-born, Keith Rupert Murdoch, incidentally, would almost certainly have adopted the name of his father, the illustrious newspaperman Sir Keith Murdoch, and would have been known as either Keith Murdoch II or Keith Murdoch, Jr. Such dynastic hankerings, however, Australians dismiss as pretentious, as also the rather portentous "K. Rupert Murdoch." In fact, Rupert Murdoch is rare in having retained his given forename intact; it is more usually contracted (Rupe) or replaced by a corruption, frequently one ending in "-y" or "-ie," such as Billy, Sammy, Richie, etc. (but also, for example, Barry and Garry become Bazza and Gazza), or a foreshortened surname (often ending in "-o," so that Thompson and Simpson become Thommo and Simmo), if no actual nickname (Bluey, Curly, Shorty, etc.) suggests itself. Very few people are known among their mates by the name their parents first bestowed upon them.

Of course, language is the great leveler, and the Australian language not only informalizes people's given names but generally "takes the piss out of" (deflates) any attempts at self-importance. (Not even place names escape this process, so that Brisbane, Hong Kong, and Wollongong become Brizzy, Hongkers, and The Gong!) The vernacular is aggressively vulgar and the humor is always self-mocking. Through both processes the dominant social values are celebrated.

The ultimate accolade in Australia is to be a "good bloke" (the female equivalent is a "good sport"), meaning someone who is gregarious, hospitable, generous, warm-hearted, and with a good sense of humor. In Australia, it availeth a man nothing if he makes himself a fortune and is not a good bloke! The worst you can be is a "wowser" (originally a teetotaller but, more generally, a prude or spoilsport) or "bludger" (originally a man who lived off a prostitute's earnings but, more generally, someone who doesn't pull his weight or carry a fair share of life's burden, e.g., a "dole bludger"). The essence of Australian mateship then is to share your good fortune with everyone not merely unstintingly but to extravagant excess, and to cop your fair share of the shit—a recipe for Polyanna socialism that is faithfully reproduced in our political system.

Given the size of the country and the isolation of its population centers, it is extraordinary that there are virtually no regional differences in speech, bar a few minor idioms. The country areas, and to some extent the whole state of Queensland including its capital, Brisbane, speak a little slower and with more pronounced nasality, but the main speech division is between broad Australian, of which the best-known exponent is the actor Paul Hogan who appears in international TV ads promoting tourism, and so-called "educated Australian," which is closer to the language of southern England and is associated with private-school affluence. However, there are many highly educated Australians—academics, learned judges, captains of industry—who speak with the broader accent. In certain areas of political and commercial life it is undoubtedly a distinct advantage to sound like an "Ocker" (a broad Australian's self-description); this identifies the speaker with the nationalistic aspirations of the vast majority of his fellow citizens. While up to a decade ago the Australian Broadcasting Corporation employed announcers with a broad accent only in its sporting and rural departments (in deference to the elocution standards established by its British mentor, the BBC), it has recently sensed a new wind blowing so that even the news is now read in a more comfortably Australian style.

Of course, the political expression of this great longing to become a classless society is the Australian Labor party (ALP), with its origins in the trade-union movement and specifically in the shearing industry unrest of the late nineteenth century. Although it has held the reins of government for only thirty-four years since federation (1901), this reformist party has always provided the dynamic of Australian politics and the policies over which generations have debated. It is traditionally the party of social welfare for the needy, of full employment and of social reform and equity. Although successive conservative parties have vigorously opposed Labor, they have nonetheless always been forced to adopt watered-down versions of the socialist platform as a way of preempting and blunting Labor's demands. The fact that currently the ALP not only holds federal office but is dominant in the major states, can be seen as a result of two processes. It is an old maxim of Australian politics that the nation turns to Labor in its hour of need (federal Labor governments were in power during the Great Depression and the Second World War), but Labor has always been the natural standard-bearer of Australian nationalism, which today is resurgent.

The present prime minister, Bob Hawke, who enjoys immense and unprecedented popularity, utterly embodies the Australian ideal. He is a tamed larrikin (a reformed womanizer and boozer) with few obvious airs and graces. He mixes easily with people, and successfully disguises his education behind a ferociously rough accent. He and his predecessor, Malcolm Fraser, in fact represent the last in a generation that completed their education at Oxford or Cambridge. Hawke's father, incidentally, was a Congregational minister, a member of that non-Anglican Protestant clergy that since World War II has contributed so notably to the Labor party on radical conscience issues like racism and Vietnam (by contrast, the traditional clerical supporters of Labor, the Irish Catholics, have been a distinctly conservative force).

However imperfectly realized, the idea of a classless and meritocratic society lies at the very core of Australia's self-image. In his heart, Ocker knows that he's as good as his master and will not bend the knee or tug his forelock to anyone. As new people in a new nation, we have the right to create this new social order. At its best, this has led historically to the early acceptance of universal franchise and of the vote for women, and in social life to the ubiquitous popularity of Chinese restaurants with their boisterous informality and sharing of dishes. At its worst, it leads to "cutting down tall poppies," a favorite pastime, which often represents a destructive unwillingness to allow individual high-flyers to reach their fullest potential.

Australians are not notably religious in any formal way, but even city dwellers live in awe of nature. The dominant motifs of our national life are the sun, the sea, and the soil (the latter providing both rural and mineral wealth). While most citizens have not seen drought first hand, they are well aware of its devastating impact on the total national economy; they will have seen minor, if not major, bushfires and flash floods. Because of nature's awesome might, there is a powerful sense of the puniness of man's efforts. This leads to a kind of fatalism on the one hand and to the characteristic self-deprecating humor on the other.

Why should a man "bust his gut" to build up his farmland when drought or flood can destroy his every effort? Conversely, why should a city-dweller carefully build up his business over a lifetime when he might be able to earn twice as much overnight through land speculation or mineral exploration or a stock exchange coup or at the racetrack or the lottery office? The perfidy of Nature, and her handmaiden Luck, dominates the Australian consciousness. It is a land where hard-luck stories and instant millionaires are part of the legend. Gambling is, quite simply, the national passion and the most obvious dislocating social force at every level. So many of our books, films and plays are a mere recounting of dramatic events, without personal conflicts and crises, just because the relationship between personal effort and final outcome is obscured when the vagaries of good luck and misfortune are so evident. (The titles of three of Australia's most outstanding books tell it all: *The Fortunes of Richard Mahony*, *A Fortunate Life*, and *The Lucky Country*.)

Australian society is materialistic and pragmatic but not notably idealistic, beyond clinging to some outrageously simplistic notions about itself. Our films and musicians reveal a high technical level of accomplishment and our writing displays a wonderful inventiveness with words, but our culture does not reveal a new perception of man's place in the universe nor indeed any other fresh ideas. Our politics is dominated by personalities and individual issues, not by major contributions to political theory; our national Parliament, whose proceedings are broadcast live on radio, is used as a forum for trading the most offensive personal insults and vituperation.

At its worst, Australia has the mentality of an arriviste. There is, at times, contempt for the Old World, for its lack of vitality and creature comforts. There is an aggressive assertion of pride in what

Australia has accomplished in a relatively short time with mighty few people. There is a belief that Australia and America share common ancestry and that Australia cannot merely achieve all that America has done but, by learning from the Great Republic's mistakes, can ultimately do better. Beating the U.S. at almost anything is not merely a cause for celebration but a harbinger of our inevitably glorious future.

Non-Australians would be amazed at the orgy of self-congratulation that broke out when the New York Yacht Club was finally divested of the America's Cup. The normally staid broadsheet, the *Sydney Morning Herald,* proclaimed: " 'The Biggest Thing Since Peace in 1945': Triumph Unites Nation." In Brisbane, a replica of the Statue of Liberty had its eternal flame replaced by an Australian flag, and a stuffed koala wearing an America's Cup T-shirt was placed in its arm. Prime Minister Bob Hawke claimed, in a frenzy of hyperbole: "It's one of the greatest moments in Australian history."

At its worst, Australia is provincial; in the past it has been racist in its dealings with its indigenous blacks and with Asians. Today, hostility to the Aborigines has been replaced by vigorous support for their cause by the educated and indifference by the ignorant. Hostility is reserved for the Vietnamese refugees, who are perceived as competitors in the job stakes.

At a government level, there is formal opposition to South Africa and acceptance of Asian immigration. For all the human tragedy of Vietnam, that terrible war did give most Australians a real sense of being part of Asia; the North was no longer merely a vast duty-free shop.

If Australians are vulgar, and they often are, it is the vulgarity of what could perhaps be quite fairly described as one of the most advanced democracies in the world. Its government is elected by compulsory voting in a preferential ballot. It is a country almost devoid of an influential elite. In embracing real democracy one simply has to put up with the authentic voice of the people.

Urban Australians travel widely within and outside their country; they are not rooted to their birthplace as are Europeans and even some Americans. They have built up all too few traditions. The natural tensions created by peoples of different origins coming together has never in this century got out of hand (in 1929, we gained our first Catholic prime minister, and in 1931 our first Jewish governor-general). It is a genuinely cosmopolitan and peace-loving country that minds its own business and is not enmeshed in historical or contemporary animosities.

For better or for worse, Australia today is very much what the rest of the world will be like tomorrow. Its life may at times lack style, but its heart may be as close to gold as mere mortals can aspire to. I have seen the future and it works, kind of.

ENDNOTES

The author's ultimate caveat: an article such as this has, of necessity, to deal in broad-brush generalizations. For a land so large and covering so many climates, Australia's lifestyle has surprising similarities from one end of the country to the other. But there are, of course, many regional differences to which I have not given fullest justice, thus reflecting my Sydneysider bias.

Gambling, for instance, is less a passion in Victoria and South Australia, where the puritan and evangelical tradition was stronger. The outdoor life—the barbecue and so on—is less to be found in Tasmania, where the winters are cold. Attitudes to the Aboriginals are more sympathetic in those cities that do not house Aboriginals. The southern cities of Australia prefer a different kind of football to most of the northern cities. Churchgoing is much stronger in the country than the cities.

And yet, to an outsider, the amazing thing is that, despite such minor regional variations, our people, who historically made separate settlements at great distances from each other, ended up speaking a similar vernacular and having such a common outlook and philosophy.

[1]For about eighty years, "God Save the Queen/King" and "Advance Australia Fair" have vied for the honor of being national anthem. During the nationalistic Whitlam government (1972–75), "Advance Australia Fair" became the national tune. The present Hawke government overhauled the words of "Advance Australia Fair," expunging residual traces of sexism and racism, and declared it the national anthem, but this has no legal force. In Queensland, for example, its status is not recognized.

[2]"Waltzing Matilda," unbeknownst to most Australians, means taking to the road with your swag (bed roll and other bare essentials). The song celebrates the fate of a swaggie who has been caught by troopers in illegal possession of a sheep and, in an act of defiance, jumps into a "billabong" (the anabranch of a river). The tune is somewhat livelier than these maudlin events might justify and for most Australians this is the national song.

[3] In May 1787, the First Fleet left England. Although there is some dispute as to the numbers, probably 778 convicts embarked for the long journey: 586 men and 192 women, plus 13 children. Seventeen convicts died and two were paroled even before sailing and a further twenty-three died along the way. Eight months later, on January 20, 1788, they entered Botany Bay, just south of Sydney Harbor.

[4]On April 25, 1915, the Australian and New Zealand Army Corps landed on Gallipoli Peninsula at a place later known as Anzac Cove. This was part of the Dardanelles campaign, which was an unmitigated disaster; before the end of that year, when all troops were evacuated, 33,512 men had died and 78,518 had been injured, of whom one-quarter were Australians. In the popular mind, much of the blame for this debacle is sheeted home to the incompetence of the British command. Australia is one of the few countries in the world that celebrates defeat rather than victory: Anzac Day, April 25, is a day to remember the sacrifices of war.

[5]The present Australian flag has a dark blue field with the Union Jack in the top left-hand quarter. It contains a large white star (with seven points representing the six states and the territories) and five smaller white stars representing the constellation of the Southern Cross, which dominates our night sky. It is very similar in design to the national flag of New Zealand and is one of the last remnants of a now depleted uniform design that once held the British Empire together. While other old dominions like Canada and South Africa have managed to evolve new national flags to represent their modern independent status, Australia is in turmoil over moves to come up with a new flag design in time for our 1988 bicentennial.

[6]The head of state of Australia is the governor-general, technically appointed by the British monarch on the advice of the Australian prime minister. When Labor prime minister Scullin in 1931 recommended the appointment of the first Australian-born governor-general, Sir Isaac Isaacs, the king complained that he did not know him sufficiently well but, after much to-ing and fro-ing, reluctantly made the appointment. It is only during the last twenty years that Australians have become properly accustomed to the idea of having an Australian as head of state, although recently some conservative politicians hoped that Prince Charles could be prevailed upon to restore a little British propriety to the office.

[7]During Japanese attacks on Darwin during World War II, 243 people officially died. However, at that time Chinese and Aboriginal deaths were considered of somewhat less importance and so this figure is probably considerably understated.

Notes on Contributors

Henry S. Albinski, born in 1931 in Chicago, Illinois, is a professor of political science and director of the Australian Studies Center at the Pennsylvania State University. His most recent books are *The Australian-American Security Relationship* (1982) and *Australian External Policy Under Labor* (1977). He has taught at various Australian and Canadian universities and serves as a consultant to both the private and governmental sectors on political risk analysis of Australia.

Geoffrey Blainey, born in 1930 in Melbourne, Australia, is Dean of Faculty of Arts and Ernest Scott Professor of History at the University of Melbourne. He is the author of seventeen books, including *Triumph of the Nomads* (1975) and *The Causes of War* (1973). He has served on various Australian federal boards and committees and as Chairman of the Australian Council.

Manning Clark, born in 1915 in Sydney, Australia, is a Professor Emeritus at the Australian National University in Canberra. He is the author of the five-volume *A History of Australia* (1962–1981), *A Short History of Australia* (1963; rep. 1981), and *In Search of Henry Lawson* (1978).

Hugh Collins, born in 1943 in Perth, Australia, attended the University of Western Australia and Harvard University. Collins is currently a Senior Research Fellow in International Relations at the Australian National University. He is the author of numerous essays on Australian politics, foreign policy, and international relations.

Jill Conway, born in 1934 in New South Wales, Australia, is president of Smith College, in Northampton, Massachusetts, and Sophia Smith Professor. She has written extensively on the role of women in America and Australia; her most recent book is *The Female Experience in Eighteenth- and Nineteenth-Century America: A Guide to the History of American Women* (1982).

Zelman Cowen, born in 1919 in Melbourne, Australia, is provost of Oriel College, Oxford, and chairman of the Press Council (U.K.). Sir Zelman was governor-general of Australia from 1977 to 1982. His recent publications include *Individual Liberty and the Law* (1975) and *Federal Jurisdiction* in Australia (second edition, with Leslie Zines, 1978).

Michael Davie, born in 1924 in Cranleigh, Surrey, England is a staff member of *The Observer* and edited *The Age* (Melbourne) from 1978 to 1981. His books include *LBJ: A Foreign Observer's Viewpoint* (1966), *The Vanishing Dream—A Report from California* (1972), and *The Diaries of Evelyn Waugh* (ed., 1976).

Donald Horne, born in 1921 in Sydney, Australia, is a professor of political science at the University of New South Wales. Horne is chairman of the Australia Council and president of the Australian Society of Authors. His fifteen books include novels, histories, biographies, and social and cultural criticism.

K.S. Inglis, born in 1929 in Melbourne, Australia, professor of history at the Research School of Social Sciences at the Australian National University, is currently a Distinguished Visiting Professor at the University of Hawaii. He has also taught at Harvard University (1982). His books include *The Australian Colonists* (1974), *This is the ABC: The Australian Broadcasting Commission 1932–1983* (1983), and *The Rehearsal: Australians at War in the Sudan 1885* (forthcoming; 1985).

Gordon Jackson, born in 1924 in Brisbane, Australia, is chairman of the Australian Industry Development Corporation and chairman or director of several resource and high-technology firms. Sir Gordon has advised Australian governments on such issues as manufacturing policy (report published 1975), policy towards Japan (1977), and foreign aid (1984). He also served as the foundation chairman of the Australian Graduate School of Management at the University of New South Wales.

Nicholas Jose, born in 1952 in London, England, is a lecturer in English at the Australian National University in Canberra. Jose, a former Rhodes Scholar, is the author of a collection of short stories, *The Possession of Amber* (1980); critical essays, *Ideas of the Restoration in English Literature, 1660–71* (1984); and a novel, *Rowena's Field* (1984).

Leonie Kramer, born in 1924 in Melbourne, Australia, is a professor of Australian literature at the University of Sydney. She is also an editorial adviser to *Quadrant, Poetry Australia,* and *Australian Literary Studies.* She is the editor of the *Oxford History of Australian Literature* (1981), and the new *Oxford Anthology of Australian Literature* (forthcoming; 1985). Dame Leonie served as chairman of the Australian Broadcasting Commission from 1982 to 1983. She is a Fellow of the Australian Academy of the Humanities, and the Australian College of Education.

T.B. Millar, born in 1925 in Western Australia, former director of the Australian Institute of International Affairs (1969–1976), is currently a Professorial Fellow in International Relations at the Australian National University. His recent publications include *Foreign Policy* (1972), *Australia in Peace and War* (1978), and *The East-West Strategic Balance* (1981).

Hugh Stretton, born in 1924 in Melbourne, Australia, is a reader in history at the University of Adelaide. Stretton, an active board member of public corporations, is a consultant to the Australian minister of finance on public enterprise questions. He is the author of several books, most recently, *Housing and Government* (1974), *Capitalism, Socialism and the Environment* (1976), and *Urban Planning in Rich and Poor Countries* (1978).

Richard Walsh, born in 1941 in Sydney, Australia, is publisher and chief executive of Angus and Robertson Publishers. He is the founding editor of both *Oz Magazine* and *Nation Review*. Walsh has also contributed articles to various magazines, journals, and books.

Bruce Williams, born in 1919 in Victoria, Australia, is director of the Technical Change Centre in London. He has served as the principal and vice chancellor at the University of Sydney (1967–1981) and as chairman of the Australian government's Committee of Inquiry into Education and Training (1976–1979). He has written numerous articles on higher education, technology, training, and employment.

Judith Wright, born in 1915 in Thalgarrah, New South Wales, is the author of twelve books of poems, in addition to literary essays, biographies, histories, and children's books. Her most recent works are *The Double Tree* (1978) and *The Cry for the Dead* (1981). An active conservationist, Wright was co-founder and president of the Wildlife Preservation Society of Queensland and founding councillor of the Australian Conservation Foundations.